A. H. Nasution and Indonesia's Elites

A. H. Nasution and Indonesia's Elites

"People's Resistance" in the War of Independence and Postwar Politics

Barry Turner

LEXINGTON BOOKS
Lanham • Boulder • New York • London

Rowman & Littlefield
Bloomsbury Publishing Inc, 1359 Broadway, New York, NY 10018, USA
Bloomsbury Publishing Plc, 50 Bedford Square, London, WC1B 3DP, UK
Bloomsbury Publishing Ireland, 29 Earlsfort Terrace, Dublin 2, D02 AY28, Ireland
www.bloomsbury.com

Published by Lexington Books
An imprint of The Rowman & Littlefield Publishing Group, Inc.
4501 Forbes Boulevard, Suite 200, Lanham, Maryland 20706
www.rowman.com
Unit A, Whitacre Mews, 26-34 Stannary Street, London SE11 4AB

Copyright © 2018 by Lexington Books

All rights reserved. No part of this publication may be: i) reproduced or transmitted in any form, electronic or mechanical, including photocopying, recording or by means of any information storage or retrieval system without prior permission in writing from the publishers; or ii) used or reproduced in any way for the training, development or operation of artificial intelligence (AI) technologies, including generative AI technologies. The rights holders expressly reserve this publication from the text and data mining exception as per Article 4(3) of the Digital Single Market Directive (EU) 2019/790.

British Library Cataloguing in Publication Information available

Library of Congress Cataloging-in-Publication Data

ISBN 978-1-4985-6011-5 (hardback)
ISBN 979-8-2163-9628-4 (paperback)
ISBN 978-1-4985-6012-2 (electronic)

Contents

Acknowledgments vii
Spelling and Translation Conventions ix
Map xi

1 Beginnings 1
2 Coming of Age 15
3 The Japanese Occupation 35
4 The War against the Dutch 47
5 Total People's Resistance and a Professional Army 85
6 Burnishing Credentials: The Idealization of Total People's Resistance 121
7 The Leper Period 153
8 Total People's Resistance as a Military Intervention in Politics 175
9 Civil-Military Cooperation Bodies 193
10 Territorial Warfare and Territorial Management 227
11 Old Age and Legacy 245

Glossary 255
Bibliography 261
Index 275
About the Author 281

Acknowledgments

I would first like to thank and acknowledge the invaluable contribution of Professor Ken Young to the development and completion of the PhD thesis upon which this book is based. We both experienced changes in our lives and places of employment during this period and I have always been most grateful for his consistent and unfailing support that encouraged me to persevere. In particular, I would like to thank him for the scholarly rigor that he sought to implant in me, and for his many valuable insights that greatly assisted me.

Brian Hill, Eric Kuntzman and Della Vache of Lexington Books and Jayanthi Chander and her team from Deanta Global were patient, helpful and efficient in having my manuscript reviewed and prepared for publication.

Greg Barton, who is currently at Deakin University, and Greg Fealey (now at the Australian National University) were helpful in providing information and guidance at the initial stages of my research.

The late Herb Feith was kind enough to assist me in compiling materials and recommending people to interview in Indonesia. Most importantly, he directed me toward the work of David Bourchier, which inspired me to examine factors other than instrumental ones that encouraged A. H. Nasution to embrace corporatist / functional forms of interest representation.

The late Daniel S. Lev was also very helpful in sharing his knowledge of 1950s Indonesian politics and personalities with me.

I was fortunate to work for Lieutenant Colonel (later Brigadier) Ken Brownrigg at the Australian Defence Force School of Languages. In a subsequent posting as Defence Attache in Jakarta, Ken was unfailingly supportive and helpful.

Bob Lowry's research into the Indonesian Army was also very useful and I greatly appreciated documents he provided to me from his archives.

A number of people assisted me in finding information in Indonesia. They include members of the Kolopaking family and Professor Rahayu Surtiati in particular. Ron Witton, Sofia Mansour and Pak Setyadi from the Bahtera email discussion forum were of very great assistance in tracking down details on Nasution's family, as was Tantono Subagyo who kindly sought information on Nasution's father-in-law from Professor Soejono. Lieutenant Colonel (Retired) Pamurahardjo and Brigadier General (Retired) Suhario Padmodiwiryo provided invaluable information. Mas Hardoyo, at the request of Herb Feith, was kind enough to put me in touch with Pamurahardjo.

I learned a great deal about Indonesian Army culture from lecturing at the Pusdiklat Bahasa (Centre for Training and Education – Languages). I am grateful to the military and civilian staff for the kindness they showed me during those visits. More recently, Lieutenant Colonel Rois Nahrudin (who was a student of mine at the Pusdiklat Bahasa) was of very great assistance in gaining approval from the Indonesian Army's Directorate of History for me to extract and translate extensively from the memoirs of Nasution's late wife, Johana Sunarti.

Dr. Sisilia Halimi from the University of Indonesia worked untiringly to seek approval for me to extract similar numbers of words from Nasution's voluminous memoirs and other works. Unfortunately, this effort met with less success because of uncertainty about ownership of intellectual property, but I was able to extract and translate sufficiently from each of them to provide insights into his personality and ways of thinking.

Of course, none of the above people are responsible in any way for the contents of this book and its shortcomings.

Finally, I would like to acknowledge my family. My late father and mother profoundly influenced me in all aspects of my life but my father was particularly responsible for my thirst for education. His formal education was cut very short by osteomyelitis that resulted in his spending extended periods of his childhood in the hospital. He was unfailingly kind and honest, admired education, and sought to inform himself as much as he could about politics. Our dinner table was the scene of many heated exchanges on issues of the day that inspired a lifelong interest in politics that ultimately led to me undertaking this thesis.

My wife, Glenys, has been an absolute rock of support throughout our married life. I thank her for her kindness, common sense and tolerance, and for checking the manuscript of this book. My children, Stephen and Sharon, have also been a source of great happiness and pride and I would like to thank and acknowledge them as well.

Spelling and Translation Conventions

The spelling system of the Indonesian language has undergone many changes over the past century, and this has made the task of according spelling conventions to names in this book somewhat complex. Originally, Dutch spelling conventions were applied but some of these were changed in the 1940s. For example, the Dutch-derived *oe* was replaced by the English-derived *u*.

The spelling system was "perfected" in 1972 and the remaining Dutch-derived conventions were dropped. For example, the Dutch-derived *sj, tj* and *dj* were replaced with *sy, j* and *j*. However, the spelling of Indonesian names is highly idiosyncratic. Many Indonesians chose to retain the Dutch spelling of their names but references to them in the media and other texts often adopt the new conventions. Organizations emerged and disappeared at different points of this continuum, leaving the spelling of their names in something of a limbo.

I have elected to use the new "perfected" spelling throughout this book, except for the names of people where they are more recognizable if older systems are retained.

In translating materials from Indonesian into English I have had to choose between an idiomatic or literal approach. As Mildred L. Larson defines the term:

> Idiomatic translations use the natural forms of the receptor language, both in the grammatical constructions and in the choice of lexical items. A truly idiomatic translation does not sound like a translation. It sounds like it was written originally in the receptor language. Therefore, a good translator will try to translate idiomatically. This is his goal.[1]

Nevertheless, Larson also goes on to note that:

translations are often a mixture of a literal transfer of the grammatical units along with some idiomatic translation of the meaning of the text. It is not easy to consistently translate idiomatically. A translator may express some parts of his translation in very natural forms and then in other parts fall back into a literal form.[2]

I have adopted the second approach. Where I have felt that naturalness was as important as accuracy I have translated as idiomatically as possible, but in a few cases I have been concerned to be as accurate as possible and employed more of a literal approach.

I have also tried to adopt a register-based approach. For example, where I have translated newspaper headlines I have adopted the journalistic register appropriate to this type of text in English.

In some cases, my translations do not accord with those in previous publications and research. For example, most texts refer to Nasution's Military Administration of 1949 as the Military Government. The term used in Indonesian is *pemerintahan*, which I believe is more accurately translated as "administration."

NOTES

1. Mildred L. Larson, *Meaning-Based Translation: A Guide to Cross-Language Equivalence*, Lanham, MD, University Press of America, 1998, p. 18, 19.
2. Ibid., p. 19.

Map

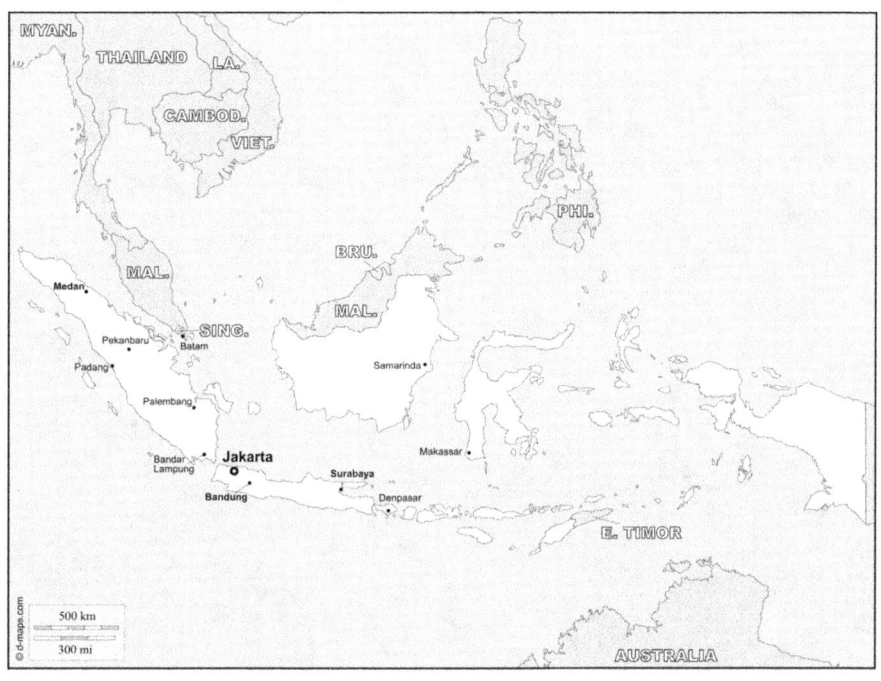

Figure 0.1 The Indonesian Archipelago

Chapter 1

Beginnings

Abdul Haris Nasution grew up in the last decades of Dutch rule over the fertile and beautiful chain of tropical islands that the colonizers called the Netherlands East Indies. His personal and family life played an important role in shaping the beliefs and political orientation that he brought to bear as a seminal military and political figure in the emergence and early years of the Republic of Indonesia. At the center of these formative networks was his beloved wife, Johana Sunarti.

They attained young adulthood when Indonesia was suffering from the turmoil of the defeat of the colonial regime by Imperial Japan in 1942, three years of Japanese occupation, and then five years of fighting and negotiations to uphold the newly declared Republic in the face of Dutch intransigence. Nasution played a leading role in the armed struggle against the Dutch and went on to lead the army in the 1950s. A book on guerrilla warfare that he wrote in the early 1950s was well known at the time and during that decade he dealt the army into emerging authoritarian political structures that became known as Guided Democracy.

Much of his thinking was based upon principles of "total people's resistance" that he had developed during guerrilla warfare campaigns against the Dutch. Although he had been a leader of an army of national liberation in what the Indonesians called a national revolution, his principles were conservative in nature in that they heavily relied upon army officers engaging with and mobilizing civilian communities through the intermediation of traditional authority figures. These principles then underpinned many of the measures for social and political control adopted by the military-backed regime of President Suharto which ruled Indonesia from 1966 until 1998.

Nasution was from the Mandailing branch of the Batak ethnic group whose homelands are in North Sumatra, to the immediate South of the Aceh region that was devastated in the 2004 Indian Ocean Tsunami. The Bataks are numerically insignificant in Indonesia, numbering just three million out of a total population of almost 200 million in 1992. [1] However, they are widely known across the archipelago and since independence have been prominent in academic, defense, political, legal and trade union affairs. They are often regarded as having adventurous personalities and a direct, straightforward approach to personal interactions.[2] Bataks are usually regarded as the polar opposites of the ethnically predominant Javanese. While Bataks often thrive in disputatious situations, such as legal proceedings, Javanese tend toward social peace and harmony.

His wife is less well-known outside Indonesia. Johana Sunarti Gondokusumo (always referred to as Sunarti in Nasution's writings) was born in the large port city of Surabaya in East Java to an ethnic Javanese economist, who had attended university in The Netherlands, and a Dutch mother. The family later moved to the West Java capital of Bandung in the Priangan Highlands where she attended the best schools that were available.

Sunarti's father was not only a member of the Javanese *priyayi* upper classes but had high Javanese aristocratic lineage. Members of this group are known for their highly refined and sometimes elaborate behavior in interpersonal situations.

Many Javanese rules of etiquette center upon the proper use of language, which is more problematic in Javanese than most other languages. When addressing someone, Javanese speakers must choose from several different levels of politeness. These "speech levels" are often expressed with words that have the same meaning, but are stylistically different. For instance, among the Javanese variations of the word "now" *saiki* is the least refined, while *saniki* is a little fancier, and *samenika* is the most elegant. Javanese has many such triads and it is not possible to speak Javanese for long without deciding whether the situation is formal or informal and the relative status of the participants.

Nasution was born in 1918 and Sunarti five years later. Two decades later, in March 1942, the colonial world that they had known was swept aside when the Japanese invaded the Indies and established their own rule over the archipelago.

The relationship between Holland and the Netherlands Indies had resembled that of the United Kingdom and India. Like India for the British, the Indies were the jewel in the Dutch crown and for centuries the "mother country" had grown wealthy from the agricultural and mineral riches of the extravagantly endowed Indonesian archipelago. Both India and Indonesia were much larger in area than their geographically diminutive colonizing powers. A comparison is often drawn between the size of the Indonesian archipelago and the land mass of the United States. Made up of more than thirteen thousand islands, Indonesia would cover more than the entire United States if projected over that country.

The archipelago has always been strategically significant. There is a maze of straits within it that must be traversed to travel from the Indian Ocean (known in Indonesia as the Indonesian Ocean) and the South China Sea and the Pacific.

The major shipping channel is the Malacca Strait that separates the large island of Sumatra and peninsular Malaysia. These days, the security of the Malacca Strait and its approaches at either end are vitally important to a number of countries and interests, including oil suppliers of the Middle East, traders shipping goods to and from Europe, and the military forces of the United States, China and Japan.

Indonesia's strategic location and vast resources had attracted other European powers in the centuries before the Dutch gained control over many of its indigenous kingdoms and principalities. By the end of the nineteenth century the British had contented themselves with peninsular Malaya and colonies along the northern littoral of the island of Borneo while the once powerful Portuguese were reduced to governing the eastern part of the island of Timor.

The indigenous rulers and particularly those on the main island of Java were heirs to rich traditions. Waves of influences from India had imprinted themselves (while not replacing) on early animistic and ancestor-worship practices. Hinduism arrived at the start of the first millennium and brought with it its caste system and artistic and literary wealth, including the *Mahabarata* (Great Story) and *Ramayana* (story of Rama) epics. Indonesian Hindu rulers built great temples, the best known of which is the Prambanan complex near the city of Yogyakarta in West Java.

Buddhism then arrived and rulers aligned with the new religion gradually gained such prominence that today the island of Bali, which lies just to the east of Java, is the only major redoubt of Hinduism. The World Heritage-listed Borobudur temple, not far from Prambanan, is the major legacy of Buddhist dominance in the region.

In turn, Islam arrived from Gujarat in India in the thirteenth century and supplanted these earlier religious influences throughout much of the archipelago. It often took on a syncretic form, accommodating earlier beliefs and forms of artistic and literary tradition.

Christianity was brought to the archipelago by the Portuguese and then the Dutch. Indonesia has strong Catholic enclaves in areas where Portuguese influences were felt the most, notably in the chain of islands between Java and Australia that is known as the Lesser Sundas. There are also many Catholics in other islands, including populous Java, while Protestant denominations are found throughout the archipelago and are particularly influential in parts of the Celebes (known as Sulawesi in Indonesia) and the Moluccan islands, including Ambon.

At the time of the Japanese invasion in early 1942, the population of the Netherlands Indies was about 65 million, of whom 250,000 were classified as Europeans. Approximately 220,000 of this latter group were Dutch citizens. At times during the 300 plus years of indirect and then direct Dutch rule there had been uprisings against the Dutch and an independence movement had gathered strength during the first three decades of the twentieth century. However, the colonial regime had found it easy to maintain control with an army of just 65,000 European and locally recruited troops. Had the Japanese not invaded it seems certain that the Dutch would have continued their policy of *Pax Neerlandica* that put an emphasis on maintaining peace and order and distancing Indonesians, as much as possible, from political mobilization.

The Japanese easily overran the colonial forces, which included a young sub-lieutenant (Ensign) Nasution, and ruled the archipelago for the next three and a half years. They immediately banned the use of the Dutch language in public and official discourse and replaced it with Malay, the *lingua franca* of the islands which the independence movement had renamed *bahasa Indonesia* (the Indonesian language). However, while initially holding out hopes for independence the occupiers cracked down on nationalist sentiment and only began to allow preparations for independence toward the end of their occupation.

The years of Japanese occupation were hard for many Indonesians. There were widespread shortages of food and young men were rounded up to work as slave laborers on projects like the Burma-Siam railway. The leading nationalists Sukarno and Hatta declared Indonesia's independence on the surrender of Japan in August 1945 and there followed five years of turmoil.

Some six weeks after independence was proclaimed, the British inserted armed units with the principal aims of disarming and repatriating the Japanese and freeing Allied prisoners of war and Dutch civilian detainees. They soon realized the strength of nationalist sentiment and advised the Netherlands Indies civilian and military leaders who were returning from exile in Australia and elsewhere to enter into negotiations with the new Indonesian government.

There followed periods of negotiation and warfare between the Dutch and the Indonesians in which Nasution played a leading role as a senior officer of the new army of the Republic of Indonesia. Toward the end of 1949 the colonial power agreed to transfer sovereignty, but even at this stage there were serious disagreements. The Indonesians insisted that the Dutch should recognize their sovereignty over the whole of the former Netherlands Indies while the former colonial power insisted upon maintaining control of the western half of the island of Papua.

The Indonesians took over an economy that had been badly damaged by the eight years of turmoil and soon political divisions began to destabilize the country. Many political parties, including the Communists who had been severely suppressed by the Dutch and defeated in an uprising against the Republican leadership in May 1948, competed for a share of power and a succession of coalitions ruled the country.

General elections were finally held in 1955 and a constitutional assembly put in place to develop a permanent constitution to replace a temporary one that had been adopted as the Dutch left. However, the general elections failed to provide a clear mandate for any of the parties and the constitutional assembly found it difficult to reach a consensus on important issues and particularly the role and status of Islam. The country veered toward a more authoritarian system of government under Sukarno, who began to transition from being a figurehead to an executive president.

The dispute with the Dutch over West Papua intensified, fanned by nationalist forces led by President Sukarno and a resurgent communist movement. Ultimately, in events in which Nasution was closely involved, nearly all the remaining Dutch residents were expelled from the country in the last two years of that decade. Their plantations, mines, oil production facilities and other companies that were the backbone of the formal economy suffered greatly as they were taken over, often by the army whose officers had no experience in running such enterprises.

With the support of the Kennedy administration in the United States, Sukarno was successful in winning West Papua from the Dutch. However, he turned almost immediately toward another external enemy, as he saw it, and began to oppose the formation of the state of Malaysia from the British colonies on the Malay Peninsula, Singapore and North Borneo. This led to a period of mostly low-level conflict and in the middle years of the sixties Australian and British troops were fighting Indonesians in Borneo.

Inflation was running at 650 percent toward the end of Sukarno's rule that ended in the long and messy aftermath of an uprising by some more junior military toward those in the general staff in late September/early October. Nasution almost lost his life when dissident soldiers tried to arrest him at his home and his younger daughter died after being hit by a stray bullet. In the capital, Jakarta, most essential services had broken down or were on the brink of doing so, including city water pumps and pipes, electricity, hospitals, emergency services and even road traffic lights.

This book will follow the fortunes of Nasution from his birth until he lost command of the army in the early 1960s. Unlike earlier biographies, it traces Nasution's relationships with Sunarti and her family. It is important to highlight them as she supported him unstintingly in their long and happy marriage and her father and his associates influenced the young Nasution's conservative political leanings and actions during the Republic of Indonesia's first two troubled decades.

For many years before Nasution met Sunarti he led a somewhat monastic existence away from his family in North Sumatra, living in a succession of dormitory-type accommodation arrangements while he studied to be a teacher and then as an army officer. The warm, welcoming, wealthy and well-connected Gondokusumo family made a major impression on him. His future father-in-law, R.P. Sunario Gondokusumo, was a political activist within the "cooperating nationalist" political movement. Although a Dutch national, Sunarti's mother was also involved in the Indonesian nationalist cause.

Sunario not only took the young man under his wing but appears to have regarded him as a son and politically mentored him. Importantly, Sunario Gondokusumo introduced Nasution to politically conservative figures from his elite *priyayi* background and the young Sumatran later mixed with other members who occupied important governmental and civil service posts when he was developing and applying his "people's war" strategies in the 1940s.

A feature of the cooperating nationalism adopted by Nasution's adopted family and their circle of acquaintances is that they sought to work for independence from within the structures of the colonial regime. They have often been overlooked by historians because "non-cooperating nationalists" (epitomized by Sukarno and Hatta) came to power in the mid-1940s and largely supplanted them, as Jamie Mackie observes:

> Although much has been written about Indonesian nationalism during recent years, little attention has been paid to the group of so-called "cooperating nationalists" or their efforts to extract concessions from the Dutch in the last years before the outbreak of the Pacific war in 1941. This is hardly surprising, since they were not only unsuccessful at that time, but were also, for the most part, swept aside by the tide of events which brought the exiled non-cooperators, Sukarno, Hatta, Sjahrir and others, to the centre of the stage.[3]

Whether or not to cooperate with the Dutch was a fundamental question for nationalists during the later years of the colonial period. Had there been an orderly and gradual transfer of power, such as in the neighboring British colony of Malaya, the outcome might have been different. Nasution was as much a political figure as a military leader and it is important to place him within one of the two major political categories of the late colonial period.

While there were differences in the political outlook within the cooperating nationalist group and it would be unjust to describe most of them as mere stooges of the Dutch, it is fair to say that many in this group desired an orderly and gradual change in constitutional arrangements that would not threaten their own position in society or adversely impact on what they saw as the welfare of the poorly educated masses. Many of the conservative cooperating nationalists with whom Nasution was associated had developed positive feelings toward Japan in the 1930s and cooperated closely with the Japanese during the occupation. Nevertheless, they tended to have in common a desire to maintain the social status quo and some sought to draw upon "traditional" paternalistic organic structures in proposing constitutional arrangements for an independent Indonesia.

Legal experts from this Javanese aristocratic/administrative class championed organicist concepts in 1945 as preparations were made to found an independent state. They advocated the adoption of a constitutional and political system that drew upon what they perceived to be organic and traditional customs, values and authority structures. Dismayed by the plethora of competing parties to emerge from the country's first general elections that were held in 1955, President Sukarno began to support organic functional forms of interest representation, whereby groups would represent functions within society, rather than political ideologies.

Some of the *priyayi* figures that Nasution met during the armed struggle against the Dutch stood by him in the 1950s when he developed means by which the military could intervene in politics and suppress the influence of the political parties by advocating organic corporatist/functional modes of interest representation. Like Nasution, they were concerned that many traditional authority figures had been marginalized by the tide of political activity—much of it from the political left—that swept through Indonesia after the proclamation of independence and gathered force again in the 1950s. Their anxiety heightened when they failed dismally in the 1955 general elections. Importantly, Nasution began to associate the principles of total people's resistance that he had developed when fighting the Dutch and this proposal for organic forms of interest representation with a reliance on traditional authority structures, rather than the parties and political leaders.

Nasution died in 2000 and was in poor health and unavailable for interview in the late 1990s when most of the research for this book was conducted for PhD purposes. However, he published numerous accounts of his life and career. Robert Cribb warns about the problematic nature of Nasution's many publications, which are used widely in this book, for those attempting to research his life and career:

> He was a prodigiously voluminous author, and he writes with unusual clarity, articulateness and plausibility. His topics are military, or military-political, and as one of Indonesia's foremost soldiers for over two decades he features extensively in his own works. Although his tone is by no means modest, he refrains on the whole from exaggerating his own role in events, and indeed often portrays himself as having been a victim, outmanoeuvred and frustrated by the

action of others. A corollary of this latter tendency, however, is that the Nasution world often seems to be inhabited by fools, knaves and those who agreed with Nasution, three mutually exclusive categories. In particular, he credits himself with insights and understandings which he appears to have developed only in hindsight. As a historian of his own ideas, therefore, he is distinctly unreliable.[4]

While it is true that Nasution was very concerned to burnish his own image, his later publications are sometimes disarmingly honest and revealing of insecurities and perceptions of his own inadequacies. When weighed up against scholarly research and the accounts of other witnesses and participants they provide important insights into his life and career, the cooperating nationalist movement of the 1930s, the Japanese occupation, the emergence and evolution of the army, and Indonesia's troubled birth and growing pains in the 1950s. They deserve to be more widely known.

This material was supplemented with scholarly research into Nasution, Indonesian history and politics, and the causes and features of military intervention in politics. It was also informed by interviews with two former army officers from the 1940s and 1950s who were involved in different ways in Nasution's intervention in politics, and interviews and email correspondence with other Indonesians who knew Nasution and/or were related to his wife.

A military posting to an embassy in Jakarta in the late 1960s and early 1970s and lengthy intelligence work relating to Indonesia provided valuable knowledge about the Indonesian armed forces. Contact with Indonesian military officers through short-term assignments to a military school in that country and other visits in the 1990s provided opportunities for discussions on Nasution and his legacy and to obtain Indonesian Army Staff College teaching materials on the army's "people's resistance" doctrines. The late professor Daniel Lev, who was associating with Nasution's main legal advisor when he was seeking to identify means of intervention that fell short of a military takeover, was generous in corresponding by email. A great deal of time was spent combing through Indonesian newspapers of the 1950s in the National Library of Australia and they greatly assisted in gaining a feel for the Indonesia of that decade and fleshing out the role that Nasution played at that time.

In exploring the influence of individuals and events on the evolution of Nasution's political orientation, the first four volumes of the most personal of his publications, *Memenuhi Panggilan Tugas* (Answering the Call of Duty) proved to be very useful. They deal with his youth and young adulthood and are much more anecdotal than his earlier publications or the later volumes in this series. While Nasution is usually reticent about his political socialization and orientation, they nevertheless provide valuable insights into his early years and the formation of his political orientation.

Information that was not available to previous researchers was found in Sunarti's *Pak Nas dalam Kenangan* (Nasution Recalled)[5] that she published in 2002 with the assistance of Ramadhan K.H. and Sugiarta Siribawa.[6] It was not difficult to identify where they had assisted Sunarti and which content was her own.

Allowing for the vagaries of hindsight and a desire to present Nasution and her family in a favorable light, the more personal parts of the book were very useful and often unlike anything Nasution himself wrote. They describe her feelings for Nasution through revealing personal anecdotes of their early life together. She recounts the hardships they shared during the guerrilla struggle, including a harrowing account of a miscarriage she suffered when the Dutch attacked Indonesian forces in 1947 and the pain she endured as they sought shelter in a series of rural villages while Nasution led his guerrilla forces.

She reveals the closeness of the relationship between Nasution and her father, providing information that has only been speculated about in the past, sometimes incorrectly. It is from this account—weighed up against Nasution's own recollections—that it was possible to gain a much more complete picture of the very close familial relationship that developed between these two men.

Sunarti's memoir provides additional insights into difficulties that arose in Nasution's relations with President Sukarno. Unlike, for example, the flamboyant and openly promiscuous Sukarno, Nasution and Sunarti were known to be faithful to each other and strongly opposed to the president's affairs and polygamous marriages.

Translated excerpts from Nasution's and Sunarti's memoirs have been included in this book, as well as the recollections of other Indonesians who grew up in the final years of the Netherlands Indies and experienced the struggle for independence and the political turbulence of the 1950s. They provide an opportunity for them to speak for themselves across time and space and reveal something of their personalities, experiences and feelings to an English-speaking readership.

Nasution's evolving conservative political orientation that championed traditional authority structures based upon his experience of formulating "people's war" strategies in the 1940s and his association of these strategies with organic structures that provided for representation based upon shared function in society, rather than the ideologies of the parties, has not been highlighted in previous research. Similarly, this book's approach of focusing upon Nasution's personal and family life is unique. It provides valuable insights into his political behavior because he and Sunarti enjoyed such a long, close and happy marriage and Sunario Gondokusumo and his associates clearly influenced the young Nasution.

Some of Cribb's publications (which appeared when the research which underpins this book was being concluded) provided valuable affirmation of Nasution's motivations. These included his depoliticization of "people's war" and reliance on "traditional" authority structures and his insightful comments that Nasution's "principal contribution to the theory of guerrilla warfare . . . was his technique for depoliticizing it" and that Nasution was concerned to depoliticize the army and prevent it from becoming a genuine "people's army" along the lines advocated by people's warfare strategists such as Vietnam's general Giap.[7]

The following observation by Cribb was also valuable in affirming conclusions drawn from the research:

> Nasution's remarks [made in the early-to-mid 1950s in his *Fundamentals of Guerrilla Warfare*—an encapsulation of his principles of guerrilla war and his interpretation of the war against the Dutch] about the organic relationship between the guerrilla and society were thus not made just for the sake of developing guerrilla strategies but also to claim for the army a direct relationship with the people, independent of the republican state, and so to establish a platform and justification for army involvement in politics.[8]

Like Cribb, this book explores the values implied within Nasution's "total people's resistance" strategies. Where it differs most from Cribb's is its concern to identify how Nasution arrived at those values and to determine how the principles of "people's war" that he developed were transformed into a means of military intervention in politics, society, and the economy in the 1950s and early 1960s.

In particular, it identifies Nasution's association between "people's war" led by organic traditional authority figures and the army in the armed struggle against the Dutch, and Sukarno's proposals for organicist forms of interest representation a decade later. It identifies how Nasution transformed his principles of "people's war" into a highly unusual form of military intervention in politics, economy and society that sought to counter the rising influence of the Communist Party. It traces his use of the army's "people's resistance" apparatus to apply these principles in support of organic corporatist/functional forms of interest representation in the mid-to-late 1950s, including a political role for the army as a functional group in its own right. It further traces how Nasution's idealized principles of army-led "people's war" became the bedrock of a comprehensive form of military intervention known as the Doctrine of Territorial Warfare and Territorial Management.

This approach and line of argument on the evolution of Nasution's political thinking and its impact on Indonesian civilian and military politics differs from that of Ulf Sundhaussen and C.L.M. Penders in their 1985 political biography of Nasution entitled *Abdul Haris Nasution: A Political Biography*.⁹ This work is particularly valuable in tracing Nasution's early years and relations with other army officers and political leaders.

Penders and Sundhaussen quote sparingly from *Memenuhi Panggilan Tugas* in their chapters on Nasution's early life, perhaps because it was still incomplete at the time they wrote and they had already amassed other material.¹⁰ Of course, they did not have access to Sunarti's *Pak Nas dalam Kenangan* and they did not delve deeply into Nasution's association with the Gondokusumo family and other Parindra-associated figures.

This is evident in their misidentification of Nasution's father-in-law as Djody (rather than R.P. Sunario) Gondokusumo. At the time of writing his 1996 PhD thesis entitled *Lineages of Organicist Political Thought in Indonesia* David Bourchier did not notice this and he also refers to Nasution's father-in-law as Djody Gondokusumo (a prominent lawyer who became a minister for justice before being convicted for corruption and pardoned by President Sukarno). Djody was not Nasution's father-in-law and not related to R.P. Sunario Gondokusumo. Bourchier later became aware of this error and assisted in clarifying the situation in email correspondence.¹¹ It is important to identify Nasution's father-in-law correctly given the influence the older man had on Nasution's political socialization.

While this book is concerned with identifying and describing how Nasution chose to dampen what he saw as harmful and dangerous divisions within society by extolling and then resorting to the socially conservative principles of "people's resistance" he had formulated in the armed struggle against the Dutch, Penders and Sundhaussen discuss the transformation of these doctrines into means of military intervention in the 1950s but do not examine in depth Nasution's motives for doing so. Indeed, these researchers found it difficult to discern his political views, remarking that Nasution's writings revealed almost nothing about his early political socialization and that they had to rely upon "a series of events and circumstances."¹²

Another point of departure is that this book was informed by important findings on the emergence of organic approaches to interest representation in Indonesia in David Bourchier's dissertation¹³ and David Reeve's 1985 *Golkar of Indonesia*.¹⁴ It draws upon the work that they did in identifying Nasution's affiliations with *priyayi* members of the aristocratically based corps of civil servants known as the *pamong praja*, members of the royal houses of Yogyakarta in Central Java, and important figures like the constitutional law academic professor Djokosutono who advised Nasution on constitutionally allowable approaches to military intervention in politics from the early 1950s and played a significant part in Nasution's embrace of organic corporatist/ functional modes of interest representation during that decade. However, with its concentration on Nasution and his principles of "people's resistance," this book goes much further than these researchers in tracing Nasution's contacts with elite members of the *priyayi* class, including the Gondokusumo family, and in identifying and tracing the emergence and application of his socially conservative principles of total people's resistance.

Susan McKemmish's unpublished 1975 MA thesis, *A Political Biography of General Nasution*,[15] is the other main scholarly account in English of Nasution's career. She not only painstakingly researches a wide range of events and influences that impacted on Nasution but is particularly concerned to identify colleagues who were involved with Nasution and the parts they played in his career. She provides a balanced and nuanced portrayal of Nasution's strengths and weaknesses, and offers insights into Nasution's personality. Her work is particularly useful in explaining Nasution's outsider status in the early 1950s vis-à-vis a large group of other officers who were linked with the Socialist Party, the shifting political allegiances in army headquarters leading up to the October 17, 1952 Affair, and Nasution's frustration and lack of decisiveness as the crisis unfolded.

Perhaps the most useful aspect of her work, from the point of view of this book, was her account of how Nasution shifted his political position after being dismissed as army chief of staff in 1952. She carefully describes the emergence of Nasution's strident anti-party stance and open dislike of the liberal-democratic system while he was on the inactive list. Similarly, she recounts the influences and factors that led to Nasution's rapprochement with Sukarno during 1955.

However, McKemmish does not explore Nasution's relationship with the Gondokusumo family and other leading conservative figures, or mention the relationship between Nasution and Djokosutono. Nor does she explore the influence of Nasution's political orientation upon his principles of "people's war," such as his reliance upon organic "traditional" authority structures.

NOTES

1. *The Library of Congress Studies*, data as of November 1992.
2. This is hinted at in the following Library of Congress description of the Batak: "Culturally, they lack the complex etiquette and social hierarchy of the Hinduised peoples of Indonesia. Indeed, they seem to bear closer resemblance to the highland swidden cultivators of Southeast Asia, even though some also practice *padi* farming." Ibid.
3. Susan Abeyasekere, *One Hand Clapping: Indonesian Nationalists and the Dutch 1939–1942*, Clayton, Vic, Centre of Southeast Studies, 1976, p. v.

4. Robert Cribb, "Military Strategy in the Indonesian Revolution: Nasution's Concept of 'Total People's War' in Theory and Practice" in *War and Society*, Volume 19, Number 2, 2001, pp. 144, 145.

5. Sunarti, *Pak Nas dalam Kenangan* (translated title: *Pak Nas Remembered*) as told to and written by Ramadhan K.H. and Sukiarta Sriwibawa. Jakarta: Pusat Sejarah dan Tradisi TNI.

6. Ramadhan K.H. was one of the two "ghost writers" of the remarkably hagiographic autobiography of former president Suharto (*Soeharto: Pikiran, Ucapan dan Tindakan Saya—Soeharto: My Thoughts, Words and Deeds*). *Pak Nas dalam Kenangan* was published by the Indonesian Army Centre for History and Tradition.

7. Cribb, 2001 *Op. Cit.*, p. 146. Another publication by Cribb where the lines of argument are similar to those developed in this book is: "From Total People's Defence to Massacre: Explaining Military Violence in East Timor" in F. Colombijn and J.T. Lindblad (eds.), *Roots of Violence in Indonesia*, Leiden, KITVL Press, 2002, pp. 227–242

8. Cribb, 2001 *Op. Cit* p. 145.

9. C.L.M. Penders and Ulf Sundhaussen, *Abdul Haris Nasution: A Political Biography*, St Lucia, University of Queensland Press, 1985.

10. Sundhaussen had previously compiled a large amount of material on Nasution for his PhD thesis that was published under the title *The Road to Power: Indonesian Military Politics 1945–1967,* Kuala Lumpur and New York, Oxford University Press, 1982.

11. Bourchier advised me of the error initially made by Penders and Sundhaussen (email dated March 20, 2005) in response to a question I raised on a discussion list. I realized that Djody Gondokusumo could not possibly have been Nasution's father-in-law as Djody was born in 1912 and Nasution's wife, Sunarti, was born in 1923 (after her father had studied in the Netherlands and returned to Indonesia). Some biographical information on Djody Gondokusumo can be found in Benedict R. O'G. Anderson, *Java in a Time of Revolution*, Ithaca, NY, Cornell University Press, 1972, p. 417.

12. Penders and Sundhaussen, *Op. Cit.*, p. 65.

13. David Bouchier, (1996), *Lineages of Organicist Thought in Indonesia*, unpublished PhD thesis, Monash University. This was subsequently adapted into a book entitled *Illiberal Democracy in Indonesia*: *The Idea of the Family State*, Routledge, Oxon and New York, 2015 but this work draws upon the thesis.

14. David Reeve, *Golkar of Indonesia: An Alternative to the Party System*, Oxford University Press, Singapore, New York.

15. Susan McKemmish, *A Political Biography of General Nasution*, Unpublished MA Thesis, Monash University.

Chapter 2

Coming of Age

Sunarti was born and grew up in a Javanese milieu in which there were important social and religious cleavages. The refined *priyayi* class, to which the Gondokusumo family belonged, generally adhered to a form of Islam that was syncretically interwoven with earlier religious influences while the *abangan* peasant masses followed less elaborate syncretic practices. Only the more *santri* Javanese (often traders) adhered to the relatively "orthodox" form of Islam that was introduced by the traders from India.

Like the British in India and Malaya, the Dutch preferred to rule the Indies through the intermediation of traditional authority figures. In Java, they relied upon the *pangreh praja* indigenous civil service whose members were drawn from the *priyayi* class. From the late nineteenth century, increasing numbers of young Indonesians from *priyayi* and similar backgrounds in other parts of the colony were educated in Dutch schools and tertiary institutes that were mostly located on Java. A small number, like Sunarti's father, attended universities in Holland.

This access to Western education often had the opposite result to that hoped for by the colonizing power. Europeans were at the top of the system of racial stratification employed in the Indies, followed by Chinese and other "foreign" Asiatics, and then "native" Indonesians. Many educated Indonesians found their categorization within this "pecking order" as *inlanders* or natives profoundly insulting. They often felt slighted in their dealings with the Dutch and heavily discriminated against when they sought employment or promotion.[1] Moreover, by the 1930s an increasing number of *pangreh praja* officials felt frustrated at being relegated to the status of junior and relatively powerless partners to the Dutch bureaucrats of the Interior Administration (*Binnenlands Bestuur*).[2]

The complexity of the situation facing these recipients of a high-quality Dutch education was often compounded by a sense of alienation from lower-class syncretic Javanese, the *abangan* majority who mainly lived in rural villages. To many *priyayi*, these were places of relative ignorance, privation and hardship and they preferred to live in the large towns and cities that had grown in number and size under colonial rule.³ Sunarti's parents were no exception, preferring to reside in the cities of Surabaya and Bandung.

Her father, Sunario Gondokusumo, held the high aristocratic title of *Raden Panji* (often shortened to the initials R.P. before his name) and could trace his lineage to the East Java-based Brawijaya dynasty⁴ of the Hindu-Buddhist Majapahit kingdom (twelfth to fifteenth century). Majapahit was something of a precursor to modern Indonesia, as it exercised influence over Java, Sumatra, Kalimantan, the Moluccas and some other coastal areas of Southeast Asia.

Sunario was at first employed as a *patih* or chief minister to the *pangreh praja* regent (*bupati*) at Mojokerto, near Surabaya.⁵ Sunarti writes that because her father was involved in anti-government activities the Dutch prevented him from going on to become a *bupati* and then exiled him to the Netherlands from 1917 to 1921 where he studied economics.⁶ Ki Hadjar Dewantoro, an exponent of traditional Indonesian approaches to education, happened to live next door to the family of Sunario's future wife, Maria Hendrika Rademaker, and introduced Sunario to her.⁷

Maria was warned by her uncle, a former Netherlands Indies Army colonel who had served in Aceh, that she would end up living in primitive conditions if she married an *inlander*. She disregarded his advice and (accompanied by her mother) moved to the Indies, following Sunario who had finished his education and returned beforehand. They would spend the rest of their lives there.

Far from sinking into a life of poverty and squalor, Maria found that the Gondokusumos were a Dutch-speaking and well-off aristocratic family.⁸ In those latter decades of colonial rule many Indonesians within their social milieu enjoyed considerable affluence, including car and electric household appliance ownership that was beyond the reach of many living in Western countries. The biographer of General Benny Moerdani, who was an Indonesian Army commander in the 1980s, shares how well-off families like his and Sunario Gondokusumo's were in those years:

> In those pre-World War II times, the Moerdani family lived in circumstances very similar to that of most of the Dutch community. Their material possessions were also similar. For example, Moerdani senior had a motor car—a "Hudson"; and their home contained both a piano and a refrigerator.⁹

Bolstered by centuries of relative privilege and equipped with marvelous cultural artifacts these elite families could be charming and congenial to mix with. This proved to be a powerful weapon when attempting to force the Dutch to recognize Indonesia's independence in the 1940s, as Tom Critchley, Australia's representative to a United Nations committee that was attempting to mediate between the Indonesians and the Dutch, remarked (in contrast to the resentful attitude of many Dutch officials):

> Besides our working relations, we also enjoyed recreational friendships with the Indonesians. For example, I regularly played tennis with Sjahrir [prime minister in the early years of the struggle].[10]

From the outset, Maria Gondokusumo decided to identify with the indigenous population but did so in a very Western philanthropic way, throwing herself into social welfare activities. In doing so, she set an example for Sunarti who was to devote much of her life to such pursuits.

Nevertheless, Sunarti also grew up with strong connections to her Dutch heritage. The Dutch language and culture were passed on to her by her mother and grandmother and she attended schools that catered to the Dutch community and the richest layer of Indonesians. Moreover, there were substantial Dutch and Eurasian communities in the cities where she grew up.

Many of the Dutch colonists loved the Indies and lived there permanently for generations, rather than returning to Holland to retire, as most British did from India and Malaya. Indeed, the percentage of Dutch or Dutch-Indonesian Eurasians in the population of the Indies and the range of occupations they followed was significantly larger than the British presence in colonial India:

> the British community in India was relatively much smaller than the Dutch in the Indies. Whereas there was one European to every 244 Indonesians, in India in 1931 there was one European (or American) to 2,750 Indians (118,000 European-born, 4,500 American-born aliens in a population of 338 million). The difference in size of these communities had certain effects on their functions. Whereas the Dutch community in the Indies followed a range of occupations from Governor-General to minor official and small shopkeeper, the British in India were purely a ruling class. . . . In addition, the Europeans in India were temporary visitors. Only a few made their homes in India, and rarely before retirement. In contrast, some 70 per cent of the Dutch community were born in the Indies, and an increasing proportion were becoming domiciled there.[11]

This relative density and pervasiveness of the Dutch and Eurasian population made a strong impact on the towns they established where there were modern shops, hotels, ice cream parlors and cinemas. Nowadays, the many publications that describe the lives of the Dutch and Eurasians in the Indies before the war recall a settled and tranquil life that they expected to continue, seemingly unaware of how precariously they ruled over a much larger indigenous population in the shadow of the rising power of Japan.

A Dutchman who migrated to Australia after the war recalls an atmosphere that, in his opinion, was free of racial tensions:

> I went to school in Surabaya. There were children of rich Arabs, Chinese children, Indos (Eurasians); ham and cheese, ham and cheese, just a bit of colour. But I don't think there was racism like under the British. If you had money to sit first class in the electric tram, you could be a Chinese with two heads, you would sit in first class as long as you had money. But if you were poor, you would sit in second class. If you went third class by train you had wooden seats. There were rich Indonesians, there were Indonesians that were in government jobs, executive positions, and they would travel first class. I never worried about colour. I don't think my father worried about colour, his partner was Chinese.[12]

The variety of occupations of the Dutch and Eurasians, some of whom had little material wealth, is also evident in his recollections:

> In 1933, with the depression, I can well remember there were white men, white Europeans, Dutch Hollanders from Holland, walking around with a little suitcase open, selling matches, shoe laces and cigarettes and things, trying to make a little bit of money.[13]

The social and economic gap between the Gondokusumo family and the uneducated, impoverished masses was very wide, as Sunarti makes clear in recollections of her childhood:

> Mother often took us children for walks in the villages. She told us stories about the actual situation in our homeland so that we could see the real situation of the people. To see the utter deprivation would inspire us when we became adults to try to find out why they lived in poverty, and to find various ways to help them so that they could improve the standard and dignity of their lives.[14]

Elite Indonesians with whom Sunarti grew up generally favored a "cooperating" style of nationalism, unsuccessfully attempting "to extract concessions from the Dutch in the last years before the outbreak of the Pacific war in 1941."[15] Most were unable to withstand the rapid succession of events that favored the noncooperators like Sukarno and Sjahrir.[16]

There was a world of difference between "cooperating nationalism" and the romantic, revolutionary "non-cooperating nationalism" espoused by Sukarno. Benedict Anderson has commented insightfully that prior to declaring Indonesia's independence, Sukarno's career had taken place "physically and politically *outside the state*" and was:

> built entirely on the mobilisation of popular forces (the nationalist movement) and in long-standing opposition to the colonial state. Not only had Sukarno

never been an official of that state, but he had been spied on by its informers, arrested by its police, tried by its judges, and imprisoned and internally exiled for almost eleven years by its top bureaucratic directorate. And many of those who spied on, arrested, and sequestered him—not to speak of those who steadfastly obstructed his political work in the periods when he was free—were Indonesian members of the state apparatus.[17]

On the other hand, many cooperating nationalists worked within the same colonial government apparatus.

Sunario Gondokusumo was a leading figure within the main cooperating nationalist party, the Greater Indonesia Party known by its acronym *Parindra*. That his party was prepared to cooperate with the Dutch is evident in the willingness of Parindra members to sit in the *Volksraad* (the Dutch-created embryonic legislative assembly which eventually consisted of Indonesian representatives who were indirectly elected through regional councils and colonial officials) and in other assemblies created by the Dutch.[18] Noncooperators refused to have anything to do with the *Volksraad* which they regarded with disdain.

Parindra was socially conservative and *priyayi* based, and included many *pangreh praja* figures.[19] The party had its roots in Indonesia's first nationalist organization, *Budi Utomo* (Noble Endeavour). Founded in 1908 by a retired *priyayi* Javanese doctor, Wahidin Sudirohusodo, the aim of *Budi Utomo* was to find a synthesis between traditional Javanese culture and the modernity of the early twentieth century. He found inspiration in Japan's victory over Russia in 1901, which debunked the myth of inherent white superiority and showed that an Asian society could become industrialized and militarily powerful.

Another leading member of *Buti Utomo* was Dr. Sutomo, a student of the colony's STOVIA School for the Training of Native Doctors.[20] Like Ki Hadjar Dewantoro, Sutomo was critical of Western education because he saw it as introducing imported and undesirable influences. He also eschewed the other major imported influences of the day: communism and political Islam.[21]

Budi Utomo was essentially an elitist *priyayi* organization. Sutherland observes that while it included "more radical students such as Tjipto Mangoenkoesoemo" who "pressed for wider social changes" leadership positions were accorded to relatively conservative establishment figures and the organization sought to improve the lot of the poor without "having to descend to their level."[22]

Soon *Budi Utomo* was joined on the political stage by the *Sarekat Dagang Islam* (Association of Muslim Merchants), which was initially aimed at seeking to unsettle the economic dominance of the Chinese in business. This organization also soon became a nationalist political party (*Sarekat Islam*). There followed a number of other new parties and organizations including the

Indonesian Communist Party (the *Partai Komunis Indonesia* or PKI), which grew out of a split within *Sarekat Islam* in 1920.

Sunario Gondokusumo was personally very close to Dr. Sutomo, to the extent that they built a holiday house together in a village near Mojokerto, located about fifty kilometers from Surabaya.[23] In 1924, Sutomo formed the Indonesia Study Club (*Indonesische Studieclub*) in Surabaya which he intended to become a national organization. However, similarly named clubs were formed in other locations as competitors, rather than subsections of the Surabaya group. Sukarno was first secretary of the Bandung Study Club and he and his colleagues quickly decided on a policy of noncooperation. On the other hand, as Dahm observes, "Sutomo's study club regarded [cooperation] as a tactical weapon for use now and then in forcing the Dutch finally to yield to the demands of the Indonesians for a share of responsibility, and thus to further the principle of genuine cooperation."[24]

In 1926 and 1927 the PKI staged what turned out to be premature and failed revolts in West Java and West Sumatra and the party was quickly banned and its leaders exiled. In 1927, Sukarno and others established the "non-cooperating" Indonesian Nationalist Party (*Partai Nasional Indonesia*—PNI).

As Sutherland notes, the appeal of organizations like the PNI "to younger Western-educated Indonesians was much stronger than that of earlier parties. If the PKI had been too radical, *Budi Utomo* too 'feudal' and *Sarekat Islam* too *santri* or too *kampung* [village], the new organizations were intellectually acceptable and satisfyingly militant."[25]

In 1928, an Indonesian Youth Congress sought to give the Indonesian nationalist movement priority over regional youth movements that had emerged in the previous decades, such as *Jong Java* (Youth of Java), *Jong Sumatrenen Bond* (Youth of Sumatra), and so on. The Congress took the historic step of adopting the "Youth Pledge" (*Sumpah Pemuda*) of "one country, one nation, one language" (Indonesian). The Dutch soon cracked down and later in the same year Sukarno was arrested, jailed and then exiled to the island of Flores before he ended up in Bengkulu, West Sumatra. Other "non-cooperating" nationalists met a worse fate, being exiled to the Boven Digul prison in the remote and sparsely populated hinterland of far-away Papua until the Japanese invasion was imminent in 1942.

In January 1931, Sutomo founded another cooperating party, *Persatuan Bangsa Indonesia* (Indonesian Unity Party), and in 1935 he merged *Persatuan Bangsa Indonesia* with *Budi Oetomo* to form *Partai Indonesia Raya* (Parindra). The aim of the new party was to achieve the independence of Indonesia through cooperation with the Dutch (including acceptance of membership of the *Volksraad*). Sutomo died in May 1938 and was replaced by the relatively ineffective aristocrat R. M. Hario Woerjaningrat, who was soon eclipsed by the fiery Jakarta-based deputy chairman M.H. Thamrin.

Under Thamrin's leadership and in an atmosphere of heightening international tensions Parindra initiated moves to form a federation of nationalist parties that became known as *Gabungan Politik Indonesia* (Gapi—Indonesian Political Federation). Gapi was ostensibly a loyal and moderate organization with the somewhat limited goal of seeking a parliament for the Indies, but it exhibited a new political toughness in its "bargaining attitude" with the Dutch authorities.[26]

By early 1939 Parindra claimed a membership of 4,500 members, although there was a surge to 11,000 members later that year as the outbreak of the Second World War gave cooperating nationalists more hope that international events might improve their bargaining position with the Dutch.[27] Parindra owned several newspapers and magazines[28] and another ten Malay language[29] newspapers and one Dutch-language magazine[30] were sympathetic to the party.

In the 1920s, Sutomo resigned from the municipal council of Surabaya as a protest against the impotence of the representatives of the indigenous population. He then sought to build on traditional *gotong royong* mutual assistance systems known as *sinoman*.[31]

The word *sinoman* is still used throughout Java to describe groups of young men who join together in communal activities.[32] The mutual assistance aspect of *sinoman* was highly developed in the urban villages of Surabaya in the final decades of Dutch rule[33] and Sutomo drew upon it to develop organizations he termed *Raad Sinoman* or *Gemeente Raad Bangsa Indonesia*[34] as alternatives to Dutch-imposed quasi-suburban governments (*wijkbestuur*) in the urban villages (*kampung*) of Surabaya.

Sutomo aimed to advise and assist the Indonesian masses to improve their lot through "self-help" organizations[35] such as the Parindra-affiliated farmer's organization *Rukun Tani* and the maritime association, *Rukun Pelayaran*. The primary meaning of the word *rukun* is pillar or cornerstone but its widely used secondary meanings are "harmony" and "like-mindedness," indicating the concern of the Parindra leaders to maintain the indigenous status quo. Their appeal to organic and traditional forms of mutual assistance, such as *sinoman* and *gotong royong* implies a similar intention. They were seeking to mobilize the masses for the nationalist cause while assuming that "traditional" fundamentals of social order would remain fundamentally unaltered. Parindra also sought to mobilize younger generations by developing the *Surya Wirawan* youth movement.[36]

Sunario Gondokusumo's association with Sutomo began in Surabaya in the 1920s. He was an organizer of Sutomo's Indonesia Study Club and other organizations, such as the *Rukun Pelayaran* and *Rukun Tani*.[37] Like her husband, Maria Gondokusumo became a member of Parindra and Sunarti recalls selling the red and white nationalist flag in the streets of Surabaya to raise funds for the construction of the *Gedung Indonesia* (Indonesian Building),[38] an object of great pride for the nationalists of Surabaya, that Sutomo and his friends initiated.[39]

On returning to Java from his studies in the Netherlands, Sunario had joined the state railway company.[40] He later became the founding director of the Parindra-owned National Bank of Indonesia in Surabaya and was subsequently appointed head of the indigenous *Bumi Putera* (Son of the Soil) insurance company in Bandung, where the family moved from Surabaya in 1937.

Sunario and Maria passed on the values of the Surabaya group of Parindra activists to Sunarti, who was introduced to rural village life thanks to the holiday house that Sunario shared with Sutomo:

> I was always raised in cities and mostly mixed with educated people. Nevertheless, from the time I was small my mother took me to rural villages (*desa*) where I mixed with the local people. Father, who participated in the struggle with Dr Sutomo, built a holiday place together [with Dr Sutomo] in the rural village of Celakat, near Mojokerto. Our family often took holidays there and my brothers and I played all day long with the village children.[41]

According to the following excerpt from a biography she provided when awarded the 1981 Ramon Magsaysay Award for charitable works, she not only visited rural villages but joined in her mother's social work in the "urban slums" of Surabaya:

> Johanna's mother, though Dutch, raised her children to be nationalists and dressed in *kain* (long wrapped skirt) and *kebaya* (long-sleeved overblouse), the Indonesian national costume. She was a leader of the Indonesian Girl Scouts until 1937 and was very active in social welfare work. She often took her daughter to help the poor in the urban slums. Johanna once wrote a high school paper about these visits and remembers the anger and astonishment she felt when her Dutch teacher returned the composition saying, "This is not your work; it looks very communistic. Please change it."[42]

A young resident of Surabaya at the time, Suhario Padmodiwiryo, recalls that the efforts of the Indonesian Unity Party and Parindra in developing "the *Suara Umum* newspaper, the *Rukun Tani* organization, the Indonesian National Bank, the People's Cooperative Bank, the Indonesian Maritime Union, village schools, and the small industry cooperatives" were "more romantic than scientific."[43] There is little doubt that the "romantic" sentiments of the Parindra activists in carrying out their noblesse oblige activities in the villages were passed on to Sunarti.

Nasution's early life could hardly have been more different from that of Sunarti's *priyayi* family. Although his family was relatively prosperous by rural village standards, his early circumstances were very different from those of Sunarti and her family.

Nasution was born in December 1918 in the Mandailing region on the border of North and West Sumatra. Huta-Pungkut, the small rural village of his birth, lies in a fertile river valley on the western side of the Bukit Barisan mountain range. Later in life, Nasution likened the Priangan mountain range near Bandung, where he was to meet Sunarti, with the beautiful mountain scenery of Mandailing. At the time, the Mandailing area was under the authority of a Dutch colonial civil service official known as a Controller.

He recalls that life in the village was very basic and not very hygienic. Villagers washed without soap and emptied their bowels in the river. He only had two sets of clothes, with a new one being presented each *Lebaran* (Muslim New Year). The older clothes were worn for a week at a time and washed in the river on Sundays. He only began to use toothbrushes (without toothpaste) and to wear underwear and footwear in Grade Six.[44]

Nasution also remembers that he and other children in the village had to protect the rice crops from birds and keep watch on the flow of irrigation water for the rice fields. Children felt like members of the same family, but one with many mothers.

Nasution's father was one of a tiny minority of villagers who were not solely dependent upon rice cultivation or other crops. He was a small-scale peddler of various wares, including textiles, and bought rubber and coffee beans from local planters to be sold to Chinese traders in the larger cities. Whereas Sunarti's family owned a car, Nasution's father transported the rubber and coffee that he traded in a hired truck or horse-drawn cart. Nasution fondly recalled these trips to cities such as Bukit Tinggi, Sibolga or Padangsidempuan.

However, his father's business was badly affected by the Great Depression in the early 1930s. They had to live from the proceeds of their rice but this was not enough to live on, let alone repay money already borrowed for buying and selling goods; a creditor once even threatened to seize their home and irrigated rice fields.[45]

Nasution did very well at school, perhaps due to the influence of his mother. One of her older brothers had been educated at the STOVIA medical school in Batavia (now Jakarta) and she had the same dream for her son. On the other hand, his father was intent on Nasution going to a religious school. A compromise was reached where he attended a government school in the mornings and a Muslim school (*Madrasah*) in the afternoons, where he learned to recite the Koran by heart.[46] He was separated from his family from the age of thirteen when he moved to a school at Kotanopan, six kilometers from Huta-Pungkut, staying there with relatives. This was his first separation from his family and he felt it deeply.

Apart from religious piety, his father's most enduring influence seems to have been his stories of the wars undertaken in the sixth century by Mohammed and in contemporary times by the Turks.[47] He was an admirer of Mustafa Kemal Pasha (Kemal Ataturk), the Turkish military and political leader, whose picture was the sole decoration in the Nasution home. McKemmish writes that Nasution "and other young Muslims were inspired by the example of Mustafa Kemal and other Turkish military commanders."[48] However, entry to the officer corps of the Royal Netherlands Indies Army or KNIL was restricted to a very few Indonesians from aristocratic and well-connected families who were sent to the Royal Dutch Military Academy in Breda. It was impossible for a village boy like Nasution to aspire to such a career.

Nasution does not record if his father admired Ataturk for taking Turkey along a Western path toward modernization, which included the disestablishment of Islam, but the Turkish leader's approach to the separation of religion and state attracted attention around the world and it is probable that Nasution heard of it.[49] It is interesting that Ataturk's "secular" approach to Islam accorded with Nasution's devotion to *Panca Sila*, the pluralistic five pillars of national life developed by Sukarno in 1945, which carefully avoids giving a special place to Islam. The influence of Ataturk might also have inspired Nasution in the 1950s when he led the army in a long and bitter war against the powerful *Darul Islam* movement that aimed to make Indonesia an Islamic state, rather than the essentially secular one that emerged from the struggle against the Dutch.

His intelligence and diligence led to unusual opportunities for education that eventually were to propel him from rural obscurity to a leading role in the struggle for independence and the political turmoil of the 1950s. In 1932, he won a scholarship to a native teacher's training school (*Sekolah Raja*) in Bukit Tinggi, West Sumatra, that was only open to the top primary school students in each region.

Life at the *Sekolah Raja* in the bustling, sizeable city of Bukit Tinggi was highly disciplined and routinized and this seems to have helped him to settle into his new life. The first-year students took it in turns to be the bell monitor, signaling time to get up in the mornings, eat, start school, go from one lesson to the other, rest, study in the evenings, etc.[50] Students also took turns to be the "officer of the week," maintaining order and supervising at meal times. They were organized into sports, art and religious clubs and senior students ensured that juniors behaved well both inside and outside the school.

Nasution, who has described this period as his boarding school years,[51] continued living an austere lifestyle in various dormitories for much of his youth and early adulthood. All the teachers, except for an art instructor, were Dutch and the three years he spent there enabled Nasution to achieve a good standard of Dutch and gave him valuable insights into how the colonizers thought and behaved. This not only assisted him when seeking to defeat their army in the 1940s but prepared him to mix with Sunarti's Dutch mother and grandfather when he was introduced to the Gondokusumo family.

The *Sekolah Raja* in Bukit Tinggi was closed due to the financial constraints brought about by the Great Depression of the 1930s, but again Nasution's keen intelligence and disciplined approach to his studies came to the fore. He was one of only four out of 100 students who passed a strict screening test to continue their education at the teacher training college in Bandung.[52] He was to study and live there in dormitories for another three years.

It is hard to imagine how unusual it was for a rural village boy to be given such an opportunity, but some statistics cast light on his achievement. In 1900 the population of the Indies was approximately forty-three million but there were only 1,500 schools in the colony. The 1930 census (the last carried out in the colony) recorded that only 6.4 percent of the non-European and non-Eurasian population were literate.[53]

Nasution was not only unusually hard-working and intelligent but something of a romantic and this no doubt spurred him on in his studies. After listening to his father's stories about the military feats of Mohammed and Ataturk he became a keen reader and intensely interested in history. His father's tales had engendered in him a special interest in military conflicts and he voraciously read Dutch accounts of their eighty-year war to achieve independence from Spain.

Nasution travelled aboard an inter-island ship for four days and nights to reach the port of Batavia, the largest city he had ever seen. He then ventured out by rail through the untidy, muddy flatlands that fringed the colonial capital and up into the gorgeously green terraced rice fields, deep gorges and swiftly flowing rivers of the Priangan mountain range to begin his studies in Bandung.

All his twenty-five classmates were from teacher training schools around the archipelago that had been closed and he began to mix with Indonesians from the main island of Java and other parts of the Indies for the first time. He soon acquired an even greater liking for history, inspired by one of his teachers, Mr. van der Werf, who was the leader of the Catholic Party in Bandung and often discussed politics with the students.[54]

Cool, elegant Bandung was home to a unique Indies style art deco architecture, much of which has been retained into the twenty-first century. It was a cosmopolitan center for education and home to the prestigious *Technische Hogeschool* (now the Bandung Institute of Technology—*Institut Teknologi Bandung*) and other academic institutions, including Nasution's teacher training school. An Australian visitor of the time, Frank Clune, described Bandung in the early 1940s as "the nearest thing on our globe to an Earthly Paradise" and:

a beautiful city of red-tiled white houses. But the glare of the red roofs is softened by a mantle of tropical green moss, laid there by the generous hand of nature.[55]

The size and location of the substantial public buildings that had been placed along the broad tree-lined avenues indicated the high expectations the Dutch had for the city. The colonial regime planned to move the center of government there from Batavia, as Jakarta was known. In 1942, the Japanese invasion put an abrupt stop to these plans and their dream ended in a nightmare when eight years later they had to cede sovereignty to an independent state led by their nemesis, the charismatic Sukarno.

Like the Dutch and so many others, Sukarno was an admirer of the West Java capital. He recalled that when he arrived there by train to study at the *Technische Hogeschool* in 1921: "It was love at first sight between me and Bandung."[56] The "Paris of Java" was at its best in the 1920s and 1930s when it:

was a beautiful, pleasant town in the mountains of West Java with a Mediterranean climate. It did not have the hectic pace of Surabaya (where Sukarno had been living); in Bandung, you did not run as in Surabaya but you strolled. The new student had no difficulty in joining the strollers.[57]

The beauty of the city in those prewar days was also evident at night, as the West Javanese novelist Achdiat K. Mihardja recorded:

Before the war, the descending twilight made a breathtaking picture of the city: the electric lights were turned on in the streets, shops, and houses. . . . As time passed, light from thousands of globes grew brighter throughout the city, finally coalescing into a sea of illumination. People, cars, and other forms of transport were on the move, like tiny fish in motion on the bed of a gleaming ocean. Red blouses, yellow dresses, gabardine suits streamed along the footpaths in front of the brightly lit shops. Packards, Fords, Erskines and Willys glittered on the roadways, forcing Fongers, Raleigh and Humber bicycles and gigs to the kerb. People were right in saying that Bandung, the "Paris of Java," began to come alive at 6 p.m.[58]

Unlike the flamboyant, well-connected, and increasingly rebellious Sukarno who had soon cut a dashing figure from his base at the *Technische Hogeschool*, Nasution was a quiet, reserved, studious and religious boy from obscure rural origins who had to make do with a much lesser institution. Rather than following Sukarno's path of noisy noncooperation with the colonial regime he was completely dependent upon the colonial government for his education, food and accommodation.

Nasution retained a close attachment to Bandung and its spectacular mountainous surroundings throughout his life but did not do well in the practical aspects of his teacher training where his austere and serious disposition failed to strike a chord with students.[59] On graduation in 1938 he returned to Sumatra (where Sukarno was by then in exile), gaining employment at a private Dutch-language school in Bengkulu for a few months. He then moved to Muara Dua in the Palembang district before moving again to Tanjungpraja, near the city of Palembang. While still in Bandung, Nasution had begun studying for the matriculation certificate that was available to graduates of Dutch Senior High Schools (*Algemene Middelbare School*—AMS). He passed the examination while at Tanjungpraja.[60]

In May 1940, the Germans invaded Holland and the Royal Military Academy at Breda was no longer available. Alarmed at the looming threat from Japan, the Netherlands Indies government established a reserve officer corps and opened a branch of the academy in Bandung. Nasution writes that he had studied for his matriculation with the aim of seeking entry to Breda before the Bandung Academy was established, even though he was aware that entry was restricted to one indigenous cadet each year.[61] Now his matriculation certificate was invaluable and the possibility of success much greater as the new academy was accepting applications from young Indonesians. Nasution was one of a dozen or so Indonesian matriculants to pass the tight selection tests.

Since his time in Bukit Tinggi he had sought refuge from dormitory life where possible in the family homes of friends or relations.[62] His new status as an officer cadet now gained him entry to more well-to-do indigenous circles in the city and he became acquainted with the Gondokusumo family.

Nasution appears to have been quite prepared to accept Sunario Gondokusumo's advocacy of cooperating nationalism as he had been attracted to that approach to politics from his time at the teacher training college in Bandung. He writes that the parents of a fellow student, Artawi, were both nationalist and members of a KNIL auxiliary organization and that Artawi's rationalization for this seemingly paradoxical situation was that Indonesians had to seize any opportunity to learn skills from the Dutch that could help their cause. For Artawi's family, this included associating with the repressive KNIL that was still mainly an instrument for safeguarding colonial rule from internal insurgency, rather than a conventional army with a focus upon external defense. In Nasution's final year of teacher training in Bandung, he and Artawi often attended open meetings held by *Indonesia Muda* (Young Indonesia), however, he says "neither of us entered a particular organisation."[63]

In 1938 when he had worked as a teacher in Bengkulu Nasution often passed Sukarno's home and the nationalist leader would always say "hello." On the one occasion when Nasution visited his home with some other young people Sukarno "gave a fiery speech" and urged him to join *Indonesia Muda*.[64] However, although Nasution considered joining *Surya Wirawan*, the youth wing of Parindra, he never followed through.[65]

Penders and Sundhaussen attribute Nasution's reluctance to become involved in the nationalist cause to such concerns as: "The failure of political parties to unite for the purpose of fighting for the independence of the country, and largely to split along religious-communal lines,"[66] and a lack of opportunity to "learn and practice in a formal context the art of intellectual dispute."[67] Perhaps more tellingly, they also write that membership of a party would have been incompatible with his search for employment as a teacher and desire to become a military officer.[68]

Mackie writes insightfully that "we can too easily slip into the facile assumption that the nationalist cause was inexorably gaining in strength and popular support, hence that sooner or later it was bound to triumph because the Dutch would eventually have had to give way to demands for a significant degree of self-government—and ultimately independence."[69] It is probable that Nasution would have continued to cooperate with the colonial regime in some way had Dutch rule not been so suddenly and cathartically ended by the Japanese in 1942.

Like other romantic revolutionaries such as Fidel Castro, Che Guevara, Napoleon Bonaparte, Lenin and Marx, leading Indonesian noncooperating independence advocates like Sukarno came from middle-class backgrounds and some like Hatta and Indonesia's first prime minister, Sutan Syahrir, had studied at universities in the Netherlands. The less well-off Nasution's most subversive act while at the Bandung teacher's college was to purchase two second-hand books by Sukarno and circulate them among his friends. The school director became aware of them but luckily the student who held them at the time did not reveal that he had obtained them from Nasution, who recalled: "He said he had found them lying on the ground outside the classroom."[70]

Sunarti writes that Nasution first visited the Gondokusumo residence because she was a member of the scouting organization *Kepanduan Bangsa Indonesia* (KBI) and the young military cadet often mixed with its members.[71] Nasution was by then a serious, deeply intelligent and good-looking young man with a high forehead and prominent cheekbones that are typical of the Batak ethnic group. A keen tennis player for much of his life, he became president of a tennis club in Bandung where Sunarti was the treasurer. She was strikingly beautiful with the Javanese features of her father but taller than most Indonesian girls. He soon became acquainted with Sunario Gondokusumo.

Unlike Nasution's primary school for *inlanders* and teacher training colleges for indigenous young people, Sunarti attended the prestigious Dutch Lyceum secondary school in Bandung and had plans to become a doctor. When the Japanese invaded, she went to Yogyakarta to continue her secondary schooling. She writes that by this time Nasution ("Pak Nas"):

seemed to feel at home within our family. It's true that Pak Nas had a different background from me. He was from the regions, not from the city like me. I was born and brought up in large cities like Surabaya and Bandung while he was born in Kotanopan, a small town in the interior of North Sumatra. I came from, it could be said, a well-off family. Even my bicycle was very nice, bought new for a rather high price. However, Pak Nas, at the time that we met—bear in mind he was far from his parents and had to be frugal—had a bicycle that he bought for 7.5 guilders, if I'm not wrong, a second-hand bicycle. But what made Pak Nas feel at home within our family—apparently because he had previously gone to school in Bandung—was to listen to father talking about idealism and nationalism and the issue of independence, in which he apparently took a great interest and enjoyed.[72]

Nasution soon became close to Sunario, a process that was no doubt assisted by his own leanings toward cooperating nationalism and his welcome into a comfortable family atmosphere after years of living in dormitories:

Our home was open to anybody. And besides that, mother and my brothers were very close to him. Even Oma—my grandmother on my mother's side—paid Pak Nas a lot of attention. Oma had family members who were officers in the Netherlands and because of that she often chatted with Pak Nas about the officer training he was receiving at the Military Academy. In short, Pak Nas found a "home" in our house and we ourselves regarded him as a member of the family.[73]

Elsewhere, Sunarti further attests to the closeness in Nasution's relationship with Sunario:

But that didn't mean that father or mother had plans to match-make between Nas and me (it didn't mean that Pak Nas was my sweetheart). Not at that time. In fact, when the two of us, Pak Nas and I, had plans to get married, father and mother put obstacles in our way because father regarded Pak Nas as his own son.[74]

Father was angry when I told him about our marriage plans. Father thought of Pak Nas as his own son and it would be like having one of his children marry another. What would people say? Especially in a critical time when conflict could break out at any time. However, finally Father became aware that our love for each other was very deep and sacred and he agreed and gave us his blessing.[75]

Another indication of Sunario's closeness to Nasution is a visit the pair made during the Japanese occupation to the Jombang/Mojokerto area in East Java where Sunario had once been *patih* to the regent. Sunario suggested that Nasution could seek shelter there "within the framework of our preparations for action."[76] While Nasution is not explicit about what sort of action was envisaged, Sunario was impressed by Japan and the intention seems to have been to prepare some sort of plan to assist them if they attacked the Indies. When this occurred, Nasution found himself having to decide whether to remain loyal to the Netherlands Indies Army or side with the Japanese. It was the first of many difficult decisions for him as he navigated his way through the turbulent and transformative three years of Japanese occupation.

NOTES

1. Kahin noted that in the late 1930s: "Except as teachers in private schools there were almost no openings within Indonesian society itself for Indonesians with a Western education." Within the civil service, Europeans occupied 92.2% of higher appointments while 98.9% of lower positions were occupied by Indonesians." G. McT. Kahin, *Nationalism and Revolution in Indonesia*, Ithaca, NY, Cornell University Press, 1952., pp. 34, 5.

2. For an account of the growing unrest and attempts at political activism on the part of some members of the *pangreh praja*, see Heather Sutherland, *The Making of a Bureaucratic Elite: The Colonial Transformation of the Javanese Priyayi*, Singapore, Heineman (ASAA Southeast Asia Publications Series), 1979, pp. 114–143.

3. As Umar Kayam illustrates in his historically based novel, *Para Priyayi*, it was possible for some villagers to climb the rungs of education and migrate to the cities where they sometimes prospered within the *pangreh praja* and founded a *priyayi* "dynasty." To such Javanese the village was a place from which they had escaped and to which they had no desire to return. Umar Kayam, *Para Priyayi: Sebuah Novel*, Jakarta, Pustaka Utama Grafiti, 1992.

4. Communication in April 2005 with Professor Soejono, a son of Sunario's brother-in-law, R.P. Soeroso.

5. Nasution, J.S. *Op. Cit.*, p. 224, 225. Nasution writes that Sunario had been an *onder-regent* in Jombang (near Mojokerto). A. H. Nasution, *Memenuhi Panggilan Tugas*, Vol Two A, Jakarta, CV Haji Masagung, 1989, p. 68.

6. Sunarti, *Op. Cit.*

7. Ibid.

8. Ibid., p. 225.

9. Julius Pour, *Benny Moerdani: Profile of a Soldier Statesman*, Jakarta: Yayasan Kejuangan Panglima Besar Sudirman, 1993.

10. Michael Wilson, Recorded Interview with T K Critchley, November 25, 1993, Oral History Section, Australian diplomacy 1950–1990 oral history project, National Library of Australia, p. 13.

11. Leslie Palmier, *Indonesia and the Dutch*, London, Oxford University Press, 1962.

12. Joost Cote and Loes Westerbeek (Eds.), *Recalling the Indies: Colonial Culture and Postcolonial Identities*, Aksant, Amsterdam, 2005.

13. Cote and Westerbeek, *Op. Cit.,* p. 108.
14. Sunarti, *Op. Cit.*, p. 7.
15. Foreword by J.A.C. Mackie in Abeyasekere, *Op. Cit.*, p. v.
16. Ibid.
17. Benedict R. O'G. Anderson, "Old State, New Society," in Benedict R. O'G. Anderson, *Language and Power: Exploring Political Cultures in Indonesia,* Ithaca, NY, Cornell University Press, 1990, p. 100. Anderson's argument highlighted the differences in background between former presidents Suharto and Sukarno.
18. A.K. Pringgodigdo comments that "This meant that Parindra was very clearly cooperative in its attitude." A.K. Pringgodigdo, *Sejarah Pergerakan Rakyat Indonesia,* 1977, Jakarta, Dian Rakyat, 1978, p. 123, f.n. 5.
19. As Anthony Reid puts it, in the late colonial period Parindra was a cooperating party which was "conservative in socio-economic matters and looked with sympathy to Japan." A.J.S. Reid, *Indonesian National Revolution 1945–50,* 1974, Hawthorn, Victoria, Longman, p. 9.
20. *School tot Opleiding van Inlandsche Artsen.*
21. B. Dahm, *Sukarno and the Struggle for Indonesian Independence.* Ithaca, NY: Cornell University Press. Translated from the German by Mary F. Somers Heidhues, 1969, pp. 60, 61.
22. Sutherland, *Op. Cit.,* 1979, p. 59. Tjipto Mangoenkoesoemo was exiled to the Netherlands at roughly the same time as Sunario Gondokusumo.
23. Sunarti, *Op. Cit.*, p. 43.
24. Dahm, *Op. Cit.,* pp. 55, 56.
25. Sutherland, *Op. Cit.*, p. 116.
26. Abeyasekere, *Op. Cit.*, p. 15.
27. Ibid., p. 28.
28. Such as *Suara Umum* (Voice of the Public), *Tempo, Bangun* (Arise), *Suara Parindra* (Voice of Parindra) and *Suara Soerja Wirawan* (Voice of *Surya Wirawan*).
29. The Indonesian language (*bahasa Indonesia*) was known as Malay until the Youth Pledge of 1928 when it was renamed for nationalist reasons. It was often referred to as Malay until the Japanese occupation period.
30. *Nationale Commentaren Hindia Belanda* edited by Dr. Ratu Langie.
31. There are many types of *gotong royong* systems in villages throughout Indonesia. For a description of three types of *gotong royong* in a rural village in Central Java in the 1950s, see Widjojo Nitisastro and J.E. Ismael, *The Government, Economy and Taxes of a Central Javanese Village,* Ithaca, NY, Southeast Asia Program, Department of Far Eastern Studies, Cornell University, 1959, p. 6, 7.
32. Josko Petkovic, "Dede Oetomo Talks on *Reyog Ponorogo*," in http://wwwsshe.murdoch.edu.au/intersections/issue2/Oetomo.html, accessed February 2005.
33. "Seminar Cagar Budaya di Sastra Unair," http://www.warta.unair.ac.id/fokus/index.php?id=183, accessed January 2005.
34. Padmodiwiryo, *Memoar Hario Kecik: Autobiografi Seorang Mahasiswa Prajurit* (translated title: *Memoirs of Little Hario: The Autobiography of a Student Soldier*). Jakarta, Yayasan Obor, p. 677, 678.
35. www.Lowensteyn.com/Indonesia/nationalist.html, accessed January 2005.

36. For a summary of Parindra's development, including its subsidiary organizations, see Pringgodigdo, *Op. Cit.*, pp. 122—124.

37. Sunarti, *Op. Cit.*, p. 11.

38. Ibid., p. 6.

39. "The people of Surabaya, from teenagers to the elderly, devoted their time (every Sunday), their physical strength, and materials to complete the building in a few years. Without any assistance at all from the government construction of the Gedung Indonesia was completed in December 1931." Padmodiwiryo, *Op. Cit.*, p. 679.

40. *Ramon Magsaysay Award for Public Service* website (www.rmaf.org.ph), "1981 Ramon Magsaysay Award for Public Service, Biography of Johanna Nasution," accessed July 2004.

41. Sunarti, *Op. Cit.*, p. 12.

42. Biography, Johanna Sunarti Nasution, the 1981 Ramon Magsaysay Award for Public Service, *Op. Cit.*

43. Padmodiwiryo, *Op. Cit.*, p. 679.

44. A. H. Nasution, *Memenuh Panggilan Tugas,* Vol One, Jakarta, CV Haji Masagung, 1990, p. 16.

45. Ibid.

46. A. Prasetyo and T. Hadad, *Jenderal Tanpa Pasukan, Politisi Tanpa Partai: Perjalanan (eds.) Hidup A. H. Nasution (A General Without Troops, A Politician Without a Party: The Life Journey of A. H.* Nasution), 1998, Jakarta: Pusat Data dan Analisa Tempo: Institut Studi Arus Informasi, p. 22.

47. McKemmish, *Op. Cit.*, p. 12.

48. Ibid.

49. Penders and Sundhaussen, *Op. Cit.*, p. 66.

50. A. H. Nasution, *Memenuh Panggilan Tugas,* Vol One, *Op. Cit.*, p. 27.

51. McKemmish, *Op. Cit.*, p. 13.

52. Prasetyo and Hadad, *Op. Cit.*, p. 30.

53. Peter Lowenberg, *Writing and Literacy in Indonesia*, Studies in the Linguistic Sciences Volume 30, Number 1 (Spring 2000), p. 140.

54. Pusat Data dan Analisa Tempo, *Perjalanan Hidup A. H. Nasution*, Percetakan PT Temprint, Jakarta, p. 31.

55. Frank Clune, *To the Isles of Spice with Frank Clune: A Vagabond Voyage by Air from Botany Bay to Darwin, Bathurst Island, Timor, Java, Celebes and French Indo China,* Sydney, Angus and Robertson, 1940, pp. 158 and 162.

56. L.J. Giebels, *Sukarno, A Biography*, Amazon Kindle e-books, Loc. 547 of 10815.

57. Ibid.

58. Achdiat K. Mihardja, *Atheis*, St Lucia, Queensland, University of Queensland Press, 1972, p. 161.

59. Penders and Sundhaussen, *Op. Cit.*, p. 2.

60. Prasetyo and Hadad, *Op. Cit.*, p. 33.

61. Nasution, *Memenuhi Panggilan Tugas*, Vol One, *Op. Cit.*, p. 32.

62. Ibid., p. 27.

63. Ibid., p. 38.
64. Prasetyo and Hadad, *Op. Cit.*, p. 33.
65. Ibid., *p. 49.*
66. Penders and Sundhaussen, *Op. Cit.*, p. 67.
67. Ibid., pp. 67, 68.
68. Ibid., p. 67.
69. In Abeyasekere, *Op. Cit.*, p. v.
70. Prasetyo and Hadad, *Op. Cit.*, p. 32.
71. Sunarti, *Op. Cit.*, p. 11.
72. Ibid., p. 13.
73. Ibid.
74. Ibid.
75. Ibid., p. 33.
76. Nasution, *Memenuhi Panggilan Tugas*, Vol. Two A, *Op. Cit,.* p. 68.

Chapter 3

The Japanese Occupation

When the Japanese suddenly and finally ended Dutch control over the Indies in March 1942 it was soon evident that cooperating nationalism had been an uneasy marriage of convenience for many who had adopted this stance. The invasion put a violent and humiliating end to claims of white invincibility and prestige that had enabled the Dutch to rule over tens of millions with a small colonial army and gave a massive spur to hopes for an independent state of Indonesia. It was to propel Nasution on a trajectory that saw him desert from the KNIL, cooperate with the Japanese in their paramilitary organizations, and then apply his Dutch officer training in the armed struggle against the colonial power in the second half of the 1940s.

The Japanese invasion was an event that many Indonesians, including Sunario and Nasution, had anticipated. Together with Siam (now Thailand), it was one of only two truly independent Asian countries in the 1930s. Its spectacular naval victory over a Russian fleet in 1905 had made a strong impression on many members of the "native" population and had given impetus to the founding of *Budi Utomo.*

Nasution had been impressed with Japan's achievements. While living in Muara Dua in the late 1930s he obtained a copy of the Indonesian nationalist Ratu Langie's book *Indonesia in de Pacific,* which argued that the balance of power around the Indies might change and implied, rather than expressed openly, that this might affect the continuity of colonial rule over the Indies.[1]

Nasution also seems to have had a regard for aspects of the German Nazi regime. Tahi Bonar Simatupang, a Christian Batak and fellow cadet at the Royal Military Academy in Bandung has said that Nasution admired Baldur von Shirach, the Hitler Youth leader "and sought a state in which the youth was organised and militarised."[2]

Simatupang is a revered figure in Indonesian military history who wrote a moving account of the armed struggle for independence and then led the armed forces in the early 1950s. By the 1980s, when he made this comment, he had fallen out with Nasution. Nevertheless, it seems unlikely that he would have lied about such a matter, particularly as Nasution was still alive and able to counter the allegation.

A fascination with paramilitary organizations does seem to fit with Nasution's long fascination with and romanticization of military life. His frustration at being trapped within the teaching profession and inability to further his military ambitions appears to have turned him into what might now be called a military nerd. His response to Simatupang's charges was that while he might not have disagreed with von Schirach's views (because he knew little about fascism and Nazism) he did not see the German as a role model. Rather, as always, he looked to heroic individuals and great deeds in history for inspiration.[3]

It is likely that this was, in fact, what attracted him to von Schirach, rather than an attraction to fascism or Nazism. Images of the smartly uniformed Hitler Youth were often seen in newsreels of the 1930s and many conservatives throughout the world saw Hitler as a bulwark against communism. They favoured his apparent rescue of Germany from defeat, economic collapse and demoralization, and drew an association with his militarization of the German society. The rapid German military victories in the early years of the war, including the rapid capitulation of the Netherlands, no doubt also impressed Nasution.

There was apparently little anti-Nazi sentiment among the Dutch population in the Indies until Germany invaded the Netherlands. This is not surprising in a transplanted European society where substantial numbers drew upon ideas of white superiority to justify their rule over a much larger indigenous population. The Dutch National Socialist Party, which was visited by its leader Anton Mussert in 1935, had many supporters in the colony, including senior military officers who permitted their facilities to be used by fascist youth organizations.[4]

There was even an indigenous Indonesian Fascist Party (*Partai Fasis Indonesia*—PFI), established in Bandung in 1933 by a Dr. Notonindito. While Mussolini's version of fascism looked back to the values and glory of the Roman Empire, the small and short-lived PFI based its philosophy on the resurrection of the culture of the pre-Dutch kingdoms of Indonesia. This emphasis on resurrecting ancient culture had similarities with Supomo's idealization of village authority structures and values but the party was roundly criticized in the nationalist movement for wanting to restore a feudal Indonesia rather than moving toward participatory democracy.[5]

Abeyasekere writes that Japanese cruelty toward the Chinese in their invasion of that country during the 1930s did not arouse widespread condemnation among Indonesians. This was "partly because of anti-Chinese feeling among Indonesians, and partly because many of them approved of Japan's rationale that the conflict was really between Japan, representing Asia, and the Western colonial powers which were exploiting China."[6]

She also notes an article in *Soeara Parindra* speculating that a Japanese invasion of the Indies might be beneficial.[7] Nazi Germany's increasing closeness to Japan, that country's assertive stance toward both China and the European colonizing powers, and the growing influence of Sunario appear to have further stimulated Nasution's awareness that Japan might in some way be associated with Indonesia gaining its independence.

That some in Parindra had pro-Japanese leanings was evident when the Indies governor general was informed in December 1940 that the Japanese were mainly directing their attempts to enlist support from Indonesian leaders and organizations at that party.[8] The leading Parindra identity, M.H. Thamrin, was suspected of channeling Japanese financial support to Parindra through his association with the Japanese consul-general in Jakarta (who directed Japanese espionage in the Indies).[9]

Sunario Gondokusumo clearly had pro-Japanese sentiments. As the invasion became imminent he "gave a signal"[10] to Nasution to try for a posting to the Central Java royal city of Surakarta where his brother, the Parindra leader Mr. R.P. Singgih, was planning an uprising against the Dutch "at the appropriate time."[11] Nasution requested the posting but was instead sent to Surabaya.[12] He writes that it was only after the Japanese arrived in Indonesia that he knew of the plan for the uprising in Surakarta, but it seems likely that Sunario had given him an intimation of it.[13]

It seems unlikely that Sunario was in contact with the Japanese before the invasion. Nasution does not mention it and Sunarti writes that when the Japanese entered the city of Bandung on March 7, 1942 her father and a group of fellow nationalists debated whether it was "necessary to welcome the foreign troops or not—that was the problem that had emerged. Finally, it was decided not to give them a welcome. That's what my father said when he returned home from the meeting."[14]

Sunario's pro-Japan sentiments extended to placing himself in danger by hiding and then organizing medical treatment for a Japanese pilot who was shot down in the Ciwidey area near Bandung where the Gondokusumo family had sought refuge.[15] He was given a letter of gratitude for his efforts by the Japanese authorities.

Sunario was far from alone in immediately and enthusiastically supporting and cooperating with the occupation authorities. The Australian military doctor, Edward (Weary) Dunlop, was working in a hospital in Bandung when the Japanese arrived. How unreal the situation seemed to some Dutch is evident in his recollection of a Dutch woman arriving at the hospital in her car and stammering: "I need an officer to come quickly to my house. There are Japanese soldiers there and they are looting it."[16]

This was the beginning of the end of the Dutch population's comfortable life in Bandung, as Dunlop's biographer records:

> The houses in the European quarter surrounding the hospital were large and solidly comfortable. Owners had ignored the order to provide billets for the occupying troops, so Japanese soldiers just marched in and ejected the occupants. The often luxurious surroundings were reduced to untidy squalor.[17]

The despair felt by the Dutch and many Eurasians was in stark contrast with the welcome many Indonesians gave to the Japanese. Weary Dunlop recorded that while the British, Australian and Red Cross flags continued to fly outside his hospital, "the streets of Bandung had broken out in an ingratiating flurry of Japanese bunting from windows and flagpoles."[18]

Nasution claims to have concluded early in the occupation that Japan and Germany would ultimately be defeated. However, he writes that some nationalists, including his father-in law, maintained a belief that the Japanese would prevail until the end was in sight: "Mr Gondokusumo was one of those senior men who for a long time did not believe that Japan would be defeated."[19]

He contacted senior Parindra figures in his spare time in Surabaya before the Japanese began to bomb the port and military installations. He recalls that as the Japanese clearly began to gain ascendancy over the defenders, Dutch nationals deserted their posts in disarray.[20]

His unit was assigned to the north coast to prepare for an enemy landing but was pulled back to the interior before this eventuated. There was chaos on the roads as they moved inland before stopping near the city of Jember. There, as the Indies state was dissolving in turmoil and disarray, Nasution deserted his post at dawn one morning while on duty as officer in charge of the guard.[21]

This was a far-reaching and consequential decision for the usually cautious Nasution. It was a clean break from the cooperating path he had taken and the first of a series of reactive decisions that he would take as he tried to navigate his way through the chaotic change that gripped his country in the coming decades.

It could be argued that as a junior officer he was obliged to show loyalty to his army and the men in his unit and that he had wider obligations to the Netherlands Indies and its instrumentalities. After all, the colonial authorities had picked him out as an unusually promising young boy and then nurtured and given him an education—an almost priceless commodity for a rural village boy in the Netherlands Indies. On the other hand, Nasution was at heart a nationalist with obligations to his own people and the ideal of an independent Indonesia.

Importantly, his desertion meant that he burned his bridges. It would have been very difficult for him seek reentry to the KNIL or to the colonial apparatus, had the Dutch succeeded in reestablishing colonial rule.

His tried to melt into the Indonesian population and pass himself off as a peasant (he would do so again when seeking to direct operations against the Dutch in 1949), making his way furtively along roads crowded with Dutch military vehicles until he came to a large town. There his Parindra contacts were of great assistance and possibly saved his life. He knocked on the door of a house with a Parindra *Rukun Tani* sign on the door. Not long after he was ushered in the adjutant of his battalion pulled up outside the *pangreh praja* subdistrict (*Kecamatan*) office across the road.[22] It turned out that the occupants immediately trusted and agreed to conceal Nasution because they were relatives of his teacher college friend, Artawi, and he further established his bona fides by talking of his relationship with Sunario Gondokusumo.[23]

They procured a bicycle for him and he began to make his way back to Bandung. In the East Java city of Mojokerto he approached an aristocratic Parindra luminary and uncle of Sunarti, *Raden Panji* Soeroso, with whom he was to become further acquainted during the armed struggle against the Dutch and again in the political turmoil of the 1950s. Soeroso told him not to show himself to the Japanese as they were believed to be acting savagely and might shoot him. He pressed on over the border to West Java and toward Bandung where he found accommodation with a fellow cadet who was under house arrest. However, he soon asked Nasution to move on so as not to endanger him and he left for the West Java city of Sukabumi. He then wandered around West Java before returning to Bandung where he sought advice from Sunario Gondokusumo.[24]

Sunarti writes that her father arranged an amnesty for Nasution with the Japanese by contacting an officer of the *Kempetai*, the Japanese military police, to explain that Nasution was a friend who had planned with him to oppose the Dutch when the moment arrived. Sunario's assistance to the downed pilot stood him in good stead and the officer agreed not to arrest Nasution.[25] Sunario gave him accommodation in his *Bumi Putera* insurance company building, which was close to the Gondokusumo residence. He was to reside there for the remainder of the occupation.

Nasution writes of continuing high-level contact with Parindra figures through his open access to the Gondokusumo family home[26] and Sunario once took Nasution to Surabaya to meet with Parindra figures.[27] He continued to enjoy a close relationship with all the members of the Gondokusumo family and particularly Sunarti. When Sunarti went to study in Yogyakarta (accompanied by her mother) Nasution kept in touch, frequently visiting her there[28] and sometimes staying with them for weeks.[29]

Sometimes small gestures are most effective in revealing the closeness of a relationship. This is evident in Nasution's recollection that Sunarti's mother sewed underpants for him (from canvas) as economic conditions deteriorated and fabric was in very short supply in the final stages of the occupation.[30]

Nasution soon began to cooperate with the Japanese by mobilizing young people into militaristic organizations. The head of the teacher training college in Bandung had once joked that he should have trained to be a *dominee* (Dutch reformed minister) rather than a teacher because of his serious nature.[31] Nasution soon showed that he was better suited to paramilitary organizations where he could lead and teach but within a highly disciplined and regimented format.

Nasution had been a volunteer drill instructor for the West Javanese youth organization *Yayasan Obor Pasundan* while he was still a cadet and it was then that he often met with members of the scouting organization *Kepanduan Bangsa Indonesia* and the Parindra youth movement *Surya Wirawan* at the Gondokusumo residence.[32] His interest in paramilitary youth organizations resurfaced when he emerged from hiding in Bandung and decided that unlike "all his other cadet friends" who had "applied for and obtained employment with the occupation administration as mid-ranking civil service officials" he would not do so because of "his feelings" and he did not want "a commitment."[33] Rather, he earned money from giving lessons in the Malay [Indonesian] language to Japanese soldiers.

It seems likely that his intention to go his own way emerged in large part from his strong and romantic attraction toward military life and uniforms. This is indicated in the unusual step that he took of obtaining three sets of boy-scout uniforms "complete with short pants and sleeves," which "were to be my uniform throughout the occupation period."[34]

Nasution attributes his involvement in paramilitary training to a desire to further the nationalist cause and no doubt there is truth in this. However, his adoption of a personal "uniform" was highly unusual behavior and lends veracity to Simatupang's claim that Nasution was attracted to militaristic youth movements of the *Hitler Jugend* type. Certainly, none of the other former military academy cadets seem to have adopted such a course of action and it seems that life in uniform, even one of his own creation, was much more attractive to him than joining his classmates in their less glamorous civil service occupations.

Meanwhile, the Japanese decided to begin to mobilize young men by developing a youth (*pemuda*) movement called the *Barisan Pemuda Priangan* (Priangan Youth Front) and the mayor of Bandung appointed Nasution its leader, enlisting him as an employee of the city government. Nasution began to view paramilitary training as a sort of vocation and records that he was highly energetic in organizing youth leaders in fourteen village-level branches and in establishing a central training center and an agricultural training center: "That period is really a beautiful memory for me, when I never felt tired or weak at all."³⁵ However, the relative freedom Nasution enjoyed in establishing *Barisan Pemuda Priangan* was short lived. At the end of 1942 the Japanese went on to establish *Seinendan*, a much more militarized and tightly controlled organization. The new organization had branches at the *kabupaten* level throughout Java, the membership was more restricted, and some of the training was given by Japanese.³⁶

This was a development that disappointed many in the Parindra movement. Suhario Padmodiwiryo, who remained in Surabaya during the occupation, recalls that the high hopes of the Parindra leaders to be included in aspects of the occupation government were soon crushed. By the third week the Indonesian red and white flag was banned and political organizations including Parindra were "frozen."³⁷

Together with other young men from throughout Java who were chosen to be *Seinendan* leaders, Nasution was sent on an intensive three-month indoctrination and training course in Jakarta, renamed from Batavia by the Japanese. The occupation army instructors were much harder task masters than the Dutch and he was mortified when they shaved his head and subjected him to highly rigorous, and sometimes humiliating, training.³⁸ His relations with the Japanese began to sour after these and other humiliations in his paramilitary career.

David Bourchier observes insightfully that "Nasution's experience in Japanese military and paramilitary organisations has been played down in assessments of his thinking, though he spent more time in Japanese formations than in the KNIL."³⁹ Through his intimate involvement in this system of "security and people's defence" Nasution was absorbing valuable lessons that he would put into effect when he began to develop his principles of "people's war" during the struggle against the Dutch.

At a personal level, Nasution might have felt closer to his KNIL instructors than the Japanese because he had been brought up by Dutchmen since his dormitory days in Bukit Tinggi and there was no language barrier between them. Moreover, he enjoyed friendly and familial relations with Maria Gondokusumo and her mother.

There is nothing in Nasution's writings that indicate that Japanese culture had any impact on him, apart from the growing feelings of distaste, but their methods of youth mobilization and militarization and the contacts he gained among other young Indonesians in Japanese-auspiced paramilitary and military organizations were to be invaluable to him in the armed struggle against the Dutch. The most important of these was the light infantry force known as PETA (*Pembela Tanah Air*—Defenders of the Homeland) that the Japanese formed in October 1943 when they intensified their efforts to mobilize the Indonesian people in support of their war effort.

The mayor of Bandung urged Nasution to join PETA but his sometimes proud and prickly nature came to the fore when he explained that at twenty-five years of age and a senior and influential figure within the paramilitary organizations he would only have become a platoon commander (*Shodancho*). Another reason was that the training given by the Japanese was likely to be much more basic than he had received within the KNIL.[40] His growing distaste for the Japanese might have been another factor in his decision.

There were to be far-reaching consequences when the occupation was over and a new army was being formed. He was to be categorized within the ranks of the former KNIL officers when a deep and sometimes traumatic rift opened between them and the much larger group who had acquired fierce and uncompromising Japanese approaches to discipline and combat from their PETA training.

Importantly, he maintained contact with PETA officers when he was appointed as a member of the executive board of the Priangan Soldiers Assistance Body (*Badan Pembantu Prajurit Priangan*) that was intended to assist them. His duties allowed him considerable independence and freedom of movement within West Java and with the help of friends in the railways (who provided free tickets) he also travelled and made important contacts throughout Central Java and parts of East Java.

The final and most successful civilian mass organization to be formed by the Japanese was the People's Loyalty Organisation (*Jawa Hokokai*—known in Indonesian as the *Perhimpunan Kebaktian Rakyat*). *Jawa Hokokai* had branches down to village level and included women's and youth groups. Unlike an earlier mobilizing attempt known as *Putera* and led by Sukarno (who was freed by the Japanese and immediately began cooperating with them in the hope of achieving independence) and other nationalist leaders, the *Jawa Hokokai* was administered in the regions by the *pangreh praja*.

This latter aspect of *Jawa Hokokai* was something of an about-face for the Japanese. They had not only established cooperative relationships with nationalists such as Sukarno and Hatta, but accorded a greater recognition to the political forces of Islam through the creation of Masyumi (*Majelis Sjuro Muslimin Indonesia*—Consultative Council of Indonesian Muslims), an umbrella organization for Muslim groups. However, by the time the occupation government formed *Jawa Hokokai*, the occupation authorities had become aware of the important role that traditional *priyayi* influences in the form of the *pangreh praja* could play in their efforts to engage grassroots populations.[41]

A system of neighborhood associations augmented by paramilitary and other organizations was created and a further effort was made to mobilize the youth in the form of the attachment to the *Hokokai* of the paramilitary *Barisan Pelopor* (Vanguard Corps).[42] The basis of the system of security and people's defense was the family. Several families were organized into a *kumi* and a number of *kumi* were organized into a *cokai*. The heads of each *cokai* reported to the village chief.

This innovation has proved to be durable in Indonesia which is the only one of the occupied territories to retain the *kumi* and *cokai* neighborhood system. The modern version of the *kumi* is the *rukun tetangga* or neighborhood association found in Indonesian cities. The *cokai* has become the *rukun warga* or intermediate administrative unit whose head reports to the village chief.

Now that the *pangreh praja* were once again in charge, Sunario Gondokusumo gained Nasution a paid position within Hokokai.[43] However, Nasution writes of a growing sense of frustration with the indigenous leaders of this organization because of their failure to appreciate that Japan would probably be defeated, lack of plans to seize independence in the power vacuum that was likely to ensue, and ready acceptance of Japanese militarism.

He recalls than under these new arrangements, the residents, regents (*Bupati*), district heads (*Wedana*), subdistrict heads (*Camat*) and village heads (*Lurah*) automatically became the leaders of mass organizations, except for women's associations where the wife of the relevant official was in charge.

> These fascist totalitarian methods were strengthened by the spirit of Dutch colonial bureaucracy (*ambtenaarisme*) and feudalism which still attached itself to Indonesian officials.[44]

Nasution was not alone in having such feelings.[45] A generation gap had opened between the older nationalist leaders, most of whom had received a high standard of Western education in the more settled atmosphere of the Dutch colonial regime, and the younger generation or *pemuda,* whose ranks included the PETA officer corps. The higher education system had been gravely disrupted by the war and the formative experiences of the *pemuda* generation had been gained in the militarized and mobilized atmosphere of the Japanese occupation. Whereas many of the older nationalists believed that Indonesia could not possibly prevent the return of the Dutch through force of arms, much of the *pemuda* generation was committed to an unremitting armed struggle (*perjuangan*). Some PETA units mounted resistance to the Japanese in the dying stages of the war and PETA personnel were involved in the confused lobbying of political leaders a day or so before the proclamation of independence.

Nasution, who was a few years older than the members of the *pemuda* generation, straddled both the older and the younger groups. He had received a Dutch education, although not of the same quality and level as many of the older nationalists. His military education within the KNIL had been curtailed by the war and he had been caught up in Japanese attempts to mobilize the population. Nevertheless, Nasution was a leader of the mobilization efforts in the Bandung area, rather than a relatively immature participant.

Until the Japanese capitulated, Sukarno and Hatta cooperated closely with the occupation authorities and refused to proclaim Indonesia's independence without their approval. However, many *pemudas* became impatient with the older political leaders and concerned that a Japanese-approved proclamation of independence would be regarded as a tarnished "gift" from a vanquished foreign power.

Attempts by some influential *pemudas* to persuade the nationalist leaders to defy the Japanese and immediately proclaim independence gained momentum when news of the US nuclear attacks on Japan became known in Indonesia. On August 15, 1945, a group of *pemudas* spirited Sukarno and Hatta to a PETA unit in the small West Java town of Rengasdengklok. On the morning of August 16, the PETA unit rebelled, seizing the town, disarming the Japanese and hoisting the national flag.[46]

Sukarno and Hatta refused to comply with the demands of the *pemudas* until they were assured that the Japanese would not retaliate. Sukarno was finally convinced when he returned to Jakarta and held discussions with a senior and influential Japanese intelligence official, Vice Admiral Tadashi Maeda, and he and Hatta proclaimed Indonesia's independence on August 17.

While Nasution was critical of the older leaders for their timidity in dealing with the Japanese as they suffered a series of crushing military defeats at the hands of the Allies, he himself was not particularly at ease in fluid situations that could lead to unforeseen consequences. He felt most at home in structured, hierarchical and militaristic organizations in which he could play a clear leadership role, rather than in the myriad of freer-flowing and less disciplined contexts that began to emerge after the proclamation of independence, and he was to throw in his lot with the emerging republican army. These tendencies and a growing authoritarian dimension to his romanticization of the military are also evident in his constant endeavors during the armed struggle against the Dutch to impose discipline over the various fighting forces associated with the Republic and either to "regularise" them within the army or disarm and demobilize them.

NOTES

1. Nasution, *Memenuhi Panggilan Tugas*, Vol One, *Op. Cit.,* p. 51.
2. David Jenkins, *Suharto and His Generals: Indonesian Military Politics 1975–1983*, Ithaca, NY, p. 226.

3. Ibid., p. 227.
4. Abeysekere, *Op. Cit.*, p. 35, 39.
5. "Kaum pergerakan di Hindia Belanda 1930-an, reaksi terhadap fasisme," Prisma 10, Okt 1994, cited in http://www.hamline.edu/apakabar/basisdata/1998/08/04/0013.html, accessed August 2004.
6. Abeyasekere, *Op. Cit..*, p. 20.
7. Abeyasekere cites Palau, a democratic-socialist Indonesian who was concerned that all parties, with the exception of Gerindo (formed in 1937 as a more radical and staunchly anti-fascist alternative to Parindra) tended toward being pro-Japan. Ibid., p. 21.
8. Ibid., p. 77.
9. Bourchier, *Op. Cit.*, p. 57. Thamrin actually taunted the Dutch, coining the expression *Koloni Orang Belanda akan Jepang Ambil Seantero Indonesia* (Japan will take over the whole of the colony of the Dutch) from the name of the leader of a Japanese economic mission to the Indies in 1940, Kobojashi. Thamrin was arrested, together with a number of other Indonesians, including Ratu Langie, on suspicion of disloyal relations with the Japanese. He died while under house arrest in January 1941.
10. Nasution, *Memenuhi Panggilan Tugas*, Vol One, *Op. Cit.*, p. 82.
11. Sunarti, *Op. Cit.*, p. 13.
12. Nasution, *Memenuhi Panggilan Tugas*, Vol One, *Op. Cit.*, p. 82. R.P. Singgih often stayed with the Gondokusumo family in Bandung during the occupation period. A. H. Nasution, *Memenuhi Panggilan Tugas*, Vol 2B, Jakarta, CV Haji Masagung, 1994, p. 174.
13. Ibid.
14. Sunarti, *Op. Cit.*, p. 13, 14.
15. Ibid., p. 14.
16. Sue Ebury, *Weary: The Life of Sir Edward Dunlop*, Penguin Books, 1994. P. 316.
17. Ibid., p. 317.
18. Ibid., p. 316.
19. Nasution, *Memenuhi Panggilan Tugas,* Vol One, *Op. Cit.*, p. 96.
20. Ibid., p. 82.
21. Nasution, *Op. Cit.*, Vol One, pp. 82–84.
22. Ibid, p. 84.
23. Ibid, p. 85.
24. Ibid, p. 87.
25. Sunarti, *Op. Cit.*, p. 14.
26. "Parindra leaders came time and again from Bandung, Jakarta, Solo [Surakarta] and Surabaya to meet at Pak Gondokusumo's residence, so I had the opportunity to follow their discussions." Nasution, *Memenuhi Panggilan Tugas*, Vol One, *Op. Cit.*, p. 95, 96.
27. Sunarti, *Op. Cit.*, p. 15.
28. Ibid., p. 16.
29. Nasution, *Op. Cit.*, Vol One, p. 102.

30. Ibid., p. 104.

31. Penders and Sundhaussen, *Op. Cit.*, p. 2.

32. Sunarti, *Op. Cit.*, p. 11.

33. Ibid, p. 95. Nasution is presumably referring to his Military Academy friends who remained in the Bandung area as Simatupang studiously avoided such involvement. T.B. Simatupang, *The Fallacy of a Myth*, Jakarta: Pustaka Sinar Harapan, translated and introduced by Peter Suwarno,1996, pp. 90—102.

34. Nasution, *Memenuhi Panggilan Tugas*, Vol One, *Op. Cit.*

35. Ibid., p. 98.

36. Benedict Anderson writes that the *kabupaten*-level (Regency) focus of Seinendan gave it a "primarily urban character," 1972, *Op. Cit.*, pp. 26, 27.

37. Padmodiwiryo, *Op. Cit.*, p. 685.

38. "By comparison, the military training [at the Military Academy] in the Dutch period was certainly not as hard." Nasution, *Memenuhi Panggilan Tugas*, Vol One, *Op. Cit.*, p. 99.

39. Bourchier, *Op. Cit.*, p. 118.

40. Nasution, *Memenuhi Panggilan Tugas*, Vol One, *Op. Cit.*, p. 101.

41. Ibid. A. Kurasawa, *Mobilisasi dan Kontrol*, Jakarta, Gramedia, 1993, pp. 394–98 describes ways in which the Japanese came to rely upon the *pangreh praja*, rather than the nationalist leaders, for the mobilization of local populations, as does J.A.A. van Doorn, "Kelampauan Adalah Kekinian Yang Kental: Konflik Belanda-Indonesia dan Bertahannya Pola Kolonial," in A.B. Lapian and P.J. Drooglever, *Menelusuri Jalur Linggarjati,*Jakarta, Grafiti, 1992, p. 266.

42. Anderson, 1972 *Op. Cit.*, p. 29, 30.

43. Nasution, *Memenuhi Panggilan Tugas*, Vol One, *Op. Cit.*, p. 102.

44. Ibid., p. 102.

45. Ibid., p. 105. See Anderson, 1972 *Op. Cit.*, pp. 25–60 for an account of the growing estrangement of many young educated Indonesians from the Japanese and their concern that the older generation of nationalists were placing too much trust in the occupation government.

46. Cribb, 1991 *Op. Cit.*, p. 49, 50.

Chapter 4

War against the Dutch

The armed struggle against the Dutch that broke out in late 1945 eventually drew Nasution back to village society, but in West Java and then Central Java, far from his childhood home in North Sumatra. He was to extol, idealize and mythologize the support that he received from relatively simple peasants and their village and subdistrict heads after the conflict ended when he codified and published his principles of guerrilla warfare and people's resistance.

It is not unusual for urban middle-class professionals from small rural towns to feel nostalgia for their recollections of a simpler way of life and it is possible that such emotions influenced Nasution in his praise for village elders and residents. He had left his own village at a young age and was brought up thereafter by foreigners in institutional settings. Childhood images of traditional rural authority figures might have remained fixed within his consciousness and influenced him to hold them in high esteem.

The elite status of the Gondokusumo family and their *pangreh praja* links might also have made him receptive to and grateful for the support he received from members of the indigenous civil service that early in the revolution was renamed the *pamong praja* or "servants of the people" in line with the democratic ethos of the new Indonesian state. The support that many of them gave when he greatly needed it seems to have reinforced a natural predisposition toward conserving and preserving traditional authority structures that was to be a feature of his political stance in the 1950s and 1960s.

Always seeking to create order out of chaos, throughout the conflict and afterward he made repeated attempts to reduce the influence of the parties over the fighting forces that were aligned with the Republic and reorganize and drastically reduce the size of the army in the face of sometimes strident opposition (particularly from left-wing officers and politicians) and this no doubt strengthened his innate conservatism. Finally, his direction of a major operation to suppress an uprising by Communist Party elements in 1948 also bolstered his conservative instincts and respect for traditional authority figures.

The armed struggle in which he would begin to develop and apply his socially conservative strategies began in earnest some weeks after the surrender of Japan and it would continue at low levels permeated by two periods of intense conflict for the next four years. Japanese occupation forces remained in formal control after their surrender was announced on August 15, 1945 as the sudden end of the war had not given the Dutch or the Allied command time to plan for the insertion of troops. The Americans had bypassed most of the archipelago and the Australians had confined their operations to parts of the Eastern islands, but eventually British forces arrived. The Netherlands was still recovering from occupation by the Germans and was in no position to insert large military forces in the short term, but their military units that had withdrawn to Australia began to arrive, as did members of the diasporic Indies administration led by Lieutenant Governor van Mook. Initially the British were concerned to repatriate civilian and military prisoners of the Japanese but they soon clashed with irregular *laskar* militia and military units who suspected that their intention was to restore order with a view to handing the archipelago back to the Dutch.

This early period of what became known as the Indonesian revolution was a time of heroic poses and romantic gestures. Many *pemudas* took oaths not to cut their hair until the Dutch were expelled from Indonesia and a new wave of writers, such as Pramoedya Ananta Toer and Chairul Anwar, became known as the *Angkatan* 1945 (1945 Generation). Like the adoption of the term *citoyen* (citizen) to express the revolutionary aims of liberty, equality and fraternity in the French Revolution, the term *Bung* (Brother) became widely used to the extent that senior nationalist figures of the period are still known as Bung Karno (Sukarno), Bung Hatta, etc.

It was also a time of rampant gangsterism in the name of the independence struggle that is remembered as the *bersiap!* ("get ready!") period for the rallying call that summoned young men armed with sharpened bamboo poles and any other weapons that were available to fight suspected enemies of the Republic. Many of their victims were Dutch and Eurasian civilians who were terrorized and often killed when they sought to leave the terrible conditions of their internment camps. Ethnic Chinese were also resented and targeted in *bersiap!* actions because of their dominance of the economy and suspected pro-Dutch sympathies.

Younger generations of Indonesians had been conditioned for such a campaign. Sukarno had been given considerable latitude to address the Indonesian people by radio and in the hope that Japan would grant independence when the war was over he rallied support for the occupation regime's efforts to mobilize the population with bloodthirsty slogans such as *Amerika kita seterika, Inggris kita linggis!* (We will iron Amerika [flat], we will break England open with a crow bar!). These efforts seem to have particularly affected younger people who were most associated with the *bersiap!* actions.

A committee convened by the Japanese in the final months of the war to prepare Indonesia for independence had adopted a constitution whose main drafter was Professor Supomo, a constitutional law expert. His speeches to the Preparatory Body for Indonesian Independence (*Badan Penyelidik Usaha Persiapan Kemerdekaan Indonesia*—BPUPKI) included favorable references to Nazi Germany[1] and Imperial Japan,[2] which might have been intended to appease Japanese observers. More forcefully and consistently, the professor argued that the new state should provide for corporatist means of interest representation that are associated with (but by no means confined to) these two Axis regimes:

> the [role of] the state is not to guarantee the interests of individuals or groups, but to guarantee the interests of the whole of society as a unified entity. The state is a societal structure that is integral. All its groups, all its components, all its members are closely linked to each other and constitute a unified societal entity that is organic. What is most important in a state based on integral thinking is the way of life of the people in their entirety. The state does not side with the strongest group, or the largest one. It does not focus upon the interests of the individual. Rather, it guarantees the wellbeing of the whole of the people as a unified entity that cannot be divided.[3]

This was in keeping with a view that law "had to grow organically out of the history and circumstances of specific communities"[4] Supomo stressed the importance of traditional customary law structures and values, making it clear that he regarded individualism and the open contestation of ideas leading to voting[5] as contrary to the norms of Eastern civilization. He harked back to what he saw as the cooperative norms of the Indonesian rural village (*desa*),[6] such as *gotong royong*[7] or mutual self-help (communal working bees to assist in such projects as building a house or a mosque) and decision-making through an exhaustive process of consultation leading to consensus (*musyawarah sampai mufakat*),[8] rather than Western-style political campaigns and voting.

Supomo advocated the traditional collectivist concept of *kekeluargaan* (the family principle).[9] His idea of *kekeluargaan* envisaged the various members of society (the national family) working cooperatively in accordance with their roles in society. Families tend to be hierarchical (more so in Supomo's day), and implicit within this vision was a repudiation of such ideas as equality and individual rights. Rather, he envisaged members of the national family taking on mutual obligations aimed at fostering and preserving the harmony and welfare of society, in accordance with their status and/or occupation.

Supomo also championed the concept of *kawula-gusti*, derived from ancient Javanese philosophies, explaining it in almost mystical terms:

> the spirit of inner life, the spirituality of the Indonesian people is characterised by and has the aim of achieving unity of life, the unity of *kawulo* and *gusti*, i.e. unity between the outer world and the inner spiritual world, between microcosmos and macrocosmos, between the people and their leaders. . . . Human beings as individuals cannot be separated from other individuals or from the outside world, from groups of people, indeed from all groups of creatures, everything is mutually interactive and mutually connected, everything influences everything else and is interlinked. This is the totalitarian idea, the integralistic idea of the Indonesian people, which actually exists within authentic constitutional structures.[10]

Supomo's studies at Leiden University in the Netherlands undoubtedly influenced him in his identification of these "traditional" values. Bourchier writes that the Leiden scholars had "discovered" that there were some basic similarities in traditional customary *adat* law throughout Indonesia and held to the idea that:

> a nation's law and government should reflect its unique culture and traditions. The other was that Indonesian culture is quintessentially communally-oriented, spiritual and harmony-loving—the mirror image of mainstream western culture, which the Leiden scholars saw as individualistic, materialistic and conflict-ridden.[11]

Supomo "saw inherent value in what he perceived to be the traditional status quo,"[12] perhaps because his own "status quo" was one of relative privilege as a member of the *priyayi* class.

The final outcomes of the BPUPKI's deliberations were not as Supomo had advocated in May 1945. As it became increasingly likely Japan would be defeated by the Allies, power flowed toward the Indonesian nationalists and away from the occupation government. Whereas in May he had interchangeably used the terms "totalitarian" and "integralistic" to describe his organicist ideas,[13] by the time that Japan surrendered on August 15, 1945 he had replaced them with *kekeluargaan*.[14]

Supomo encountered opposition from members of the BPUPKI who were concerned that the proposed constitution lacked any reference to basic human rights or whether sovereignty was to reside in the people or the state.[15] Moreover, while Sukarno liked to resort to indigenous imagery, he was not content for the state and its legislative apparatus simply to emerge from within the "*volksgeist*" of an Indonesian rural village as organicist thinking seemed to call for. Rather, he was concerned to adopt an inspirational approach that would arouse Indonesians to embrace the Indonesian nationalist ideology that he had shaped over many years.[16]

To complicate matters, Sukarno had to contend with proponents for establishing an Islamic state or at least ensuring that the new Constitution gave Islam a special place in national life (both of which Supomo flatly rejected). The followers of other religions and particularly those in predominantly Christian or Hindu areas might have balked at joining a new nation where Islam was accorded a special status.

On July 1, 1945 Sukarno gave an historic address in which he put forward his *Panca Sila* or Five Principles formulation as the philosophy of the new state. While resorting to indigenous imagery in summing up the principles as a *gotong royong* formulation, he was highly creative in attempting to bridge and incorporate all the proposals put forward by the various factions in the BPUPKI. The five principles were:

- Nationalism (*Kebangsaan*)
- Internationalism or Humanitarianism (*Internasionalisme atau peri-kemanusiaan*)
- [Decision-making through] Consultation and Representation (*Musyawarah dan perwakilan*)
- Social Welfare (*Kesejahteraan sosial*)
- Ketuhanan (*Belief in God*)

In view of the tensions on whether and how to incorporate a recognition of Islam within the Constitution, the final *Sila* was the most significant. Sukarno had formulated an abstract noun incorporating a word for God (*Tuhan*) that is used by adherents of Christianity and Islam but more by the former than the latter (Indonesian Muslims more frequently choose the Arabic term *Allah*). The term *ketuhanan* was vague, and no doubt intended to be so. Although *ketuhanan* may be translated as belief in God, as above, it can also mean "to display the characteristics of God" or "(everything) that is associated with God."[17]

The complexity of Sukarno's thinking in arriving at the term *ketuhanan* is apparent in the following remark by an Indonesian admirer on the eve of his hundredth birth anniversary in 2001:

> Bung Karno took some time before he included *ketuhanan* within the system of his "philosophy." Apparently, he needed to consider the status of the other religions so that he could include a wider basis of *ketuhanan* than just Islam.[18]

Ketuhanan was reworded to become *Ketuhanan Yang Maha Esa* and the three additional words are generally translated as "The Almighty One" or

"The Almighty." However, a literal translation "Who/Which is the Most One and Only" indicates the highly expressive yet abstract nature of the formulation. That all three additional words were derived from Sanskrit, rather than Arabic, perhaps further satisfied those members of the BPUPKI who took pride in cultural vestiges of Java's Hindu/Buddhist past that were still prominent there and were concerned at the possibility of Indonesia becoming an Islamic state. Sanskrit is associated with Javanese traditional beliefs that emerged from the Hindu-Buddhist empires of the pre-Islamic era whose culture still informs that of the modern *priyayi* class.

However, organicist thinking was largely sidelined in the final version of the Constitution. For example, it states that sovereignty resides within the people. As Bourchier points out, this is "a philosophy which contradicts directly the integralist or organicist idea that the state and society are essentially one and the same."[19]

The 1945 Constitution also provides for voting in the legislatures (Article 2 (3)), contradicting Supomo's advocacy of what Bourchier describes as "village style" consensual decision-making[20] (*musyawarah sampai mufakat*). On the other hand, it did not guarantee individual rights or provide for parties and elections.[21]

Bourchier concludes that the constitution embodies "contradictions between integralism and popular sovereignty" and that this "laid the foundations for later disagreements and confusion about what the 'founding fathers' had intended."[22]

Although the 1945 Constitution was formally adopted at the time of the Proclamation of Independence, its effective life was very short. The capitulation of Japan left the collaborationist Sukarno and Hatta and *pangreh praja*-associated members of the committee exposed as a rising tide of demands from other sectors of the community, particularly from the *pemuda* (youth), became overwhelming. Many young activists favored the social democrat, Sutan Sjahrir, who had been imprisoned by the Dutch for his nationalist activities in the 1930s but refused to cooperate when released by the Japanese occupation government. Sjahrir was obviously much more acceptable to the Allies, who by this stage had gained a foothold in Indonesia, than Sukarno and others who were badly tainted by cooperation with the Japanese. Like Quisling in Norway, Pierre Laval in France and Anton Mussert in the Netherlands, Sukarno might have been put on trial and even sentenced to death for his behavior during the occupation had the Dutch been able to return more speedily and with greater effect.

The formation of a single state party, named the *Partai Nasional Indonesia* (PNI—Indonesian Nationalist Party), was announced on August 22. It was named in honor of Sukarno's old "non-cooperating" party of the same name but was a direct descendant of the major Japanese-auspiced Hokokai movement that had been intended to mobilize Indonesians in support of their war effort.²³ However, many opposed this concept, including those like Sjahrir who had kept their distance from the Japanese occupation government, and the initiative was "postponed" on August 31.

By late October, Sjahrir and his supporters had joined a quasi-parliament formed upon the basis of the preparatory committee and known as Central Indonesian National Committee (*Komite Nasional Indonesia Pusat*—KNIP) and before long he was appointed prime minister, a position not envisaged in the Presidential 1945 Constitution. By November 3 the Sjahrir government was urging that political parties be formed and the multiparty system that followed was a major rebuff to the *pamong praja*-associated advocates of traditional means of interest representation who had cooperated with the Japanese.²⁴

Importantly, echoes of Supomo's homages to traditional authority structures were to find their way into Nasution's principles for fighting guerrilla campaigns and this strongly differentiated them from similar strategies of the political left in nearby China and Vietnam which saw landlords and officials from old regimes as class enemies to be overthrown in the name of the proletariat. A reliance upon traditional authority structures was to feature in Nasution's principles of "people's resistance" during the fight against the Dutch and then in his attempts to tone down political divisions and counter the appeal of a resurgent PKI in the 1950s. No doubt there was a strong element of expedience in this but there is no reason to conclude that he did not deeply believe in what he was advocating.

Political parties soon mushroomed in the embryonic new state and irregular *laskar* military units sprung up that were often aligned with them. The *laskar* forces emerged in part from Japanese-sponsored paramilitary organizations, including the *Barisan Pelopor* (Vanguard Corps) led by the radical nationalist, Dr. Muwardi,²⁵ the village-based paramilitary *Keibodan* (vigilance corps), and the *Seinendan* with which Nasution had been associated.²⁶

In the final year of the occupation the major Muslim party, Masyumi (*Majelis Syuro Muslimin Indonesia*—Consultative Council of Indonesian Muslims), was given permission to form the *Hizbullah* (Army of God) youth militia. Early on in the occupation period the Japanese had sought to influence and gain the cooperation of the Muslim community in Indonesia as evidenced by a 1943 Japanese initiative to incorporate the various and fissiparous Muslim organizations into the Masyumi umbrella organization.

In addition to *Hizbullah*, in November 1945 the *Sabilillah* (Way of God) citizen militia, which was originally intended as a type of home guard, was established. This organization was also associated with Masyumi.²⁷ The cadre of 500 Hizbullah leaders who had been trained by the end of the occupation formed the nucleus of a *laskar* force that fielded two divisions in the Muslim heartland of West Java and was strongly represented in Central and East Java. By early 1946 *Hizbullah* claimed a membership of 300,000.²⁸

On November 10 and 11, Amir Sjarifuddin (who was to become minister for defense) sought to form a single *pemuda* youth organization with a socialist program at a meeting of twenty-eight major youth organizations in Yogyakarta. However, only seven organizations came together to form the Pesindo (Indonesian Socialist Youth—*Pemuda Sosialis Indonesia*), which nevertheless became the largest *laskar* organization associated with the left. The Muslim *Hizbullah* (Army of God) youth militia did not attend the conference and relations between this organization and Pesindo were often poor.

Frictions between Pesindo and some of its constituent organizations emerged when *pemudas* associated with the prominent "national Communist" Tan Malaka, and/or the radical nationalist *Barisan Banteng* (Wild Buffalo Brigade) organization (which evolved from the wartime *Barisan Pelopor*—Pioneer Brigade) moved into more clearly oppositionist roles vis-a-vis Pesindo.²⁹

During this period, there were competing visions of how "people's resistance" could or should be waged that were based as much upon attempts to shape the political orientation of the new state as the immediate imperative of defending Indonesia's independence. For example, Sjarifuddin proposed that a large people's army, including *laskar* forces, operate alongside an elite, well-trained and equipped military force.

A more radical concept was put forward by Tan Malaka. An aristocrat from the Minangkabau (West Sumatra) ethnic group, he had been educated in the Netherlands before he became the chairman of the Indonesian Communist Party in 1921 and was then exiled from the Indies. He took up residence in China, where he became the Comintern representative in Southeast Asia, before moving to Manila in 1925. He warned against plans by the PKI to stage a putsch in the Indies and began a letter-writing campaign when his warnings were ignored. Many PKI members blamed his activities for the failure of revolts in West Java in November 1926 and West Sumatra in January 1927.

He then formed the *Partai Republik Indonesia* (Republic of Indonesia Party—PARI) to take up the struggle from the shattered PKI and became increasingly estranged from the international communist movement. As Anderson—who presents a sympathetic portrayal of Tan Malaka in Java in a Time of Revolution—puts it, "Thereafter he seems to have led an increasingly lonely and isolated life, largely in the coastal cities of China."³⁰

He fled south to Singapore in the wake of the Japanese attack on China before moving to Jakarta in July 1942.³¹ Anderson's account of Tan Malaka's activities after returning to Jakarta differs from that of the American journalist and long-time observer of Indonesia, Arnold Brackman. While Anderson states that Tan Malaka worked as a clerk in a Japanese-owned coal mine in the Banten area of West Java,[32] quoting unnamed "Indonesian sources," Brackman writes that after Tan Malaka's arrival in Jakarta in 1942 he worked "behind the screen" for the Japanese intelligence figure, Admiral Maeda, "recruiting such youths as Adam Malik, who directed a 'national communist' cell in the Sendenbu, and attracting the support of erratic radical nationalists such as Sukarni Kartodiwiryo and Chaerul Saleh."[33]

Popular resistance had held off British forces from imposing control over the city of Surabaya (the Battle of Surabaya) for some time and this made a strong impression upon Tan Malaka. British troops and some Dutch officers from the NICA (Netherlands East Indies Civil Administration) had landed in Surabaya in mid-September. Before long there were clashes between British soldiers, units of the nascent Indonesian Army and various *pemuda* groups. Sukarno, Hatta and Sjarifuddin were flown to Surabaya by the British and managed to achieve a ceasefire but some *pemudas* continued to attack and the British commander, General Mallaby, was killed by a grenade. This led the British to impose an ultimatum, insisting that all Indonesians report and surrender their weapons by October 10. The ultimatum was not obeyed and there ensued a bloody confrontation in which the British deployed battle-hardened troops with air and naval support. Inspired by this popular resistance, in 1946 Tan Malaka wrote a paper entitled *Muslihat* (Strategy) in which he advocated guerrilla warfare against the Dutch[34] and followed it up with a treatise on guerrilla warfare entitled Gerpolek (*Gerilya, Politik, Ekonomi*—Guerrilla Warfare, Politics and Economics).[35]

Seeing himself as a rival for the office of the president, he attempted to persuade Sukarno to appoint him as his political legatee. Sensing personal danger, Sukarno eventually named Tan Malaka as one of a group of four legatees.[36] Tan Malaka subsequently became involved in discussions with Prime Minister Sjahrir that appear to have centered around the prospect of one or the other replacing Sukarno. While there are different versions as to who instigated this association the two men subsequently fell out.[37]

Controversially, the Japanese disbanded PETA with the acquiescence of Sukarno. Salim Said writes that the President and others who had collaborated with the Japanese allowed this to happen without protest because they were afraid of being tried as war criminals by the Allies:

> It is known that Sukarno and his friends—the older generation—before and even after the formation of his cabinet, were not only afraid of the Japanese but also of the Allied armies. This was because they already knew—from Allied radio broadcasts—that they were the first targets of the incoming Allies, especially the Dutch re-occupation troops. By not having any army, Sukarno and his friends were hoping to show the Allies that they were not the Japanese collaborators the Dutch had portrayed them as.[38]

A *Badan Keamanan Rakyat* (BKR—People's Security Agency) consisting mainly of former PETA officers was formed on August 20, but this was at best an interim measure as BKR units were not provided with a centralized command and officers held and maintained their positions through patron-client (*bapak-anak*—father-child) relationships. Mulder writes that in Javanese culture such relationships "focus on a leader who becomes the binding element of the group, horizontal bonds among the members tending to remain weak. The loyalty to the leader is of course a function of his capacity to provide his followers with moral or material benefits and if he is reasonably successful in doing this he may enjoy the respect that is due to his status."[39] This somewhat spontaneous and locally organized birth of an embryonic national army was to give rise to a belief within sections of the officer corps that the army that emerged within the revolution was not just a tool of the state but an equal stakeholder in upholding the country's independence.

The security situation deteriorated as *bersiap!* actions gathered force and incoming Allied troops clashed with local forces. On October 5, the Sjahrir administration established a more professional military force, the *Tentara Keamanan Rakyat* (People's Security Army—TKR). Nasution decided to join it, a decision no doubt made easier by his severing of links with the colonial army when he deserted his unit in East Java and his work with the Japanese paramilitary Seinendan. However, other former KNIL officers who had not deserted made the same decision. While Nasution had clearly cast aside any vestige of loyalty to the Dutch in 1942, they regarded their earlier oaths of loyalty to the Dutch queen as null-and-void because of the surrender of the Netherlands Indies to the Japanese.

The *Tentara Keamanan Rakyat*, like the BKR, was intended to uphold security within the new state while the political leadership conducted negotiations with the Allies and the returning Dutch. On January 1, 1946, its name was changed to *Tentara Keselamatan Rakyat*—People's Salvation Army—implying a widening of its terms of reference. Meanwhile, Amir Sjarifuddin had increasingly assumed responsibility for defense matters and was made minister for defense on October 14, 1945. He appointed Urip Sumohardjo, a retired KNIL major and graduate of the Royal Netherlands Military Academy in Breda, to be chief of staff of the new military force.

After fighting broke out between *pemudas* and the British in November 1945, Bandung was divided into northern (British) and southern (Indonesian) zones. *Pemuda* groups asserted dominance over the older civilian leaders in the southern zone and in this context Nasution assumed command of the local TKR from an older former PETA officer, Arudji Kartawinata, whom many *pemudas* blamed for failing to secure arms in the early weeks of the revolution and for being too accommodating to the Japanese and the British. He became chief of staff of the West Java Command of the TKR under the

Breda-trained Didi Kartasasmita but not long afterward Didi was transferred to the Ministry of Defense in Jakarta and Nasution was appointed commander of III Division (Priangan region). Sunarti writes that she and her family were proud of him "although rather taken aback because he was only 27 years old. He didn't even have a TKR uniform, other than his boy-scout uniform."[40]

However, nearly all the former KNIL officers soon suffered major setbacks when many former PETA officers and particularly those in Central and East Java were resistant to Urip's orders. PETA officers had been trained in the heightened atmosphere of the occupation where the Japanese had emphasized the inculcation of *semangat* or (fighting) spirit through intensive propaganda and physical endurance activities and the ethos that they had acquired was more akin to the *samurai* spirit of the Japanese warrior than the more technical ethos of Western armies.[41]

On November 11 Sumohardjo held a meeting in Yogyakarta to sort the situation out. Former PETA officers demanded a vote on who should occupy a new position of commander-in-chief (*Panglima Besar*) and Urip allowed this to proceed. The charismatic Central Javanese former PETA officer, Colonel Sudirman, was elected to the top post, having negotiated "the acquisition in his Banyumas area of the largest supply of Japanese arms outside Surabaya" and "moral authority as an ascetic, strong-minded exemplar of traditional Javanese values, with a fatherly concern for his men's spiritual and material welfare."[42] In a classic Indonesian face-saving compromise that upheld the will of the majority while preserving the dignity of everybody involved, Sumohardjo was confirmed his old position of chief of staff. Both were promoted to the rank of lieutenant general and went on to enjoy a cordial and mutually respectful relationship thereafter.

The same meeting also proposed that the pro-Republic young sultan of Yogyakarta, Sri Sultan Hamengku Buwono IX, be appointed minister for defense. Prime Minister Sjahrir was apparently not aware of the meeting and while the government hesitantly accepted the election of Sudirman as *Panglima Besar* it stood fast in confirming Sjarifuddin as minister for defense.

Nasution's lack of interest in disturbing the indigenous social order solidified during the early period of the revolution into a strong distaste for radical politics. This is evident in his reaction to the intense political activity of the early years and the formation of *laskar* units by local identities and political parties. Among the divisional commanders on the island of Java, he displayed an unusual level of concern to exert army control over the *laskar* and was relentless in disbanding or incorporating them into the army.

Urip Sumohardjo was less strident and issued a statement in which he attempted to spell out the respective roles of the army and the *laskar*. He asserted the army's differentiation from civil society: "the army is released from all other work aside from national defence, and its livelihood is guaranteed by society," while also stating that the army was not a separate "'caste' standing above the community." Going to an issue which was central to the rivalry between the *laskar* and the army he referred to the shortage of arms on the Republican side, stating that if it proved possible the military would "arm the people" but "for the present the embryonic army [was] not in a position to do this."[43]

When tensions arose between some *laskar* and army units in Central Java, local commanders did not resort to disbanding or co-opting them as zealously and enthusiastically as Nasution. The regular and irregular forces coexisted best in East Java where, Anderson observes, the largely PETA-trained officer corps "came closer than the KNIL veterans to sharing the ideology of the *pemuda* groups."[44]

Penders and Sundhaussen have contrasted the treatment of the *laskar* by Nasution's West Java *Siliwangi* Division with their counterparts in Central and East Java, noting that the Javanese divisions and irregular forces in those provinces generally adhered to the spirit of their traditional *ksatria* (knights) over which had been layered Japanese Bushido notions. They were not as interested in "organisation, tactical planning, and strategy" as Nasution's West Java division.[45]

Panglima Besar Sudirman took a benign view of the various components of *perjuangan*. As Said remarks, "For Sudirman, the armed *pemuda*, regardless of whether they were in the army, left-wing *laskar* or right wing *laskar*, were all 'sons' of the *panglima besar*."[46] He also states that Sudirman's sympathy for the *laskar* was based on his concept of the army as a people's army that was not differentiated from civil society.[47]

An instinctive lack of empathy with the romantic and unruly aspects of the revolution, together with his background in the KNIL and leadership role in the paramilitary organizations of the occupation period, no doubt influenced Nasution's approach to the *laskar,* but they do not fully account for the unusually intense nature of his distaste for them. He endured humiliating experiences at their hands, such as being ordered to show his identity card when entering the "territory" of *laskar* organizations, even though they knew he was the local TKR divisional commander.[48] On one occasion, he was even forced to strip naked so that he could be searched.[49]

Perhaps more importantly, the politically aligned *laskar* units represented competing visions for the nature and political orientation of the new state and threatened those who desired the maintenance of the colonial era's peace and order (*rust en orde*) stemming from respect for "traditional" authorities and governance structures. As McKemmish puts it, "The civilian politicians, especially of the older generation, had more to lose in terms of their prestige and positions of power in a society torn apart by revolution."[50] Nasution and his West Java command came to be associated with this conservative outlook by opponents who nicknamed the *Siliwangi* "the *rust en orde* division"[51] and he was often accused of being a NICA agent intent on suppressing armed opposition toward the Dutch.[52] While Nasution doesn't mention it, Sunarti's Eurasian ancestry and her home life with her Dutch mother and grandmother must have further inflamed these suspicions.

The Republic moved from Jakarta to Yogyakarta in early 1946 when clashes with returning Dutch forces in Jakarta threatened the leadership. Sjahrir and his cabinet, who stayed in Jakarta to negotiate with the Allies and the Dutch, became greatly concerned about the unruly and violent *laskar* and *bersiap!* actions in and around the city which greatly embarrassed them when they were trying to impress upon Allied commanders that they had the security situation under control.

The situation was exacerbated when the *Laskar Rakyat Jakarta Raya* (Greater Jakarta People's *Laskar*—LRJR), many of whom were criminals, refused a government directive that all armed units (regular and irregular) leave Jakarta by September 19, 1945, only complying much later. When the LRJR carried out acts of social revolution on the outskirts of Jakarta (together with other irregular groups) that entailed overthrowing members of the *pamong praja* the Sjahrir government was again greatly concerned.[53] Nasution's remit did not extend to Jakarta but his highly energetic and committed stance against the *laskar* might have extended to discussing joint action against them with Dutch forces.[54]

He was supported by Sutoko, who had been trained by Nasution within the *Seinendan* organization.[55] He had been the leader of the Post, Telegraph and Telecommunications Youth Force (*Angkatan Muda Pos, Telegrap dan Telepon*—AMPTT) before it amalgamated with Pesindo and then led the local Pesindo organization.[56] Nasution employed a mixture of personal contacts, persuasion, and force in incorporating the *laskar* in the Priangan area into the *Siliwangi* Division. An example is his forcible suppression of the radical API (*Angkatan Pemuda Indonesia*—a radical *pemuda* organization formed on September 1, 1945) organization in Bandung. Van Dijk has recorded Nasution's description of his suppression of API as follows: "Well, at a given moment, it was in Bandung, I recruited 50% of them [the *laskar* groups] to form one regiment with me. The rest refused. Thereupon I secretly disarmed a fourth or third of them within the space of a few hours one night. After that the remainder came of their own accord."[57]

That Nasution was displeased at the intense political activity that nurtured the *laskar* phenomenon is apparent in his many publications. For example, in the first volume of *TNI,* an account of the armed struggle that he wrote in the 1950s, he wrote of his dismay at the proliferation of the parties and their *laskar* forces following Sjahrir's appointment as prime minister, with parties forming their own "armies" that were under their control and not necessarily responsive to the government.[58]

He disparaged long-haired *pemuda*s striking romantic poses at the outset of the revolution: "Standardised regular uniforms were considered inappropriate; rather one had to have an appearance and a uniform which expressed the Rebel—with long hair, belts full of bullets, etc."[59]

Sunarti shared his distaste for the political impetus in many *laskar* organizations. She attended Sjahrir's conference of *pemuda* groups in Yogyakarta as a member of the PRI (*Pemuda Republik Indonesia*—Youth of the Republic of Indonesia) but left when that organization (which she recalls as "pure and free of party associations") was incorporated within Pesindo. Instead, she devoted herself to the Indonesian Red Cross.[60]

In 1948, radical Pesindo elements were heavily involved in triggering a significant uprising by left-wing politicians and army officers around the city of Madiun in East Java which became known as the Madiun Affair. Nasution, who deployed the *Siliwangi* to crush the uprising, later teased Sunarti: "If you had not left [Pesindo] I would have been forced to arrest you."[61]

In the first eighteen months or so of the revolution the *Siliwangi* Division became known for its responsiveness to Sjahrir and his cabinet in Jakarta, rather than the Yogyakarta-based army headquarters.[62] In return, the *Siliwangi* were given privileged access to scarce funding which helped Nasution ensure the loyalty of his officers.

The government expected Nasution to be militant enough to ensure that nationalist sentiments were assuaged while demonstrating sufficient military capability to persuade the Dutch that it would be more prudent to negotiate with the Republic than attempt a military solution. An important aspect of this strategy was to reassure the Dutch that an independent Indonesia would still be a safe place for their investments. It motivated both Amir's funding of the *Siliwangi* Division and Nasution's concern to disarm unruly *laskar* organizations.[63]

In late 1946 the British had inflicted humiliation on the *Siliwangi* Division by successfully demanding that all Indonesians evacuate the northern half of the city of Bandung. The difficulty of Nasution's balancing act was then underlined in March 1946 when Sjahrir ordered him to evacuate his forces from the restive southern part of the city of Bandung in response to a British ultimatum.[64] In response, Sudirman's army headquarters in Yogyakarta sent Nasution a telegram ordering him to "defend every inch of our land."[65] While Sukarno, Hatta and Urip seem to have argued with Sjahrir to allow at least the *laskar* to remain,[66] the *Siliwangi* ordered the evacuation of all the inhabitants and fighting units from the crowded urban villages to appease the government and then torched them to show a measure of defiance to the Allies.[67] This episode, which became known as *Bandung Lautan Api* (Bandung Sea of Fire), was quickly mythologized as a symbol of popular defiance of the Allies and the Dutch and inspired two very popular songs.[68]

While in the heated and uncertain atmosphere of the time Nasution continued to depend to a considerable extent upon the good will of his subordinates, his behavior during the incident can be viewed as an early example of a cautious and reactive attitude in times of crisis and a tendency to allow subordinates to make the running. His senior colleagues, including his friend Sutoko, set in train the scorched earth strategy on their own initiative and he seems to have opted to go along with them by formally issuing the instruction.[69] While Sjahrir was satisfied with this compromise, the army headquarters was not, and as Said comments: "It took a few weeks for Nasution to straighten out his decision with the headquarters."[70]

The army headquarters continued to follow a different approach to Nasution and the Sjahrir government. This was highlighted when *Panglima Besar* Sudirman became openly associated with Tan Malaka and the cause of armed struggle (*perjuangan*), rather than Sjahrir's preferred option of negotiation that became known as *diplomasi* (diplomacy).

On December 22, 1945, Sudirman spoke at a meeting at Purwakarta that Tan Malaka had organized to oppose Sjahrir's policy of *diplomasi*. Tan Malaka used the occasion to demand the formation of a popular front which would have the aim of achieving "*100% Merdeka*" (100% independence) and later announced a "minimum program" that made a litany of demands, including a "people's army," "people's government" and the nationalization of foreign assets,[71] all of which was anathema to Sjahrir and his cabinet who were pursuing their policy of *diplomasi*.

By late February Sjahrir was under such pressure that he offered his resignation to Sukarno. However, his Socialist Party retained a majority within the quasi-parliament and on March 2, the president, who continued to be wary of Tan Malaka, appointed him to form a new cabinet. The highly principled Sjahrir did so and quietly continued in his quest for a negotiated settlement with the Dutch.

By mid-March the government had resolved to destroy Tan Malaka's Union of Struggle (*Persatuan Perjuangan*) as it might jeopardize an agreement resulting from Sjahrir's negotiations. Tan Malaka was arrested and detained until late 1948 when he was released and formed the "national communist" *Murba* Party. In the aftermath of a major Dutch offensive in December 1948 he attempted to lead the guerrilla struggle, claiming that the Sukarno/Hatta government had been wiped out, but he was killed by an army unit in East Java in 1949.

On June 27, Vice President Hatta announced that Sjahrir's negotiating position was to concede Dutch authority over areas outside Java, Sumatra and the island of Madura (near the East Java capital of Surabaya) and to agree to the Republic's participation as a state within a federal Indonesia which would join a Netherlands-Indonesia union. In exchange, the Dutch would recognize the Republic's de facto control over those areas. Opposition to these terms from within the army was evident when troops kidnapped the prime minister on the day of the announcement.

After an appeal by President Sukarno, Sjahrir was released and the government cracked down on dissent and on July 2, several opposition politicians were arrested. In the early morning of July 3, 1946, a major Sudarsono (who claimed he was acting upon Sudirman's orders) and a group of leading Tan Malaka associates went to the president to present a petition that he dismiss the cabinet. Sudarsono was arrested upon leaving Sukarno's office.[72] Sudirman could not be contacted until he reported to the palace on the evening of July 3, and his involvement in what became known as the July 3 Affair remains unclear.[73]

Sudirman's association with Tan Malaka was particularly worrying for the government because the *Panglima Besar* was immensely popular within the predominantly Javanese army. Known for his soulful addresses to his troops, he could call upon essentially Javanese symbols to rally their support. He often spoke of the "sacred" nature of the struggle for independence and once ordered his men to fast for three days so that they would be more aware of the spiritual dimension of the revolution.[74] Remarking upon the "pervasive sadness" of a radio address Sudirman made to his troops on April 9, 1946, Anderson insightfully comments:

> But Sudirman knew his audience, and spoke out of the culture he shared with his listeners. In his stress on spiritual purity and sincerity, on the moral qualities of the soldier, and on the need for austerity and self-sacrifice, one can see a harmonious blend of ancient Javanese conceptions of the *satria* [noble]-warrior and the values of the Japanese military ethos at its best.[75]

While Sudirman epitomized the PETA idea of *semangat*, Nasution lacked his charisma and took care not to associate himself with Tan Malaka's radical-left program. Once again, the contacts he had made with leading Bandung *pemudas* in Japanese paramilitary units came to his assistance when his ally Sutoko distanced the Bandung branch of Tan Malaka's Union of Struggle from the national organization.

The relative closeness to the government of the former KNIL officers and its wariness toward those with a PETA background was brought into sharper focus when Sjarifuddin sought to reorganize the army in early 1946, renaming it the *Tentara Republik Indonesia* (Army of the Republic of Indonesia—TRI). As Cribb points out, the former KNIL officers may not have shared Amir Sjarifuddin's left-wing political views but "they had many other things in common in the context of 1946, notably Western education and an interest in discipline, hierarchy and effective military organisation." Their desire to establish an army that could meet international standards of professionalism led them to cooperate closely with Sjarifuddin in forming the TRI.[76] On June 3, 1947, the name of the army was again changed to *Tentara Nasional Indonesia* (Indonesian National Army or TNI) which was to comprise the TRI, *laskar* units and other armed groups.

Tensions had originally emerged between the anti-fascist prime minister Sjahrir and the former PETA officers when he published a pamphlet entitled *Perjuangan Kita* (Our Struggle) on October 21, 1945. He angered many former PETA personnel by declaring that "democracy" rather than nationalism "should be the primary objective of our revolution" and calling for a purge of all "political collaborators of the Japanese fascists"[77]

When Sjahrir became firmly identified with the policy of *diplomasi* the rift between the more hardline former PETA officers and his government widened. Sjahrir's reasons for favoring *diplomasi* have been succinctly summarized by T.B. Simatupang who, like most of his fellow former KNIL officers, supported the prime minister's approach:

> The most urgent issue was how to resolve the conflict between us and the Dutch. At first, a political faction emerged which supported negotiations with the Dutch because the international situation could benefit us if we were skillful in showing that we were a democratic movement with peaceful intentions, and because we (and also the Dutch at that time) were unable to resolve the conflict with armed forces. Accordingly, this faction believed that there was room to solve conflict through negotiations, so that we would not lose time, materials, and lives in a war, and we could immediately start upon development programs. This faction was mainly associated with Sutan Sjahrir.[78]

This support for Sjahrir from former KNIL officers widened the gap between them and those who had been trained within PETA.

The closeness of the government to the KNIL officers was reflected in its statement that the TRI was to be "organised on international military foundations." and was to "undergo revision of its organisation in accordance with sound military forms and foundations."[79] This "revision" or review of the TRI was to be implemented by "a committee comprising military experts and other experts considered necessary."[80] Former KNIL officers dominated the committee that was headed by Didi Kartasasmita.[81]

The committee sought to reduce Sudirman's influence while bolstering Defense Minister Sjarifuddin and the former KNIL officers. It reorganized the defense apparatus into a general headquarters (responsible only for operational matters) under General Sudirman, and a military section that was subordinate to an expanded Ministry of Defense in which key positions were accorded to former KNIL officers.

However, former PETA officers continued to dominate the field commands in Central and East Java, with Nasution becoming the only former KNIL officer to gain and retain a field command when he was reappointed commander of the *Siliwangi* Division. Most of the older prewar Breda-trained KNIL officers found it impossible to cope with the somewhat anarchic nature of the emerging Republican Army and gradually retreated into relatively ineffectual positions or were deposed, while Nasution's fellow Military Academy cadets felt most comfortable in a headquarters environment under the avuncular mentorship of Urip Sumohardjo.[82]

One of the former Military Academy cadets who worked with Urip was T.B. Simatupang, who wrote that Nasution chose to serve in the *Siliwangi* Division rather than in a staff appointment at army headquarters in Yogyakarta because of his interest in tactical-organizational matters.[83] However, Nasution's background as a gifted and determined boy from a rural village in North Sumatra and his singlemindedness about pursuing an education and a military career set him apart from the other former Bandung Military Academy cadets.

His adoption of a boy-scout uniform after he was no longer entitled to an official one and deep involvement in Japanese paramilitary units, rather than accepting a civil service appointment, meant that by the time independence was declared he had more to offer than the technical military skills he and his classmates had acquired at the Military Academy. The other former KNIL officers were not steeped in Japanese paramilitary mobilization and training techniques and lacked the personal links he had built up with influential *pemudas* like his faithful ally Sutoko. In effect, he had developed the sort of *bapak-anak* links that were a feature of the Central and East Java commands.

The ethnic composition of the city of Bandung was also in his favor. By the twentieth century the city was not as closely tied to an ethnic group as more "indigenous" cities like Yogyakarta and Surakarta. Rather, it had become a center of learning and administration for young people from throughout the archipelago who were prepared to accept and adopt "outsiders" like Nasution.

Nasution only came into his own as a "people's warfare" strategist in July 1947 when the Dutch launched an offensive that they somewhat cynically termed a "police action." The origins of the attack can be found in an agreement reached between the Dutch and Sjahrir in the mountain resort of Linggarjati in November 1946. As Simatupang writes, this was a watershed in Dutch-Indonesian relations:

> After this agreement, our strategic goal changed, because we and the Dutch had agreed that one day there would be a sovereign United States of Indonesia (RIS). Neither we nor the Dutch could get out of the main points of this agreement after it became a historical reality which had national and international significance.[84]

In accordance with the stance that he had developed during the negotiations that preceded the agreement, the prime minister had acknowledged Dutch authority over areas outside the islands of Sumatra, Java and Madura and agreed to a decolonization plan that would lead to the creation of a Netherlands-Indonesia union. While moderates like Simatupang supported the agreement, those who adopted a harder line, and particularly the Tan Malaka-inspired opposition, were enraged. Hardline members of the Dutch parliament also found the agreement difficult to accept because they believed it gave too many concessions to the Republic, and only ratified the agreement when clarifications were attached to some of its points to the effect that they did not reflect the intentions of the Dutch negotiators.[85]

Opponents within the Republic were deeply suspicious that the Dutch intended to prosecute a policy of divide and rule of the sort that had served them well in their three centuries in the archipelago. They had already established a federal state (*negara*) of East Indonesia (*Indonesia Timor*) in early 1946, which covered the swathe of islands from Sulawesi (Celebes) to Bali and the East and Lesser Sundas. They had also set about developing other *negara*s and special districts (*daerah istimewa*) in "outer islands" where the Republic was weak, while building up their forces through the imposition of conscription in the Netherlands.

The Dutch later claimed that the Linggarjati Agreement had broken down because of continued efforts to win over international opinion by the Republic and violations by regular and irregular military forces associated with it, necessitating their "police action." In mid-1947 they attempted to impose further conditions, serving an ultimatum that a "transitional government" be formed, under which the Republic was not permitted to carry out its own diplomatic relations. Moreover, the ultimatum required the Republic to agree to Dutch police entering its territory to secure Dutch enterprises.

Sjahrir conceded 95 percent of the Dutch demands in the last week of June but his position became untenable and he resigned as prime minister in June 1947. His successor was Amir Sjarifuddin, who now led a large left-wing coalition known as the Left Wing or *Sayap Kiri*. On July 15, the Dutch delivered a new ultimatum to Indonesia, demanding that Republican forces withdraw ten kilometers from a demarcation line that had been negotiated on October 14, 1946, and then launched their offensive when they claimed that Sjarifuddin's response was unsatisfactory.

The Netherlands was still in the early stages of recovery from the economic devastation caused by the German occupation. Their Indies administration was similarly hard pressed and sought to restore their fortunes by gaining access to prime export-earning areas of Java and Sumatra and to deep-water ports, as they made clear in naming the "police action" Operation Product. By this time, the Dutch forces were sufficiently numerous, mechanized and trained. Moreover, they had the advantage of air and naval support while the Republic's air force and navy were still rudimentary and unable to provide operational support.

The Dutch rapidly occupied major population centers in West Java (except for Banten), the island of Madura and the Eastern salient of Java, the city of Semarang and surrounding areas in Central Java, the plantation areas around Medan in North Sumatra, and oil and gas fields in the Palembang and Padang areas of Central Sumatra. They did not extend their offensive into the Republican heartland around the cities of Yogyakarta and Surakarta, although their commander, General Spoor, wished to do so.[86]

Nasution was left feeling devastated and depressed. The Republic appeared to have suffered a devastating blow and in West Java he faced disappointment and recriminations. His lowest point was when many officers in the army headquarters in Yogyakarta were duped by a message transmitted by the Dutch but purporting to be from within the *Siliwangi* (using the *Siliwangi* code) to the effect that he had capitulated.[87] However, he was to rebuild his career and reputation when he developed his strategies of "people's war" from the rural hinterland of West Java, an episode in his life that he was later to portray as something of a "road to Damascus" experience that laid the foundations for Indonesia's future defense doctrines.

The term "territorial" began to be used in Indonesia in the aftermath of the defeat as Heijboer writes, citing Nasution: "At the time [of the rout of the Siliwangi Division] this [territorial warfare] was just an idea that emerged in my thoughts. Later I would channel it into other functions, and make it the foundation for principles of war in Indonesia."[88]

Forces engaged in territorial warfare strive to maintain government functions and the sovereignty of their state to the maximum degree possible within their pockets of national sovereignty. This form of warfare envisages army commanders moving beyond purely military concerns such as battlefield tactics and strategies and taking the reins of government in cooperation with civilian authorities and organizations in areas that are relatively free of enemy influence. It is political in the sense that military commanders need to forge alliances with certain individuals and entities and disregard or even oppose others. This often necessitates them adopting political roles at the grassroots in dealing with political differences within their societies. As the Yugoslav expert on this form of warfare, Lieutenant General Kveder, points out, guerrilla leaders need to: "independently solve many political problems. . . . This is a necessity which cannot be avoided in such a war, regardless of the desire of many officers in European armies to refrain from politics in the exercise of their military profession."[89]

The strategies that Nasution developed between 1945 and 1948 accorded with the basic tenets of territorial warfare in that they were aimed at wearing down the technologically superior Dutch forces while maintaining enclaves of national sovereignty. His reliance upon traditional authority structures in the form of the *pamong praja* and village administrations to do so meant that he was upholding a certain political vision of the nation and the state and this was where the politics can be found within his principles of guerrilla warfare.

Before the offensive Nasution had sought to prepare for a mechanized onslaught by adopting flexible strategies that allowed for the possibility of retreat, while also attending to directives from the army command in Yogyakarta to conduct a linear defense. Heijboer states that he was among the commanders who advocated a more flexible approach as he had a very long front to defend, was aware of the superiority of the weapons systems the Dutch would bring to bear, and understood that the mountainous areas of West Java were suitable for guerrilla warfare.[90]

He divided his West Java command into six zones into which he placed his brigades. Fortunately, although each brigade was positioned to conduct a linear defense of a strategic location, they were intended to be administratively self-sufficient and located close to an area of mountainous terrain into which they could retreat if necessary.[91]

In despair at the ease with which the Dutch routed his forces and ashamed that his *Siliwangi* Division had let down the people of West Java, he recalled a journey by packhorse through the hinterland of West Java in the wake of the offensive, accompanied only by an adjutant:

> Along the entire length of the road we encountered groups of soldiers who were retreating or lost, often accompanied by their families. My discussions with them were not pleasant for me, because what I heard were expressions of despair or indifference.
> All along the road I tried to think "what can I do," but my thought processes ran into a dead end and there was still no way out.[92]

However, Priangan-based *Siliwangi* units gradually regrouped in the interior of West Java:

> Many of the troops who withdrew became scattered and often the commanders didn't know the whereabouts of their subordinates. Before long the main roads could no longer be used, which meant that the TNI could only use village roads and walking paths that criss-crossed the interior. However, it was apparent that the dispersed troops, groups, and even individuals all headed back to their bases in their places of origin. This was also the case for the commanders. The senior officers sought out their juniors, while they in turn looked for their commanders.[93]

In the rural hinterlands of West Java Nasution and other officers developed principles of territorial warfare that were intended to maintain Republican sovereignty within guerrilla pockets from where they could harass the Dutch. He writes that he became fully aware of the potential of this form of warfare after trekking for two weeks to the south from the city of Tasikmalaya and realizing that the Dutch were only in control of a limited number of strong points. Moreover, the people in rural villages were still loyal to the Republic and were assisting and looking after the retreating troops.[94]

He recalls that reading about guerrilla warfare helped him devise the strategies that he began to employ:

> Our military leaders had not received appropriate education and training. We had to train and educate ourselves without any teachers apart from experience, desire, and clear thinking. We didn't have overseas books or writings that could be used, but I had acquired a book from a friend in Singapore about the experiences of Brigadier General Wingate. This greatly assisted my thought processes and the term Wingate became widely used within the TNI.[95]

Following the example of Wingate's infiltration of troops behind the Japanese lines in Burma (Myanmar) he was inspired to create guerrilla bases which the Dutch could not easily reach. His forces would avoid large-scale encounters and focus instead on mounting surprise attacks upon their military posts and lines of communication.[96]

Some of Tan Malaka's ideas about "people's warfare" also appear to have struck a chord with Nasution, as he quotes his *Gerpolek* extensively in Volume Two of *TNI*.[97] He and his officers were also influenced by Edgar Snow's *Red Star Over China*.[98] However, other factors also influenced him, not the least of which was the "people's resistance" apparatus established by the Japanese.

He made clear his admiration for these occupation structures in *Memenuhi Panggilan Tugas*, recalling that resistance was organized from the household level upward. A group of households were organized into a *kumi* and several *kumi* were amalgamated into a *cokai*. Village heads were subordinate to the *Cokaico* (head of a *cokai*). Each village administrative unit (kelurahan) had its own youth brigade (*barisan pemuda*) to participate in civil defense. Heads of regions from the *bupati* (regents) to the *lurah* village heads led their own youth brigades. Schools were formed into companies headed by teachers with military training.[99]

Nasution was also assisted by the nature of the Japanese-auspiced PETA, which had many of the characteristics of a territorial warfare force. It was never accorded a central command structure and each battalion was an autonomous unit with close links to its local area from which most of its members were recruited. As Mrazek points out: "the structure of the PETA was to be 'territorial.' The PETA was to consist of battalions and companies that would be permanently stationed in one area and all the maintenance of the troops was to be provided from the resources of this area. There was virtually no provision for a logistical support of the units from a centre outside the region. Indeed, no central staff of the PETA was established at all."[100]

More recently, Nasution had been influenced by the torching of the southern part of Bandung in the *Bandung Lautan Api* incident of March 1946. He later wrote that it gave him faith that the people were at one with the army and claimed that the evacuation had convinced him that the people were highly responsive to the leadership of the army in emergency situations, and that a duality of command between the army and civilian-led *laskar* umbrella organizations was undesirable and unnecessary.[101] He went on to recall that the incident taught him that the TRI was a "people's army":

> The *Bandung Lautan Api* incident convinced me that the unity between the people and the army was strong, and that therefore the idea of a "people's army" was a fact of life in the field.[102]

However, Nasution also saw his "people's army" as occupying a leadership position over civilian populations, with the right to lead them and the civil authorities in critical situations. He recalls that while the civil authorities were normally obedient to the government's instructions, during emergencies they obeyed the divisional commander instead and that this had a great influence in how he thought and acted in future army leadership positions.[103]

At a more technical level, prior to the "Police Action" the German term *Wehrkreis* began to be used by a group of army headquarters (Yogyakarta) staff officers known as the younger generation officer corps, whose leader was T.B. Simatupang. He recalls that the term was taken from German books and then became widely used during the armed struggle when combat areas had to be controlled and defended as functional areas of the Republic, even though Dutch troops occupied several points within them.[104] The *Wehrkreis* system had its origin in Prussian mobilization techniques that were later practiced by the German Army. Although a literal translation for the term is "defensive circle," a more meaning-based translation is "military district."[105] Recognizing the likelihood that Indonesia's linear defenses might not survive against a Dutch offensive, this concept advocated that a territorial strategy be pursued.

There are similarities between the *Wehrkreis* system and Nasution's advocacy for different tiers of forces (one offensive/mobile and the other more supportive and partisan in nature) during the revolution.[106] There are also similarities between the *Wehrkreis* concept and the form of warfare that Tito's Yugoslav forces described as "territorial." Kveder wrote that armies that adopted this form of warfare did not countenance the prospect of surrender to a stronger enemy. Rather, they avoided linear methods of defense and operated freely within a particular territory, liberating and relinquishing areas in accordance with the flow of battle. They attacked only when they stood a reasonable chance of defeating enemy forces.[107]

Cribb attributes Nasution's initial impulse to create the *Wehrkreis* to a need to "restore a sense of hierarchy within the *Siliwangi* Division" whose units had been "scrambled" in the retreat from the Dutch offensive, and to assert responsibility for the entire province of West Java after the Ministry of Defense "stripped him and the *Siliwangi* Division of responsibility for the security of the province in the wake of the apparent debacle of July 1947."[108]

In October 1947 Nasution formed five *Wehrkreis* sectors throughout West Java. In December, he extended the *Wehrkreis* system downward to include Military District Commands (KDM—*Komando Distrik Militer*) and Subdistrict Military Commands (KODM—*Komando Onder Distrik Militer*).

Nasution made plans for three phases of resistance. At first the Dutch were to be harassed wherever possible while the *Siliwangi* Division regrouped. *Siliwangi* units were then to enter their *Wehrkreis* sectors where they were to reinstitute and/or consolidate civil governmental institutions so that the de facto authority of the Republic reached to the village level. In the third stage, *Siliwangi* forces were to cut lines of communication between enemy concentrations:

> Troops were sent through enemy territory, infiltrating into empty areas, particularly in the northern area. Several battalions were moved from the mountain areas in the south to the northern plain, a journey that took several weeks. Territorial officers were appointed to maintain public relations with the civil administrators and the public. A long-term program was initiated to enlarge the pockets gradually in all directions, even into the outskirts of big towns occupied by the enemy. People in the villages were still loyal to the Republic, and the important thing was [to work out] how to organise them. Tactics aimed at tiring the enemy, tying him down wherever he was, forcing him to disperse his strength, and rendering him immobile were gradually improved.[109]

The Dutch were heavily reliant on road transport to move troops and supplies between the population centers that they controlled and *Siliwangi* troops had some success in waging guerrilla warfare against them. Heijboer writes that Dutch soldiers began to call certain stretches of highway (such as between Cirebon and Ciamis and Cirebon and Cikijing) "death roads" because of frequent *Siliwangi* ambushes.

> Mental tiredness had a great deal to do with the disappointing experience that almost everywhere the TNI was still capable of launching violent actions, and moreover were practically impossible to reach.[110]

Indonesian forces also systematically destroyed roads and bridges upon which the Dutch depended.

> Dutch traffic in occupied areas was not only disturbed by gunfire, but—sometimes more effectively—by various forms of damage to the roads. The Dutch Army had to admit that in this regard their enemy was demonstrating considerable creativeness and perseverance. On more than one occasion bridges were dropped into ravines the day after they were erected by the engineers corps.[111]

Guerrilla warfare was not confined to West Java. Heijboer writes that it was highly successful in occupied parts of East Java:

> after all of the sacrifices of the Dutch Marines and X Brigade in seizing the road to Malang, they continually became the targets of sabotage. The troops that carried out this harassment stayed close to cities for long periods. It was only after September with air and artillery support that large-scale actions were launched against such cities as Ngadipuro, Nongkojajar, Krewek and Batu, that the situation for the Dutch around Malang, Blimbing, and Singosari became secure.[112]

With their territorial focus, close ties with local communities and loose structures of command and control, Indonesian forces were well-suited to this sort of asymmetric warfare. The Dutch had little rapport with Indonesians and the mechanized forms of transport that had afforded overwhelming superiority to them in the early part of their offensive now had the effect of separating them from the populace. They were vulnerable to guerrilla attacks and of little use off the highways in the muddy labyrinths of rice fields and the dense jungles of West Java.

At a divisional meeting in December 1947 the Siliwangi leadership formally decided that their emphasis would shift to "total people's resistance." A West Java Leadership Political Note was issued to that effect, jointly signed by Sewaka (the West Java Governor) and Nasution, and planning was put into place to establish "guerrilla pockets" throughout West Java to the perimeters of the major cities of Jakarta, Bogor and Bandung. Territorial operations were to be led by the subdistrict head (*Camat*) and subdistrict (*Kecamatan*) territorial officers (*Opsir Teritorial Kecamatan*—OTK).[113] For Nasution, an important objective of the "Political Note" was to establish a single civil-military leadership for West Java, replacing Regional Defense Councils (*Dewan Pertahanan Daerah*) that had been established at each Residency because he saw them as unwieldy structures that were comprised mainly of party-affiliated civilians who sought to interfere in military matters.[114]

While guerrilla attacks reminded the Dutch that the forces aligned with the Republic had not given up the fight, Nasution's "people's resistance" structures were not able to turn the tables and force the Dutch to withdraw from their strong points. They were only established in a few areas where his influence was strong and the central government never recognized Nasution's province-level defense council.[115] Nevertheless, the "Political Note" issued by Nasution and the West Java Governor and the appointment of Subdistrict *Kecamatan* Territorial Officers was highly significant as it entailed the formation of territorial commands that shadowed the civilian *pamong praja* system of administration, pioneering the idea of a partnership between the army and the *pamong praja* where army officers played the leading role in waging "people's warfare."

The territorially based corps of civil servants remained largely intact in the areas under his control and extended down to the *pamong desa* (village administration) level. Nasution was being pragmatic in attempting to assert Republican sovereignty over these areas through the civil service but also a political choice. His strategies followed logically from his attempts to co-opt or disband the party-affiliated *laskar* organizations in that they were intended to impose order and "depoliticise" resistance to the Dutch by supporting and relying upon organic "traditional" authority structures. Under a joint army-*pamong praja* leadership, the mobilization of "the people" was much more likely to follow the traditional (*kawula-gusti*) lines extolled by Professor Sutomo than those espoused by political figures such as Tan Malaka.

The noted guerrilla warfare researcher Walter Laqueur has observed that *Fundamentals of Guerrilla Warfare* reminded him "of Mao with the politics left out."[116] However, Laqueur might not have been aware of the indispensable support many *pangreh praja* officials provided to the colonial regime in its crack-downs on noncooperating nationalist political leaders. That Nasution looked to them for support in waging guerrilla warfare, rather than the political parties, was no doubt based on necessity but it also accorded with his own political leanings.

The political nature of Nasution's choice is evident in his references in the early-to-mid 1950s to his wartime reliance upon traditional authority structures. For example, in *Fundamentals of Guerrilla Warfare* he lauded the reliability and authenticity of "traditional" *pamong praja* and *pamong desa* (village) officials in the "people's war" campaign of 1947. He particularly praised the village heads (*lurahs*), asserting that *Pa'* (Father) *Lurah* was "still the one and only" person who could be relied upon to lead their community, even though they might not be well-educated or informed about wider events and circumstances.[117]

Nasution's disdain for the parties was to come increasingly to the fore in the 1950s, and his idealization (and mythologization) of a time when traditional authority figures held sway over rural populations under the leadership of military officers is evident in this excerpt from *TNI* that was published in that decade:

> Experience in the first military action showed that in times of guerrilla warfare within the guerrilla enclaves it was clearly not the party leaders who became the leaders and protectors of the people, but the *lurah* [village head], *camat* [subdistrict head] and local military commanders.[118]

His praise for these traditional leaders in his recollections of his guerrilla warfare strategies reveal the socially conservative instincts that were at the heart of the principles that he developed.

The political nature of Nasution's reliance upon traditional authority figures is also evident when contrasted with the views of Tan Malaka. In caustically criticizing the *pamong praja*, Tan Malaka wrote that the social order in the Dutch colonial period was "rotten to the core."[119] While he was concerned to enlist the support of what he described as "enlightened" members of the *priyayi* class,[120] he proposed the redistribution of land that was the property of "hostile aliens and aristocratic parasites of the Dutch."[121] It is likely that had the struggle spawned a large left-wing revolutionary army, the *pamong praja* would have been a prime target as presaged when social revolutionary movements acted against some of its members in the early stages of the struggle against the Dutch.

Perhaps the best known of the social revolutions that took place in Java was the so-called "Three Regions" (*Tiga Daerah*) Affair which took place in Brebes, Pemalang and Tegal in the Pekalongan area of North Central Java. Very briefly put, the affair was precipitated in part by *santri-abangan* rivalries when orthodox Muslim youth replaced some village heads with members of the *santri* community. The unrest culminated in action by left-wing forces who replaced the resident of Pekalongan with a member of the secret PKI. This event provoked a reaction by Indonesian Army units whose officers had been recruited from local *priyayi* families.[122] Later in the revolution, members of the *pamong praja* were targeted by left-wing forces during the September 1948 Madiun Affair.[123]

Tan Malaka asserted that "The Indonesian revolution cannot just be wrapped up within a national revolution."[124] This was a remark that could have been directed specifically at Nasution who drew upon an innate conservatism and fondness for discipline and order in responding to the widespread politicization of society, the emergence of unruly *laskar* groups, and the civil disorder that accompanied this process.

Tan Malaka urged that a "people's army" be formed whose obligation was to: "implement the people's political programs of the *Murba* (proletariat). In the revolutionary period, the people's army is a revolutionary army, that is an army of revolutionary politics."[125] His ambitions for the army and disdain for the *pamong praja* contrast with and serve to highlight the strong, albeit implicit, political dimension to Nasution's strategies for "people's war" and the views that he was to express in the 1950s.

Unlike Nasution, Tan Malaka never had the opportunity to put his principles into practice and Anderson has cogently argued that his imprisonment and the defeat of his movement were decisive blows to any prospects of the struggle against the Dutch turning into a social revolution. As George Kahin remarks in his foreword to *Java in a Time of Revolution*, "Anderson believes that this defeat over the issue of immediate social revolution not only reinforced the position of the political moderates in Indonesian society but considerably reduced the likelihood that, once national independence was attained, far-reaching social reforms would actually be carried out."[126] Of course, such a turn of events might have posed a costly and perhaps even lethal threat to indigenous elites like the Gondokusumo family.

Nasution indicates his concern for the maintenance of rural social stability and his fear that traditional patterns of authority might easily be disturbed in such statements as: "the intellectual levels" of *lurahs* and village officials needed "to be raised in order that they might follow the developments confronting them but in wartime it was difficult to make improvements."[127]

Nasution's praise of the *lurah* and the *camat* and castigation of political leaders was no doubt self-serving, as he wrote his best-known work in the early 1950s when he was deeply frustrated and chagrined by opponents in the parliament. Nevertheless, there is little doubt that Nasution found loyal members of the *pamong praja* and *pamong desa* to have political views that were compatible with his own and that they performed invaluable services for him and his *Siliwangi* Division in the "people's war" against the Dutch.

Conversely, the young *Siliwangi* commander appears to have been held in high regard by many of the loyal *pamong praja* officials in West Java. In the 1955 general elections, Nasution (who had stood down from the army leadership) formed a small and ultimately unsuccessful party known as IPKI (*Ikatan Pendukung Kemerdekaan Indonesia*—League of Supporters of Indonesian Independence). IPKI received most of its votes from West Java where it was supported by a well-motivated group of *Siliwangi* officers and *pamong praja* officials.[128]

There was another personal and emotional dimension to Nasution's recollections of the services village administrations and populations provided in the second half of 1947, as they were also extended to Sunarti, whose memoir supports Nasution's idealization of traditional village leadership structures and values. Their relationship began in earnest in the early period of the revolution when Sunarti nursed Nasution after he was injured while observing a test of hand grenades:

I looked after his wounds and covered them with a bandage. I had to use a few of them, and they even covered his left eye. He looked very gallant, like a freedom fighter. I was enthralled and my heart was beating strongly. Before this took place, we had only had a friendly, family style relationship because he was like a son to my father and mixed with us every day in our home.[129]

After Sunarti had studied law for a year at Gadjah Mada University in Yogyakarta, Nasution visited and "poured out his longing for her":

Without my presence at his place of duty he was very lonely. I was only too well aware of his intense need for me to be beside him as he fulfilled his immense responsibilities. So, we became engaged and exchanged rings on the 17th of February 1947. I gave him one condition—that after we were married I wanted to continue my studies and he agreed.[130]

The Gondokusumo family and Sunarti's Red Cross Post had evacuated to Ciwidey in the mountains outside Bandung and the young *Siliwangi* commander clearly found their home there a haven of loving and secure domesticity that he had not truly known since leaving North Sumatra. It became, like his own parent's house had been, a place that he could come home to and relax because "we all need something of a 'base' in the form of a family or parents."[131]

Sometimes it is the *non-dit* or things that are left unsaid that can be most revealing. Neither Nasution nor Sunarti have written about the delicate situation faced by the mixed-race Gondokusumo family during the occupation and the early years of the armed struggle against the Dutch.

When the Japanese arrived, Maria, her mother and the children were in a delicate position in the racial cross-currents that evolved under the colonial regime. The Japanese tried to encourage Eurasians to feel and act more like Asians with very limited results:

Their words fell on deaf ears of both Eurasians and Indonesians. The Indonesians were convinced that the differences between the Indonesians and the Eurasians were too deeply rooted to be eradicated overnight. The response of the Eurasian group was fairly reactionary. It utterly rejected the idea of being equated with the Indonesians. Some went so far as to say that they would rather die than be treated as an Indonesian.[132]

Maria and her mother seem to have been exempted from internment by the Japanese when they rounded up Dutch citizens, probably because Sunario could protect them. However, given the high percentage of mixed marriages in the colony and Maria's uncle's service in the KNIL, it is also possible that they were able to claim some Indonesian ancestry which might have spared them.

In seeking refuge for his family in Ciwidey, Sunario might have been motivated to escape the violence perpetrated against Dutch and Eurasians in the *bersiap!* period. Fears for the safety of Sunarti and her family might also have influenced Nasution in his antipathy toward unruly *laskar* elements.

Nasution and Sunarti married in May 1948 and Sunarti then followed Nasution to the large town of Tasikmalaya, where his headquarters were located. During the Dutch attack in July Sunarti miscarried and had to be treated under an operating table because of fears of air raids. Still weak and losing blood, she was evacuated from the city. She was to move thirteen times from hamlet to hamlet to avoid the Dutch, often losing contact with Nasution. They eventually reunited but were separated again when Nasution had to leave for the Tasikmalaya area.[133]

When Nasution returned, he and Sunarti took refuge in another series of villages, ending up in the hamlet of Bojong Gambir, where the divisional meeting that formalized the Siliwangi's emphasis on "people's resistance" took place. Sunarti had a small typewriter and she typed Nasution's orders to his commanders.

Sunarti appears to have been well-disposed toward village life. She writes of visiting the *lurahs* and *ajengan* (religious teachers), recalling one (Pidoli) who meant well in seeking to give Sunarti religious instruction but was much too slow. Eventually she asked her to speed up the instruction because she had studied at the Lyceum on Bandung and in the law faculty of Gadjah Mada University.[134]

The emotional pressure experienced by Nasution after the rout of his division at the hands of the Dutch was no doubt heightened by Sunarti's miscarriage and flight from Tasikmalaya. The opportunity to have a baby soon afterward was apparently not available or taken up and their first child was born five years later in 1952. It is reasonable to assume that these experiences impacted on Nasution when he began to idealize traditional village authority structures after his dismissal in 1952, as it was the *lurah*s and villagers who gave refuge and cared for her.

Nasution and Sunarti found time to nurture their marriage and the following excerpt from her memoir reveals the emotional intensity they experienced:

> After the Dutch occupied Taraju, Pak Nas built a bamboo hut in the middle of a forest for us to evacuate to. It was in a valley that was watered by a small river with clear water. The hut was at the edge of the river and shaded by lush overhanging branches. I had to use a bamboo footbridge to go down to the river.
>
> I was there for about a week and it is my most beautiful memory. On that last day before we left for Yogyakarta, Pak Nas and I just sat there for hours to imprint our beautiful memories in our minds. We could hear birdsong and the sounds of animals around the valley. We bathed in the clear little river. We felt

that we never wanted to leave because we were at one with the beautiful natural surroundings. And we were aware that after we left we would be separated and we did not know when we would meet again. We were entering a period of uncertainty.[135]

That this period was also very significant for the normally phlegmatic and reserved Nasution is evident in his description of their time in the villages as "a beautiful memory for us."[136]

On the other hand, both portray their return from the forests to the cities as something of a fall from grace. Whereas the people of the villages had been simple, uncomplicated and steadfast, the politicians in the big cities seemed unaware of the achievements and importance of the *Siliwangi* Division and town dwellers less likely to be loyal and supportive.

The "period of uncertainty" that Sunarti alluded to arose when she and Nasution were compelled to leave their sanctuary in West Java in early February 1948. International pressure had forced the Dutch to resume negotiations with the Republic, and Australia and India had successfully called upon the United Nations Security Council to mediate. A Good Offices Committee was formed which comprised representatives from the United States (to chair the group), Australia (nominated by Indonesia) and Belgium (nominated by the Netherlands). Following the second police action in December 1948, the powers of this committee were increased and its name changed to the United Nations Commission for Indonesia (UNCI).

The resumed negotiations took place under international auspices in the neutral territory of a United States naval vessel (the USS Renville) in January 1948 and produced what became known as the Renville Agreement. The Republic agreed to recognize the military gains made by the Dutch (along a line of demarcation that became known as the van Mook line, after the lieutenant governor) and was required to remove its forces from large areas of Java and Sumatra. The *Siliwangi* Division was the most affected, having to leave the hinterland of West Java for Republican-held areas in Central Java.[137]

The Dutch benefited economically and politically from the terms of the ceasefire, gaining access to the plantations and oil fields that had been their objective in launching the "police action." In line with the divide and rule federalization process they had set in train before and after the Linggarjati Agreement, they established the federal states of Pasundan (West Java), East Sumatra, South Sumatra, Madura and East Java in their newly occupied areas.

Nasution clearly felt that the "people's war" strategies he developed had salvaged his reputation and that of his *Siliwangi* Division, particularly after the army headquarters had lost faith in him and his command. Later in life he was to complain that the civilian leaders who negotiated the ceasefire had failed to recognize his achievements and those of the *Siliwangi*, and that

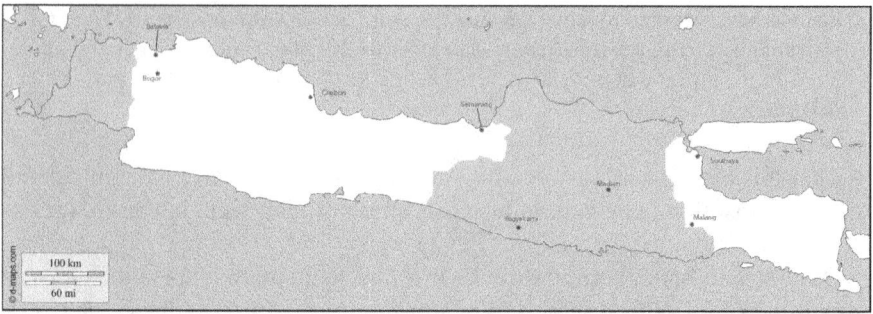

Figure 4.1 The van Mook Line. *Source*: D-Maps, modified by Sharon Turner-Chapman (http://d-maps.com/carte.php?num_car=133892&lang=en).

some had thought that his division had been reduced to scattered remnants that needed to be rescued from slaughter by vastly superior Dutch forces. He considered that in signing the ceasefire the civilian leaders had not only neglected the interests of rural civil servants and villagers who had been loyal to the Republic but created a vacuum that was quickly filled by *Darul Islam* insurgents who were intent on replacing the essentially secular state with an Islamic one and would remain a serious threat throughout the 1950s.[138]

According to Heijboer, by the time of the withdrawal Nasution was planning a large-scale assault on the South Priangan area and was at first reluctant to withdraw to Central Java, only doing so when he realized that some of his troops had received the order before him and were proceeding to assembly points. Heijboer states that the Dutch were surprised when some twenty thousand Siliwangi troops reported at assembly points for evacuation from West Java.[139]

Sunarti recalls that she suffered humiliation at the hands of city people after Nasution departed for Yogyakarta. On arrival in the city of Garut nobody would assist her, even when she explained that she was the wife of the *Siliwangi* commander, and she ended up travelling to Bandung perched on a truckload of firewood.[140]

Nasution alludes to this sort of humiliation in his memoirs:

> Our guerrilla fighters had to separate from their families who were left behind in the mountains with nobody to safeguard and look after them. Alternatively, they had to ask their families to go into the occupied cities where they were subjected to insults and misery or bring their families with them which meant, of course, that they suffered in other ways. They had to farewell the guerrilla civil servants who had loyally and unstintingly devoted themselves to the Republic, leaving them in their posts without any guidance. They had to leave behind the ordinary people who had united with them in the guerrilla war to such an extent that they had become like family.[141]

No doubt Nasution's recollections of his time in the villages were self-serving and perhaps embellished, but it is reasonable to assume that many were not confected. They were to influence his focus on village administrations in the plans for "people's resistance" he developed after he evacuated to Central Java:

> In investigating which organisation of people's defence and guerrilla government would be most efficient for our needs, I concluded that it was the villages and *lurah*s and other village officers that must be their foundations. They could not be allowed to be altered and weakened. Rather, they had to be strengthened so that the fullest possible benefit could be won from them for the people's struggle.[142]

NOTES

1. Excerpt from a speech by Professor Supomo included in Muhammad Yamin, *Naskah Persiapan UUD 1945*, Vol One. Extracted from Marsillam Simandjuntak, *Pandangan Negara Integralistik*, Jakarta, Grafiti, 1994, p. 88.
2. Ibid., p. 89.
3. Ibid., p. 85.
4. Bourchier, *Op. Cit.*, p. 6.
5. Simandjuntak, *Op. Cit.*, p. 99.
6. Ibid., p. 101.
7. Ibid., p. 91.
8. Ibid., p. 91.
9. Ibid, various, for example, p. 91.
10. Ibid., p. 89, 90. Supomo went on to say: "This is the totalitarian idea, the integralistic idea of the people of Indonesia that is achieved also in an original constitution."
11. Bourchier, *Op. Cit*, p. 5, 6.
12. Bourchier, *Op. Cit.*, p. 83.
13. Supomo's speech to the BPUPKI, Simandjuntak, *Op. Cit.*, p. 89, 90.
14. Bourchier, *Op. Cit.,* p. 91.
15. See Ibid. pp. 86–94 for a discussion on the tensions that emerged within the BPUPKI over such issues as human rights, people's sovereignty and whether the legislatures would resolve debates through voting.
16. Ibid., p. 82.
17. W.J. S. Poerwadarminta, *Kamus Umum Bahasa Indonesia*, Pn Balai Pustaka, Jakarta, 1976, p. 1094.
18. G. Moedjanto, "Pemikiran Bung Karno Menuju Pancasila: Catatan Bung Karno Seratus Tahun," *Bernas*, May 20, 2001, extracted from the Indomedia Bernas website in February 2005.
19. Bourchier, *Op. Cit.*, p. 93.

20. Ibid., p. 94.
21. Ibid.
22. Ibid., p. 93.
23. Anderson notes: "The single most important aspect of this PNI was its direct continuity with the *Hokokai*." He bases this conclusion on the composition of its top leadership (Sukarno and Hatta) and the involvement of former leaders of arms of the Hokokai, such as military (*Barisan Pelopor*) and women's organizations. 1972 *Op. Cit.*, p. 93.
24. As Lance Castles puts it, "the '*pamong praja*' figures who had close relations with the Japanese" and whose "blueprint" had provided for a dominant executive and a single state party but had not mentioned elections or individual rights had proved to be "too narrow to deal with revolutionary demands." Lance Castles, "Pengalaman Demokrasi Liberal di Indonesia (1950–1959)," Education on Democracy and the Civil-Military Dialogue Seminar June 11, 1998, www.csps-ugm.or.id/artikel/Ndi-lance.htm, accessed November 2004, p. 1.
25. Anderson, 1972 *Op. Cit*, p. 29, 30.
26. Ibid., p. 26.
27. See C. Van Dijk, *Rebellion Under the Banner of Islam: The Darul Islam in Indonesia*, The Hague, M. Nijhoff, 1981, pp. 76–7, for a brief account of the origins of *Sabilillah*.
28. Ibid., p. 75.
29. For a list of these organizations and an account of the events leading to and immediately following the formation of Pesindo, see Anderson, 1972 *Op. Cit.*, pp. 252–60. Sjarifuddin's attempts to impose a socialist philosophy on the *pemuda* movement is often said to have resulted in a breakdown of *pemuda* solidarity after the Yogyakarta conference. (Ibid., p. 260).
30. Anderson, 1972 *Op. Cit.*, p. 274.
31. Ibid., pp. 269–75.
32. Ibid., p. 275.
33. Arnold Brackman, *Indonesian Communism,* New York, Frederic A. Praeger, 1963, p. 39. Sendenbu was the Japanese propaganda organization in Indonesia.
34. Anderson, 1972 *Op. Cit.*, p. 287, 288.
35. A. H. Nasution, *TNI* (Vol Two), Jakarta, Seruling Masa, 1968, pp. 216–26.
36. Anderson, 1972 *Op Cit.*, pp. 277–80.
37. Kahin, *Op. Cit.*, p. 149, 167, and Anderson, 1972 *Op Cit.*, pp. 280–283.
38. Salim Said, *Genesis of Power: General Sudirman and the Indonesian Military in Politics 1945–1949*, North Sydney: Allen and Unwin,1992, p. 11, 12.
39. N. Mulder, *Individual and Society in Java*, Yogyakarta, Gadjah Mada University Press, 1992, p. 49.
40. Sunarti, *Op. Cit.*, p. 26.
41. See Peter Britton, *Profesionalisme dan Ideologi Militer Indonesia*, Jakarta, LP3ES, 1996, pp. 37–42, for a succinct account of PETA training and indoctrination methods.
42. Reid, *Op. Cit.*, pp. 78–9.
43. Anderson, 1972 *Op Cit.*, p. 265, 266.
44. Ibid., p. 267.

45. Penders and Sundhaussen, *Op. Cit.*, p. 31.
46. Said, *Op. Cit.*, p. 89, f.n. 69.
47. Ibid., p. 66.
48. Penders and Sundhaussen, *Op. Cit.*, p. 30.
49. Prasetyo and Hadad, *Op. Cit.*, p. 42.
50. McKemmish, *Op. Cit.*, p. 22.
51. Nasution, *Memenuhi Panggilan Tugas*, Vol One, *Op. Cit.*, p. 262.
52. Prasetyo and Hadad, *Op. Cit.*, p. 42.
53. Cribb, 1991 *Op. Cit.*, pp. 49–57.
54. Ibid., p. 135, fn 16.
55. McKemmish, *Op. Cit.*, p. 50.
56. Penders and Sundhaussen, *Op. Cit.*, p. 28.
57. Van Dijk, *Op. Cit.*, p. 78.
58. Nasution, TNI (Vol One), *Op. Cit.*, p. 154.
59. Nasution, *TNI*, translation excerpted from Anderson, 1972 *Op. Cit.*, pp. 236, 237.
60. Sunarti, *Op. Cit.*, p. 24.
61. Nasution, *Memenuh Panggilan Tugas*, Vol One, *Op. Cit.* p. 180.
62. According to Kahin, Sudirman's control over the Siliwangi Division was "largely nominal. [It] looked chiefly to the Minister of Defence . . . for [its] orders." Kahin, *Op Cit.*, p. 185.
63. Cribb, 2001 *Op. Cit.*, pp. 146–149.
64. Anderson, *Op Cit.*, p. 296.
65. Said, *Op Cit.*, p. 42.
66. Anderson. 1972 *Op Cit.*, p. 330, f.n. 65.
67. Penders and Sundhaussen, *Op Cit.*, p. 33.
68. The songs are *Halo Halo Bandung, Bandung Selatan* (South Bandung) and *Sapu Tangan Sutera dari Bandung* (A Silk Handkerchief from Bandung).
69. McKemmish, *Op. Cit.*, pp. 27–31.
70. Said, *Op Cit.*, p. 42.
71. Anderson, 1972 *Op Cit.*, p. 290.
72. Said, *Op Cit.*, p. 63.
73. Anderson, 1972 *Op Cit.*, pp. 370–402, Said, *Op Cit.*, pp. 63–66.
74. Britton, *Op. Cit.*, p. 42, 43.
75. Anderson, 1972 *Op. Cit.*, pp. 375–378.
76. Cribb, 1991 *Op Cit.*, p. 108.
77. Brackman, *Op. Cit.*, p. 46.
78. T.B. Simatupang, *The Fallacy of a Myth*, Jakarta, Pustaka Sinar Harapan, 1996, p. 114.
79. Nasution, *TNI* (Vol One), *Op. Cit.*, p. 259, 260.
80. Ibid., p. 260.
81. Harsja Bachtiar, *Siapa Dia: Perwira Tinggi Tentara Nasional Angkatan Darat (TNI-AD)*, Jakarta, Djambatan, 1998, p. 164.
82. Britton, *Op. Cit.*, p. 46.
83. Simatupang, *Op. Cit.*, p. 110.
84. Simatupang, 1996 *Op. Cit.*, p. 115.

85. Pierre Heijboer, *Agresi Militer Belanda: Merebutkan Pending Zamrud Sepanjang Katulistiwa 1945/19* (*The Dutch Military Aggression: Seizing the Girdle of Emeralds Around the Equator*), Jakarta: Gramedia Widiasarana Indonesia in Cooperation with Koninklijk Instituut voor Taal, Land-en Volkunkende (KITLV), Translated by W.S. Karnera, 1998, p. 28.

86. Ibid., p. 109.

87. Ibid.

88. Ibid., p. 52.

89. Dushan Kveder, "*'Territorial War': The New Concept of Resistance,*" Foreign Affairs, Vol 32, Nos. October 1–4, 1953–July 1954, p. 97.

90. Heijboer, *Op. Cit.*, p. 30.

91. Cribb, 1991 *Op Cit.*, p. 157.

92. Nasution, *Memenuhi Panggilan Tugas*, Vol One *Op. Cit.*, p. 311.

93. Nasution, *TNI*, Vol Two, *Op. Cit.*, p. 92.

94. Nasution, "Kita Belum Cukup Dewasa," 1995 *Op. Cit.*, 48 49.

95. Nasution, *TNI*, Vol Two, *Op. Cit.,* p. 94.

96. Heijboer, *Op. Cit.*, p. 52.

97. Ibid., pp. 216–226.

98. In *The Indonesian Doctrine of Territorial Warfare and Territorial Management* (The Rand Corporation, p. 9) Guy Pauker discusses Nasution's use of tactics associated with Wingate's Raiders. See also Nasution, *TNI* (Vol Two), *Op. Cit.*, p. 94.

99. Nasution, *TNI* (Vol One), *Op. Cit.*, p. 91.

100. R. Mrazek, *The United States and the Indonesian Military 1945–65: A Study of Intervention*, Prague, Oriental Institute in Academic, 1978, p. 27.

101. Nasution, *Memenuhi Panggilan Tugas,* Vol One, *Op. Cit.*, p. 235.

102. Ibid., p. 236.

103. Ibid., p. 236.

104. Simatupang, *Op. Cit.*, p. 120.

105. See George Forty's translation in George Forty, *German Infantryman at War*, Hersham, United Kingdom, Ian Allen Publishing, extracted from http://print.google.com/print/doc?isbn=0711029296, July 2005.

106. For example, Forty writes: "Before general mobilisation in June 1939, each military district [*Wehrkreis*] had two components in its headquarters, a tactical component, which became the corps HQ in the field, and a second component that remained the military district and was responsible for training and reinforcement. Older, less fit men unable to take part in active operations normally staffed this component." Forty, *Op. Cit.*

107. Kveder, *Op. Cit.*, p.95.

108. Cribb, 2001 *Op. Cit.*, p. 148. Sudirman had given responsibility for the recovery of West Java to the large Divisi *Gerilya Bambu Runcing* (Guerrilla Division of the Bamboo Spears) *laskar* organization that was formed on the basis of elements of the West Java *Laskar Rakyat*. Cribb, 1991 *Op Cit.,* p. 158.

109. Nasution, *TNI* (Vol. Two), Op. Cit., p. 98, 99. Translation extracted from Penders and Sundhaussen, *Op. Cit.*, p. 35, 36.

110. Heijboer, *Op. Cit.*, p. 112.

111. Ibid.
112. Ibid.
113. Prasetyo and Hadad, *Op. Cit.*, p. 52.
114. Nasution, *Memenuhi Panggilan Tugas,* Vol One, *Op. Cit.*, p. 262.
115. Ibid.
116. W. Laqueur, *Guerrilla*, p. 368. Excerpted from Penders and Sundhaussen, *Op. Cit.*, p. 46.
117. Nasution, *Fundamentals of Guerrilla Warfare and the Indonesian Defence System Past and Future*, Jakarta, Information Service of the Armed Forces, undated, pp. 265–7.
118. Nasution, *TNI* (Vol. Three), Jakarta, Seruling Masa, 1971, p. 48.
119. Anderson, 1972 *Op Cit.*, p. 286, 287.
120. Ibid.
121. Ibid., p. 286.
122. Anton Lucas, *One Soul, One Struggle: Region and Revolution in Indonesia*, Sydney, Allen and Unwin, 1991, provides a comprehensive account of the *Tiga Daerah* affair.
123. See Anderson, 1972 *Op. Cit.*, pp. 332—369 for an account of the patterns of social revolution that took place in Java during the revolutionary period.
124. Ibid., p. 217.
125. Nasution, *TNI* (Vol Two), *Op. Cit.*, p. 222.
126. George McT. Kahin, "Foreword" to Anderson, 1972 *Op. Cit.*, p. ix.
127. Nasution, Fundamentals, *Op. Cit.*, p. 267.
128. Penders and Sundhaussen, *Op Cit.*, p. 100, 100A. Brackman, *Op. Cit.*, p. 218.
129. Sunarti, *Op. Cit.*, p. 26.
130. Ibid., p. 32.
131. Nasution, *Memenuhi Panggilan Tugas,* Vol One, *Op. Cit.*, p. 234.
132. E. Touwen-Bouwsma, *Japanese minority policy; The Eurasians on Java and the dilemma of ethnic loyalty*, in Bijdragen tot de Taal-, Land- en Volkenkunde, Japan, Indonesia and the War: Myths and realities 152 (1996), no: 4, Leiden, 553–572.
133. Sunarti, *Op. Cit.*, pp. 36–39.
134. Ibid., p. 42.
135. Ibid., p. 45, 46.
136. Nasution, *Memenuhi Panggilan Tugas,* Vol One, *Op. Cit.*, p. 41.
137. The *Siliwangi* preferred to use the term *hijrah* to describe their departure, recalling Mohammed's flight from Mecca to Medina from where he mustered his forces and returned to seize Mecca.
138. Nasution, *TNI* (Vol Two), *Op. Cit.*, p. 113, 114.
139. Heijboer, *Op. Cit.*, p. 126.
140. Sunarti, *Op. Cit.*, p. 48, 49.
141. Nasution, *TNI* (Vol Two), *Op. Cit.*, p. 113, 114.
142. Nasution, *Fundamentals, Op. Cit.*, p. 267.

Chapter 5

Total People's Resistance and a Professional Army

Nasution made some important alliances and friendships after he arrived in Yogyakarta. He found allies in the government who appreciated his strong antipathy toward unruly *laskar* elements and desire to professionalize the army. In the hinterland after the Dutch attacked the Republic again in December 1948, he would also establish firm friendships with a group of socially conservative senior *pamong praja* figures who would support him as he began to deal the army into political life in opposition to the multiparty system and a resurgent Communist Party in the 1950s.

After the failure of Republican forces to mount an effective linear defense in July 1947, the way seemed to be more open for Nasution to professionalize the army. The parliament enacted far-reaching legislation that provided for the reorganization and rationalization (*re-dan-ra—reorganisasi dan rasionalisasi*) of the army. The largely ethnic Javanese units from Central and East Java were reorganized into three territorial divisions,[1] while the *Siliwangi* Division was headquartered some sixty-five kilometers from Yogyakarta in the city of Surakarta and designated as a General Reserve Unit (*Kesatuan Reserve Umum—KRU*).[2] In January, the Sjarifuddin government limited *Panglima Besar* Sudirman's scope of responsibility to that of *Panglima Besar Angkatan Perang Mobil* (commander-in-chief of the Mobile Armed Forces) and placed him in charge of a *Markas Besar Pertempuran* (Combat Headquarters).

At the Ministry of Defense, a more powerful *Staf Umum Angkatan Perang* (Armed Forces General Staff) was formed. It was headed by the Bandung Military Academy alumni Air Commodore Suryadarma and Colonel T.B. Simatupang who reported directly to Prime Minister Sjarifuddin.

Urip Sumohardjo had strongly disagreed with the concessions made in the Renville Agreement and resigned his position. He died not long afterward.

The emotions set in train by the agreement and attempts to reorganize the army are evident in Sudirman asserting that Urip had committed a form of "mental *hara kiri*" because of "spiritual anguish."[3]

Sudirman resented the changes but had little choice other than to delegate the management of technical military matters to Nasution, as he had done with Urip, as he had contracted pulmonary tuberculosis. He had lost a lung when operated upon in mid-1948 and left detailed military planning largely in Nasution's hands.

Sjarifuddin was not in office long enough to ensure that all the changes he envisaged took place. Just as Sutan Sjahrir had been forced to resign because of controversy over the Linggarjati Agreement, Sjarifuddin became embroiled in similar controversy after negotiating the Renville Agreement and resigned as prime minister in early 1948. President Sukarno appointed Vice President Hatta as prime minister and Sjarifuddin became leader of an opposition coalition known as the *Front Demokrasi Rakyat* (FDR—People's Democratic Front) and began to oppose the professionalization plans that he had favored as prime minister.

A graduate of the Dutch-established Law School in Jakarta, Sjarifuddin was (like Nasution) a Mandailing Batak but had converted from Islam to Christianity. He was at first a noncooperating nationalist and served a term of imprisonment in the 1930s for his nationalist activities, but worked for the colonial government after his release and was on friendly terms with members of the Dutch community.[4] As the Indies faced capitulation at the hands of the Japanese the director general of the Department of Education, P.J.A. Idenburg, provided him with funds to establish an underground movement. The Japanese arrested him and he was only saved from execution through the intervention of Sukarno. However, he was imprisoned until August 1945 and his antipathy toward fascism was no doubt reinforced by the cruelty he suffered at the hands of the Japanese.

The Indonesian Communist Party was beginning to reassert itself after its shattering reversals in the 1920s. Musso, an exiled communist leader, had returned briefly to the Indies in 1935 to establish an "Illegal PKI" which remained an underground organization until a faction within it declared the party to be operative again in October 1945. However, no major figure from the party appears to have been in Indonesia when independence was proclaimed and it had taken the party time to regroup.

Brackman has summarised the PKI's motives in remaining concealed:

A number of reasons dictated the policy of concealment. By playing an open, prominent role early in the post-war Indonesian revolution, the Communists would have handicapped the Republic when the time came to solicit Western recognition and assistance. This also would have played into the hands of the

Dutch, who, after first seeking to depict the Republic as a Japanese fiction, then labelled it a Communist creation. Thus, the Communists would only have antagonised Indonesian nationalism—especially in view of the PKI's supra-national character. Then, too, by delaying its emergence above ground, the PKI provided its scattered leadership abroad with time in which to return to Indonesia. Underground, the PKI enjoyed a breathing space while awaiting a clarification of the post-war Communist line and the revolutionary situation at home. It is also conceivable that the PKI chose to remain underground to await the reception accorded the Allies on their landing. If the Republic collapsed, the PKI's emergence would have proved premature. Abroad, the Communists were treating the Republic disdainfully. Radio Moscow ignored the proclamation of independence, and in Holland, the Communists—Indonesian and Dutch alike—denounced the Republic as the handiwork of Japan. Certainly, between August and November, the Indonesian situation must have confounded Moscow. From afar, the Republic appeared to be controlled by collaborating nationalists of Trotskyite coloration.[5]

From the time Sjarifuddin formed the FDR he became increasingly close to the PKI and eventually claimed to have been a secret member since Musso's visit. This resurgence of the left was to have ramifications for attempts to reform the army. Hatta took over the reorganization and rationalization program and directed it against recalcitrant Javanese units and Ruth McVey writes of "an alliance" being formed "between the army leaders and the conservative [Hatta] regime whereby, in return for military support for the government's program, the army was freed of civilian interference, and both irregular forces and army units of dubious loyalty to the central command were dismantled in the name of retrenchment [sic] and rationalisation."[6]

While still constrained by the proximity and influence of Sudirman, Nasution was supportive and he reestablished the sort of symbiotic relationship with the government in which his *Siliwangi* Division had supported the Jakarta-based government and vice versa.[7] Unlike independence fighters in nearby Vietnam, the Republic lacked a land border with a country that might have provided means of obtaining weapons. They were always in very short supply throughout the army but less so in the *Siliwangi,* thanks to Sjarifuddin's generosity.

An immediately controversial element of Nasution's plans for "total people's resistance" was his proposal that the army be divided into three types of forces: strike units with a weapon to personnel ratio of 1:1, territorial elements with a ratio of 1:3, and territorial cadre forces who were to lead the resistance at the village, *kecamatan* and *kabupaten* levels.[8] Nasution had a number of examples to draw upon, such as the forces of Mao Tse Tung, Vo Nguyen Giap and Tito. Mao Tse Tung is perhaps the best-known proponent of the development of such forces.[9] For some two decades Mao and his comrades developed both guerrilla and conventional forces to the point where they controlled much of the hinterland of China. At the same time that Nasution was making plans for "total people's resistance," Mao's forces were conducting a series of general offensives that were to culminate in the destruction of the Chinese Nationalist regime on the mainland and the establishment of the People's Republic in October 1949.

A similar combination of conventional and guerrilla forces was being developed in Indonesia's near neighbor, Vietnam. The Vietnamese military leader, Vo Nguyen Giap, developed village-based guerrilla infrastructures from 1946 while building his offensive forces up to the point where he inflicted a devastating blow against the French at Dien Bien Phu in 1953. However, the war in the South of Vietnam followed a different course from that in China. The Viet Cong never developed large-scale mobile offensive forces and it was the arrival in strength of conventional forces from the North following the United States withdrawal in 1973 that was a decisive factor in the defeat of the Saigon regime. In Europe, Yugoslavia had been the center of a people's war during the Nazi occupation of that country. Tito's army evolved from a force of partisans into a combination of partisan and conventional forces.[10]

While the *Siliwangi* could be content at becoming the elite and relatively well-armed General Reserve Unit, the designation of the remaining Javanese divisions as territorial forces reminded them of their lack of support from the government and seemed to relegate them to second-class status. The *laskar* forces (many of which by then had been organized by Sjarifuddin into a body known as the *TNI-Masyarakat*—People's TNI) were to be disbanded altogether.[11]

Again, Nasution quickly became caught up in rumors that he was pro-Dutch. Within the officer corps of the Javanese divisions there was an intense degree of suspicion regarding moves to reform the TNI so that it accorded more closely with "international" standards and many Central and East Javanese opponents of Nasution's *re-dan-ra* plans suspected that he, his former KNIL colleagues at the headquarters, and the *Siliwangi* Division more generally had a hidden agenda of securing themselves advantageous positions in the army of a future federal state formed through negotiations with the Dutch.[12] As Anthony Reid remarks, "Whatever the military merits of such drastic pruning, it was a complete political impossibility short of civil war."[13] Such a conflict erupted in September 1948 in the form of the Madiun Affair.

Nasution also developed comprehensive strategies for the formation and defense of Republican enclaves based upon his planning in West Java the previous year. His Strategic Order No. 1/1948 (that Sudirman signed on June 12, 1948) provided for the army to switch to territorial warfare, with the support of the *pamong praja* and village administrations, in the event of a further Dutch attack. It contained the following key elements:

- The army would no longer mount a linear defense.
- It would endeavor to obstruct the enemy advance (by nonlinear methods), buying time for the total evacuation of the Republic's civil service, which would be used to maintain the administrative apparatus of the Republic in guerrilla strongholds, and the implementation of a scorched earth policy which would deny assets of economic importance.
- Its basic task was to form guerrilla pockets (military subdistrict commands *Komando Onder-distrik Militer* or KODMs) at the *kecamatan* level of the *pamong praja* within which "totalitarian" guerrilla governments would maintain the authority of the Republic. A number of *Wehrkreis* were to be established in mountain strongholds within which more mobile forces would conduct a war of attrition.
- Troops from West and East Java who had been evacuated from their home regions under the terms of the Renville Agreement were to return to these districts and form guerrilla enclaves.

Inspired once more by British guerrilla operations in wartime Burma, this strategy, which envisaged the whole of the island of Java becoming a theater for guerrilla warfare, was to become known as "Operation Wingate." Another source of inspiration was the Long March of the Chinese Red Army in the 1930s, when Red Army forces marched for thousands of kilometers from the Shanghai area to the relatively safe region of Yenan in the north of China. When the maneuver was put into effect at the end of 1948 it became known as the Long March of the *Siliwangi*.

Nasution's experience in West Java was evident in establishing the *pamong praja* territorial administrative system as the basis for guerrilla enclaves. These civil servants were to form mobile civil administrations that could be moved about the countryside within geographically fluid liberated areas in accordance with the ebb and flow of territorial warfare.

He recognized that the condition of Indonesian forces and the localized nature of this form of warfare would not enable guerrilla administrations to function effectively above the level of the *kecamatan*, located immediately above the *kelurahan* village administrations and responsible for a cluster of them. The *camat* had always been responsible for representing the outside world to the villagers and for mobilizing people. Accordingly, his planning concentrated on the village and *kecamatan* levels.

Legge recorded the importance of this latter level of administration in communicating and mediating between the outside world and the villages in the subdistrict:

> At the base of the [*pamong praja*] pyramid the *camat* or sub-district officer has maintained the vital link between the government and the rural population

in general. He conveys information concerning national policies as far as they affect the village and, indeed, may be said to provide the village with its picture of the outside world. He mobilises support for novel projects. He is an arbiter between conflicting pressures. He is, in effect, the government.[14]

Nasution provided for the *lurah*s to remain in charge in their villages[15] and to ensure their effective cooperation, they were to be "assisted" by army-trained village cadres.[16] He wrote and widely distributed a pamphlet entitled *Village Defence* (*Pertahanan Desa*), which provided guidance for guerrilla administration and operations in the event of a second Dutch attack. An important task of the village cadres was to prevent the *lurah*s from coming under the influence of the Dutch. Both the Dutch and the Indonesians were aware of the importance of the *lurah*s who, as the foundations of public administration in Indonesia, came under heavy and sometimes lethal pressure from both sides.[17]

The *camat*s were expected to operate their mobile administrations under the supervision of the commanders of KODM subdistrict military commands, but his planning envisaged army officers being the "top official"[18] at all levels of administration above the village. In effect, he sought to alter the direct relationship between the *lurah* and the *camat* as the *lurah*s were to be responsible to the KODM commander.[19] At the next level of military administration, he provided for the regents (*bupati*) and residents (*residen*) to be "intermediaries, inspectors and planners."[20] They were to assist the military district (*Komando Distrik Militer*—KDM) commanders. Heads of *Keresidenan* (Residencies) were subordinated to STM (*Sub Territorium Militer*) commanders.

In keeping with this emphasis on army leadership of guerrilla administrations, Nasution sought to do away with the "dualistic" command structure under the Regional Defence Councils that he had opposed in West Java.[21] Indeed, in *Fundamentals of Guerrilla Warfare* he makes it clear that he was determined to avoid repeating this experience by forming "a concentrated form of leadership."[22] His antipathy toward these earlier bodies is evident in *Fundamentals of Guerrilla Warfare* where he referred to his experiences in West Java in 1948 and again praised the *lurah*s. He claimed that although "total people's defence" during the armed struggle was often lauded there had been a serious lack of coordination and cooperation between the various governmental instrumentalities and a dearth of concerted effort from the political parties which often had to await instructions from their national executives. However, it was "fortunate that the *lurah*s . . . at least retained some authority, and we made ample use of this situation."[23]

In the event of a Dutch assault, Nasution was to occupy the position of commander of the Java Troops and Territory (*Komando Tentara dan*

Territorium Jawa), with another former KNIL officer colonel Hidayat occupying a similar command in Sumatra.

Nasution summed up his ideas for guerrilla administrations and operations in classic territorial warfare terms, except that unlike territorial warfare forces of the political left he firmly allied himself with organic traditional authority figures. He spoke of the need for permanent military administrations led by army territorial officers that the people would know were always there. They would include civil administrative structures and officials so that the Republic would maintain de facto authority of the people and be mobile, evacuating when enemy patrols approached. Officials were to be taught to play hide and seek with the Dutch.[24]

Nasution's reliance on the *pamong praja* and village administrations no doubt accorded with the political attitudes of the people with whom Nasution associated most closely at a personal level during 1948. While living in Central Java Nasution renewed his acquaintance with Sunarti's uncle, the former Parindra identity R.P. Soeroso, who he had first met on his way back to Bandung after deserting from the KNIL. The older man was married to Sunario Gondokusumo's younger sister and was living in the city of Surakarta.[25]

Born in 1893, in the 1920s Soeroso had formed the Federation of Civil Servants' Unions (*Persatuan Vakbonden Pegawai Negeri*—PVPN) that had grown to a membership of some forty-two thousand by the time of the Japanese occupation.[26] He had been a *Volksraad* member during the colonial period and was one of three Indonesians to be appointed a resident (political head of a Residency and responsible for several regencies) by the Japanese.[27] He had been deputy chairman of the BPUPKI preparatory committee on Indonesian independence where he advocated the separation of "church" (Islam) and state.[28] He subsequently became a member of the successor body to the BPUPKI, the *Panitia Persiapan Kemerdekaan Indonesia* (PPKI—Preparatory Committee for Indonesian Independence) formed in August 1945.[29]

In response to professions of loyalty from the *pangreh praja* soon after the Proclamation, Sukarno had reassured the civil service that the leadership of the Republic would by no means regard them "simply as secretaries, clerks or petty foremen. We are not going to lower the *pangreh praja*. We are going to give it the proper place it deserves."[30] It is probable that as part of this rapprochement between Sukarno and the *pangreh praja*, senior members of the corps were given prominent positions, including Soeroso being appointed governor of Central Java on August 19, 1945.[31]

Surakarta and Yogyakarta housed the two royal courts of Java, both of which had been rendered militarily insignificant by the inroads made by Dutch imperialism, as Frank Clune observed in a visit to Yogyakarta in the dying days of the Indies government: "In the *Kraton* [Palace] the Sultan maintains ancient ceremonial with a bodyguard of futile feudalists armed with old-fashioned swords, shields, bows and arrows."[32] However, unlike Yogyakarta, where the staunchly nationalist sultan enjoyed widespread support, the relatively low prestige of the royal courts of royal houses of Surakarta was worsened by the disturbances of the Japanese occupation and weakness on the part of the young Susuhunan, whose father died in the final year of colonial rule. Moreover, unlike the junior Pakualaman royal house in Yogyakarta, the smaller hereditary Manguknegaran refused to accept a subordinate relationship to the Susuhunan when negotiating with the government of the Republic on the future status of the principalities.

The ailing Sudirman spent a great deal of time in Surakarta after it had become known as the "wild west" because disaffected military and civilian elements had coalesced there into a center of opposition to the government's plans for *re-dan-ra*. In view of his previous closeness with Tan Malaka and suspicions that he had supported the July 3 Affair, he aroused suspicion in some quarters by often spending weekends at the nearby hill station of Tawangmangu where the "national communist" and his adherents were detained.

On the other hand, Nasution and Sunarti also frequently spent weekends in Surakarta, but with R.P. Soeroso[33] whose conservative views were apparent in the platform of the tiny renewed Parindra party that he formed in November 1949 as a successor to the eponymous prewar party. Feith notes that the new Parindra was one of only two parties in the parliament that expressed reservations about democracy (the other was the Great Indonesian Union Party or *Persatuan Indonesia Raya*—PIR). Both were aristocratically led and used similar language to that of Supomo in his address to the BPUPKI by calling for an "Eastern democracy" and "democracy with leadership."[34]

During 1948 Soeroso moved to Yogyakarta to become a senior official in the Ministry of Internal Affairs (the successor to the colonial *Binnenlandsch Bestuur* and responsible for administering the *pamong praja* throughout the Republic). At the time, Nasution was making preparations in case the Dutch launched another offensive, including planning for a military administration, and "often discussed politics and regional government matters with him."[35] Sunarti describes their relationship in similar terms: "Pak Nas often discussed politics and the situation that was developing in the country with Pak Soeroso."[36] Nasution also mixed with the aristocratic R.P. Gondoadikusumo, another well-connected relation of the Gondokusumos who lived in Yogyakarta.

Married life and his engagement with Sunarti's extended family were clearly a revelation to Nasution after years of living in an austere and self-sufficient manner:

> In Yogyakarta *Ibu* Ning, my wife's aunt who lived in Bausasran Street, was part of our family. While at Senior High School during the Japanese occupation my

wife had stayed with her. For us, Bausasran was a place for family reunion. I felt that I had been "absorbed" into my wife's family. Possibly the same thing would have happened to her if we had been in Sumatra.³⁷

Unlike his years of dormitory life and shared accommodation, in Yogyakarta Sunarti paid careful attention to household matters that he had often neglected.³⁸

Sunario Gondokusumo continued to reside in Bandung and Sunarti makes no further reference to him mentoring Nasution. After the Dutch attack in December 1948, Sunario and some other nationalists in that city were jailed for issuing a statement condemning it.³⁹

Given the socially conservative nature of Nasution's association of his principles of "total people's resistance" with the *pamong praja,* it is perhaps not surprising that the first use of these strategies was to counter internal opponents from the left of politics in the form of the Madiun Affair where the *pamong praja* were a particular target.

Following the return of Musso in August 1948 the PKI had regrouped and was playing an increasing part in the political life of the Republic. In early September, the major parties in the *Front Demokrasi Rakyat* merged with the PKI, Sjarifuddin announced his secret membership of the party, and Musso made pro-Soviet statements which the government feared would harm its efforts in seeking United States' support in its negotiations with the Dutch.⁴⁰

The situation became extremely tense when Nasution's intentions to demobilize or downgrade units associated with this broad left movement became clear. Clashes occurred between these units and the substantial *Siliwangi* presence in the Surakarta area.

On September 18, a *laskar* leader took control of the city of Madiun and proclaimed a "revolutionary" local government. Always solicitous of the irregular militias that supported the Republic, Sudirman incurred Vice President Hatta's wrath by trying to negotiate with the leaders of the uprising.⁴¹ Then on September 19 President Sukarno acted, calling upon the people of Java to choose between the current leadership and that offered by Musso. In turn, Musso denounced Sukarno and Hatta as Japanese Quislings and declared that he would fight to the finish.

While East Javanese units approached Madiun to counter the uprising, a much larger force was deployed from the West by the *Siliwangi* Division. Pro-PKI forces retreated to the south as pro-government forces took town after town until they occupied Madiun on 30 September. Sjarifuddin and Musso were among those killed and other leaders of the left were imprisoned, dealing a heavy blow to the PKI. The swift and effective action attracted American support for the Indonesian cause, which was to become vitally important after the Dutch launched their second "police action."

In restoring order, Nasution's plans for the army to assume wide political and economic powers with the *pamong praja* as its junior partner were put into practice for the first time in Central and East Java. The Republic-held territories of East Java were declared a special military area (*Daerah Militer Istimewa*) and Colonel Sungkono was appointed as military governor.[42]

Soebijono, a veteran of the guerrilla war who remained in the army and participated in developing the doctrine of territorial warfare and territorial management in the 1960s, points out that because of the death and disappearance of civil servants who had been targeted by the PKI in areas where that party had been dominant, the army took over many of the functions of the *pamong praja*.[43]

Most of the territorial officers during the period of military administration were secondary school and university students, with the former being assigned to villages and the latter to *kecamatan* subdistricts. According to Slamet Danusudirdjo, this was because "it was difficult to find members of the regular army to be assigned to territorial duty."[44] The assignment of young, relatively well-educated Indonesians as territorial officers had its origins in a decision in 1947 to use cadets from the Military Academy to impart military training to the best-educated young men from the villages. They, in turn, were to form the basis of military cadres who were to assist the *lurah*s in preserving the sovereignty of the Republic in their administrative areas and in providing support for the army. Soebijono writes that this was "intended as an interim arrangement" but was still in place when the second "police action" was launched in December 1949.[45]

The Madiun Affair strengthened Nasution's position within the army by purging many left-wing officers and cemented his good relations with Hatta and the government. His intense dislike of the *laskar* forces and particularly those of the left is evident in a remark he later made that the affair was "a blessing in disguise." It had enabled him to "move against groups he had long regarded with distrust and enmity, including critics from the political left who had slighted him and the *Siliwangi* Division."[46]

He continued to plan for a campaign of "people's resistance" that would entail the army exercising authority over the civilian administration. However, opposition from Sudirman to important aspects of the reorganization plans and the distraction of the Madiun Affair left him no time to form the different tiers of forces he had envisaged. Consequently, when the *Siliwangi* departed on their "long march" to West Java in December there was no clear distinction between Republican units in the campaign that followed the Dutch assault.

The first confirmation of the military intentions of the Dutch was the appearance of aircraft over Yogyakarta's Maguwo airfield. Bombs fell and fighter aircraft strafed the installation unopposed before paratroops descended. A cabinet meeting was hastily convened where it was decided that President Sukarno, Vice President Hatta and those cabinet ministers who were in Yogyakarta at the time would remain in the city. This meant that they would submit to capture by the Dutch rather than follow the army leadership in waging a guerrilla war in the hinterland of Java, despite having previously undertaken to do so.[47] The lack of psychological preparedness of the older civilian leadership for a military conflict was apparent when (as an afterthought and at Simatupang's urging) Hatta commissioned an emergency government of the Republic of Indonesia (*Pemerintah Darurat Republik Indonesia*—PDRI) to be based in Sumatra under the minister for welfare, Sjafruddin, who happened to be there at the time.[48]

Perhaps more shamefully, the chief of the Armed Forces General Staff, Air Commodore Suryadarma, also allowed himself to be captured. His deputy, Simatupang, escaped from the city and significantly, although ordered by Sukarno to stay in Yogyakarta[49] Sudirman made a hurried and dangerous departure. The handful of government ministers who remained at large in Central Java[50] formed a "Commisariat" of the emergency government in Sumatra under Home Affairs Minister Sukiman, with Soeroso appointed to handle "internal affairs matters."[51]

The decision by the civilian leadership not to avoid capture remains controversial. It is likely that perceptions that the Republican forces had performed poorly against the Dutch in the first "Police Action" weighed upon the civilian leadership in making their decision. According to Simatupang, the cabinet concluded that even if it left Yogyakarta it was likely to be captured within days.[52]

Although they had demonstrated great moral courage by choosing the noncooperating nationalist path that had led to years of detention under the colonial regime, the civilian leaders might also have doubted their ability to adapt to the physical hardships and dangers of the guerrilla struggle.[53] The difficulties encountered by older civilian leaders who become engaged in guerrilla warfare has been summed up well by Regis Debray:

> It has been widely demonstrated that guerrilla warfare is directed not from outside but from within, with the leadership accepting its full share of the risks involved. In a country where such a war is developing, most of the organisation's leaders must leave the cities and join the guerrilla army. This is, first of all, a security measure, assuring the survival of the political leaders.... In Latin America, wherever armed struggle is the order of the day, there is a close tie between geology and ideology. However absurd or shocking this relationship may seem, it is nonetheless a decisive one. An elderly man, accustomed to city living, moulded by other circumstances and goals, will not easily adjust himself to the mountain nor—though this is less so—to underground activity in the cities. In addition to the moral factor—conviction—physical fitness is the most basic of all skills needed for waging guerrilla warfare; the two factors go hand in hand.[54]

Sukarno claims that he resisted pleas from General Sudirman to evacuate to a guerrilla area because he wished to remain in a position where he could "bargain for us and lead."[55] Heijboer writes: "In a cabinet session held in a rear room of the palace because bombs were falling, Sukarno explained to the ministers that what was important was to surrender with honour. [He would be] surrendering to an enemy who had unilaterally ended a cease-fire, and this would become known by the whole world."[56]

In a similar vein, Hatta has stated that he was confident that the Dutch would be forced by international pressure and their own reluctance to continue with an "unprecedented war" to negotiate. He wanted to be readily available for this eventuality.[57]

In carrying out his duties as the Australian representative on the United Nations Good Offices Committee, Tom Critchley was accommodated at the hill station of Kaliurang which overlooked Yogyakarta when the Dutch attacked. He was having breakfast with Vice President Hatta which had "hardly begun before it was interrupted by the sight of Dutch planes dive bombing and strafing Yogyakarta's airport. Hatta excused himself, called for his car and set off down the hill towards Yogyakarta."[58] Critchley, who was deeply immersed in the Republic's efforts to negotiate a resolution of the dispute, agrees with the decision of the leadership not to avoid capture:

> There has been criticism of Sukarno for not accepting General Sudirman's invitation to accompany the Republican Army into the jungle. But the cabinet decision seems much the wiser course. Had Sukarno joined the guerrillas, he would have been an obvious target. Consequently, he would have had to remain hidden and might well have been eliminated. On the other hand, as a prisoner of the Dutch he remained at the forefront of international and United Nations pressures to have the Republican leaders released and re-established in Yogyakarta.[59]

The course adopted by the civilian leadership was successful in drawing international attention and sympathy to the Indonesian cause. Although the Dutch launched their offensive at a time that they calculated would draw minimum world attention—a few days prior to the end of the final session of the UN General Assembly for 1948 and during the Christmas recess of the US Congress—some members of the UN Security Council were meeting in Paris. Thanks to prompt action by the outraged Critchley, a few days after the offensive began the Council called for a cessation of hostilities. Some member countries, including Australia and New Zealand, boycotted Dutch commerce, far exceeding Dutch fears of possible retribution.[60]

The United States had been torn between refraining from directly criticizing the Dutch, who were an ally in the looming Cold War, and support for the Republic which had just annihilated the PKI in the Madiun Affair.

The situation worsened considerably for the Dutch when Washington questioned whether the Dutch were misusing their Marshall Plan aid for the postwar reconstruction of Europe to prosecute their war in the Indies and linked this with a demand that the captured leaders, who were being detained in Sumatra, be immediately returned to Yogyakarta. In Indonesia, the Dutch experienced another major setback when the leaders of their federal "puppet" states also expressed their outrage at the "police action" and stated that they would take no part in negotiations with the colonial power until the leaders of the Republic were returned to Yogyakarta.

Once outside the city, the critically ill Sudirman entrenched his heroic reputation by taking to the interior on a stretcher, accompanied by a handful of staff. He was gaunt and very thin and photographs of him at that time show him in an oversized Australian army greatcoat and wearing a Javanese *blangkon* head dress made of batik cloth. A large statue of the austere general wearing that simple attire has been erected at the top of the main General Sudirman Avenue in Jakarta—perhaps an ironic location for it as he stands sentinel over multistory office buildings, luxury hotels, cafes and restaurants. He was to remain hidden from the Dutch, moving from place to place for six excruciating months.

Simatupang later wrote movingly of his own departure:

> Yogyakarta had fallen. The President, Vice President and our other senior officials had been captured. Did this mean that our Republic had died? There was a writer, if I'm not wrong it was Machiavelli, who said something to the effect that the last bastion of a state is in the hearts of its soldiers. Whether our Republic would live or die now depended primarily upon whether it still lived on in the hearts of the officers, non-commissioned officers and soldiers of the army. The answer would be given in the coming days and weeks and months. And my own fate, Colonel Tahi Bonar Simatupang of the Indonesian National Army, depended upon that answer.[61]

Nasution was out of Yogyakarta when the attack came and took up his designated command near the city. On this occasion, he was not accompanied to guerrilla enclaves by Sunarti who was visiting Surakarta when the Dutch attacked. She made her way back to Yogyakarta, narrowly avoiding being kidnapped by PKI remnants, and was detained by the Dutch for a time and then released.

Nasution's abiding frustrations with the duality of command that had prevailed in West Java in 1947 were reflected in the code he devised to signal that a state of war was imminent (*DPD dirobah*—"Regional Defence Councils are altered") and the code for an actual state of war ("*DPD hapus*"—"Regional Defence Councils are abolished").[62]

He first established his command post in the village of Kepurun on the Yogyakarta/Surakarta border as this was an area that was not frequently patrolled by Dutch units from Yogyakarta or Surakarta but close to Yogyakarta.[63] He proclaimed a military administration throughout Java on December 25,[64] dispatching twenty officers to circulate the Proclamation and "Working Instructions" for the military administration.[65] Sudarno recalls that a week after these documents were circulated throughout Java, "a letter arrived from the Deputy Chief of Staff of the Armed Forces, Colonel T.B. Simatupang, and from Minister Sukiman, stating that the government of the Republic of Indonesia ratified the policy steps taken by Nasution as the Commander of Java Command to continue the struggle to save the Republic of Indonesia."[66]

He was fastidious to a fault in issuing instructions and guidance:

> On that first night, the tasks that awaited us were outlined and allocated between us. In fact, some of [my officers] had already departed to perform tasks. Drawing upon experience in West Java and bearing in mind preparations that had been made in Yogyakarta, which were still in the early stages, there was no need to think about this or that.
>
> So, I immediately wrote instructions by hand, and representatives of Headquarters Java Command (*Markas Besar Komando Djawa*—MBKD) left in various directions. On 20 December 1948, I drew up the first MBKD Proclamation: "In relation to the war situation, based upon Government Regulations No. 3 and No. 70 I hereby proclaim a military administration for the whole of [the island of] Java."
>
> This was very necessary because those regulations provided for military government arrangements to be [in the hands of] the military governors and STC (Residency) commanders. The central government had always been reluctant to give the same authority to the Armed Forces Headquarters.[67]

Reid writes that "Nasution was unable to co-ordinate activity even in Java, and initiative rested more than ever with the unit commander."[68] While this state of affairs is not unusual in the early stages of guerrilla warfare where commanders typically have wide autonomy, the difficulty of coordinating the Republic's diverse and highly autonomous units and the outbreak of the Madiun Affair before the "police action" got under way severely constrained him from developing better command and control systems.

For some days, Simatupang joined some of the *Siliwangi*, who were often accompanied by their wives and children, on their arduous journey:

> For four days as I walked to the West with those *Siliwangi* troops I saw wives and children also walking through the darkness of the night, crossing rivers, and climbing up steep and slippery hills. I heard of children being carried away by strong currents when soldiers and their families crossed rivers that were almost in flood. How true it is that our independence was not received as a gift.[69]

Nasution appears to have been intent on preserving the army so that it would remain intact as a credible force when the conflict ended while doing what he could to assist in the holding of enclaves as an assertion of continuing Republican control over parts of Java. He later wrote that the TNI only "brought to a deadlock" the struggle against the Dutch and gave credit to the civilian negotiators for ending the conflict:

> our guerrillas did not defeat the enemy in the sense of removing him from Indonesia's soil. We only frustrated his attempts; we did not defeat him in the usual military sense of the word.
>
> The fact that the enemy finally surrendered, that he was willing to recognise a return of all the areas to the Republic and the army, that he was willing to transfer sovereignty under certain conditions, and was willing to withdraw his troops were all hastened by international political pressure. Consequently, we did not have to prolong our guerrilla war which at a certain point would have required the formation of a regular army to launch an offensive.[70]

While the military conflict was not in itself decisive, the tactics employed by Nasution's guerrilla forces seriously weakened the capability and resolve of the colonial power and pressured it to return to the negotiating table, as Penders and Sundhaussen conclude:

> What many of the internationally more celebrated guerrilla leaders achieved in the course of many years, often with aid from the outside, Nasution and his forces accomplished—admittedly against a weaker opponent than most of the other leaders had to face—within a few months.[71]

They believe that Nasution brought it home to the colonial power that it would never be able to raise an army of sufficient size to defend the positions they occupied, and to seek out and destroy Republican forces.[72] Perhaps overstating their case, they assert that the politicians interned by the Dutch resolved to negotiate despite the army leadership's categorical rejection of such a course because they were afraid that the TNI would seize all the glory of achieving independence.[73]

George Kahin, who was a highly sympathetic witness of the Indonesian struggle, recalls that the Dutch army soon found itself in a difficult position and that by the end of January their 145,000 troops spent more time defending themselves than conducting offensive operations. They could only carry out operations from strongholds during the day before returning at dusk and then fighting for survival against Indonesian forces at night. Between their occupied cities they held strong points but could only travel to and from them with heavily armored convoys. Eventually they had to withdraw garrisons from some major towns, and plantations were abandoned as they could not defend them, and the city of Madiun was isolated throughout January and had to be supplied by air.[74]

Despite their ability to tie down the Dutch, TNI units were also constrained and generally unable to take and retain territory. Simatupang recalls that a stalemate developed in which neither side could inflict a decisive blow on the other:

> Not far from Kenteng there was a Dutch post, at Banter. This post was not very strong, I estimate that Dutch strength there was [at the level of] one company at the most. . . . on three occasions, our side had launched attacks on the post with forces assembled from our troops in its vicinity and augmented with troops specially brought in from other places, including from around Wates. However, we were not able to take the Dutch post and the Dutch remained in Banter. This is an example of our inability to take or drive out a Dutch post which was not very strong, even though we had assembled all the forces available to mount an attack on it.[75]

Republican forces did mount some limited offensive actions, the best known of which is a six-hour "general offensive" on Yogyakarta led by Lieutenant Colonel (later president) Suharto on March 1, 1949. Like the 1968 Tet Offensive in Vietnam but on a much smaller scale, it aimed to shock the defenders and give the appearance of a wholesale revolt against them. Suharto's forces apparently caught the Dutch by surprise and occupied parts of the city for some six hours. Due, in no small part, to his role, the "offensive" was the subject of *Janur Kuning* (literally Yellow Coconut Leaves), a major motion picture in the late 1970s, and a detailed Indonesian Army Staff and Command College (Seskoad) publication.[76] Another example is a three-day attack on the city of Surakarta in mid-March, when the Indonesians only desisted at the request of representatives of the United Nations.[77]

Kahin only refers to Nasution once in his classic account of the revolution,[78] and the Java Commander's role in the guerrilla struggle attracted some adverse comment at the time. Nasution recalls that his small and covert headquarters was sarcastically referred to by some, including politicians who stayed in the towns waiting to see who would win, as the "Headquarters Travelling Around Java" (*Markas Besar Keliling Djawa*—MBKD), a play on the words *Markas Besar Komando Jawa*. He remembers allegations that the TNI only knew how to retreat and that this was because of his reorganization and rationalization of the army.[79]

In countering such arguments Nasution wrote that his role was not to command troops in an operational sense. Rather it was "to lead, to provide understanding and directives about methods of organization, operations, administration, etc. in guerrilla conditions. This enabled all officials to determine their activities for themselves."[80]

Nevertheless, there is something unusual in Nasution's passion for the administrative and legal aspects of the military administration and his lack of direct involvement in the fighting. He never seems to have displayed a detailed and technical interest in combat operations, taken part in fighting, or directed troops in a military engagement. After his retirement, he showed little interest in weapons or the technical aspects of the military profession. His military education as a KNIL officer cadet might have been higher than most other officers in the TNI but was quite limited by international standards and (through no fault of his own) he never engaged in any significant further officer training.

Nasution's major legacy to the TNI from the guerrilla campaign was his blueprint for operating a military government in partnership with the *pamong praja* and *pamong desa*. Salim Said has noted that the 1945 generation of army officers, who went on to form the backbone of Suharto's regime, came to regard his military administration as an example of "how government should be conducted, which has been a powerful influence on their behaviour ever since."[81]

An indication of Nasution's passion for the legal-administrative aspects of his position is that even though he was aware that he was being hunted by PKI elements[82] as well as the Dutch who had begun to patrol the area more frequently, he "never went out of the house during daylight hours" and "forced himself" to stay on in Kepurun:

> to finish the most important instructions for operations and the guerrilla administration, even though the danger that I faced increased because PKI remnants were always searching for me so that they could murder me.[83]

His instructions were distributed by couriers and an air force radio transmitter located to the south of Yogyakarta.[84] He also enlisted a government radio *Radio Republik Indonesia* employee, Maladi, to broadcast the news of the guerrilla struggle to the emergency government in Sumatra and overseas through a transmitter on Mount Lawu.[85]

Nasution's instructions were sufficiently numerous to occupy many of the two hundred pages of *Fundamentals of Guerrilla Warfare* that he set aside for archival material from the military administration.[86] They include general appreciations of military and political developments, instructions on procuring supplies of food and other requirements, maintaining the education system, securing communications, handling captured goods, and dealing with irregular troops. He also issued guidance on noncooperation with the enemy, the extinction of rumors, the roles of the *camat*s and *lurah*s in maintaining guerrilla administrations, and the roles of village guerrilla troops vis-à-vis village administrations. His concern to operate within the law and to establish a sense of order is evident in a detailed instruction he issued in May 1949 entitled "Emergency Regulation Governing Military Courts of the Military Government, Civil Courts of the Military Government and Special Military Tribunals, and Concerning the Methods of Implementing Sentences of Imprisonment."[87]

He sought to establish a "Defence Bank" modeled on existing "village banks" so that the wealthy would be able "to declare their good will . . . by giving some of their money to form the Bank's capital."[88] In another section of the same instruction, he outlined measures to maintain public health, including the administration of polyclinics and people's hospitals, and recommendations for using medicines that could be obtained from plants to treat such illnesses as intestinal problems, coughs, malaria, and skin diseases.[89]

To try to ensure that his instructions were sanctioned at the highest available level, Nasution sought and gained general approval from a Commissariat of Ministers who had joined the troops, headed by Home Affairs Minister Sukiman.[90] He later praised their cooperation, stating that during the guerrilla period there was no "short circuit" between the civilians and the military.[91]

The *pamong praja*, was an ideal ally for Nasution in his efforts to promote order and stability in Republican areas by "depoliticising" the populace. Accordingly, he worked hard to ensure that they remained loyal and immune to enticements from the Dutch. He writes that the Dutch soon realized that they could not reestablish *rust en orde* by military means alone and tried to induce village administrations and their populations to side with them by distributing food and medicines, and by suddenly surrounding villages and forcing their inhabitants to listen to propaganda. He records that the army was particularly careful to ensure that the Dutch were not successful in attracting the *lurah*s and the *camat*s.[92]

Ultimately, sufficient numbers of *pamong praja* officials were prepared to work with the army in upholding pockets of Republican sovereignty. Indeed, Kahin writes that the level of civilian noncooperation was a "stunning surprise" to the Dutch: "Outside the towns and just back from the main roads Republican civil servants, though frequently on the move to escape Dutch patrols, maintained the Republican civilian administration as best they could."[93]

The Sultan of Yogyakarta played a vitally important role in ensuring noncooperation with the Dutch and the loyalty of the *pamong praja* to the Republican cause. His immense authority and prestige within the city and surrounding areas and policy of neither cooperating nor dealing with the Dutch was a major setback for them.

Kahin found (from a "candid" Dutch official) that almost all the civil servants in the Yogyakarta area refused to work for the Dutch: "Out of about 10,000 civil servants in the Yogyakarta area no more than 150, he stated, were working for the Dutch administration."[94] Those civil servants in Yogyakarta who refused to work with them endured considerable personal hardship as the relatively little food that was entering the city was reserved for the Dutch and cooperating civil servants.[95]

The former civil servant, Sudarno, provides a particularly complete and illuminating account of how *pamong praja* agencies in the Malang area of East Java withdrew to guerrilla strongholds and worked with their army counterparts in the civilian administration. For example, he records that 1,100 officials and their families (a total of 5,000) in the Kawi area of East Java and another 450 officials and their families (totaling 1,800) had to be provided for so that they could "keep the wheels of government rolling." His account describes the collection of taxes, rice, and corn (for which emergency government promissory notes were issued) to maintain the administration and the troops in the field.[96]

Wiliater Hutagulung, a former army territorial officer, has described a close relationship between the army and *pamong praja* officials. He recalls Java Command instructing him in early January 1948 to convene a meeting between senior *pamong praja* officials and military officers. Given that this was very soon after the seemingly lethal Dutch attack on the Republic it is impressive that he could assemble the governor of Central Java (Wongsonegoro), two residents (Salamoen and Boediono) and two *bupatis* (Sangidi and Sumitro Kolopaking). From the army side, the divisional commander (Colonel Bambang Sugeng), a regimental commander (Lieutenant Colonel Sarbini) and Hutagulung (territorial officer) were present.

The discussions confirmed that the civilian governor would function as an adviser to the military governor and that throughout the period of emergency the decisions of the military governor would be binding. On the other hand, the military were forbidden to intervene in the "internal affairs" of the *pamong praja,* and the civilian administration below the *kabupaten* regency level was to function as smoothly as possible. The responsibilities of *lurahs* and *camats* and procedures for the provision of sustenance for refugees and the military were determined.[97] In February Hutagulung successfully convened another meeting with the same officials present, this time to plan (in Nasution's absence) a "general offensive" against the Dutch in March 1949.[98]

Below the ranks of the *pamong praja* were the village administrations headed by the *lurah*s. Nasution's writings in the 1950s that stressed the role of village leaders in carrying on "people's resistance" were similar to the wording of a pamphlet that he wrote in August 1948 to highlight how essential the villages and village administrations were to his strategies:

> In implementing such a form of state administration, the regional unit that is sufficiently compact and able to be directly led is the rural village [*desa*]. Because

of this, the village leaders, i.e. the *lurah*s, are the foundations of the maintenance of the government of the Republic of Indonesia. . . . the *lurah* is elected by his own people whom he knows intimately and knows about all the ins and outs of the village. The *lurah* must be protected and respected. Members who are seconded to the villages, such as village cadres, must be under the authority of *Pak Lurah*. The *lurah* must himself embody the authority of the military administration.[99]

In relying on the *lurah*s in this way, Nasution was, in effect, bolstering traditional patterns of authority, as Cribb observes, although this scholar's portrayal of the *lurah* differs markedly from Nasution's:

This [decision to rely upon the *lurah*] was a telling decision, because the *lurah* were at the centre of village tensions, distrusted for their former role as agents of the colonial government. True, many *lurah* had been replaced in village administrations in 1945 and 1946, but the institution remained a conduit for the delivery of supplies and labour from the village to the authorities of the outside world, and Nasution sought to make use of this relationship in his guerrilla struggle. His enthusiastic espousal of the *lurah* as the pivot of his people's defence system reflected his general willingness to preserve the social order rather than seeking to transform it.[100]

Cribb also observes that Nasution attempted to distance his forces as much as possible from the general population[101] and to make his forces as self-sufficient as possible, to the extent of providing opium to the *Siliwangi* to finance their operations when they returned to West Java.[102]

He goes on to remark that in Vietnam the "old village order" was overthrown by the resistance and replaced with "a new one better geared to the struggle."[103] The Vietnamese resistance was a socialist-led one. Many existing village heads were loyal to the Saigon government and not in sympathy with the socialist cause, as pointed out in a 1964 US State Department report that observes that the Viet Cong "were attempting to achieve" the "breakdown of administration and the decline of faith in the government." It was necessary for the guerrillas to replace them both to build up alternative administrations that would support them and influence local populations to lose faith in Saigon.[104]

While a new administrative order in the villages of Java might have been better able to mobilize resources for the army (and this is debatable given the long history of the *lurah*s in providing supplies to "the outside world") such an overhaul could easily have given rise to political forces that Nasution opposed. To sum up, Nasution's reliance on the *pamong praja* and *pamong desa* meant that the mobilization of the people to support the armed struggle accorded with his concern not to disturb the existing social order.

The instructions Nasution issued during the period of the military administration also appear to have percolated down to the village level. He writes that while on a journey to the Wonosobo area he came across a village meeting where the *lurah* himself was explaining the latest instructions from Java Command. He could not follow what was said because they were speaking Javanese but his interpreter was able to assure him that all his instructions were complete and had been delivered in a bundle to the village head.[105]

While this event might have been stage-managed for his benefit, Republican forces seem to have been generally well supported by the villages. For example, Suhario Padmodiwiryo writes that in the Malang area of East Java:

> The village *lurah*s in our area had been given sufficient information about the situation and what activities we expected from them. For example, that they should avoid stockpiling too much rice and it would be best if stocks of food such as rice, yams, corn, and cassava should be dispersed and concealed. With the full understanding of the *lurah*s and village elders we began to dig covered trenches and tunnels in protected forest areas on the slopes of Mount Kawi in preparation for a headquarters that we might have to use in emergency situations, depending on the intensity of fighting in the future.[106]

He also describes how his wife, who joined him in his guerrilla enclave, assisted in setting up a village school in cooperation with local teachers and that "their influence was very good for the school atmosphere because they brought innovations in teaching."[107]

Conversely, Anthony Reid writes that the involvement of such urban refugees in village life was to leave a strong and generally positive impression upon them.

> Army officers, politicians, officials and refugees of all sorts from the occupied cities were thrown on the hospitality of uneducated villagers. The contact was not always without friction, but its impact on both sides was profound. For many villagers, the presence of these refugees and their cat-and-mouse encounters with Dutch patrols was the first real experience of revolution. Some of the townspeople organised schools and development projects in the villages, and even encouraged distribution of village or plantation land to poor peasants in order to encourage commitment to the Republican cause. For the townspeople themselves the guerrilla supremely symbolised the hardship, the comradeship, and the solidarity of the common struggle. Most powerfully affected were perhaps the *Tentara Pelajar* (Student Army) of Central and East Java, most of whom were still at school during the 1945–46 upheavals, but who by 1949 formed an enthusiastic and disciplined volunteer army of the young elite. The solidarity which the guerrilla period forged between these future leaders and young army officers, and the populist legitimacy it seemed to confer on the leadership of both, were important elements in post-independence national life.[108]

Even in the economic field, the Republic seems to have enjoyed some success at the village level. Salim Said provides an interesting account of the imposition of taxes and the utilization of plantation crops by local commanders,[109] while Suhario Padmodiwiryo provides a first-hand account of the exploitation of coffee plantations in the South Kawi area by Republican forces, and the use of women vendors or *bakul* for trade activities with areas under Dutch control.[110]

In his pamphlet on village defense Nasution affirmed that "Indonesian currency must be the only one that is valid. Dutch currency must be obliterated."[111] This appears to have been successful, as Kahin writes that peasants who brought "slim supplies of food" into Yogyakarta would only accept Republican currency.

> One significant effect of this, a factor which helped buoy Republican morale, was that the rate between the N.E.I. guilder and the Republican rupiah prevailing among Chinese shopkeepers in Yogyakarta, which had fallen from 1:50 before the Dutch attack to 1:500 a few days thereafter, had climbed back to 1:150. Some Chinese shopkeepers with whom the writer spoke in Yogyakarta at this time stated a preference for Republican currency over N.E.I. currency, explaining that they had to have the former in order to buy rice. Ten days after the writer left the ratio was back to 1:110 and by the end of January it reached 1:90. The faith of the Indonesian peasant in the Republican regime and its dog-eared paper notes with the picture of Sukarno on them appeared to be exerting a greater power over the relative values of the currencies than Dutch military might.[112]

Importantly for his future involvements in politics, as the conflict dragged on Nasution became increasingly acquainted with members of the Central Java aristocracy who were working with the military administration. After three months of writing all the instructions that he felt were necessary to the military administration he moved to Boro where he maintained a more secure and complete headquarters for another three months. While at Boro he attended a meeting in the mountains near Wonosobo where he met the Javanese aristocrat Sumitro Kolopaking.

Sumitro Kolopaking was the sixth *Bupati* of Banjarnegara. He could trace his ancestry to the Central Java-based Mataram kingdom, which was originally a Hindu kingdom whose capital was to the north east of the Dieng Plateau (the location of Banjarnegara). Mataram later converted to Islam and unsuccessfully attacked Batavia in 1629 under the leadership of Sultan Agung Hanyokrokusumo. The name Kolopaking is said to have been bestowed upon *Tumenggung*[113] Kolopaking I for giving "dried coconut" (*kelapa aking*) to Sultan Agung's successor, Sultan Amangkurat I (reigned 1646–77).[114]

Mataram was divided by the Dutch East India Company into the principalities of Yogyakarta and Surakarta before becoming bankrupt in 1799 when all its territories were taken over by the Dutch administration in Batavia. Prince Diponegoro of Mataram fought the Dutch in a prolonged conflict that became known as the Java War (1825–1830). Raden Adipati Tumenggung Kolopaking IV supported Prince Diponegoro and the Kolopaking family were stripped of the *kabupaten* of Kebumen. Instead, the senior member of the family was installed as *Bupati* of Banjarnegara with the proviso that the name Kolopaking no longer to be used.[115]

However, Sumitro Kolopaking was successful in reversing this edict when the Dutch prevailed upon him to leave his position of *Komisaris Besar* (chief commissioner) of police and go into training to take over as *bupati*. He accepted the offer on condition that he and his siblings could again use the Kolopaking name.[116]

Kolopaking had been one of the "senior conservative civil servants" who had been appointed a member of the BPUPKI.[117] He had been installed as Resident Ad Interim of the Pekalongan area in the wake of the Three Regions Affair.[118]

Later in the revolution he became a member of the executive of the *Persatuan Indonesia Raya* (Greater Indonesian Union Party)[119] that was formed by "older-generation civil servants having aristocratic backgrounds,"[120] and became a member of parliament for this party in 1950. The anti-party, secular, paternalistic and socially conservative nature of the PIR is evident in this summary of its views by Kahin:

The PIR is to be a mass-backed party without the religious orientation of Masyumi and without being based upon Western political concepts of the PNI. It is to be based upon traditional Indonesian political and socio-economic concepts partially modified and adapted to those of the West. The present is regarded as a transitional period between the old authoritarian society and the more Western-oriented Indonesian society that is yet to come. The ballot cannot alone serve to ensure that the interests of the common people will be looked after. Not only will many of the common people not vote, but when they do they may well vote in a way that does not serve their interests. They are not individualistic enough to look after their own interests directly and are accustomed to expect authority from above.

The great danger is that the peasant vote will go to irresponsible demagogues who do not understand the people and are not able to represent their interests. The people need and expect guidance from above; this has been ingrained in them for centuries. The people themselves are not accustomed to pushing their own interests in a politically articulate manner and cannot overnight be expected to become politically responsible individualists of the character of people living in the Western democracies.

Some means must be found for giving real representation to the agrarian population. Such representation was given them in the past by the civil servants because they went out and among the people and learned what their interests and desires were. Somehow this virtue must be incorporated into the structure of the Indonesian government. The leaders of the government must be able to know the interests of the people and to a very large extent depend upon themselves, rather than upon the people, to ascertain what their interests are. The character of the Indonesian government that is to be developed must allow for "fatherly authority" from above to look after the needs of the peasantry.[121]

That Nasution shared such views, and particularly the dangers of "demagogues," is evident in *Fundamentals of Guerrilla Warfare*. He argued that agrarian village communities were unable and often unwilling to change quickly and accept new ideas. However, they were "the government's most obedient citizens." Although there had been "agitation" against the *lurah*s during the colonial period, such as a requirement to work on their lands, do other communal work and pay taxes, traditional relationships had generally not been altered greatly. However, he lamented, during the armed struggle it had been difficult to restore order in village communities that had been subjected to the depredations of armed gangs or rendered chaotic by agitators.[122]

The views of the PIR were also consonant with those expressed in Professor Supomo's contributions to the BPUPKI debates. For example, Supomo had described individualism[123] and the open contestation of ideas leading to voting[124] as contrary to the norms of Eastern civilization and advocated decision-making through consultation leading to consensus (*musyawarah sampai mufakat*),[125] rather than voting. It is not surprising that Supomo became a member of the PIR in 1951.[126]

Kolopaking and other *pamong praja* identities from the guerrilla era in Central Java were to become mainstays of Nasution's IPKI organization in the 1950s and Kolokaping became general chairman.

Nasution's admiration for the older aristocrat and the "traditional" values he embodied is strikingly clear in his recollections of their meeting:

> *Bapak* Kolopaking, a person of aristocratic descent, carried on the way of life of the aristocrats of the past; that is, he lived simply, had strong personal discipline, and unobtrusively mixed a great deal with the people. . . .
>
> *Bapak* Kolopaking is still a close friend of mine. When in 1954 I formed IPKI he spontaneously joined in, together with the *Bupati* of Wonosobo whom I also met at the Division III Headquarters, and all the other Residents of Central Java who had of course all participated in the guerrilla struggle. I met all of them at the Division III Headquarters, although they were all still holding *Bupati* appointments.[127]

It is evident that the guerrilla experience was not only a defining event for Nasution but also for these conservative allies in the *pamong praja* and *pamong desa*. Nasution and his *pamong praja* associates had been "cooperating nationalists" under the Dutch and had not enjoyed the heroic stature of those who opposed the colonial regime outright and suffered for it. They also lacked the democratic credentials that Sjahrir and Sjarifuddin had gained as "non-cooperators" with the Japanese.

Conservative *pamong praja* identities such as Kolokaping had been largely swept aside in the emergence of pluralist politics when Sjahrir came to power, and Nasution had often been accused by *laskar* and other political interests of being authoritarian, militaristic and a stooge of the Dutch. However, by the time the Dutch recognized Indonesian sovereignty Nasution and these *pamong praja* identities had obtained much improved nationalist credentials, while some of those who had been more favored at the outset of the revolution but then submitted to capture by the Dutch or poked fun at the guerrilla campaign from occupied cities had lost some of their moral authority.

In the 1960s, Margono Djojohadikusumo, a high-status *priyayi* who had familial *pamong praja* connections, commented along somewhat similar lines in comparing the *pangreh/pamong praja* and the civilian political leaders:

> Throughout the Netherlands Indies administration this service was the intermediary that connected the Dutch authorities with the people. This was an instrument of the state that was often condemned and belittled by people. And let me say frankly that I often did so, but now my views have been tempered. Because in the Japanese occupation period and then when the Dutch mounted their two military actions I saw many examples of quiet patriotism and courage on the part of *pamong praja* officials who set examples that were worthy of emulation by most of the politicians.[128]

It was during this second guerrilla war that Nasution's ideas for "total people's resistance" became firmly associated with traditional values and authority structures. Nasution was to idealize the period as a critical time in the life of the Republic when the army had worked selflessly together with the people and organic "traditional" authority structures while the politicians had submitted to capture and were negotiating with the Dutch.

Moreover, the restoration of the reputation of the *pamong praja* under the military administration was not a case of swimming against the broader political tide. Anthony Reid has observed that an unusual aspect of the Indonesian Revolution was that "it moved slightly to the Right, rather than to the Left, over a five-year period."[129] Amir Sjarifuddin and some other leaders identified with the PKI were killed after the Madiun Affair. After the Dutch attack, Tan Malaka allied himself with sympathetic Republican troops and declared that he was now the leader of the Republican cause but was hunted down and killed by other army units.

Through such processes the officer corps on Java gradually shed itself of most of its more left-wing officers and its largely junior *priyayi* recruitment base meant that it was not particularly sympathetic to political Islam. Moreover, many more orthodox *santri* officers had preferred to remain within the Hizbullah or Sabilillah or separated from the army after the *Siliwangi* and other Republican forces found that they had to combat a growing *Darul Islam* movement from 1949. As McVey comments, by the early 1950s a *santri* officer was a "rare bird."[130]

The army that emerged from the armed struggle was one of only four postcolonial forces that Janowitz has described as armies of national liberation, in that it was established "during the struggle for national liberation."[131] In this respect, it had similarities with revolutionary Marxist forces, such as those of China and Vietnam. However, unlike those revolutionary armies that were attached to Communist parties, the army had no institutional links with a political movement. Rather, like Nasution, many officers had acquired a distaste for potentially divisive local politicians during their endeavors to mobilize rural populations in support of guerrilla forces.

For example, in *Report from Banaran*, T.B. Simatupang writes that the idea of banning political activities was discussed in Republican circles before the second Dutch "police action" and "became more powerful, particularly in certain armed forces circles" during the period of military administration.[132]

The instructions of some field commanders provide examples of attempts to unify contending forces. On January 22, 1949, Colonel Sungkono, in his capacity as military governor of East Java, issued the following order:

> The Struggle has only one aim, that is the victory of the Republic of Indonesia. Accordingly, all the other interests that citizens have must succumb to the general interest. No interests of any parties or groups should be entertained. The struggles of the parties and groups for the time being should be suppressed, so that all physical and spiritual powers can be mobilised for the benefit of the struggle of the Republic of Indonesia.[133]

Similarly, in March 1949 Lieutenant Colonel Slamet Rijadi, commander of the 5th Brigade, Second Division, Java, issued an instruction warning that political frictions had begun to appear in a number of places. He urged guerrillas to ensure that the people did not become divided by party ideologies that might impede them from wholeheartedly supporting the national struggle.[134]

Nugroho Notosusanto, a former student army member who became a Suharto regime ideologue also recalls the suppression of political activities during the period of military administration:

> There were some political party leaders in our *kecamatan*, notably from PNI and Masyumi, but they seemed not to be very active, perhaps because the

Military Administration prohibited acts that might endanger the unity of the people in our *kecamatan*. Anyway, they did not belong to the "ruling elite" in our *kecamatan*.[135]

Sunarto, a young military subdistrict commander in the Temon area during the guerrilla war asked the people to cease carrying out partisan political activities until the end of the war. According to Sunarto, as a result "the many political parties in Temon simply cancelled their activities during the period of guerrilla war."[136]

Writing about the situation in East Java, Sudarno recalls:

It can be said that throughout the Second War of Independence there were no activities carried out by the political parties in the areas held by the Republic. All the attention of the leaders, whether they were party leaders or in the administration (civilian and military), was totally focused on finding the best method of winning the war. The exceptions were the followers of the Murba Party who up until March 1949 in East Java were the backbone of the unit led by Sabaruddin which operated in the Nganjuk area.[137]

While the armed forces on the side of the Republic continued to defy and harass the Dutch, in mid-1949 the captured leadership entered into negotiations that culminated in the Indonesian representative, Mohammad Roem, signing an agreement with van Roijen of the Netherlands to return the captured civilian leadership to Yogyakarta. Military leaders registered their opposition to the civilian leadership negotiating a ceasefire and Nasution asserted that the military administration remained in control. He issued an order for Republican troops to step up their activities and consolidate their positions as the Dutch could be forced to submit to all of Indonesia's conditions if the fighting was permitted to continue until September.[138]

However, after Sukarno returned to Yogyakarta, Nasution decided to call off the guerrilla war and made his way from his guerrilla headquarters into the city where Sunarti was eagerly awaiting him:

Finally, the moment I had been awaiting arrived. He arrived with Lieutenant Suranto, wearing a sarong and a bamboo hat like a rural villager. My husband looked thin and he was no longer clean-shaven like in the past. That was a very emotional moment. Pak Nas remarked that I was very thin. That was true as I only weighed 48 kilograms. He immediately shaved off his moustache and beard.[139]

Disgusted with the compromise reached with the Dutch, Sudirman declined to join him there and only agreed to do so when persuaded by a special emissary of the Sultan of Yogyakarta (colonel, later president, Suharto).

Now terribly thin and still clad in his greatcoat and Javanese cloth cap, he inspected guerrilla forces in a highly emotional ceremony. He tendered his resignation to Sukarno who countered by stating that he, as supreme commander, would also resign if Sudirman did so. Sudirman subsequently drafted a profoundly bitter and eloquent letter of resignation but was dissuaded from submitting it by Nasution, who by then had also returned to the capital.[140]

Sudirman's determination not to make concessions to the Dutch impacted on the outcome of the conference to settle the issue of the decolonization of the Netherlands Indies (termed the Round Table Conference) that was convened in The Hague. The leadership of the TNI, and particularly Sudirman, were adamant that the TNI would form the core of the army of the state that was formed from the Round Table Conference but were not confident that the civilian negotiators would maintain their position. As Ian MacFarling points out, this led Sudirman to take the highly unusual step of sending:

> a military mission as part of the Republican delegation to the Round Table Conference. . . . The notion that an official delegation from a nation should include an independent military group which had a separate directive that differed from the national political delegation's terms of reference is still astonishing today.[141]

Simatupang was successful in ensuring that the TNI, rather than the KNIL, would be the core of the postrevolutionary army.

While the guerrilla campaign might not have been decisive in bringing about the return of the captured leaders and the Round Table Conference, Tom Critchley listed it as the first of three important developments that the Dutch failed to foresee when mounting the second "police action" (the others being failure to gain cooperation from the Sultan of Yogyakarta and lack of support from the Federal States):

> Firstly, although after their December [1948] military action the Dutch could command major centres and the main communication routes, they continued to be harassed in the countryside by guerrilla troops that had the support of the Indonesian people.[142]

In summary, Nasution's principles of "total people's resistance" provided guidelines for action, rather than detailed operational orders, but they played a significant role in providing a framework for effective guerrilla operations that helped push the Dutch toward a compromise. They also helped ensure that the army would not be disbanded or absorbed into a postcolonial force commanded by those who had fought against the Republic.

His determination to put the army on a more professional footing, while emphasizing that asymmetric warfare was the only course of action open to it, was another important legacy of his service during the struggle against the Dutch. His antipathy toward what he saw as disruptive elements and particularly those from the left of politics culminated in his role in suppressing the Madiun insurgency and that outcome played an important part in ensuring American support for the Republic in the negotiations following their second "police action."

Susan McKemmish effectively sums up the reputation that Nasution had acquired by the time the conflict ended:

> In some respects, he had been peculiarly ill at ease in the atmosphere of heightened nationalism, revolutionary fighting spirit and millenarian expectations of the revolutionary years. Although he had advocated the armed revolutionary road to national independence, in his pragmatic, almost clinical approach to the tactics and strategies of guerrilla warfare he tended to downgrade the importance of the revolutionary fighting spirit, which to the more *semangat*-oriented guerrilla fighters was the very essence of their struggle. On the other hand, using the opportunity provided by the revolutionary experience to display his considerable organisational and administrative skills, he had become by the end of the revolution an officer whose reputation in these areas was unsurpassed.[143]

The Round Table Conference left two major problems that were to plague Dutch-Indonesian relations throughout the 1960s. The first was their insistence that the new Indonesian government take over the debts of the Netherlands Indies, including the costs of military operations against the Republic. The second and most significant was their refusal to concede that West New Guinea (later known as West Irian and now West Papua) be included within the new state. Sukarno and the PKI were to draw upon this issue throughout the 1950s to influence the political debate and it was to impact greatly upon Nasution as he sought to navigate his way through the political and economic turmoil that gathered force in that decade.

NOTES

1. Division I (Western Central Java), Division II (Eastern Central Java); Division III (Republican remnants of East Java).

2. Nasution, *Memenuhi Panggilan Tugas*, Vol Two, Op. Cit., p. 14.

3. Sudirman's strikingly eloquent and bitter letter of resignation is reproduced in Nasution, *TNI* Vol Three, *Op. Cit.*, p. 69, 70.

4. Cribb, 1991 *Op. Cit.*, p. 94.

5. Brackman, *Op. Cit.*, p. 54, 55. See Ibid., p. 55 for a brief account of the reformation of the above-ground PKI in October 1945.

6. R. McVey, "The Post-Revolutionary Transformation of the Indonesian Army (Part 1)" in *Indonesia*, No. 11, (April 1971), p. 137.

7. See Said, *Op. Cit.*, pp. 66–80 for an account of Sudirman's political behavior and his relations with Nasution during 1948.

8. A. H. Nasution, *TNI* Vol. Two, *Op. Cit.*, p. 160, 161.

9. See, for example Mao Tse Tung, "Mobile Warfare, Guerrilla Warfare and Positional Warfare," in Mao Tse Tung, *Selected Military Writings of Mao Tse Tung*, Peking, Foreign Languages Press, 1963, pp. 244–248.

10. Kveder, *Op. Cit.*, p.95.

11. Reid, *Op. Cit.*, p. 135.

12. A. H. Nasution, "Bertugas Dengan Sri Sultan," in Atmakusumah (ed.), *Tahta Untuk Rakyat: Celah-celah Kehidupan Sultan Hamengku Buwono IX*, 1982, p. 180.

13. Reid, *Op. Cit.*

14. Legge, 1961 *Central Authority and Regional Authority in Indonesia: A Study in Local Administration*, Ithaca, N.Y., Cornell University Press, p. 16. For a description of the relations between *lurah* and *camat* in a Central Javanese village in the 1950s, see Nitisastro and Ismail, *The Government, Economy and Taxes of a Central Javanese Village*, 1959 Op. Cit., p. 13, 14. In a similar vein to Legge, these researchers describe the *camat* as "the backbone of the system."

15. A. H. Nasution, *Fundamentals*, p. 54, 112.

16. According to Chaidir Basrie, these cadres, known as *pasukan gerilya desa* (*pager desa*—village guerrilla troops), were former *laskar* personnel who did not enter the regular forces (*Bela Negara: Implementasi dan Pembangunannya*, 1988, p. 28).

17. Heijboer, *Op. Cit.*, p. 124.

18. Ibid.

19. Said, *Op. Cit.*, p. 102.

20. Nasution, *Fundamentals, Op. Cit.*, p. 114.

21. Nasution, *Memenuhi Panggilan Tugas,* Vol Two, *Op. Cit.*, p. 84.

22. Nasution, *Fundamentals, Op. Cit.*, p. 54.

23. Ibid., p. 94, 95.

24. Ibid., p. 113.

25. Correspondence by fax from R.P. Soejono (Soeroso's son) dated May 17, 2005.

26. Donald K. Emmerson, *Indonesia's Elite: Political Culture and Cultural Politics*, Ithaca, NY, 1976, p. 45, f.n. 22.

27. Kahin, *Op. Cit.*, p. 121.

28. "Piagam Jakarta: Kompromi Tak Kunjung Padam," http://www.*tempo*.co.id/harian/fokus/39/2,1,98,id.html.

29. Anderson, 1972 *Op. Cit.*, p. 63, 64.

30. *Antara-Domei* (Jakarta), September 3, 1945, excerpted from Ibid., p. 113.

31. https://profil.merdeka.com/indonesia/r/r-p-soeroso, accessed July 2017.

32. Clune, *Op. Cit.*, p. 174.

33. Nasution, *Memenuhi Panggilan Tugas,* Vol Two, *Op. Cit.*, p. 28. Sunarti, *Op. Cit.*, p. 54.

34. H. Feith, *The Decline of Constitutional Democracy in Indonesia*, Ithaca, NY: Cornell University, 1962, p. 38.

35. Nasution, *Memenuhi Panggilan Tugas*, Vol Two, *Op. Cit.*, p. 29.

36. Sunarti, *Op. Cit.*, p. 54.

37. Nasution, *Memenuhi Panggilan Tugas*, Vol Two, *Op. Cit.*, p. 29. Sunarti's Aunt Ning was a younger sister of Sunario Gondokusumo and R.P. Soeroso's wife. Written communication via intermediary with Professor R.P. Soejono, Jakarta, April 1, 2005.
38. Ibid., p. 42.
39. Nasution, *Memenuhi Panggilan Tugas*, Vol Two, *Op. Cit.*, p. 126, 127.
40. M.C. Ricklefs, *A History of Modern Indonesia*, London, MacMillan Education, 1981, p. 216.
41. Said, *Op. Cit.*, p. 77.
42. Sudarno et al., "Presidential Determinations of 1948, No. 22," in Sudarno 1993) *Sejarah Pemerintahan Militer dan Peran Pamong Praja di Jawa Timur Selama Perjuangan Fisik 1945–1950* (translated title: *The History of the Military Administration and the Role of the Pamong Praja in East Java during the Period of Physical Struggle 1945–1950*), Jakarta: Balai Pustaka, p. 45.
43. "They had to be capable of keeping the wheels of the government and the economy turning and restoring the life of the community, in addition to carrying out their security tasks." Soebijono, "Dwifungsi ABRI Sebagai Konsep Politik" (translated title The Indonesian Armed Forces Dual Function as a Political Concept) in Soebijono et. al. (eds.), *Dwifungsi ABRI*, Yogyakarta, Gadjah Mada University Press, 1992, p. 17. See Said, *Op Cit.*, p. 104 for an interview with Slamet Danusudirdjo, a member of the Student Army (*Tentara Pelajar*), who was assigned the role of a territorial warfare officer "to accompany the troops and to take charge of areas already liberated from enemy control."
44. Slamet Danusudirjo, *Serangan Umum: 1 Maret 1949 di Yogyakarta, Latar Belakang dan Pengaruhnya* (Army Staff and Command College, General Offensive: March 1, 1949 in Yogyakarta, Its Background and Influence), Seskoad (Army Command and Staff School).
45. Soebijono, *Op. Cit.*
46. McKemmish, *Op. Cit.*, p. 44. McKemmish notes that Nasution made such statements in two interviews.
47. Penders and Sundhaussen, *Op Cit.*, p. 42.
48. Simatupang, 1961 *Op. Cit.*, p. 10.
49. Suryohadiprojo, *Op. Cit.*, p. 85, 86.
50. Said, *Op Cit.*, p. 112.
51. Indonews, March 20, 2000 (http://www.mail-archive.com/indonews@indonews.com/msg06592.html, accessed November 2004. Another minister, Supeno, evacuated Yogyakarta but was ambushed and killed by the Dutch in February 1949.
52. Simatupang, *Op. Cit.*, p. 10.
53. Reid, *Op. Cit.*, p. 101.
54. R. Debray, "Guerrilla Doctrine Today," in W. Laqueur (ed.), *The Guerrilla Reader: A Historical Anthology*, New York: New American Library, 1977, p. 215. Heijboer, *Op. Cit.*, p. 144.
55. Said, *Op Cit.*, p. 100.
56. Heijboer, *Op. Cit.*, p. 144.
57. Ide Anak Agung Gde, *Renville*, Jakarta, Sinar Harapan, 1991, p. 211.

58. Critchley, *Op. Cit.*, p. 22.
59. Ibid.
60. Heijboer, *Op. Cit.*, p. 166.
61. T.B. Simatupang, , *Laporan dari Banaran* (translated title Report from Banaran), Penerbit Sinar Harapan, second edition, Jakarta, Pembangunan, p. 13.
62. Nasution, *Fundamentals*, *Op. Cit.*, p. 134. Nasution's "Working Instruction for the Military Administration Throughout Java," which was issued together with his proclamation of the military administration in December 1948, advised: "b. Regulation No. 79 abolishes DPDs and people's defence bodies that are not in accordance with the instruction of the *Panglima Besar* of the Armed Forces dated November 9, and gives responsibility to heads of regions at each level, and instructions from heads of regions [in the form of] residents, *bupati, camat,* and *lurah* to all civilian instrumentalities in their regions." Nasution, "Working Instructions for the Military Administration Throughout Java" in Sudarno, et. al., *Op. Cit.*, p. 51, 52.
63. Nasution, *Memenuhi Panggilan Tugas*, Vol Two, *Op. Cit.*, p. 102.
64. This created a different situation to that in Republican areas in Sumatra where civilians were more clearly in charge following the formation of the emergency government (PDRI).
65. "Java Command Headquarters Proclamation No. 2 MBKD" and "Working Instructions for the Military Administration Throughout Java" (in 1993) *Sejarah Pemerintahan Militer dan Peran Pamong Praja di Jawa Timur Selama Perjuangan Fisik 1945–1950* (translated title: *The History of the Military Administration and the Role of the Pamong Praja in East Java during the Period of Physical Struggle 1945–1950*). Jakarta: BalaiPustaka, p. 50.
66. Ibid., p. 60.
67. Nasution, *Memenuhi Panggilan Tugas*, Vol Two, *Op. Cit.*, p. 83.
68. Reid, *Op. Cit.*, p. 155.
69. Simatupang, *Laporan dari Banaran, Op. Cit.*, p. 21.
70. Nasution, *Fundamentals*, *Op. Cit.*, p. 20.
71. Penders and Sundhaussen, *Op Cit.*, p. 49.
72. Ibid.
73. Ibid., p. 44.
74. Kahin, *Op. Cit.*, p. 391.
75. Simatupang, *Op. Cit.*, p. 44.
76. Seskoad, *Serangan Umum*, 1990, *Op. Cit.*
77. Heijboer, *Op. Cit.*, p. 175.
78. Kahin, *Op. Cit.*, p. 185.
79. Nasution, *TNI*, Vol Three, *Op. Cit.*, p. 36.
80. Nasution, *Memenuhi Panggilan Tugas*, Vol Two, *Op. Cit.*, p. 127.
81. Said, *Op. Cit.*, p. 3.
82. Nasution, *Memenuhi Panggilan Tugas*, Vol Two, *Op. Cit.*, p. 103.
83. Ibid., p. 142.
84. Ibid., p. 83.
85. Ibid., p. 129.
86. Nasution, *Fundamentals*, *Op. Cit.*, pp. 108–338.

87. Ibid., pp. 255–264.
88. Ibid., p. 311.
89. Ibid., pp. 321–332.
90. Nasution, *Memenuhi Panggilan Tugas*, Vol Two, *Op. Cit.*, p. 150.
91. Ibid., p. 151.
92. Ibid., p. 90.
93. Kahin, *Op. Cit.*, p. 391, 392.
94. Ibid., p. 396.
95. Ibid.
96. See Sudarno et. al., *Op. Cit.*, pp. 94–253 for accounts of such activities, including orders issued by regional branches of the administration in East Java and records of taxes and other contributions collected by the *pamong praja*.
97. Wiliater Hutagulung, *Tiga Episode Perang Kemerdekaan* (translated title Three Episodes from the Independence War), extracted from www.mail-archive.com/siarlist@minipostgresql.org/msg02842.html, accessed January 2005.
98. Ibid.
99. Nasution, *Memenuhi Panggilan Tugas,* Vol. Two, *Op. Cit.*, p. 35, 36.
100. Cribb, *Op. Cit.*, pp, p. 153.
101. Ibid., p. 151, 152.
102. Robert Cribb, "Opium and the Indonesian Revolution" in Modern Asian Studies, Volume 22, Number 2, 1988, pp. 717–720.
103. Ibid.
104. US State Department, SNIE 53-2-64, "The Situation in South Vietnam," October 1, 1964, US Department of State, Office of the Historian, *Foreign Relations of the United States, 1964–1968,* Volume I, Vietnam (Washington, DC), Document No. 368, (http://www.mtholyoke.edu/acad/intrel/pentagon3/snie53.htm).
105. Nasution, *Memenuhi Panggilan Tugas,* Vol Two, *Op. Cit.*, p. 145.
106. Padmodiwiryo, *Op. Cit.*, p. 280.
107. Ibid., p. 272.
108. Reid, *Op Cit.*, p. 155.
109. Said, *Op. Cit.*, pp. 101–8.
110. Padmodiwiryo, *Op. Cit.*, p. 269.
111. See Nasution, *TNI* Vol Two, *Op. Cit.*, p. 202.
112. "Kahin, *Op. Cit.*, p. 396, 397.
113. A title, usually of a *bupati*. Heather Sutherland, *The Making of a Bureaucratic Elite*, p. xvii.
114. www.kebumen.go.id, *Sejarah Terjadinya Kabupaten Kebumen* (translated title History of the Establishment of the Regency of Kebumen), accessed December 27, 2004, http://country studies.us/Indonesia/8.htm. accessed December 27, 2004.
115. Raden Tirto Wenang Kolopaking, *Sejarah Dinasti Kanjeng Raden Adipati Tumenggung Kolopaking 1677–1832: Pendopo Panjer Roma Kebumen* (translated title History of the Dynasty of Raden Adipati Tumenggung Kolopaking 1677–1832), location and publication not stated, 1997, p. 16, 17.
116. Ibid., p. 19.
117. Bourchier, *Op. Cit.*, p. 73.

118. Anderson, *Op. Cit.*, p. 341, 342. Anderson writes that Kolopaking did not enjoy real authority in this position and was replaced in May 1946.

119. Ibid., p. 111.

120. Kahin, *Op. Cit.*, p. 324.

121. Ibid., p. 325. Kolopaking was not the only PIR member to become associated with Nasution's "total people's resistance" strategies. Governor Sewaka of West Java, who authorized Nasution's plans from Bojonggambir in 1947 was also a PIR member.

122. Nasution, *Fundamentals, Op. Cit.*, p. 266.

123. Supomo's speech to the BPUPKI, Simandjuntak, *Op. Cit.*, p. 99.

124. Ibid.

125. Ibid., p. 91.

126. Reeve, 1985 *Op. Cit.*, p. 110.

127. Nasution, *Memenuhi Panggilan Tugas,* Vol Two, *Op. Cit.*, p. 146.

128. Margono Djojohadikusumo, *Kenang-kenangan dari Tiga Zaman: Satu Kisah Kekeluargaan Tertulis* (translated title Memories of Three Eras: A Family Story). Jakarta, Indira, 1970, p. 101. Margono was a senior official in the Netherlands Indies, Japanese Occupation and Republican administrations. He lost two sons in an attempt to seize arms from the Japanese in 1945 and was the father of the noted economist Professor Sumitro Djojohadikusumo, who associated himself with the PRRI/Permesta rebellion and fled to Malaysia where he remained until the advent of the New Order. Margono fled with him and his opinions about Indonesian political leaders (Sukarno in particular) were often quite bitter. His grandson, Prabowo, married into the Suharto family and achieved considerable notoriety over his actions in East Timor and during Suharto's downfall. In 2014, he stood unsuccessfully in presidential elections and appears to be preparing to run again in 2019.

129. Reid, *Op. Cit.,* p. 171.

130. The emergence of centrist attitudes within the army officer corps has been commented upon by Ruth McVey. McVey, 1971 *Op. Cit.*, p. 138.

131. The countries listed by Janowitz were Indonesia, Burma and Algeria. M. Janowitz, *The Military in the Political Development of New Nations*, Princeton, NJ, Princeton University Press, p. 10, 13.

132. Simatupang, *Report from Banaran: Experiences During the People's War* (English language translation), Ithaca, NY, Modern Indonesia Project, Cornell University, c1972, p. 130. Excerpted from Said*, Op Cit.*, p. 111.

133. Instruction of the East Java Military Governor, dated January 22, 1949, CMI Document no. 5682, CAD, CG 58, The Netherlands Defence Ministry Archives, extracted from Said, *Op Cit.*, p. 110–111.

134. Guide for Guerrillas, Issued by Lieutenant Colonel Slamet Rijadi, commander of the 5th Brigade "Penembahan Senopati," Second Division, Java, dated March 23, 1949. Extracted from: Nasution, *Fundamentals, Op. Cit.,* pp. 224–225.

135. Nugroho Notosusanto, "Some Effects of the Guerrilla War (1948–49) on Armed Forces and Society in Indonesia," in Nugroho Notosusanto, *The National Struggle and the Armed Forces in Indonesia*, p. 105. Extracted from Said, *Op Cit.*, p. 111.

136. Ibid., p. 106.

137. Sudarno, *Op. Cit.*, p. 369, 370.
138. McKemmish, *Op. Cit.*, p. 47.
139. Sunarti, *Op. Cit.*, p. 85.
140. For an account of these events, see Said, *Op Cit.*, pp. 114–22.
141. I. MacFarling, *The Dual Function of the Indonesian Armed Forces*, Canberra, Australian Defence Studies Centre, 1996, p. 43, 44.
142. Critchley, *Op. Cit.*, p. 25.
143. McKemmish, *Op. Cit.*, p. 48.

Chapter 6

Burnishing Credentials
The Idealization of Total People's Resistance

The emergence of the Republican army as the core of the new national army meant that officers like Nasution who were still in their early thirties occupied senior positions that would have been given to highly trained men in their forties and fifties in most military forces. Nasution's childhood dream of an outstanding military career seemed to have been fulfilled when he was appointed army chief of staff in 1950. However, his memoirs reveal that he experienced a crisis of confidence that manifested itself in anxiety and inability to sleep at night.

Feelings of deflation and lack of affinity with everyday life are common among service personnel who have been exposed to conflict situations. In Nasution's case they were triggered by concern that he was inadequately qualified and experienced for his new role, internal problems of unity and commonality of purpose within the army, and criticism from political figures. His unease was exacerbated because he found himself once again among professionally qualified KNIL officers.

Perhaps because they had not experienced a decisive military defeat, the Dutch were behaving as if an orderly decolonization process was still possible. They used the term "transfer of sovereignty" to describe their formal relinquishment of the Indies while nationalist Indonesians referred to the same process as "recognition of sovereignty," holding fast to their standpoint that the country had been independent since August 17, 1945.

Many Dutch civil servants remained in place pending the assumption of their roles by Indonesians, large Dutch business enterprises dominated the economy, and a sizeable Dutch and Eurasian community continued to live in the country. Significantly for Nasution, the terms of the transfer provided for a Netherlands Military Mission to advise the TNI as it transitioned to a more professional status. His KNIL background and Sunarti's Dutch ancestry led to more charges that he was pro-Dutch and hampered his efforts to professionalize the army.

The old schism between former PETA and KNIL officers was exacerbated by the presence of the Military Mission and what some PETA officers saw as a preparedness by the former KNIL cadets like Nasution to resume their tutelage by Dutch officers who had recently fought against the republic. Their resistance to the mission attracted support from some politicians and this added to Nasution's frustrations and tensions. Eventually, he began to seek out a path for the army to involve itself more in politics, with disastrous results.

Nasution had to work within a political system that had been worked out the previous year in Round Table negotiations between The Netherlands and the Indonesian Government. The 1945 Constitution had been discarded in favor of a liberal-democratic system of parliamentary rule that provided for a bicameral parliament with a House of Representatives (*Dewan Perwakilan Rakyat*—DPR) and a Senate.

Two categories of politicians and bureaucrats emerged that Feith describes as "administrators" and "solidarity makers."[1] Feith's "administrators" were "leaders with the administrative, technical, legal, and foreign-language skills required to run the distinctively modern apparatus of a modern state."[2] Sjahrir and his *Partai Sosialis Indonesia* (PSI) exemplified the "administrators," although they were also represented in the Masyumi and smaller parties, including the *Partai Persatuan Indonesia Raya* (PIR), the Catholic Party (*Partai Katolik*) and the Protestant Christian Party (*Parkindo*). The "administrators" sought to use the skills they had developed in the colonial period to work within the system of parliamentary democracy to solve the immediate administrative, developmental and financial problems with which the republic was faced.

On the other hand, the solidarity makers were "leaders skilled as mediators between groups at different levels of modernity and political effectiveness, as mass organisers, and as manipulators of integrative symbols."[3] President Sukarno was the leading exponent of "solidarity making" and placed nation building and the development of a national spirit above all other issues. The *Partai Nasional Indonesia* (Indonesian Nationalist Party—PNI) that had formed in 1946 and modeled itself on Sukarno's party from the late 1920s of the same name (the later version lacked Sukarno's direct involvement) and *Murba*, the party formed by Tan Malaka supporters, were the leading "solidarity makers." The PNI represented "Javanism." Its leaders were drawn from the *priyayi* class and it drew a great deal of support from the *pamong praja*. The Murba presented itself as both "radical nationalist" and "radical socialist" but it actually conveyed "an inchoate messianistic radicalism," refusing to "recognise the practical difficulties of governments."[4] The administrators were ascendant in the first three cabinets that followed the recognition of Indonesian sovereignty by the Dutch.

Although this was a relatively prosperous period due to increased sales and prices for commodity exports thanks to the Korean War, many Indonesians became frustrated and disillusioned with the fruits of independence. Often, those most disappointed were young *pemuda*s who had reached adulthood in the heightened atmosphere of the occupation and were not members of the elite Dutch-educated circles that produced the administrators. They lacked social prominence and highly paid positions in the routinized postrevolutionary system and craved more charismatic leadership that would give the sort of meaning to their lives that they had found in the revolution. Anti-Dutch feelings, reinforced by a growing perception that the Dutch were being intransigent in refusing to hand over West Irian, led to a belief within this group that the revolution had been derailed and the post-1949 system of government was a mere facsimile of the former colonial regime.

Having been a cooperating nationalist in colonial times and benefited from a Dutch education before becoming involved in Japanese paramilitary organizations and serving in the army, Nasution straddled the *pemuda* and older generations. In this new period of his life Nasution worked closely with Hatta (who continued as prime minister), his academy classmate Simatupang (Nasution's superior and in charge of the armed forces), the Sultan of Yogyakarta (defense minister) and Ali Budiardjo (the secretary general of the Ministry of Defense). All were "administrators" and in a policy sense Nasution seems to have been closer to that camp at this stage of his career. He agreed with those in the Ministry of Defense/armed forces leadership that there was a need to drastically reduce the army's size and introduce much greater efficiency and technical expertise. According to Feith, "close cooperation was possible between Nasution on the one hand and Simatupang on the other because they shared an approach to the building up of a modern, cohesive and powerful army." However, in other respects Nasution did not fit easily into either of the "administrator" or "solidarity maker" categories.[5]

According to Feith, in the early 1950s Nasution was an "administrator"[6] but Susan McKemmish doubts the validity of this categorization. She also disagrees with Sundhaussen's categorization of Nasution as one of a group of former KNIL "administrator-type" officers (in *The Political Orientations and Political Involvement of the Indonesian Officer Corps 1945–1966: The Siliwangi Division and Army Headquarters*, the thesis upon which he based *Road to Power*). McKemmish observes that Nasution was not associated in any way with the PSI as was Simatupang, and states that he admired the "solidarity maker" Sukarno more than "administrator" Hatta.[7]

Sukarno remained an indispensable rallying figure for the Indonesian masses but had lost some of his influence within the military for choosing not to avoid capture in Yogyakarta.[8] In the final year of the revolution he had been eclipsed in day-to-day political processes by Hatta and was largely a figurehead president whose most important formal role was to appoint a cabinet *formateur* from within the parliament when it was necessary (as was often the case) to form a new government.

Sukarno was not the only political force that the liberal-democratic system failed to accord a preeminent position. On the island of Java and elsewhere where it had become a sizeable force, the army had to surrender the political authority it had gained through the military administration.[9]

Both the constitution and the parliament were temporary, pending the holding of general elections. These were not only intended to choose a new parliament but a constitutional commission (*Konstituante*) whose function was to draw up a permanent constitution. One of the primary tasks of the interim parliament was to enact the necessary legislation to hold these elections.

Importantly, the new state was a federation known as the United States of Indonesia (*Republik Indonesia Serikat*—RIS). In accordance with the processes set in train at Linggarjati, the original republic was a member state and retained its capital in Yogyakarta. Two-thirds of the 146 members of the House of Representatives were from the "federal" states (*negara*s) established by the Dutch to counter the power of the Republic of Indonesia, while the republic and each of the other states provided two members each to the Senate.

After leading the Republic's delegation to the Round Table Conference, Hatta served as prime minister until August 1950 when he resumed vice-presidential duties. Republican leaders and particularly Hatta had emerged from the revolution with much greater moral authority than those from the federal states.[10]

Once the Dutch were no longer able to prop up this federal construct it quickly collapsed and the resignation of the Hatta cabinet coincided with the replacement of the federation with a unitary state known as the Republic of Indonesia. The Senate was abolished and a unicameral system installed but the composition of the DPR lower house remained largely as it had been, meaning that two-thirds of members were from the old federal states. The provisional constitution was largely unchanged and provisions remained in place for general elections for a new parliament and *Konstituante*. Mohammed Natsir of the Masyumi party formed the first government of the unitary state.

Nasution often felt under great stress. He had doubts that he was technically qualified enough to perform his duties competently and was concerned that Dutch officers (many of whom had been his seniors within the KNIL) and other foreigners might regard him as too young and inexperienced to be chief of staff. Frustrated at his inability to resolve problems, he was often unable to sleep at night.

> Sometimes I would just lie awake on the couch in the guest reception room. I was envious of my wife who could sleep soundly.[11]

When he visited India soon after becoming chief of staff in 1950 he felt ill at ease with the much older and more technically trained officers of the Indian Army:

> The commander of the Calcutta military area . . . was a big man with a long moustache. He asked me how old I was and I replied that I was 31. He laughed . . . and said that he had served in the military for more years than I had been alive. I felt rather slighted by that old Two-Star General.[12]

Although Nasution never raises it, his desertion from the KNIL might also have been on his mind. He writes of feeling slighted on a flight with a Dutch military aircrew from Makassar to Bali with Sultan Hamengku Buwono when nobody spoke with them apart from the steward.[13]

Nasution had never lived in steamy and untidy Jakarta and he felt uneasy there. The coastal city had never been attractive like Bandung or possessed a *kraton* palace district like the smaller court city of Yogyakarta. After the Japanese occupation and the tumultuous years of revolution, buildings across the city were run down with faded and moldy whitewashed exteriors. Their ground floors were often obscured by a tangle of pop-up food stalls, makeshift shelters for the homeless and informal micro businesses.

He and Sunarti often spent weekends in Bandung and he was so reluctant to return to the capital that he sometimes stayed on afterward, spending his time "walking alone in the places I enjoyed in the colonial and Japanese periods while mulling something over in my mind but feeling that my brain was clogged up and at a dead end." He writes revealingly of experiencing a stress-related "crisis," and seems to have experienced symptoms of depression after the emotional intensity of the guerrilla campaign and the military administration:

> It was a big contrast with the period of guerrilla warfare, the period of Java Command Headquarters, which was so filled with activity, although not actual operational activity but outlining, instructing, coordinating etc. within the framework of overall resistance.[14]

He recalls gaining satisfaction from helping friends who had similar experiences, but was perhaps speaking mostly about himself and his own situation:

> There were . . . some who felt ill at ease with their outward appearance as heads [of organisations] because at home they were in the opposite position.[15]

It is possible that Nasution's reference to being in "an opposite position" at home might have described difficulties in his own marriage. For her part, Sunarti writes that she always encouraged Nasution to spend the extra days in Bandung:

> to calm his mind in dealing with the disorder that continued to exist, not only in West Java but in other regions as well. I always advised him that it was necessary to calm his mind in such ways. I saw many officers who felt ill and regularly went to the doctor but really didn't have anything physically wrong with them.[16]

There were frictions between Nasution and Simatupang, often due to perceptions that Simatupang was intervening in the running of the army. In line with Simatupang's claim that Nasution had been an admirer of Baldur von Shirach, he and other officers close to the PSI[17] seem to have been wary of Nasution because of "Bonapartist" tendencies.[18]

Simatupang appears to have been more robust and self-confident than Nasution. For example, he visited India on the way to the Round Table Conference in 1948 but appears to have experienced none of the feelings of insecurity that Nasution has described. Simatupang's background in the revolution was largely as a negotiator and he was present at all the major negotiations with the Dutch, including the Round Table Conference. Although he had some misgivings about the outcomes of this conference he appears to have been generally satisfied that the outcome had achieved all that was possible. As a "stakeholder" in the Round Table Conference he was committed to developing the international and Western-style army that both sides agreed to in principle.

Simatupang was sufficiently forthright in his opposition to militarism to ask Sukarno not to wear military uniform to avoid the experiences of militarist states like imperial Germany where the Kaiser was never photographed in civilian clothes.[19] He writes that one of his "obsessions" in the early 1950s was to professionalize the army to avoid mistakes made in other countries where people's wars for independence had resulted in communism (China) or a never-ending cycle of coups (Latin America).[20]

Plans were made for Nasution to step down from his position of army chief of staff at the end of 1951 so that he could study for a year at the Netherlands

War College (*Hogere Krijgschool*).[21] Nasution wanted to pursue further military education[22] and Sunarti was keen to accompany him (her expenses were to be paid by Sunario Gondokusumo).[23] However, he suspected that the proposal had been inspired by Simatupang to remove him.[24] The proposed assignment was later amended to a study tour to a number of countries[25] and then cancelled due to rising tensions associated with an anti-parliament demonstration that became known as the October 17, 1952 Affair.

Nasution had to shape a national army out of the regular and irregular forces on the side of the republic and KNIL personnel who elected to join the TNI. A major demobilization program was put in place that was reasonably successful (particularly in the case of students returning to their interrupted studies) but far too many wished to remain within the army. Unfortunately, many of them lacked the skills to gain employment of similar status in civilian life or to fit into a professional army that no longer relied so much upon guerrilla warfare.

With the departure of the Dutch the country was divided into seven territorial regions (*Tentara dan Territorium*—T&T)[26] whose locally sourced commanders were accustomed to operating with a very high degree of autonomy. During the revolution, the army headquarters staff had often found it difficult to control these commands and the situation was exacerbated when Sudirman was critically ill and Nasution recognized that local commanders and officials had to be left to "determine their activities for themselves."[27] The regional commanders and senior officers on the army general staff were similar in terms of age and combat experience, adding to Nasution's feelings of frustration and helplessness.[28]

> A meeting of unit or regional commanders at that time was like a meeting of "shareholders" in the Republic, with the result that not only was I subjected to criticism but the Cabinet and the President were criticized freely. Tendencies towards *bapakism* [patron-client relationships] and warlordism were a reality.[29]

Relations between the new army and KNIL forces that had not yet been demobilized continued to be poor after the recognition of sovereignty. Many on the Dutch side felt that they had been militarily superior in the field but stabbed in the back by the United States and other countries who had pressured the Dutch to relinquish their colony. In the cities where Dutch forces had congregated, there were clashes with the army "that had to be handled quickly so they didn't explode into armed conflict between the two armies."[30] The most serious of these occurred in January 1950 when a former Dutch captain, "Turk" Westerling, staged a revolt in Bandung that resulted in many army casualties. Westerling had created a well-armed force (the *Angkatan*

Perang Ratu Adil—APRA—*Army of the Just King*—of some 800 men) with the support, albeit hesitant, of the *negara* of Pasundan.[31]

The Dutch garrison commander in Bandung persuaded Westerling's force to leave Bandung but some began to infiltrate Jakarta (with the backing of the pro-Dutch sultan Hamid of Pontianak) to stage a coup. However, Westerling's forces were driven out of Jakarta and he was subsequently spirited out of Indonesia by the Netherlands military.[32]

Meanwhile, in West Java and the border areas of West and Central Java the *Darul Islam* movement, given impetus when the *Siliwangi* Division departed to Surakarta under the terms of the Renville Agreement, gathered intensity. To complicate matters, remnants of Westerling's forces began to cooperate with *Darul Islam* elements in the West Java hinterland.[33] Suspicion of Dutch nationals in Indonesia grew and was often directed at members of the Netherlands Military Mission (NMM) who were disparagingly referred to as *Nederlandsch Mata-Mata* (NMM—Dutch Spies).[34]

Nasution was cooperating with the NMM.[35] For example, in October 1951 he announced plans for the Netherlands to provide the bulk of military training to Indonesia. One hundred officers per year were to be sent abroad for training, 90 percent of whom were to go to the Netherlands. Places for Indonesian officers at the *Hogere Krijgschool* were to be increased from two to four.[36]

However, Nasution was in a difficult position in his dealings with the mission because of his sponsorship of renewed reorganization and rationalization of the army (that was often perceived to be in line with Dutch objectives to exert control over the army), his KNIL background, and his wife's Dutch ancestry. He was friendly with the head of the mission, Major General Pereira,[37] but appears to have tried to keep his distance from the Dutch in public and only attended those NMM functions where he felt that it was essential for him to do so.[38]

However, Sunarti was understandably popular with the NMM officers because of her ancestry and fluent Dutch. The ambiguity of her position and those of her mother and her relations is evident in her recollection of Dick, a relative of her mother who had been sent to Indonesia with the Dutch Army:

> He longed to become an Indonesian citizen but because he had been in the Netherlands Army he could not gain entry to ours. When the Westerling Affair broke out he secretly assisted Major Jubroh, the Assistant for Intelligence of the *Siliwangi* Division.[39]

With her mother accompanying her in the Saint Carolus Hospital, Sunarti gave birth to their first child, a girl named Hendrianti (Yanti), on February 24, 1952. This was an occasion for great joy, particularly after she had miscarried at the outset of the first guerrilla war in 1947. From the Netherlands, Dick sent her a pram and fabric for clothing: "He was really very close to our family."[40]

Difficulties with their marriage that Nasution hints at[41] might have stemmed in part from her attempts to persuade him to accept invitations from Dutch officers that were extended to her but included her husband:

> But this attracted unfounded gossip regarding my husband. It was said that Pak Nas enjoyed mixing with the Dutch officers and had close relations with them. There were even those who said that this had led to the negotiations regarding the future of West Irian being unable to be concluded.[42]

Sunarti seems not to have fully understood at first that this was not a good time for Nasution to be associated with the officers from the Military Mission. Nationalism was at its zenith and many Indonesians felt deep repugnance for the former colonial power. Dutch names for localities and their monuments that had been expunged by the Japanese were not restored and the new Indonesian rulers soon exhibited a lack of regard for much of the built environment that the Dutch were handing over. Unlike Hanoi and Ho Chi Minh City in nearby Vietnam, the substantial old Dutch colonial buildings in what is now called the Old City (*Kota Lama*) soon decayed in the tropical conditions and they remain largely in that state today.

The new authorities seemed only to be interested in maintaining a small number of prestigious buildings from that era with any degree of care. Chief among these was the president's palace, now known as the *Istana Negara* or State Palace, which had housed a succession of Dutch governors general, and the beautiful old Bogor Palace, just outside Jakarta. Both were highly prized by Sukarno who clearly enjoyed living in them.

Unlike the former British colonies of Singapore and Malaysia, where English is still widely spoken, this expunging of memories also applied to the Dutch language that had been used in the archipelago for centuries. It was still spoken in private by many older educated Indonesians but no longer understood by those who grew up after 1950.

Within a short time, there was not a single Dutch street name left in Jakarta and all the suburbs with Dutch names had been given Indonesian ones. For example, the Jakarta suburb of Weltevgreden was renamed Menteng and Meester Kornelis, where the Dutch had a military school, was now called Jatinegara.

The venerable old *Hotel Des Indes* (The Indies), once a rival to the Raffles in Singapore and the Empire and Orient in Penang, had been renamed the *Duta Indonesia* (Indonesian Envoy). The name was apparently chosen to save replacing the crockery which was emblazoned with the initials H.D.I. Frank Clune stayed there in 1940:

> Talk about the vast open spaces of Australia! These rooms in the Des Indes are quarter-acre blocks and air-conditioned to a temperature of 72 degrees, which is very welcome, as Batavia is only 7 degrees 30 minutes south of the Equator.[43]

This Jakarta landmark had already declined significantly by late 1947 when Tom Critchley, stayed there:

> There was no air conditioning, running water was only available at stipulated times and disruption of electricity was frequent. The beds were encased in fly screen, or I should say mosquito screen cages—we referred to them as "meat safes." Breakfast was usually served cold. We believed the eggs must have been fried the night before. But Kirby was particularly concerned about the cold toast and insisted on the importance of it being brought to the table hot. A day or two later when its arrival was delayed, we went to investigate and found the cook taking the bread as soon as it was toasted and slapping it quickly under his arm pit. We lost all interested in warm toast.[44]

This powerful reminder of Dutch privilege was one of the first buildings to be confiscated in political unrest that made life in Indonesia impossible for the Dutch in the late 1950s and inexperienced management accelerated its decline. Describing it as once "one of the great hotels of the East," Critchley writes "I regret it was razed and not preserved like some other landmarks like Raffles Hotel in Singapore." Its demolition was a terrible loss to the architectural fabric of the city.[45]

Of course, there were no longer any Dutch public statues. A large one of the colonial governor Jan Pieterszoon Coen that had been a landmark in the city had been removed and destroyed by the Japanese occupation forces.

Nasution writes that frictions soon emerged between the army leadership and sections of the parliament over the NMM. He recalls that members of parliament continually attacked him over the mission, even though it had been created by those who had taken part in the Round Table Conference.[46]

Signs of resentment toward the presence of the NMM also began to appear in the press. For example, on February 7, 1951 the Bandung daily *Pikiran Rakyat* reported that students at the Army Officers' Training Centre in Bandung had questioned the speaker of parliament, Mr. Sartono, on why Dutch officers were still being permitted to give lectures in the Dutch language.[47]

On March 10, 1951 Simatupang wrote in the Ministry of Defense journal *Perwira* that with the failure of discussions between the Netherlands and Indonesia on Irian, the Indonesian Armed Forces needed to approach the issue of the Netherlands Military Mission on the basis of whether Indonesia gained or benefited from its presence. Simatupang's view was that Indonesia needed to look at the matter rationally and without sentiment and that it should be separated from the Irian dispute. Although the foundation of Indonesia's army was "people's defence" and some were asking whether use of the Dutch military would distance the armed forces from their origins, he believed that Indonesia had much to gain because the Dutch language was the most widely used foreign language in Indonesia and cooperation with a small power like the Netherlands was more in line with Indonesia's foreign policy of non-alignment with any of the major powers.[48]

The future of the system of "people's defence" was also raised within the context of an emerging controversy over Nasution's plans for reorganization and rationalization. By March 1952 two Masyumi-led cabinets (the Natsir and Sukiman cabinets) had been replaced by a PNI-led Wilopo cabinet (April 1952–June 1953). The proposed rationalization program became a difficult issue for the Wilopo cabinet from the time of its formation.

Nasution had "learnt a great deal" from his previous experience of attempting to reorganize and rationalize the army in Yogyakarta and he had made sure that the cabinet and the minister for defense authorized his plans. Nevertheless, he was again a target for criticism because he "was indeed their architect."[49]

Nasution proposed that the army be reduced in number from 200,000 to 100,000 men, comprising a force of 100 battalions. The new "core" army was to be mobile and highly trained. It was to rely on a large militia (based on compulsory national service) that could be activated in time of emergency and volunteer groups such as the revolutionary-period Village Guerrilla Troops (*Pager Desa*).[50]

He was criticized within the army and the parliament on the grounds that he was seeking to downgrade the TNI's identity as a revolutionary force that was close to the people and had engaged in people's defense. In fact, his plans were remarkably consistent with those he had developed for three tiers of forces in 1948, with the more professionally trained one being a cadre army capable of carrying out more mobile and offensive operations.

Many army personnel became concerned at the emphasis of the *re-dan-ra* program on selecting officers for retention or demobilization based upon educational level and professional military qualifications. Officers who felt that they had served the country well during the revolution but lacked formal qualifications were incensed by Nasution's warning "that those who did not meet the requirements for higher positions must be prepared to fill lower positions."[51]

Suhario Padmodiwiryo writes that the Dutch term *klein en hanteerbaar* (small and manageable) came to be used disparagingly to describe efforts of this type to downsize and professionalize the army.[52] This officer also recalls hearing that the *re-dan-ra* program meant that the Army Headquarters Territorial Section, where he worked, would be closed:

What this point of view amounted to was disagreeing with the TNI's total people's defence system and it was in line with the KNIL's ethos as a police army that was used against the people of Indonesia during the Dutch colonial period.[53]

A leading army solidarity maker and distant relative of Sukarno,[54] Colonel Bambang Supeno, led the resistance to this early 1950s iteration of *re-dan-ra*. McVey writes that he began to advocate retention of "a mass force that possessed close ties to its civilian surroundings and was oriented towards local defence."[55]

An indication of the small size of the Indonesian elite at the time is that Supeno was also related to Sunarti. He had supported Nasution's plans for *re-dan-ra* in 1948 and served as Nasution's chief of staff for territorial affairs during the period of military administration.[56]

Supeno was particularly affected by Nasution's plan to build a Staff and Command School. He had already established a *Candradimuka* Academy near Bandung, the term *Candradimuka* being the name of the volcanic crater in which *Gatot Kaca*, the mythological hero of the Indonesianized Ramayana / Mahabharata epics, forged his strength and fighting spirit before flying out to engage in battle. Supeno's choice of this name indicated his concern to draw upon indigenous cultural influences to reinforce the ethos of the revolutionary TNI.

The emphasis of the *Candrimuka* Academy was on maintaining *semangat*. It was no doubt intended also to counter the influence of the Netherlands Military Mission, and officers with a KNIL background were never invited to participate in its courses.[57] A lasting influence of the academy is the *Sapta Marga* or Seven Oaths of the Indonesian officer corps that was developed there. Although the academy was favored with visits by President Sukarno,[58] Nasution moved to disband it in 1952 so that the limited funds available to the army could be diverted to a more conventional staff and command college.[59]

Supeno proposed directly to President Sukarno that Nasution be sacked and received an encouraging reaction. He began to campaign within the officer corps for his removal as chief of staff and gained strong support from the Officers' Association of the Republic of Indonesia (*Ikatan Perwira Republik Indonesia*—IPRI) that at the time was chaired by the East Java commander, Bambang Sugeng.[60]

Supeno was carpeted before senior officers but walked out after being strongly criticized. Undeterred, he again went outside the chain of command by writing to the prime minister and the minister for defense and sending copies to the president and Zainul Baharuddin, the chairman of the parliamentary committee on defense. Four days later Nasution suspended Supeno from duties.

Simatupang, Nasution and Hamengku Buwono arranged a meeting with the president to seek clarification of reports that he favored Nasution's removal. Simatupang records that he did nearly all the talking from the defense / military side in what became a very heated exchange that led to an irrevocable breach between Simatupang and the president and hastened the processes that led to the affair.

The president eventually admitted to having spoken to Supeno and indicated that he was not opposed to removing Nasution. Simatupang flatly told the president that he had made a terrible mistake that could have profoundly negative consequences for the democratization process in general and the professionalization of the army. When the president angrily claimed that Simatupang was trying to "corner" him the meeting was over. Simatupang declined to shake hands on leaving and appears to have slammed the door on the way out (he later wrote that while others recalled this, he could not remember doing so).[61]

In September and early October claims were made in the parliament by "solidarity makers" that the army leadership was failing to pay due regard to *semangat* and tradition, that KNIL and PSI-associated officers were being favored, and that Bambang Supeno's suspension was illegal. Zainul Baharuddin moved an unsuccessful motion of no-confidence in the Ministry for Defense and the armed forces and army leadership and demanded changes to their policies. Sukarno exerted influence behind the scenes and the motion was worded in more subtle terms that called for a commission to review the defense organization with a view to making improvements in both leadership and organization.[62] Nasution and officers loyal to him became bitterly resentful at what they regarded as insulting treatment that amounted to meddling in internal military affairs and considered bringing some sort of pressure to bear upon Sukarno to dissolve the parliament.[63]

Nasution writes that in the days leading up to October 17 he gradually stepped back from a leading role because he became aware that some of the officers involved wished to remove him as chief of staff.[64] On October 17, a group of officers drew up a list of points to be conveyed to Sukarno the following day, which Nasution "after some procrastination" signed.[65] Meanwhile, a close Nasution ally from his Java Command Headquarters days, Brigadier General Dr. Mustopo, arranged for demonstrators to assemble outside the palace. A dentist by profession and head of the army dental service, Mustopo had skills in this area, having mobilized underworld elements in the fight against the Dutch. He had close links with village gangs in the Jakarta underworld and some were paid for taking part in the demonstration.[66] On October 17, Mustopo's "spontaneous" civilian supporters assembled at the Presidential Palace together with army units. In a show of force, guns were directed at the building⁶⁷ while a group of officers met with Sukarno to demand changes to the parliament.

As was the case when he had met with the president together with Simatupang and the Sultan, Nasution did little talking and his seeming lack of self-assuredness and assertiveness in these encounters bore similarities with his earlier role in the *Bandung Lautan Api* affair. Again, he seems to have been carried along by subordinates who made the running; a pattern of behavior that was to be repeated at other crucially important times in his life.

Sutoko started by explaining that the army leadership was concerned about the composition and behavior of the parliament and called for the president to form a new assembly before handing Sukarno a petition signed by sixteen officers. Colonels Simbolon (Commander T&T I/North Sumatra) and Kawilarang (Commander T&T III/*Siliwangi*) then spoke along similar lines. The president reminded the delegation that the army should not involve itself in politics but promised to discuss the issues they raised with the cabinet and others.⁶⁸ Sukarno then went to the front of the palace and employed his considerable prestige and oratorical skills to persuade the demonstrators to disband. They duly did so and army personnel were withdrawn.

That afternoon the army banned several newspapers, arrested six parliamentarians and imposed a curfew but the rebellion soon fizzled out. After a few days, all the detainees were set free and restrictions lifted.⁶⁹

There are varying opinions on the extent of Nasution's involvement in the October 17, 1952 affair. Feith believes that at first Nasution planned to use *Siliwangi* forces to mount a coup but was opposed by Simatupang and the Sultan and deterred by indications that Sukarno would not endorse a program of arrests that he intended to implement.⁷⁰ Ruth McVey notes Feith's generally sympathetic treatment of Nasution and his assertion that the incident was planned by a small group within the general staff and the Jakarta city commander.⁷¹ While agreeing that this could indeed have been the case, she cites a tendency of officers to "feign reluctance while quietly encouraging impatience on their subordinates' part." She further notes that in confronting Sukarno at the palace the spokesman for the officers' group was Nasution's old ally, Lieutenant Colonel Sutoko, while two regional commanders, Colonels Simbolon and Kawilarang, made supporting statements. "Nasution's own formal role was only to introduce the speakers."⁷²

Sunarti believed that Nasution's role in the affair was a minor one:

According to Kemal Idris [a prominent guerrilla fighter and then army General who took part in the protest], Pak Nas's role was only a minor one. It was Bambang Supeno who caused the problem but Pak Nas said that he would take responsibility by resigning. Even though he didn't do it, he felt that he had to take responsibility.⁷³

There has been considerable debate on the legality and propriety of the October 17 affair. For example, Crouch writes that although the affair was on the surface an attempt to redress a situation in which civilian politicians were meddling in purely military affairs, those involved "cannot have been unaware, however, that the dissolution of parliament at their behest would have placed them in a very strong position from which to make further political moves."[74] McVey contends that "it seems clear that the military chiefs did not intend their move as a bid for direct army rule, but sought, maximally, an arrangement whereby Sukarno would serve as the leader and legitimator of a regime which would provide a much-enhanced role for the army."[75] Simatupang has written that the armed forces leadership never intended to mount a coup when it staged the October 17, 1952 affair because this would have led to an endless cycle of coups.[76] Nasution himself later used the term "semi coup" in "informal" conversations because his aim was to have the provisional parliament disbanded while retaining the leadership of Sukarno and Hatta.[77] That the discontented officers fell at the hurdle of negotiating with Sukarno was a reminder of the president's considerable prestige and political skills.

There were divisions within the section of the leadership that mounted the action and large sections of the officer corps opposed it. Rivalries within the officer corps as a whole subsequently intensified with senior officers lining up as for or against the affair. Three regional commanders, Colonel Suwondho in East Java, Colonel Gatot Subroto in South Sulawesi, and Lieutenant Colonel Kosasih in South Sumatra, were overthrown or detained by subordinates who opposed their alignment with the officers involved in the affair.

By the end of the year Nasution had resigned from the appointment of army chief of staff and was placed on the nonactive list where he would remain until his reinstatement in November 1955. In 1954 Simatupang's Armed Forces the chief of staff position was abolished.

Sunarti recalls that she had a premonition that he would suffer a defeat as tensions rose before the affair took place.[78] In its aftermath, Nasution entered what he called his "leper period."[79] He was warier of Sukarno than before and his treatment at the hands of the parliament greatly reinforced his long-standing dislike of civilian politicians "meddling" in army affairs.

While Nasution had failed to assert himself in confrontations with Sukarno and was intensely frustrated at his failure to reorganize and rationalize the army, behind the scenes in the comfort and security of his home in Menteng he embarked upon another course of action that he would pursue throughout the rest of his life. As the army entered a period of virtual leadership paralysis in which its material and human resources declined sharply, he began to work assiduously at burnishing his reputation as a military strategist who had developed formidable "people's resistance" strategies in the guerrilla war against the Dutch.

Like Nasution's reorganization and rationalization programs of the revolution, the debate in 1952 had in fact been over differing visions of how best to achieve an army based upon "people's resistance." Nasution wished to preserve the people's base of the army, while professionalising it, through a system of militia reserves and trained civilians. On the other hand, Bambang Supeno appears to have seen the army as filling both the regular and militia functions.[80]

Guy Pauker writes that between "1950 and 1958" Indonesian Army personnel appeared to have forgotten the lessons of guerrilla warfare they had learned in the struggle against the Dutch.[81] However, the territorial structures of the revolutionary period in parts of Java and Sumatra had not disappeared with the recognition of sovereignty and were extended throughout the country when the TNI spread into the previously Dutch-occupied areas in the early 1950s.

Indeed, Nasution writes that the army's territorial organization was heavily involved in installing the republic's *pamong praja* and *pamong desa* administrations in West Java before the Dutch ceded sovereignty. He remarks that the Dutch sometimes referred accusingly to "Nasution's shadow administration" in complaints that the TNI was exceeding its authority by shadowing local Dutch-sponsored administrations in territories that they had not ceded to the Republic. On one occasion, the conduct of a UNCI-brokered meeting within the stately art deco surrounds of Bandung's Savoy Homan Hotel was disrupted when a Dutch representative angrily walked out of over the issue, prompting an apology from the UN military representative.[82]

Nasution's account is supported by a September 1949 Australian Department of External Affairs report complaining of Republican "interference" in the civil administration of the federal areas of Central and East Java, and in Pasundan [West Java]:

> In Pasundan [West Java] they [the Dutch] have said that they will garrison their troops by the end of the month but this will probably depend on the outcome of their present demand that the Republic withdraw its administration. In East Java, the Dutch are pressing for the Republic's complete military and civil withdrawal. The F.C.A. [Federalists] are supporting the Dutch, claiming that the presence of Republican administrations is inconsistent with the *Negara* status of Pasundan and East Java as recognized by the Republic at the Inter-Indonesian Conference [a meeting between the Republic and the various *negara*s held in Yogyakarta from 19–22 July 1949]. The Republicans appear genuinely anxious that a withdrawal on their part from Pasundan and East Java will considerably strengthen the positions of the *Darul Islam* and Tan Malaka groups, both of which are opposed to the Hatta Government and to the R.T.C [Round Table Conference].[83]

That the army intended to retain links with its "people's resistance" origins after the transfer of sovereignty is evident in the command structures that it introduced from late 1949. The seven territorial commands were intended to carry out guerrilla warfare independent of command and provisions in the event of attack. They were comprised of both combat troops and a military administrative unit capable of taking over administrative and political functions in the event of war.[84]

In principle, the troops in these regional commands were to be drawn from the ethnic groups in the areas in which they operated. A number of regiments were formed which had particular areas allocated to them while military district commands had the primary task of liaison with local populations. Regiments were allocated to particular territories while military district commands had the primary responsibility of liaison with civilian populations.

Another indication that the army intended to remain in touch with its revolutionary origins was the establishment of the territorial section within army headquarters[85] where Suhario Padmodiwiryo was assigned as deputy head of territorial affairs. While the *Tentara dan Territorium* operated in the regions, the section was to liaise at a national level with civil authorities. It was to draw up plans for territorial defense and was to ensure good relations between army units and local communities.[86]

Nasution's ally in taming the *laskar* in the Priangan area and the October 17 Affair, Lieutenant Colonel Sutoko, was in charge of territorial affairs in the army headquarters. Sutoko was one of two deputies to Nasution (the other was Colonel Suprapto). Suprapto looked after operational affairs while Sutoko was in charge of territorial affairs and intelligence.

According to Suhario Padmodiwiryo, the propensity of Suharto-era territorial affairs officers to intervene in politics was evident from that time. He states that following the transfer of sovereignty the section attracted officers with a family background in the *pamong/pangreh praja* and that, like their forebears in Dutch colonial times, they busied themselves collecting information on the political parties throughout Indonesia.[87]

The section conducted courses for army officers on territorial affairs in Bandung, the first of which was run in January 1951.[88] In his biography, Padmodiwiryo writes that when he attended advanced infantry officer training in the United States in 1956 he felt that he did not have much to learn from the American instructors on one subject offered in the curriculum: the planning and operation of a military government.[89]

In July 1951, the *Siliwangi* Division opened its own training course for territorial officers. Present at the opening ceremony were the Divisional/*Tentara dan Territorium* III Commander, Colonel Sadikin and representatives of the West Java provincial administration. Both the military and civilian guests stressed the need for relations between the army and the community.

All officers of the *Tentara dan Territorium* were to undertake this training, which was to take place in four phases of one and a half months. Fifty percent of the course material was to be in the area of military studies while the other half was to include constitutional law, people's defense, and general knowledge. Apart from military instructors, lecturers were to be drawn from the *pamong praja*, the police and the Department of Information.[90]

The newspapers of the early 1950s indicate some concern to maintain the strategy of "total people's resistance." Announcing plans to demobilize 80,000 military personnel on June 24, 1950, an army spokesman (speaking on behalf of Nasution) said that with the cessation of the conflict with the Dutch, large numbers of personnel who had been mobilized were now no longer required and would be returned to civilian life. The government had determined that Indonesia's defense policy would be based on total people's defense:

> This does not mean that every member of our populace will be armed. Rather, what is meant by that is the realisation of the greatest possible defence potential based on the strength of the people. This system can be arranged and directed towards a militia system that provides for every citizen to have an obligation to defend the country. Meanwhile, our army which will be the core of this total people's defence will undergo training and improvement.
>
> if it eventuates that in the coming years we are dragged into conflict, with the existence of total people's defence we will have put into place preparations for a return to guerrilla tactics . . . a defence that is based on total people's defence is the most appropriate for Indonesia because it is clear that in the next three to five years Indonesia will not possibly be able to develop armed forces that are of a similar standard to those of our neighbouring countries around the Pacific.[91]

When the Hatta cabinet resigned in August 1950 the new defense minister, A. Halim,[92] expressed concern that the army remain close to the people in an "order of the day":

> Our armed forces must continue to foster close and good relations with the people and the community, so that our army can truly be called a real people's army. Most of you know from personal experience that the guerrilla war could not possibly have been waged to the finish if [the army] had not been supported and upheld by the general public. Because of this, in carrying out further steps towards the perfection and consolidation of the armed forces, [your] close relations with the people should never be forgotten.[93]

On October 4, 1950—in preparation for the first commemoration of the Battle of Surabaya since the recognition of sovereignty—Colonel Gatot Subroto's Central Java *Tentara dan Territorium* announced that all the village heads (*lurah*s) from throughout the province who had assisted the army during the guerrilla war would be assembled, entertained and thanked for their service.[94]

In December 1950, the government linked the maintenance of a defense policy of "total people's resistance" with the country's nonaligned or "free and active" foreign policy. "Government circles" stated that it was important that the foreign and defense policies be intertwined. Referring to the need to form an army rapidly during the revolution, the involvement of the army in security duties since the transfer of sovereignty, and the increasing tensions that were evident in the international arena, the "government circles" said that

> For these reasons "total people's resistance" will remain Indonesia's defence principle until such time that the Indonesian armed forces are organised in such a manner that they can confront an external threat.[95]

A defense policy of "total people's resistance" was also compatible with the government's nonaligned foreign policy because it would not entail large-scale purchasing of weapons from countries with military alliances and entanglements. The "government circles" quoted above went on to state unequivocally that the government would not become reliant upon international arms providers as that would compromise its nonaligned policy.[96]

In January 1951, Gatot Mangkupradja, the political figure who had in 1943 proposed the establishment of PETA, linked the total people's defense policy with a free and active foreign policy in a series of articles in the Bandung daily *Pikiran Rakyat*. He idealized the territorial links of the forces established by the Japanese, such as PETA and Hizbullah, and urged the army to reestablish what he recalled as warm relationships between these forces and the people. Gatot laid claim to a continuing relationship with the villages who had protected townsfolk and the army during the guerrilla conflicts but was scathing in his criticism of those who he asserted had reclaimed their high offices and who "have not only never visited the humble dwellings of the peasant farmers but have never even sent a letter of thanks. Those who sit upon the thrones of high office cannot, of course, hear what these farmers have to say but my comrades and I who continue to enjoy family-like relationships with them hear and feel the disappointments of these small people, even though they do not express them openly."[97]

Three days later Lieutenant Colonel Saragih, territorial affairs officer in Territory III/*Siliwangi* lamented attempts to separate the army from the people by those who were upset by the army's attempts to clamp down on militia groups.[98]

President Sukarno joined in the call for the continuation of people's defense in his address to commemorate the Battle of Surabaya:

a system of defence in which, alongside the armed forces, the people will be prepared to take part in the defence of their homeland in an organised manner.[99]

The threats to security that the army faced in the early 1950s were all from within the country and required a counterinsurgency response. Regional insurrections began to emerge after the federal structure, which the Round Table Conference had put in place, was disbanded in 1950 in favor of a unitary state.

In West Java, *Darul Islam* forces continued to struggle for the establishment of an Islamic state and over time were joined by insurgencies in parts of Central Java (*Angkatan Umat Islam*—Forces of the Muslim People), South Sumatra (where in January 1952 forces led by Kahar Muzakar declared this region to be part of the *Darul Islam* established in West Java), Kalimantan (where Ibnu Hadjar established the *Darul Islam*-aligned *Kesatuan Rakyat Tertindas*—Union of Oppressed People in 1950), and Aceh (where forces led by Daud Beureu'eh aligned themselves with the West Java *Darul Islam* movement from September 1953).

The institutionalization of the army's role as a mobilizer of the people for counterinsurgency operations began to take shape in the mid-1950s in West Java, where the *Darul Islam* insurrection continued and intensified after the transfer of sovereignty. In 1956 the commander of the Tasikmalaya-based 11th Infantry Regiment (East Priangan region), Major Suwarto, formulated an integrated military, economic and sociopolitical strategy to separate *Darul Islam* insurgents from local communities.[100] His ideas on counterinsurgency gained wide attention in April 1956 when he announced a "Five-Year Plan" to end the *Darul Islam* rebellion.[101]

However, the newspapers of the period indicate that the army's involvement in a range of nonmilitary affairs aimed at winning the "hearts and minds" of populations where insurgencies took place, and the mobilization of civilians for counterinsurgency purposes, began four years before Suwarto's plan was announced.

On April 25, 1950, the commander of the *Siliwangi* Division, Colonel Sadikin, ordered that with effect from May 1, all military personnel in his division were to donate 1 percent of their salaries to a Community Development Implementing Agency to repay the great debt of honor that military personnel owed to the people.

> it was the people who from the time of the independence struggle provided necessities for forward scouts and the military, who provided guidance, food, places to sleep, etc. throughout the guerrilla times, who were casualties of battle and cleansing actions, with the result that now hundreds of thousands of them are suffering, have no houses and nothing to eat.[102]

Previously, on March 22, the West Java Commander had put forward a proposal to construct housing for people displaced by the conflict between the army and *Darul Islam* forces that was a precursor to more coordinated efforts by the army to carry out civic mission projects.

> Villagers who previously evacuated to the towns are now, since the TNI carried out cleansing operations, returning to their villages. Their situation is very sad as their houses have been burned and they no longer possess farming implements. Sadikin hoped that attention would be given to this matter.[103]

In May 1951 *Pikiran Rakyat* reported that the people of the East Priangan area had ceased to be passive bystanders and were assisting the army in the fight by the army against *Darul Islam* insurgents.

> The passive attitude of the people [that was apparent] when the army began its pursuit and cleansing [operation] has now changed to active participation to guarantee security and assist the army in carrying out its task. . . . the change in attitude has not only been achieved by information programs, particularly concerning religion, but given impetus by the quick reactions of army and police units towards any acts on the part of the [insurgent] gangs. Moreover, thanks to the wise training of troops by commanders, interaction between the army and the people that in the beginning was often mutually hurtful has given rise to a positive spirit of mutual assistance. This is evident in no fewer than 8,500 villagers taking part in pursuing and surrounding insurgents to the south of Tasikmalaya with satisfying results from 10 to 17 May.[104]

A June 1951 report describes the mobilization of 1,000 villagers in a cleansing operation on the island of Kalimantan. Village officials were tasked with sending seven of their villagers to participate in the operation for periods of one week at a time.[105]

In August 1951, army personnel and villagers in the Bogor area of West Java staged a people's defense exercise involving 5,000 villagers that was attended by the police, *pamong praja* and the press. The somewhat idealistic—and perhaps unrealistic—exercise scenario began with a group of "insurgents" armed with Lee Enfield rifles, Sten guns and machetes entering a village with the purpose of seeking food. The village head struck a gong as a signal for villagers to mobilize. Armed with sharpened bamboo poles and machetes the villagers surrounded the insurgents, yelling out "advance" and "we are ready." After being cut off from their line of retreat by soldiers who had heard the alarm, the insurgents fired their weapons wildly and soon ran out of ammunition. Finally, they were captured by the villagers.[106]

Nasution's consciousness of the importance of "total people's resistance" to the identity of the army and the medium-term defense and security of the nation is evident throughout his writings. His account of the "infiltration" of the army's territorial system into Dutch areas has been discussed. When he visited India in 1950 he was acutely conscious of the differences between the Indian and Indonesian armies because of their differing backgrounds:

> I asked them how much time was set aside for them to live together with the people, something that I regarded as very basic in the education of an officer. They answered that in fact that was not a part of their planning. I explained how we had lived and struggled together with the people in wartime, and were accommodated and fed by them. One of them replied firmly that they did not desire such a situation precisely because they did not wish to "burden" the people.[107]

By mid-1951 Nasution was seeking to reemphasize "total people's resistance" within the officer corps. He had issued his plans for a force of 100 battalions in a booklet that outlined some basic problems with which the army would have to deal, the system of training envisaged (from recruit training school to the staff college) and the salary system. However, the opposition to these plans that culminated in the October 17, 1952 affair was beginning to mount.

He writes that a speech by President Sukarno on Independence Day 1952 on the need to return to the spirit of the proclamation, including "a true national unity, and not just the unity of families or the unity of groups"[108] inspired him to conduct a series of lectures in the major cities and write articles in the army newspaper on total people's defense as the core identity of the army.

Using themes that were to be the bases of *Fundamentals of Guerrilla Warfare* he advocated a continuing focus on "total people's resistance" because "total people's warfare" was the form of conflict that typified the twentieth century. He decried the neglect of proper planning for "people's war" in the early stages of the revolution and stressed the need for leadership of such conflicts to be centralized, even though it was typically fought at local levels.

He placed his advocacy for "total people's resistance" within the context of the three types of forces he had recommended: the regular army as the mobile strike element, a reserve militia force that assisted and supported the regulars, and a trained civilian component.[109] He emphasized that there was no question of frontline forces being allocated exclusively either to conventional or guerrilla warfare but to both. Guerrilla warfare was defensive in nature and a regular conventional force was needed to take the offensive:

> guerrilla warfare, especially in a total context is very damaging both physically and psychologically with the result that its effects are very difficult to overcome. So, this is a very expensive form of warfare. Accordingly, we will not undertake

guerrilla warfare because we love it or because of a guerrilla "ideology," but because we are forced to, because our army is not yet sufficiently mature to undertake conventional warfare.[110]

By the end of the following year, when Nasution was still on the inactive list, he began to go further than advocating "people's defence" for technical reasons and to idealize the army's "total people's resistance" experience. In his *Fundamentals of Guerrilla Warfare,* he took up his arguments from 1951, asserting that it was still necessary to rely upon guerrilla warfare.

He declared that it would be some ten to fifteen years before Indonesia could hope to develop an army of international standard and fifteen years to build such a navy. Even then, Indonesia would lack the industrial base necessary to support a modern war machine and was unlikely to acquire one in the foreseeable future. For the next ten years, he argued, "guerrilla warfare will be the main item on our program of defence."[111] However, guerrilla forces had to have strong ideological convictions that conventional forces were unlikely to possess.[112]

Fundamentals of Guerrilla Warfare was something of a blueprint for the style of military intervention in politics that Nasution would later fashion. For example, Cribb has noted perceptively that it was in *Fundamentals of Guerrilla Warfare* that Nasution began to cite the continuing need to prepare for guerrilla warfare to formulate a role for the army that steered a middle course between being a mere instrument of the state and taking over the running of the country, hinting at an approach to intervention in politics that he would introduce in the 1950s and called the "middle way":

> A member of a guerrilla army, fighting for an ideology, can not only be used as a country's tool to be ordered to carry a gun; but also as an ideological pioneer, he must be active in ideological matters and in politics. How can he be the vanguard of an ideology or fight for a political aim if he is merely to be a tool to be ordered around with no voice in political decisions. It is not sufficient for him to be merely acquainted with political matters, but he must champion and propagandise them. An army which is merely a country's tool does not have the inner strength to withstand a violent guerrilla war.[113]

In another part of *Fundamentals of Guerrilla Warfare,* Nasution presaged another step that he would take, this time in late 1955, when he created an Inspectorate General of Territorial Affairs and People's Resistance, arguing that there should be an inspectorate with army headquarters to take charge of territorial affairs, such as reserve and guerrilla forces.[114] Relating this idea to the problem of reorganizing and rationalizing the army, he also stressed the need for further planning and training in territorial affairs.[115]

Penders and Sundhaussen have argued that Nasution's political orientation was based on "no other ideology but nationalism and the *Pancasila*."[116] However, their characterization does not sufficiently take into account Nasution's social conservatism, concern to maintain existing authority structures, distrust for politicians (particularly of the radical variety), and attachment to "traditional" authority structures and values.

As previously noted, such attitudes were strikingly evident in *Fundamentals of Guerrilla Warfare*. For example, Nasution criticized "petty politics" in favor of an amorphous all-embracing nationalism based on *Panca Sila* while seeking to extend into peace time a continuing leadership role for the army based upon guerrilla warfare remaining the basis of Indonesia's defense policy:

> For us, who for many years to come must concentrate on guerrilla and antiguerrilla warfare in which the army and the people's partisans must cooperate, it is not possible to say that a soldier is a soldier, and politics is politics, and that the soldier must keep away from politics.
>
> By using the word politics, we do not mean "petty politics" in the sense of parties and groups fighting only for positions in the government as is usually the case in peacetime. It is politics in the wider sense; it is statesmanship; it is fighting and defending a greater policy as is implied in the proclamation [of independence] and the preface of our original Constitution of 1945 [which includes the *Pancasila*]. With such ideas, we do not mean to say that the soldier must belong to this or that party, but that he must adhere to the wider political horizons.
>
> Involvement in the "petty politics" going on daily around them in the struggle for position is dangerous, and to avoid them they must be steeped in the proper political ideology.[117]

In *Fundamentals*, Nasution also attached considerable importance to an organic relationship between the army and the people that was to be expressed through links between the army and the "traditional" leaders of the people: the *pamong praja* and *pamong desa* village administrations. In his planning for "people's resistance" he had made detailed provision for army, *pamong praja*- and *pamong desa*-led guerrilla administrations that made no mention of the parties or representative institutions. In particular, he had praised and sought to maintain the authority of the *lurahs*.[118]

By the time he was placed on the inactive list, Nasution was already fully immersed in ways of thinking which predisposed him to develop systematically affinities between his strategies of "total people's resistance" and a "traditional" conservative vision of the proper relationship between state (including the military) and society. After the turmoil and despair of his first tenure as chief of staff, Nasution began to idealize the military administration of 1949. He portrayed it as a harmonious time in which there was an all-embracing sense of nationalism and an absence of divisive politics. Instead, the people were united under the leadership of the army and traditional authority structures.

It is easy to be cynical about Nasution's efforts to promote his role in the struggle against the Dutch and that of the army, but translations of his *Fundamentals of Guerrilla Warfare* became widely read in army training establishments around the world, including Australia. Knowledge of this was a source of pride for the army officer corps and no doubt added to their esprit de corps and sense of solidarity during the difficult times ahead.

He was to employ these concepts when he resumed the leadership of the army and began to deal it into the authoritarian structures that began to replace liberal democracy in the latter years of the 1950s. The army was to be a conservative counterweight to the Communist Party, and a renewal of its involvements with the people that Nasution had advocated during the struggle against the Dutch was to be its means of engaging in politics at the grassroots level.

In the midst of the turmoil that seemed to have thwarted his hopes for a military career he found solace in his home life with Sunarti:

> In our daily lives, if a problem was taking up a lot of his attention I never directly asked him about it. He had to relax and calm down first. Once had done so he would broach the subject himself. I never urged him to explain anything, even though I thought it important. Usually, when dealing with a problem he would pray for guidance.[119]

Like her mother, Sunarti was active in welfare work, principally for the families of soldiers. She had started to do so in 1948 when the *Siliwangi* Division was evacuated from West to Central Java under the terms of the Renville Agreement. After the Dutch took Yogyakarta she was centrally involved in organizing a new Army Wives Association (*Persatuan Isteri Tentara* or Persit) within Dutch-occupied Yogyakarta and became its deputy head. There she became friendly with Sukarno's second wife, Fatmawati, who had also been left behind in the city.

> On bicycles or by horse and cart we became active in visiting and helping the wives of soldiers who had been left behind when their husbands went to the battlefields. To console them, Fatmawati participated in visiting the widows of soldiers who were missing or had been killed.[120]

This relationship was to be important when Sukarno sought to take a second wife (he was divorced when he married Fatmawati) and then a third.

Sunarti and the Persit organization, which she chaired once Nasution became chief of staff, were strongly opposed to polygamy and Nasution was to institute strict laws that greatly limited the scope for army personnel to take more than one wife at a time. Nasution's staunchly puritanical outlook, backed by Sunarti, was to be a source of friction with the president when these two very dissimilar men forged an uneasy alliance from the mid-1950s.

NOTES

1. Feith, 1962 *Op.Cit.* This categorization is probably the best-known element of Feith's seminal work.
2. Ibid., p. 113.
3. Ibid.
4. Ibid., p. 132.
5. Ibid., p. 254.
6. Ibid., p. 171.
7. McKemmish, *Op. Cit*, p. 53.
8. McVey, 1971 *Op. Cit.*, p. 131. Feith, *Op. Cit.*, p. 171.
9. Although Feith notes that the leadership was not interested in creating a Western-style nonpolitical army and expected to be able to exert political pressure on the central government. Ibid., p. 209.
10. Kahin writes that the *negara*s, with the exception of East Sumatra where a social revolution by left-wing forces had seriously alienated local middle-class republicans, had attracted support largely from "members of the local aristocracies who feared loss of their political and economic positions under Dutch rule, and political opportunists dissatisfied with their positions under the Republic." Kahin, *Op. Cit.*, p. 352.
11. Nasution, *Memenuhi Panggilan Tugas,* Vol Two, *Op. Cit.*, p. 294.
12. Ibid., p. 217.
13. Ibid., p. 206.
14. Ibid., p. 211.
15. Ibid., p. 294.
16. Sunarti, *Op. Cit.*, p. 99.
17. McKemmish, *Op. Cit.*, p. 52, 53.
18. Ibid., pp. 52–54. Feith writes that the possibility of a military coup was raised in parliament on October 14, 1952, with a reference to the recent Nasser-Naguib coup in Egypt. Subsequently, *"Najib-najiban* ('doing a Naguib') became part of Jakarta's political vocabulary." Feith, *Op. Cit.*, p. 257.
19. Simatupang, 1996 *Op. Cit.*, p. 130.
20. Ibid., p. 130, 131.
21. "Keterangan Kol. Nasution: Milisi, pendidikan dan soal keamanan" ("Colonel Nasution Explains: Militias, education and the security problem"), *Merdeka*, October 22, 1951.

22. To overcome the gaps in his military knowledge Nasution began to read overseas military publications and visited army training centers (that had been handed over by the Dutch) to pick up what he could. Nasution, *Memenuhi Panggilan Tugas,* Vol Two, *Op. Cit.,* p. 209.

23. Nasution, *Memenuhi Panggilan Tugas,* Vol 2B, *Op. Cit.,* p. 193.

24. McKemmish, *Op. Cit.,* p. 54.

25. Nasution, *Memenuhi Panggilan Tugas,* Vol Three, *Op. Cit.,* p. 15, 16.

26. T&T I/Bukit Barisan(Aceh, North Sumatera, West Sumatera, Riau) T&T II/Sriwijaya(South Sumatera, Jambi)T&T III/Siliwangi(West Java) T&T IV/Diponegoro(Central Java)T&T V/Brawijaya(East Java)T&T VI/ Tanjungpura(Kalimantan)T&T VII/Wirabuana(Sulawesi, Moluccas—including Irian Jaya, Bali, West Lesser Sundas)

27. Nasution, *Memenuhi Panggilan Tugas,* Vol Two, *Op. Cit.,* p. 127.

28. "McVey, *Op. Cit.,* p.147.

29. Nasution, *Memenuhi Panggilan Tugas,* Vol Two, *Op. Cit.,* p. 258.

30. Ibid., p. 236.

31. Penders and Sundhaussen, *Op. Cit.,* p. 56.

32. Feith, *Op. Cit.,* p. 60, 61.

33. Nasution, *Memenuh Panggilan Tugas,*Vol Two, *Op. Cit.,* p. 236. Feith records that there were "frequent expressions of protest over reports that individual Dutchmen were involved in the bandit activity of Darul Islam." Feith, *Op. Cit.,* p. 287.

34. Ibid.252.

35. Ibid., p. 242.

36. "Keterangan Kol. Nasution: Milisi, pendidikan dan soal keamanan" ("Colonel Nasution Explains: Militias, education and the security problem"), *Merdeka,* October 22, 1951, *Op. Cit.*

37. McKemmish, *Op. Cit.,* p. 54, f.n. 17. Pereira was a former KNIL officer.

38. He did not attend lectures given by mission officers at the army headquarters (Padmodiwiryo, *Op. Cit.,* p. 396) and failed to attend the parade that transferred former KNIL officers to the TNI. Nasution, *Memenuhi Panggilan Tugas,* Vol Two, *Op. Cit.,* p. 250.

39. Sunarti, *Op. Cit.,* p. 105.

40. Ibid.

41. Nasution, *Memenuhi Panggilan Tugas,* Vol Two, *Op. Cit.,* p. 294.

42. Ibid., p. 101.

43. Clune, *op cit.,* p. 101.

44. Critchley, *Op. Cit.,* p. 11.

45. Ibid.

46. Nasution, *Memenuhi Panggilan Tugas,*Vol Two, *Op. Cit., p. 248.*

47. "Tentara dan politik: Mr Sartono depan opsir-opsir Bandung" ("The Army and politics: Mr Sartono with Bandung officers"), *Pikiran Rakyat,* February 7, 1951.

48. "Keterangan Kol. Simatupang: Kedudukan Misi Militer Belanda di Indonesia" ("Colonel Simatupang Explains: The Position of the Netherlands Military Mission in Indonesia"), *Pikiran Rakyat,* March 12, 1951. In old age Simatupang had not changed his mind regarding the NMM. See *Fallacy of a Myth, Op. Cit.,* p. 131.

49. Nasution, *Memenuhi Panggilan Tugas*, Vol Two, *Op. Cit.*, p. 175, 176.
50. Ibid., p. 176.
51. Penders and Sundhaussen, *Op. Cit.*, p. 61.
52. Padmodiwiryo, *Op. Cit.*, p. 398.
53. Ibid., p. 398, 399.
54. Penders and Sundhaussen, *Op. Cit.*, p. 81.
55. McVey, *Op. Cit.*, p. 145.
56. McKemmish, *Op. Cit.*, p. 67.
57. Padmodiwiryo, *Op. Cit.*, p. 397.
58. U. Sundhausen, *The Road to Power: Indonesian Military Politics, 1945–1967*, Oxford University Press, Kuala Lumpur and New York, 1982, p. 63.
59. Ibid., p. 63.
60. McKemmish, *Op. Cit.*, p. 68.
61. Simatupang, *Fallacy of a Myth, Op. Cit.*, pp. 134–138.
62. McKemmish, *Op. Cit.*, p. 70.
63. Ibid.
64. McKemmish, *Op. Cit.*, p. 72.
65. Ibid.
66. Feith, *Op. Cit.*, p. 262. See Cribb, 1991 *Op. Cit.*, p. 112, 113 for an account of this highly eccentric officer's involvement with underworld elements in the fight against the Dutch.
67. See Nasution, *Memenuhi Panggilan Tugas*, Vol Three, *Op. Cit.*, pp. 32–214 for his account of the October 17, 1952 Affair. For another first-hand account of the affair by one of its most controversial participants, see A. Kemal Idris: *Bertarung dalam Revolusi* (translated title: *Fighting in the Revolution*), Jakarta, Pustaka Sinar Harapan, 1996, pp. 136–142. For comprehensive accounts of the October 17, 1952 Affair and its aftermath, see McVey, 1971 *Op. Cit.*, pp. 143–157 and H. Feith, *The Wilopo Cabinet, 1952–53: A Turning Point in Post-Revolutionary Indonesia*, Ithaca, NY, Modern Indonesia Project, Southeast Asia Program, Department of Far Eastern Studies, Cornell University, 1958.
68. Penders and Sundhaussen, *Op. Cit.*, p. 87.
69. Ibid., p. 86, 87.
70. Feith, 1962 *Op. Cit.*, p. 262, extracted from R. McVey, *Op. Cit.*, p. 148.
71. Feith, 1962 *Op. Cit.*, p. 264 and McVey, *Op. Cit.*, p. 147.
72. Ibid.
73. Sunarti, *Op. Cit.*, p. 223.
74. Harold Crouch, *The Army and Politics in Indonesia*, Ithaca, NY, Cornell University Press, 1978, pp. 28–30.
75. R. McVey, *Op. Cit.*, p. 148.
76. Simatupang, *Laporan Dari Banaran, Op. Cit.*, p. 251.
77. Nasution, *Memenuhi Panggilan Tugas*, Vol Three, *Op. Cit.*, p. 220.
78. Sunarti, *Op. Cit.*, p. 223.
79. Nasution, *Memenuhi Panggilan Tugas*, Vol Three, *Op. Cit.*, p. 215.

80. Supeno's is the view that prevailed in Indonesia until the downfall of the Suharto regime, largely because troops were used extensively for internal security duties. Robert Lowry wrote in the mid-1990s that "the regular army is at least twice as big as it needs to be given the regional security situation. At least 100,000 of the approximately 150,000 men employed in the territorial structure could be replaced by reserves or militiamen if the external threat were the only consideration." Robert Lowry, *The Armed Forces of Indonesia*, Canberra, Strategic and Defence Studies Centre, Australian National University, 1993, p. 219.

81. Pauker, *Op. Cit.*

82. Nasution, *Memenuhi Panggilan Tugas*, Vol Two, *Op. Cit.*, p. 213, 224.

83. www.info.dfat.gov.au, 487 Pritchett to Critchley and Department of External Affairs, Cablegrams, The Hague 6 K340 Batavia, September 12, 1949, accessed November 2004.

84. Penders and Sundhaussen, *Op. Cit.*, p. 55.

85. *Reorganisasi TNI-AD Tahun 1984*, 1986, p.p. 13, 14. This section was retained in a reorganization of staff appointments in 1954. Ibid., p. 15.

86. *Rencana-rencana dari Komisi Perencana Angkatan Darat (Plans of the Army Planning Commission)* General Staff, Army Headquarters, 2nd Ed., 1951, 1f and 33f. Extracted from Sundhaussen, 1982 *Op. Cit.*, p. 60.

87. Interview with Suhario Padmodiwiryo, *Op. Cit.*

88. "Kursus Bagi Perwira Teritoriaal" ("Courses for Territorial Officers"), "Organisasi Territorial Tentara Harus Sempurna: Pendidikan Perwira Territorial Dibuka" ("Army Territorial Organisation Must be Perfect: Territorial Officer Education [Program] Launched"), *Pikiran Rakyat*, January 5, 1951. Suhario himself taught these courses over a number of years. Interview with Suhario Padmodiwiryo, *Op. Cit.*

89. Padmodiwiryo, *Op. Cit.*, p. 475.

90. "Organisasi Territorial Tentara Harus Sempurna: Pendidikan Perwira Territorial Dibuka" ("Army Territorial Organisation Must be Perfect: Territorial Officer Education [Program] Launched"), *Pikiran Rakyat*, July 24, 1951 *Op. Cit.*

91. "80,000 anggota tentara akan didemobiliser. Tapi pemerintah tak akan melepas sebelum ada kepastian didapatnya mata pencaharian. Politik pertahanan tetap berdasarkan pertahanan rakyat total." ("80,000 army members to be demobilized. But the government will not let them go before there is confirmation that they will have work. The defence policy will continue to be based on total people's defence"), *Merdeka*, June 24, 1950.

92. The sultan was reappointed to the position from April 1952 and he served until July 1953. H. Bachtiar, *Siapa Dia?: Perwira Tinggi Tentara Nasional Indonesia Angkatan Darat (TNI-AD)*, (translated title: *Who is He?: Senior Officers of the Indonesian Army*), Jakarta, Penerbit Jambatan. 1988, p. 118.

93. "Hubungan tentara dan rakyat harus tetap dipelihara: Perintah harian Hamengku Buwono IX dan Dr. Halim" ("Relations between the army and people must be maintained. Order of the Day from Hamengku Buwono IX and Dr. Halim"), *Merdeka*, September 12, 1950.

94. "Rempah-rempah dari Semarang: Let. Kol. Suprapto akan pindah ke Jakarta" ("Spices from Semarang: Lieutenant Colonel Suptapto to be moved to Jakarta"), *Merdeka*, October 4, 1950.

95. "Beleid pertahanan dan beleid politik L.N.: Indonesia mendasarkan pertahanannya atas pokok pikiran politik bebas" ("Indonesia's defence policy and foreign policy: Indonesia bases its defence on the principles of a free [and active foreign] policy"), *Merdeka*, December 11, 1950.

96. Ibid. A major factor in the downfall of the Sukiman government was the acceptance of its foreign minister of US military aid under the US Mutual Security act of 1951. This required accepting governments to sign agreements that were widely perceived in Indonesia to be in violation of Indonesia's nonaligned "free and active" foreign policy. See Feith, 1962, *Op. Cit.*, pp. 198–207.

97. "Pertahanan total dan politik bebas" ("Total defence and the free [and active foreign] policy"), *Pikiran Rakyat*, January 15, 1951.

98. Let. Kol. B. Saragih: Ada usaha-usaha memecah tentara dari Rakyat" (Lieutenant Colonel B. Saragih: People trying to split the army from the People"), *Pikiran Rakyat*, January 18, 1951.

99. "Pidato Panglima Tertinggi: Bangunlah sistem pertahanan yang teratur" ("Speech by the Supreme Commander: Develop a systematic defence system"), *Merdeka*, October 6, 1950.

100. Sundhausen, 1982 *Op. Cit., p.* 956, p. 138.

101. "TT-III Jalankan 'Rencana 5 Tahun' Pemberantasan Gerombolan D.I." ("TT-III Implements 'Five-Year Plan' to Eradicate D.I. Gangs"), *Merdeka*, April 16, 1956.

102. "Tentara berhutang budi pada rakyat: Instruksi Kol. Sadikin untuk pemberian sumbangan dari tentara kepada rakyat" ("Army has debt of honour to people: Colonel Sadikin instructs soldiers to donate to people"), *Merdeka*, April 25, 1950.

103. "Pembersihan di Djawa Barat" ("Mopping up in West Java"), *Merdeka*, March 22, 1950.

104. "Rakyat mulai turut aktif dalam pembersihan" ("People beginning to participate actively in mopping up [operations]"), *Pikiran Rakyat*, May 24, 1951.

105. "Di Hulusungai (Kalimantan): Rakyat membantu tentara adakan pembersihan" ("Hulusungai, Kalimantan: People assist army in mopping-up [operations]," *Pikiran Rakyat*, June 8, 1951.

106. "Latihan people defence yang pertama di Bogor: 5000 rakyat membantu tentara" ("First People's Defence Exercise in Bogor: 5000 people assist army," *Pikiran Rakyat*, August 9, 1951.

107. Nasution, *Memenuhi Panggilan Tugas*, Vol Two, *Op. Cit.*, p. 221, 222.

108. Nasution, *Memenuhi Panggilan Tugas*, Vol Three, *Op. Cit.*, p. 4.

109. Ibid., p. 6.

110. Ibid., p. 7.

111. Nasution, *Fundamentals*, p. 71, 72.

112. Ibid., pp. 22–26.

113. Cribb, 2001 *Op. Cit.*, p. 145.

114. Nasution, *Fundamentals, Op. Cit.*, p. 84.

115. Ibid.
116. Penders and Sundhaussen, *Op. Cit.*, p. 98.
117. Nasution, *Fundamentals Op. Cit.*, p. 97.
118. Nasution, *Memenuhi Panggilan Tugas,* Vol Two, *Op. Cit.*, p. 35, 36.
119. Sunarti, *Op. Cit.*, p. 223.
120. Ibid., p. 60.

Chapter 7

The Leper Period

Nasution's conservative attitudes were further reinforced in the three years that he spent on the inactive list (from late 1952 until late 1955) that he described as his "leper period." Throughout his exile he continued to portray the period of military administration as a time of social harmony when all social groups were united in an all-embracing sense of nationalism. The IPKI party that he formed was supported by senior *pamong praja* figures with whom he had become friendly in Central Java. They lauded traditional forms of leadership and argued that the Indonesian masses were not sufficiently educated to choose between the unfamiliar and divisive ideologies of the parties. Importantly, Nasution formed an increasingly close association with the University of Indonesia's professor Djokosutono, who was to guide him on how to deal the army into politics in opposition to the Communist Party short of mounting a military coup.

Some aspects of Nasution's IPKI platform accorded closely with President Sukarno's increasing doubts about liberal democracy. However, by referring to the guerrilla struggle Nasution (deliberately or otherwise) highlighted a significant point of difference between his and the President's record. Unlike Nasution and his military and civil service associates, Sukarno had allowed himself to be captured and did not share in the ownership of the guerrilla struggle.

Nasution showed a strong interest in legal and constitutional affairs as he attempted to find a legally permissible way of challenging the parliament in the lead-up to the October 17, 1952 Affair. He then sought legal advice from Professor Djokosutono, who was a colleague of Professor Supomo, the drafter of the 1945 Constitution, in dealing with an investigation by the attorney general into his role in the affair. Nasution and Djokosutono showed a strong interest in developing legal training for Indonesian Army officers and the structures they created were developed and extended until the end of the New Order period.

As he made his way through this difficult period in his life, Nasution was embittered at his ignominious resignation as chief of staff:

> At this dark time in moments of reflection I sometimes blamed myself. If in Yogyakarta after the guerrilla war I had not persuaded Pak Dirman [Sudirman] to accept again the leadership of Sukarno and Hatta it was very possible the 17 October 1952 Affair would never have happened.[1]

He continued to associate with a few of his military associates, including the former KNIL non-commissioned officer Gatot Subroto with whom he was to form the IPKI organization, but his links with other officers, including Sutoko and others in the army headquarters who had organized the October 17 Affair, suddenly ceased.[2] His stress was compounded by the possibility that he could face legal action and he frequently had to report to the attorney general who was investigating the affair. He writes, perhaps disingenuously, that he did not attend the swearing in of Bambang Sugeng as acting chief of staff because he "had to report to the Attorney General in accordance with the demands of the anti-17 October group."[3]

As chief of staff, Nasution had been allocated a large house on Teuku Umar Road, a tree-lined boulevard in the wealthy suburb of Menteng. The Dutch had named the suburb Weltevreden or "Quiet and Contented" and intended it to be a garden city. A boulevard named Jalan Iman Bonjol (which the Dutch had called Oranje Boulevard) bisected it. On either side of Iman Bonjol stood large houses built in the characteristic Indies architecture of the final decades of Dutch rule. Although in many cases the white paint work was fading and the gardens showed signs of neglect they were solid and well-built with white rendered brick walls and sharply pitched red-tiled roofs.

Nasution and Sunarti remained at Jalan Teuku Umar after his dismissal and although he was not aware of it at the time, after years of transience he had finally found a permanent place to live. He grew to love the house and remained there for the rest of his long life.

Nasution continued to spend a great deal of time with his Gondokusumo in-laws, frequently spending weekends in Bandung. Sunario Gondokusumo was often in Jakarta and stayed with Sunarti and Nasution. He provided financial support, tracing the owner of the home in Menteng (a Dutch doctor) and purchasing it for them "so we wouldn't be destitute and homeless."[4] In Bandung, Sunario and family eventually moved from nearby the old Bumi Putera complex in South Bandung to the more prestigious area of North Bandung where he built an apartment for Sunarti and Nasution above the garage because, as Sunarti put it, they continued to regard the city as their "base."[5]

After alluding to his own incorruptibility, Nasution complained in one of the campaign speeches he made for IPKI in the 1955 elections that "as a colonel and guerrilla leader during the first and second clash, and former deputy commander of the armed forces and chief of staff of the army, I can survive on my monthly salary for only two weeks. In the third week, I have to live on my royalties from my writings and for the fourth I depend on the assistance of my parents."[6]

There is little doubt that the "parents" he was referring to were the Gondokusumos. Nasution's father became ill in the early 1950s and never completely recovered.[7] He moved to Jakarta to live with him and Sunarti in 1967 before, almost blind from glaucoma, he returned to North Sumatra in the late 1970s where he died in 1981.[8] In his recollections of the 1950s, Nasution rarely mentions his other relatives except to complain that some of them expected him to provide them with "promotions, transfers, the provision of facilities," which he had to decline.[9]

Sunarti's uncle, R.P. Soeroso, continued to associate with Nasution after the October 17 Affair. In November 1949, he established the new Parindra party that Feith described as "a splinter party" led by aristocrats.[10]

It seems certain that Soeroso discussed his reservations about the suitability of democracy for the Indonesian masses and advocacy of an "Eastern democracy," a "regulated democracy" (*demokrasi teratur*), and "democracy with leadership" (*demokratie met leiderschap*)[11] with Nasution in Yogyakarta in 1949 and in Jakarta from 1950. It is probable that Nasution was sympathetic to them in view of his concern to maintain the existing social order and the contents of his writings.

Despite only leading a "splinter party," Soeroso was a member of every cabinet until the 1955 elections.[12] However, Nasution appears to have become somewhat distrustful of the older man's advice. He believed that it was at the suggestion of Prime Minister Wilopo that Soeroso advised him to "just be obedient and he even outlined that I would be freer to act if I was a civilian in the political field. Although he spoke as an uncle, I felt he was also an unofficial liaison person with [the Prime Minister] Pak Wilopo."[13] Instead, before and after the October 17, 1952 Affair Nasution was receiving advice from other quarters.

Like Professor Supomo, Djokosutono was from a well-off *pangreh praja* family in Surakarta. After receiving a Dutch secondary education he moved to Batavia in the mid-1920s to study law at the *Rechtshoogeschool* where "His thinking was strongly influenced by his Dutch teachers . . . and by the German traditions of constitutional law they were steeped in."[14] He probably remained on the staff of the *Rechtshoogeschool* as a teaching assistant before occupying a senior position in the Justice Department (probably under Supomo). During the occupation, he worked in the Department of Justice (probably still under Supomo) and after the proclamation provided legal training to officials of the republic.[15]

Djokosutono is remembered by some as a perfectionist, somewhat insecure and prone to eccentricities. For example, at a dinner to mark the death of Dr. Wertheim, who had been one of Djokosutono's teachers at the law school in Jakarta, the story was told that Djokosutono was such a perfectionist that he was always reluctant to sit exams. On one occasion Wertheim and another lecturer, Professor Logeman, turned up at Djokosutono's house and offered to take him for a trip around town by car. While discussing everyday matters, they surreptitiously inserted questions that were to be asked in a forthcoming examination, which Djokosutono easily answered. At the end of the trip they told him he had passed.[16]

Like many *priyayi* Javanese, he was a devotee of *kebatinan*,[17] a Javanese mystical belief system that combined animistic, Muslim, Hindu and Buddhist traditions. Adherents of *kebatinan* seek to find a unity with the spiritual powers of the universe through meditation and other practices. Features of *kebatinan* are a search for clarity or "clear water" (*mamayu hayuning bening*) and a desire to unite with the forces of the cosmos that are manifested on earth in harmonious relations between humans of various functions and statuses in life.

From 1946 he established an *Akademi Ilmu Politik* (Academy of Political Sciences)[18] that trained civil servants in Yogyakarta. It was subsequently fused with the prestigious Gadjah Mada University in that city. He directed the academy until the Madiun Affair of September 1948 when it ceased to function because its students dispersed to fight the PKI.[19]

Djokosutono, who was "preoccupied with legal order,"[20] had established a police academy near Malang in East Java, which then moved to Yogyakarta before being relocated permanently to Jakarta in 1950. Supomo was its dean before Djokosutono took over the appointment and retained it for nearly all the 1950s.[21] In 1952 he began to teach at the Military Law Academy.

Nasution first came into contact with Djokosutono in 1951,[22] possibly through his friendship with Sumitro Kolopaking. A half-brother of Sumitro, Mr.[23] Sunario Kolopaking,[24] was associated with Djokosutono during the last years of the revolution and the early 1950s. Sunario Kolopaking, who had been the first minister for finance of the republic in Sjahrir's first cabinet, assisted Djokosutono to set up the Academy of Political Sciences in Yogyakarta.[25]

As there was no expert in economics available, Sunario Kolopaking was appointed as the first dean of the Faculty of Economics at the University of Indonesia in Jakarta in 1950. Soon afterward he was joined by Djokosutono who returned to Jakarta. Sunario Kolopaking was a founder of the police academy that was at first headed by Supomo. Djokosutono renamed it the *Perguruan Tinggi Ilmu Kepolisian* (College of Police Sciences)[26] when he headed it in the 1950s.[27] It is likely that Sunario's interest in police matters was shared by his half-brother, Sumitro, who, as noted earlier, had been a chief commissioner of police before undergoing training to become the *bupati* of Banjarnegara.

Because of overwork and illness, Sunario Kolopaking handed over the economics faculty to Djokosutono who became acting dean before transferring it to the noted economist, Dr. Sumitro Djojohadikusumo.[28] It is possible that Djokosutono's association with Sunario Kolopaking gave some impetus to the relationship Nasution developed with Djokosutono.

By June 1952 Nasution had established a *Sekolah Hukum Militer* (military law School) in Jakarta where Djokosutono was a senior academic. In 1953 the name of this institution was changed to *Akademi Hukum Militer* (AHM—Military Law Academy) because it regarded itself as almost the equal of the Faculty of Law and Social Sciences at the University of Indonesia.[29] As David Bourchier notes, the AHM "trained almost all of Indonesia's military lawyers, including many who were to play crucial parts in constructing army sponsored corporatist organizations after 1957 and, later on, in Suharto's New Order."[30] In the early 1960s Djokosutono played a leading role in establishing a military law college (*Perguruan Tinggi Hukum Militer*) that provided degree-level training in law.[31]

By the mid-1990s the army had produced so many military lawyers that the number of senior officers in the legal corps of the TNI was second only to the infantry corps and considerably higher in number than the other arms corps (Artillery, Engineers and Cavalry).[32] These army lawyers went on to play instrumental roles in the trials of those thought to be involved in the upheaval of September 30, 1965 and drafted much of the legislation that underpinned the New Order regime.[33]

The interest showed by Djokosutono and Nasution in developing legal training for army officers was highly unusual. Armies that place such an emphasis on legal training are usually preparing for or involved in the military government of occupied territories or home areas that are under martial law.

Some research has attributed Nasution's interest in legal affairs to his training within the KNIL and the influence of his (sometimes incorrectly identified) father-in-law.[34] Nasution's leadership of the military administration of 1949 has not been given prominence in this research. It is much more likely that his experience of heading the military administration was the major impetus to his interest in legal and constitutional matters.

It is probable that he saw the establishment of legal training for officers in Jakarta as a logical continuation of the focus he had given to legal and administrative matters in the first half of 1949 and his maintenance of territorial officers within a "people's resistance" section in the army headquarters in the early 1950s. This would accord with Suhario Padmodiwiryo's observation that this territorial function entailed the monitoring of civilian populations, the training of army territorial officers to liaise with rural villagers to prepare them for "people's resistance,"[35] and the involvement of army commanders in West Java in the early 1950s in enlisting civilian populations to assist in the fight against the *Darul Islam* movement.

In line with his interest in establishing legal foundations for his initiatives, in 1952 he had sought a legal basis for mounting a "half-coup" against the parliament (while leaving the presidency and vice presidency intact). Essentially, he was attempting to find a legally sanctioned means for the army to close-down the legislative arm of government and assume wider powers in administering the civilian population. He writes that he took legal advice from Mr. Basaruddin Nasution, the director of justice in the Ministry of Defense,[36] who was a "faithful student and assistant of Professor Djokosutono."[37] Nasution strongly implies that Basaruddin was in turn seeking legal/constitutional advice from Djokosutono in the lead up to the October 17 Affair:

> Apart from the Vice President, I also always requested advice from the Head of the Justice Directorate, Mr Basaruddin. In those days, I took lessons on the Provisional Constitution [*Undang-Undang Dasar Sementara*] from him.
>
> The problem of what steps could be taken after the dissolution of parliament was very difficult to solve, because it had not yet been possible to hold general elections. However, there was a widely-held understanding that there was a way out based on the Law of the State of Emergency (*staatsnoodrecht*), where the President could act because the atmosphere in the country was such that it endangered the safety and unity of the nation.
>
> Mr Basaruddin was in continual contact with his friends at the University of Indonesia with the result that discussions on the problem of the army *contra* the parliament also took place there. Indeed, the timing was very appropriate because it was orientation time [at the University] and the newspapers that were full of news about the parliament naturally stimulated the development of discussions.
>
> I came to know from him that there were many who were sympathetic to the army's position at that time.[38]

Basaruddin was one of the handful of officials from the army/Defense Department who remained in contact with him during his "leper period"[39] and it is highly likely that he retained his conduit to Professor Djokosutono through this official.

It appears that Nasution's attempt in 1952 to seek legal and constitutional means whereby the army could intervene in the political arena short of an outright military coup against the president and vice president became a precedent for a request he made in 1958 for Djokosutono to advise him on an approach to military intervention that he called "the middle way." This resort to legal advice and unwillingness or inability to stage an outright coup would have accorded with Nasution's ambitious but essentially conservative and cautious nature.

Bourchier writes that Djokosutono was not so much an ideologue as a legal technician, along the lines of the legal and political theorist of the Weimar Republic and Nazi Germany, Carl Schmitt, and his involvement in developing the "middle way" concept for Nasution indicates that he played such a role. Bourchier argues that like Schmitt, Djokosutono:

> saw law primarily as a tool of power and the role of constitutional lawyers as adjusting the legal architecture to suit the prevailing conditions. At the same time, he held that Indonesia's legal structures should more faithfully reflect the country's *cultural* patterns, which he spoke about in terms strongly redolent of the Leiden *adat* [customary law] scholars such as van Vollenhoven, Ter Haar and Haga whom he quoted frequently and with approval.
>
> Djokosutono saw the army and Sukarno as two centres of power that were not sufficiently taken into account in the 1950 Constitution and "he played an important role as a supplier of political, legal and doctrinal formulas which would help legitimize the increasingly prominent political profile of both Nasution's army and the President."[40]

This view is supported by Daniel S. Lev, who knew Djokosutono:

> Djokosutono was in a sense, a Javanese sense, conservative, but not remarkably so. . . . Djoko was useful because he knew a lot, was very well read with something of a photographic memory, and could be called upon to fish up useful and applicable ideas for anyone who needed them.[41]

While Lev was very well placed to make such an observation, Nasution's remark that when seeking legal advice prior to the October 17 Affair he "came to know that there were many [at the University of Indonesia's Law Faculty] who were sympathetic to the army's position at that time"[42] indicates that he was more than a disinterested legal technician. Another indication is the great interest Djokosutono showed in developing the military law school, to the point of providing degree-level training.

A further sign is Djokosutono's involvement in programs initiated a decade later by the American CIA- and Rand Corporation-linked Guy Pauker in which visiting lecturers from the University of Indonesia taught and advised the officers at the Bandung-based Seskoad Staff and Command School who were developing doctrines for army intervention in politics and the economy.[43]

Djokosutono took over leadership of the Faculty of Economics at the University of Indonesia in 1958 after Sumitro Djojohadikusumo allied himself with an American-backed revolt in Sumatra (the PRRI/Permesta rebellion) and then fled to Malaysia. A former student, Subroto, recounts that Djokosutono "was the leading figure in protecting the Faculty of Economics. There was a lot of pressure to appoint leftists on the teaching staff."[44] That Djokosutono was personally loyal to Nasution as well as a legal adviser is indicated in Nasution's recollection that on one occasion after returning from giving a lecture at Seskoad, Djokosutono "reported to him" that certain officers there were opposed to him.[45]

Djokosutono's very close association with Supomo is another pointer to his political orientation. David Reeve has drawn attention to the close philosophical and research relationship that existed between Djokosutono and Supomo, in which Djokosutono shared Supomo's interest in *adat* law and, together with Supomo, wrote Indonesia's main textbook on this subject.[46] It seems more than likely that Djokosutono agreed with the political formulas Supomo advocated in the discussions of the BPUPKI and, as noted earlier, his thinking "was strongly influenced by his Dutch teachers [at the *Rechtshoogeschool*] and by the German traditions of constitutional law in which they were steeped."[47]

Djokosutono's close research and personal association with Supomo over many years and his interest in *kebatinan* indicate that he was philosophically in tune with the older man. He might well have been inspired to assist Nasution in finding constitutional formulas for an increased political role from personal belief as well as a preparedness to assist in providing technical legal advice.

Moreover, there is the web of interlocking family and professional connections between Sunario Kolopaking, Sumitro and Djokosutono that have already been outlined. It seems likely that this drew Nasution into Djokosutono's social and professional orbit, placing their association on a closer basis than that of lawyer and client.

Another indication of Nasution's socially conservative attitudes and links with Sumitro Kolopaking and other conservatives in the early 1950s is an assertion by the generally authoritative retired senior army officer, Sayidiman Suryohadiprojo,[48] that the TNI leadership sought to develop an association with the PIR.

While Djokosutono does not appear to have joined the PIR, Supomo and Sumitro Kolopaking were members. In the early 1950s the PIR had expanded from its base in Central Java by taking into its ranks some aristocrats from the federal states. It had 17 of the 232 seats in parliament and occupied powerful portfolios prior to the 1955 elections.

It continued to push for the interests of the *pamong praja*, particularly as the aristocratic nature of the civil service began to be diluted by what

Sutherland describes as "a gross and administratively unwarranted expansion of government services as politicians strove to provide jobs, reward clients and obtain a following."[49]

Sayidiman asserts:

> From 1950 the TNI leadership was aware that the army would find it difficult to achieve its political aims by itself. There were too many forces in Indonesia whose interests differed from the political aims which they wished to realise. As an organisation that was basically of a military nature, the TNI had difficulty in moving in the political arena.
>
> Therefore, the TNI sought partners within the political parties which they could invite to move forward together. At first the choice fell upon the *Partai Indonesia Raya* or PIR because the PIR was comprised of people who appeared also to adhere to the ideology of the Republic of Indonesia which was based on the Pancasila.[50]

However, he states that the link between the army and PIR was not a durable one because:

> the PIR became afflicted by the same illness that at that time greatly affected many people and those in the parties in particular. Divisions emerged within PIR because personal interests became stronger than organisational interests. The result was that PIR could not play an effective role in the Indonesian political arena in struggling for its political objectives that originally were parallel with those of the army.[51]

Sayidiman is likely to be referring to a split within the PIR in 1954 over the economic policies of the first cabinet of the PNI politician Ali Sastroamidjojo (July 1953–July 1955)[52] whose economic policies were seen to favor Javanese interests and disadvantage the export-producing outer islands. Java-based members grouped under the leadership of Mr. Wongsonegoro while those from the outer islands formed a separate grouping under Dr. Hazairin. While Sayidiman does not state who in the army leadership attempted to form this association with the PIR, he is presumably referring to officers in the army headquarters in Jakarta. It is unlikely that he was referring to Simatupang and the other PSI-associated officers and Nasution is the most likely candidate.[53]

Referring to Sayidiman's assertions, David Reeve suggests that Nasution may have come under the influence of Supomo's family principle *kekeluargaan* ideas from the time the law professor became a member of the PIR leadership in the early 1950s:[54]

> When Nasution founded IPKI in 1954, its leadership consisted of military officers close to him and senior *pamong praja* figures. Sumitro Kolopaking,

formerly on the PIR executive, became general chairman of the IPKI executive. In the late 1950s, when both men [Sukarno and Nasution] were developing ideas to reduce the influence of the parties in favour of groups with shared function in society (functional groups), they were advised (probably separately) by Professor Djokosutono, who after Supomo's death in 1958, was considered to be Indonesia's foremost constitutional law expert.

He and Supomo had co-authored a two-volume study of *adat* law and Reeve observes that there is thus a direct line of *adat* law-Supomoism in the functional group concept and the whole idea of interest representation through functional groups represents a political format for the integralistic vision of the state.[55]

The "*adat* law-Supomoism" connections Reeve draws between Sumitro Kolopaking, Supomo, Djokosutono and Nasution complement the family associations between Sumitro Kolopaking, Sunario Kolopaking and Djokosutono, the connection between Djokosutono and Nasution (on the basis of these family associations), and Nasution's keen interest in developing legal education for army officers. Most importantly, the connections that Reeve draws strongly indicate a similarity of attitudes between these influential and socially conservative Indonesians. Moreover, an essential ingredient in the similarity of political attitudes between Nasution and Kolopaking was shared participation in the "total people's resistance" campaign and military administration of 1949.

A further connection with the PIR is Nasution's and Sunarti's association with the former governor of West Java, Sewaka, with whom Nasution cosigned their political note authorizing the army to lead a campaign of "total people's resistance" throughout the province in 1947. Sewaka was a member of parliament for the PIR and became defense minister in the Sukiman cabinet in April 1951, replacing Sumitro Kolopaking (also from PIR) who was appointed but declined to be installed.[56]

Although Feith states that relations between Sewaka and the army leaders "were strained from the beginning" because he was some twenty years older and would not actively promote army interests,[57] Nasution records that the personal relationship they had in West Java had not changed and that the older man took the initiative to visit him and Sunarti.[58] Sunarti also recalls the visit, writing: "Our relationship had been close in Bandung and in South West Java during the guerrilla period."[59]

At this stage, it is appropriate to explore what it was that drew Sumitro Kolopaking and certain other Indonesians with aristocratic connections to Nasution in 1954 when he established his IPKI organization. Together with the residents of Central Java and the *Bupati* of Wonosobo, the older man supported Nasution's IPKI organization. When Nasution refrained from becoming the formal leader of the organization because he was still in the military (albeit on the inactive list) Sumitro became general chairman.

Nasution formed IPKI in May 1954 for the purpose of fighting the general elections. It is well-known that this organization was something of a predecessor to the New Order's election vehicle, *Golkar*, which started life in the 1960s as a joint secretariat for functional groups that was to function as an alternative to political parties. Like *Golkar*, IPKI participated in politics but refused to be categorized as a political party. It called for the "spirit and soul" of the Proclamation and the 1945 Constitution to be protected and nurtured, presaging the New Order's "simplification" of the parties by advocating the amalgamation of those with a similar orientation. Thus, it seems to have flagged Nasution's interest in returning to the 1945 Constitution and signaled that Nasution was on a somewhat similar quest to Sukarno who was fond of claiming that the revolution was not yet complete. Moreover, IPKI strongly criticized the parties and the multiparty/liberal-democratic system as being at odds with Indonesian political culture and this was something that Sukarno was about to take up with gusto.

Kolopaking had been one of the more conservative members of the BPUPKI. He was one of the *"pamong praja"* figures whose "blueprint" had called for a dominant executive and a single state party and made no mention of individual rights.[60] Nasution began to express regret that the idea of a single state party did not come to fruition in 1945 and registered doubts about the readiness of the Indonesian people for a multiparty democratic system, particularly in times of crisis and imminent conflict.

> This [the formation of *laskar* organizations] was in line with efforts to oppose the formation of an Indonesian National Party, which they thought smacked of fascism or totalitarianism, and which became the source of divisions in the future. Because of this, the Indonesian people who were seething for independence were theoretically given the go-ahead to implement democracy 100% which was said to be intended to give the impression to the Allies that we weren't an appendage of fascist Japan but a democratic country, even though it was clear that we weren't ready and were unable to do this, and even though all countries that are at war set aside party affairs and even their representative institutions to concentrate all their energy and thoughts on winning the war.[61]

IPKI performed very poorly in Indonesia's first general elections that were eventually held in September 1955, achieving four seats in parliament (three in West Java and one in Central Sumatra). The relative success of the organization in West Java was largely due to the concerted support of a group of *Siliwangi* officers and *pamong praja* officials.[62] In Central Java Nasution was supported by almost all the residents and *Bupatis* who had participated in the military administration[63] but was unsuccessful in getting candidates elected.

Noting that Sumitro Kolopaking became general chairman of the IPKI executive and his PIR antecedents, Reeve contends that IPKI's endorsement of "society as a 'harmonious unity' supported by all regions and groups" in its Manifesto Number 1 was in accordance with the thinking of the framers of the 1945 Constitution.[64] However, the organization voiced support for ethnic minorities and greater regional autonomy and this was a factor in Sultan Hamengku Buwono gradually pulling back from IPKI.[65] The more junior Paku Alam remained a supporter and took Nasution's seat in parliament after he reentered the army.[66] Nasution also advocated a return to organic "traditional" means of interest representation found at the village level along lines that are strikingly similar to that of Kahin's (previously noted) description of the PIR's objectives and doubts about the ability of the uneducated masses to resist attempts by parties with imported ideologies to manipulate them:

> We will fight for an electoral law which will force political parties of a similar outlook to combine, by changing the current legislation inherited from the Dutch into one based on our traditional ways of electing village heads. In short, we would like to change the current system, which is voting for a party, to our traditional system of voting for a person.
>
> The system of electing a village head is a personal election, not a system of voting for isms. I think our people, who are not individualistic like Western peoples, cannot choose which "ism" is better. It is not the theory behind an "ism" which is important but the character of the individuals who represent them. It doesn't matter how good an "ism" is if it is implemented by bad people.[67]

This call was also redolent of his support in his pamphlet on village defense written in 1948 for the leadership role of the *lurah* as the basis for guerrilla administrations.[68]

In speeches during the general election campaign Nasution continued to idealize the values of the guerrilla struggle, contrasting them with what he saw as the divisiveness and disunity of the 1950s:

> If [in 1945–49] we had put the interests of parties and isms above the national struggle, if we had fought then only for our own "isms," I am sure our Republic would have been wiped out by the Dutch a long time ago.
>
> People are divided because of their commitments to their political parties; those who were formerly united in the guerrilla struggle against the colonial power are now enemies. Worse still, they are willing to be friends with people who betrayed our struggle providing they belong to the same party. Furthermore, these divisions along party lines have penetrated the family, creating frictions between father and son, older brother and younger brother.[69]

At the heart of IPKI's emergence was an alliance between army supporters of Nasution, *pamong praja* leaders with "clean political backgrounds," and the royal families of Yogyakarta. The *pamong praja* supporters had in common the fact that they had not been federalists or absent from the revolution.

While dismayed at what they saw as the erosion of organic "traditional" values and authority structures caused by the multiparty system, they had sound nationalist credentials.

Unlike most *pamong praja* members who, as Sutherland points out, "found it expedient to lie low and cultivate influential patrons"[70] they felt able to oppose aspects of liberal democracy and speak out in support of "traditional" values, together with Nasution and other officers who had been their partners in the military administration. They could criticize the "isms" of the parties on the basis that they had united and "put the national struggle above party interests" "to save our state during the first and second clash [with the Dutch]."[71]

Pride in the "total people's resistance" campaigns of the revolution was also indicated in IPKI's defense policy which promised to "fight for the implementation of a people's defence system by introducing a people's army [militia] based on conscription, compulsory military service, compulsory training, and an efficient civilian reserve."[72] Nasution was to attempt to reemphasize the idea of "people's defence," although not along the lines proposed in his IPKI speech, when he was reinstated in November 1955, an event that was initiated by an old comrade from the military administration.

His return to the army was facilitated by Sukarno's increasing pessimism about liberal democracy. There were similarities in the doubts about this form of government voiced by Nasution in his IPKI material and those expressed by the President.[73]

However, Nasution was not merely imitating Sukarno. In calling upon his experiences in the guerrilla campaigns of the revolution he was implicitly drawing a line between those who had been present during the military administration and those, notably Sukarno, who had not. By espousing "traditional" notions on how the state should relate to society and rejecting the party system, he was nurturing the images that he had begun to propagate in *Fundamentals of Guerrilla Warfare* and continued to promote in the first volume of *TNI* and *Tjatatan-Tjatatan Sekitar Politik Militer Indonesia* ("Notes on Indonesian Military Policy" that appeared in 1955). His socially conservative instincts that were offended by what he saw as growing and unending political turmoil were embodied within these publications that idealized (and mythologized) the "people's resistance" campaigns of 1947 and 1948/49 as golden ages when political antagonisms were largely absent and all sections of society were united in a common national purpose.

Meanwhile, in Nasution's absence conflicts within the army had not abated. The minister for defense in the Ali Sastroamijoyo government was Iwa Kusuma Sumantri, who had been a supporter of Tan Malaka. This was a strange choice as Iwa was neither liked nor trusted by conservative army officers. Frictions arose between these officers and the civilian leadership, partly because of this antipathy.[74]

When the Ali cabinet took decisions affecting the sensitive area of promotions and appointments a number of officers made attempts to present a united front to protect what they saw as the corporate interests of the army from further encroachments. In mid-1954 there was an attempt at reconciliation between officers who had been for or against the October 17, 1952 Affair and in early 1955 a reconciliation of sorts was achieved when army leaders from all factions met in Yogyakarta in February 1955 and hammered out a Charter of Army Unity (*Piagam Keutuhan Angkatan Darat*). A major objective of the meeting (which the "inactive" Nasution did not attend) was to try to ensure that the government appointed a successor to army chief of staff, Bambang Sugeng, who was acceptable to the army leadership.

An attempt by the cabinet to disregard the outcome of the Yogyakarta meeting and appoint an officer who had not been recommended by the army leadership led to a crisis in which they boycotted the swearing-in ceremony. Colonel Zulkifli Lubis, who had been acting army chief of staff since May 2, 1955, was dismissed following his refusal to hand over to the cabinet's appointee.

This had grave political ramifications and culminated in Iwa's resignation on July 12, 1955 and the demise of the cabinet a week later. A Masyumi-led coalition led by Burhanuddin Harahap (August 1955–March 1956) took over and Zulkifli Lubis was reinstated as acting chief of staff.

The revolt by the army leadership was a strong indication that powerful sections of the officer corps would no longer tolerate "interference" in matters they regarded as internal to the army. Unlike the fiasco of the October 17, 1952 Affair, the concept of civilian supremacy over the army had suffered a considerable blow as the officers corps had shown its potential to influence political events as long as it was sufficiently united and resolute.[75]

Meanwhile, long-awaited general elections were something of an anticlimax for those seeking a stronger government. The elections exacerbated tensions and failed to solve the problem of cabinet instability. The four parties which received most of the votes were the secular nationalist Indonesian National Party (PNI), the Masyumi Party, the Muslim Scholar's Party (NU), and the PKI which gained most of its support in Java. Rather than slimming down the number of parties in parliament to more manageable levels, twenty-eight gained representation—eight more than in the old assembly. Moreover, the vote gained by the four majors was split fairly evenly between them meaning that none emerged as outright winners:[76]

With the exception of the PKI, which had made a startling comeback after its involvement in the 1948 Madiun Affair, the election results had failed to satisfy any of Indonesia's major interest groups. The Java-based "traditional" Muslim NU (*Nahdatul Ulama*) had separated from the "modernist" Masyumi in mid-1952 and was operating as a separate party and its third place, like the PKI's fourth, gave that party a fillip. However, the combined vote of these two major Islamic parties only amounted to 39.3 percent of the total vote and the combined vote of all the Muslim-oriented parties was only 43.5 percent.

Table 7.1   Major Party Results in the 1955 General Elections

Party	% of Valid Votes	% of Parliamentary Seats
PNI	22.3	22.2
Masyumi	20.9	22.2
NU	18.4	17.5
PKI	16.4	15.2

Indeed, the outcome of the elections clearly exposed schisms within the Muslim community of Indonesia.[77] In the ethnic Javanese areas of Central and East Java, Masyumi and the predominantly Javanese and *santri*-based party, *Nahdatul Ulama* (NU) competed for the votes of the *santri* community. Masyumi's modernist style of Islam was, as Ruth McVey notes, "most visible socially as the 'Protestant ethic' of an emergent urban entrepreneurial class."[78] The NU on the other hand, represented a *kolot* or old-fashioned style of Islam. As McVey puts it:

> Politically, the *kolot* position is represented archetypically by the Nahdatul Ulama Party, the leading element of which has consisted of the moneylenders and landholders of hinterland Java, together with traditionalist religious teachers and scholars. Hence the *kolot* position has come to be identified with rural and small-town wealth as well as with theological conservatism, though in fact the overwhelming majority of those who adhere to it are poor and a considerable number are urban.

She also states: "Outside the Javanese ethnic areas, Masyumi was associated with" anti-Javanese sentiment rather than from theologically or socially *moderen* [modern] enthusiasm.[79]

Nahdatul Ulama came third due to its support in densely populated Java, gaining 18.4 percent of the vote.[80]

Within the context of the politicization of Indonesian society in the 1950s, the schism between the modern and *kolot* forms of Islam was not as sharp as that between *priyayi* and *abangan*, based as the latter was on issues of social class, rather than religio-cultural orientation. Until the upheaval of the independence struggle and the politicization of grassroots Indonesia in the lead up to the general elections, differences between these two groups tended to be masked or overwhelmed by the "ideological domination" of the *priyayi* group over the *abangan* masses.[81] The inclusive, syncretic nature of *abangan-priyayi* belief systems had generally mitigated against the expression of open or articulated division between the two social classes.[82]

Right-wing elements within the PNI, a party whose power base was the *pamong praja* and whose major constituency was the *abangan* masses, had perhaps even better reason than the anti-PKI Muslim parties to be concerned at the PKI's resurgence. Although the PNI was comprised of both radical and conservative elements, the loyalty of the *abangan* masses was increasingly being transferred to the PKI. This was evident in the size of the vote achieved by the PKI in the general election and the large number of previously PNI-voting Indonesians who were attracted to the PKI in the 1957 regional, district and municipal elections.

Even less satisfied than the PNI (which gained first place in the poll) were members of the small number of conservative parties that had done poorly in the elections. The PIR's parliamentary representation fell from eighteen to two, Parindra was wiped out, and as mentioned, IPKI only gained four seats.

Conservative *pamong praja*-associated organizations of this type were not only disappointed with their poor showing in the elections but alarmed at the rapid growth of the PKI. While in the mid-to-late 1950s the potential for disruptive *abangan-priyayi* class struggle was generally mitigated by PNI and PKI members tending to concentrate their resentment on the common enemies of their *abangan-priyayi* cultural entity (the *santri* and Indonesia's small but economically dominant Chinese ethnic group), the electoral gains of the PKI in the 1955 elections alarmed members of the *priyayi* elite and the *santri*. Like the landlords and traditional elites of China and other communist states, their power, prestige and wealth would be jeopardised in the event of an outright PKI victory in future elections.

Disappointment at the inconclusive results of the elections led to President Sukarno becoming increasingly vocal, claiming Western models of liberal democracy were artificial implants in the Indonesian environment and parties were ideologically divisive and thus not able to provide Indonesia's much needed "political unity."[83]

After the elections, the Burhanuddin cabinet had to appoint a new army chief of staff, a decision in which President Sukarno played a major role. After a series of discussions with Sukarno a rapprochement was achieved and Nasution was reappointed in November 1955.

Yet again he was assisted by associates from the guerrilla struggle in Central Java. The rapprochement was brokered by Maladi, a Radio Republic of Indonesia employee who had broadcast news of the 1949 campaign to the outside world in his capacity as information officer at Nasution's Java Command Headquarters.

Nasution had unofficially involved Maladi in his IPKI organization but writes that it was not appropriate for him to be formally involved in the election campaign because by this time he had become head of the national broadcaster. During the campaign Maladi had informed Nasution that the president was pleased with his themes of "purifying and finalizing the revolution of 1945," "returning to the 1945 Constitution," and reuniting forces that had participated in the revolution but had since rebelled against the central government.[84] Maladi also reported to Nasution that the president had been moved when told that his picture was still on the wall in Nasution's office.[85]

The candidates put forward by army headquarters for the chief of staff position were Colonels Simbolon, Zulkifli Lubis, Kawilarang, Jatikusumo and Nasution.[86] Penders and Sundhaussen write that Nasution was, in Sukarno's eyes, the "least objectionable" of the candidates and the only officer who might be able to quell the increasing assertiveness within the army. Reflecting Sukarno's diminished support for the parliamentary system since the October 17, 1952 Affair, they contend that in 1955 Sukarno would have been more sympathetic to the sort of requests that Nasution made in 1952.[87]

It is likely that a bargain was struck between Nasution and Sukarno before the former's reinstatement, as they met beforehand and apparently reached substantial agreement on the problems besetting the country and the means to overcome them.[88] Reeve comments that "It appears that Sukarno undertook to cooperate with Nasution's plans to reassert central control over the army while Nasution agreed to cooperate with Sukarno's emerging plans to reform the political system."[89] Penders and Sundhaussen conclude that Nasution had always believed his true vocation was the army, and IPKI's poor performance in the general elections made it unlikely he could make a mark on the political scene.[90] Feith has also pointed out that army politics were Nasution's overwhelming concern,[91] while McVey writes that "he was a strong centralist who sought to preserve the unity of the nation (and to enhance his own power) by strengthening the army chain of command and imposing Jakarta's will on the outlying regions."[92]

Maraden Panggabean, a former chief of armed forces staff and cabinet minister in the 1970s, believed that President Sukarno felt able to approve the nomination of Nasution because on the one hand he was known to be "legalistic" and thus less likely than Lubis to mount direct challenges to civilian rule, and because while campaigning for IPKI Nasution had urged a return to the values and spirit of the revolutionary period and particularly the Proclamation of Independence and the 1945 Constitution. He had affirmed that the "revolution was not yet finished," a favourite theme of Sukarno.[93]

Nasution's disappointment with IPKI's performance was no doubt compounded by the disappearance from the parliament of his natural allies in the previous parliament—conservative *pamong praja* interests in the PIR and Parindra. He thereafter became increasingly distant from IPKI.[94] As noted earlier, the Paku Alam took Nasution's seat in parliament when he was reinstated to his army post. Sumitro Kolopaking took the seat of Nasution's close supporter, Gatot Subroto, who was also reinstated in the army,[95] becoming Nasution's deputy chief of staff in August that year.

Nasution began moves to fashion the army into a major center of political power—albeit one that was still largely excluded from the processes of government.[96] In doing so he further developed ideas that he had presented in his IPKI material into means of military intervention.

NOTES

1. A. H. Nasution, *Memenuhi Panggilan Tugas,* Vol Three, *Op. Cit.*, 1983, p. 176.
2. Ibid., p. 204.
3. Ibid., p. 203.
4. Ibid., p. 218.
5. Sunarti, *Op. Cit.*, p. 136.
6. Excerpts from Nasution's IPKI Campaign Speech, Penders and Sundhaussen, *Op. Cit.*, p. 238.
7. Nasution, *Memenuhi Panggilan Tugas,* Vol Three, *Op. Cit.*, p. 273.
8. Sunarti, *Op. Cit.*, p. 227.
9. Nasution, *Memenuhi Panggilan Tugas,* Vol Three, *Op. Cit.*
10. Feith, 1962 *Op. Cit.*, p. 144.
11. Ibid., p. 38.
12. Bourchier, *Op. Cit.*, p. 116.
13. Nasution, *Memenuhi Panggilan Tugas,* Vol Three, *Op. Cit.*, p. 204.
14. Bourchier, *Op. Cit.*, p. 120, 121.
15. Ibid.
16. Wahana, *Selamat Jalan Prof Dr. Wertheim* (Farewell, Professor Dr. Wertheim), www.hamline.edu/apakabar/basisdata/1998/11/06/008.html, accessed February 2005.
17. Reeve, *Op. Cit.*, p. 150.
18. Ibid., p. 120.
19. Gadjah Mada University Website, http://web2.ugm.ac.id, accessed December 2004.
20. Bourchier, *Op. Cit.*, p. 120. Djokosutono renamed the academy the *Perguruan Tinggi Ilmu Kepolisian* (College of Police Sciences).
21. Ibid.
22. Jenkins, *Op. Cit.*, p. 269.
23. *Meester in Rechten*—Master of Laws.
24. Sumitro and Sunario were half-brothers (children of the *bupati* of Banjarnegara, Tumenggung Djojonegoro II). Email from Kolopaking family, December 28, 2004. Sumitro's mother was the *bupati's* first wife, while Sunario's was his second. R.T.W. Kolopaking, *Sejarah Dinasti Kanjeng Raden Adipati Tumenggung Kolopaking 1677–1832* (History of the Dynasty of H.R.H. Kolopaking 1677–1832, *Pendopo Panjer Roma Kebumen*, location and publisher not stated, 1997, p. 18.

25. Bourchier, *Op. Cit.*, p. 120, f.n. 36.
26. Kolopaking, *Op. Cit.*, p. 18.
27. Bourchier, *Op. Cit.*, p. 120.
28. University of Indonesia Faculty of Economics website, www.fe.ui.ac.id, accessed December 2004. Bourchier, *Op. Cit.*, p. 121, f.n. 39.
29. *Panduan Memilih Perguruan Tinggi* (Guide for Choosing an Institute of Higher Learning) www.pdat. co.id, accessed February 2005.
30. Bourchier, *Op. Cit.*, p. 121.
31. In 1994 this institution was renamed the *Sekolah Tinggi Hukum Militer* and provided legal education to the doctoral level. *Panduan Memilih Perguruan Tinggi, Op. Cit.*
32. Arms corps are the combat branches of an army, while service corps (e.g., Transport, Logistics) play supporting roles to them.
33. "Closer analysis of the data shows that these officers played a major role in the aftermath of the failed coup attempt of 30 September 1965 acting not only as prosecutors, attorneys general and judges but also as the drafters of the laws that support the New Order." MacFarling, *Op. Cit.*, p. 158.
34. Sundhaussen, 1982 *Op. Cit.*, p. 95 and Bourchier, *Op. Cit.*, p. 119. As previously noted, Bourchier relied upon the incorrect identification of Nasution's father-in-law by Penders and Sundhaussen. This led him to believe that Nasution's father-in-law was the lawyer Djody Gondokusumo.
35. Interview with Suhario Padmodiwiryo, *Op. Cit.*
36. Nasution, *Memenuhi Panggilan Tugas,* Vol Three, *Op. Cit.*, p. 169.
37. Ibid., p. 170.
38. Ibid., p. 169.
39. Ibid., p. 215.
40. Bourchier, *Op. Cit.*, p. 122.
41. Email from Lev, September 6, 2004.
42. Nasution, *Memenuhi Panggilan Tugas,* Vol Three, *Op. Cit.*, p. 169.
43. David Ransom, "Ford Country: Building an Elite for Indonesia," in Steve Weissman (ed), *The Trojan Horse: A Radical Look at Foreign Aid*, Palo, Alto, California, Ramparts Press, 1975, pp. 101–104.
44. "No Ivory Tower," www.fordfoundation.org, accessed June 2005.
45. Nasution, *Memenuhi Panggilan Tugas*, Vol Four, p. 313.
46. Reeve, *Op. Cit.*, p. 24.
47. David Bourchier, *Op. Cit.*, p. 120, 121.
48. Sayidiman Suryohadiprojo trained at the republic's military academy in Yogyakarta in the late 1940s before joining the *Siliwangi* Division as a junior officer. He undertook junior officer military training in the United States and later studied at the Feuhrungsakademie in West Germany and undertook the International Defense Management course at the Naval Post Graduate School in the United States. He served as a battalion and Kodam (Military Area) commander, deputy chief of staff of the armed forces and governor of the National Defense Institute (Lemhannas), ambassador to Japan and ambassador at Large for the African region. Upon retirement, he taught at

various institutions within and outside the military and became a well-known media commentator on military affairs. He has written a number of books, including *Kepemimpinan ABRI* (The Leadership of ABRI) 1996 *Op. Cit.* While something of a New Order ideologue in the sense that he was a prominent supporter of Sishankamrata and the *Pancasila* state, he is outspoken and generally regarded as a credible commentator on military affairs.

49. Sutherland, *Op. Cit.*, p. 155.

50. Sayidiman Suryohadiprojo, "Hubungan ABRI dan Golkar Pada Masa Mendatang," ("Relations between the Armed Forces of the Republic of Indonesia and Golkar in the Future"), *Pelita*, October 20, 1988, p. 7. Reeve drew attention to this article in David Reeve, "The Corporatist State: The Case of Golkar," in Arief Budiman (ed.), *State and Civil Society*, 1990, Centre of Southeast Asian Studies, Monash University, p. 158.

51. Suryohadiprojo, 1988 *Op. Cit.*

52. The Wilopo cabinet fell in July 1953 as a result of a dispute over foreign investment. After a fifty-eight-day period of political stalemate, Ali Sastroamijoyo of the PNI formed a cabinet.

53. Citing Reeve's "The Corporatist State: The Case of Golkar," Bourchier, *Op. Cit.*, writes that the connection Reeve describes was between IPKI and the PIR. This does not seem to be immediately evident in Reeve's paper.

54. Supomo joined the PIR's political section. Bourchier, *Op. Cit.*, p. 114.

55. Reeve, 1990 *Op. Cit.*, p. 161.

56. Feith, 1962 *Op. Cit.*, p. 180, fn. 4.

57. Ibid., p. 210.

58. Nasution, *Memenuhi Panggilan Tugas*, Vol 2B, p. 172.

59. Sunarti, *Op. Cit.*, p. 101.

60. Castles, *Op. Cit.*, p. 1.

61. Nasution, *TNI* (Vol One), *Op. Cit.*, p. 158.

62. Penders and Sundhaussen, *Op Cit.*, p. 100. Indeed, the election results showed that the vast majority of IPKI voters were from West Java. Ibid., p. 100A. See also Brackman, *Op. Cit.*, p. 218.

63. As Feith puts it, "various *pamong praja* officials with clean revolutionary records" were candidates for the League in the 1955 elections. Feith, 1962 *Op. Cit.*, p. 405.

64. Reeve, 1985 *Op. Cit.*, p. 111.

65. Penders and Sundhaussen write that Nasution's support for greater regional and village autonomy cost him the support of the sultan. Penders and Sundhaussen, *Op. Cit.*, p. 100.

66. Ibid., f.n. 67.

67. Excerpts from Nasution's IPKI Campaign Speech, Penders and Sundhaussen, *Op. Cit.*, Appendix 2, p. 242.

68. Nasution, *Fundamentals*, *Op. Cit.*, p. 114.

69. Excerpts from Nasution's IPKI Campaign Speech, Penders and Sundhaussen, *Op, Cit.*, p. 238.

70. Sutherland, *Op. Cit.*, p. 155.

71. Excerpts from Nasution's IPKI Campaign Speech, Penders and Sundhaussen, *Op, Cit.*, p. 241.
72. Ibid., p. 244.
73. McKemmish, *Op. Cit.*, p. 105.
74. M. Panggabean, *Berjuang dan Mengabdi* (translated title Struggling and Serving), Jakarta, Pustaka Harapan, 1993, p. 208.
75. Soebijono comments that "From that moment, the Armed Forces (*cq* the Army) in a de facto sense became an active social and political force." Soebijono, *Op. Cit.*, p. 23.
76. Ricklefs, *Op. Cit.*, p. 238.
77. As Ramage points out, "although 87.1% of Indonesians profess Islam as their religion (according to the 1980 government census), many of them do not seek to channel their political ambitions through Islam. In what is widely regarded as the most 'fair' and accurate of Indonesian elections, the 1955 parliamentary polls gave all Islamic-oriented political parties a combined total of only 43.5% of the vote." D. Ramage, *Ideological Discourse in the Indonesian New Order: State Ideology and the Beliefs of an Elite, 1985–1993*, PhD Dissertation, University of South Carolina, p. 61.
78. R. McVey, "Nationalism, Islam and Marxism: The Management of Ideological Conflict in Indonesia," Introduction; Introduction in Sukarno, *Nationalism, Islam and Marxism*, Ithaca, Cornell Modern Indonesia Project, 1969, p. 13.
79. Ibid.
80. Masyumi won between one quarter and one half of the votes in all regions except the Christian areas and Hindu-Buddhist Bali, three quarters of the vote in Aceh and was the largest party in the strongly Muslim province of West Java. However, in Central and East Java it only won 12 percent of the vote while NU won 30 percent in these provinces. Ricklefs, *Op Cit.*
81. McVey, 1969 *Op. Cit.*, p. 15.
82. McVey has pointed out that the possibility of class struggle between *priyayi* and *abangan* was largely absent in the rivalry between Masyumi and Nahdatul Ulama. Ibid.
83. Yong Mun Cheong, "The Indonesian Army and Functional Groups," in *Journal of Southeast Asian Studies*, Vol VII No. 1, March 1976. pp. 92–3.
84. Nasution, *Memenuhi Panggilan Tugas*, Vol Three, *Op. Cit.*, p. 129.
85. McKemmish, *Op. Cit.*, p. 105.
86. Nasution, *Memenuhi Panggilan Tugas*, Vol Three, *Op. Cit.*, p. 302.
87. Penders and U. Sundhaussen, *Op. Cit.*, p. 104.
88. Ibid., pp. 104–5.
89. Reeve, 1985 *Op Cit.*, p. 142.
90. Penders and Sundhaussen, *Op. Cit.*, p. 305.
91. Feith, 1962 *Op. Cit.*, p. 115.
92. McVey, 1971 *Op. Cit.*, p. 158.
93. Panggabean, *Op. Cit*, p. 217.
94. Nasution, *Memenuhi Panggilan Tugas,* Vol Three, *Op. Cit.*, p. 314.
95. "Gatot Subroto diganti Sumitro Kolopaking" ("Gatot Subroto replaced by Sumitro Kolopaking"), *Merdeka*, March 9, 1956.

96. Lev supported this view: "He [Nasution] believed IPKI would actually win lots of votes in 1955 because the army and its many families and friends would vote for it. They didn't, at least not in enough numbers. So, in effect, when he was re-appointed commander, he simply set about transforming the army into something of a political party." Email from Lev, September 6, 2004.

Chapter 8

Total People's Resistance as Military Intervention in Politics

Restored to office, Nasution became increasingly caught up within a swirling vortex of politics as the liberal-democratic institutions and conventions agreed to at the Round Table Conference were jettisoned in favor of Sukarno's evolving authoritarian structures. Paradoxically, the old revolutionary called his new system "guided democracy," a name previously favored by socially conservative patricians like R.P. Soeroso who doubted the ability of the masses to cope with liberal democracy.

While the president and Nasution now shared a distaste for the parties, Sukarno soon began to take care to counterbalance the army's leadership, whose power was considerably strengthened when martial law was declared in 1957. He did so by encouraging and accepting support from the Communist Party. At a personal level, Nasution seems not to have been able or willing to build the sort of cooperative relationship with the president that he had enjoyed with Sjarifuddin and then Hatta. While admiring Sukarno for his leadership of the independence struggle and recognizing his immense popularity and prestige, he and Sunarti were repelled by aspects of the president's behavior and personality, including his incorrigible search for new sexual partners and polygamous marital situation.

The resurgence of the PKI gave additional impetus to Nasution's predisposition toward socially conservative political views. As Sukarno began to advocate ideas for corporatist representation he began to associate them with a quest to have the army recognized as a functional group with a role to play within the political process and legislative bodies, and with the development by his people's resistance apparatus of army-backed and army-controlled civil-military functional groups. This latter means of military intervention in politics was intended to provide a means of engaging with the populace at the grassroots that might enable him to exert a measure of control over the mass organizations of the parties, including the highly effective offshoots of the PKI.

The political tumult that ushered in guided democracy accelerated a decline into economic chaos as the country's commercial, transport and industrial sectors, which had languished since the end of the Korean War, received a stunning blow when the Dutch enterprises that still dominated the formal economy were seized and taken over in response to intransigence over the West New Guinea issue. The expertise required to run them disappeared in a few months when all Dutch citizens were expelled. Army-backed organizations associated with Nasution's revived people's resistance apparatus were involved in the confiscations and, like the *Bandung Lautan Api* episode and the October 17, 1952 Affair, Nasution appears to have been a somewhat reactive bystander.

However, he was at first preoccupied with the perennial problem of disunity within the army. This became a major headache for him as regional commanders began to rebel against his headquarters and then, in a full-scale insurgency, the central government.

The origins of regional dissatisfaction were many and complex, including a perception that political life was becoming dominated by the Javanese ethnic group (heightened in November 1955 when the outer islands-oriented Burhanuddin Harahap Masyumi-led government fell and was replaced by another Ali Sastroamijoyo PNI-led cabinet), and that government expenditure was unfairly focused on Java. Many devout Muslims in these so-called "outer islands" were concerned at the rising influence of the PKI, whose power base was on Java, and that President Sukarno was too close to the PKI.

At a personal level, Nasution was in sympathy with this anti-PKI sentiment. However, although he was from the outer islands he had by then spent most of his life on the island of Java and was concerned to assert control over the territorial commanders. Some were particularly resistant to the idea that they should be rotated through a series of appointments. They were *putra daerah* or "local sons" and, under the *bapak-anak* patron-client system of command relationships that had persisted after the revolution, tended to be resistant to the authority of army headquarters. Rather, they relied upon the support of their troops.

Government expenditure on the army had declined to "catastrophic" levels after 1952 and corruption had become endemic throughout Indonesia. A factor in the resistance of local commanders to being transferred was reluctance to give up well-established and lucrative local business arrangements that often allied their interests with those of local civilian elites.[1]

Nasution was initially cautious about transferring them but by mid-1956 he had stepped up the pace. The outspoken Colonel Lubis, who was to be posted from the army headquarters to North Sumatra (to replace an also reluctant Colonel Simbolon[2] as commander of Territory I / North Sumatra), began plotting against Nasution.

Lubis was personally antipathetic toward Nasution, a fellow Batak, and extremely disappointed that Nasution, rather than he, had been chosen to lead the army. Lubis found new allies who had in some cases supported Nasution in the October 17, 1952 Affair.

Attempts to move Colonel Simbolon (North Sumatra), Colonel Kawilarang (West Java) and Colonel Warouw (East Indonesia) were to result in considerable unrest in their regions, and disaffection with Nasution. Simbolon, who held similar claims to the chief of staff position, was to be replaced by Lubis. The removal of Warouw from the lucrative Eastern Indonesia Command, where army smuggling activities were conducted openly, to an overseas diplomatic post proceeded reasonably smoothly when an appropriate officer of Sulawesi origin replaced him. However, Lubis sought to forestall the posting of Kawilarang by taking advantage of escalating tensions between the outer islands and the central government when Hatta, who was born in Sumatra, resigned as vice president in August 1956. A supporter of Lubis detained the foreign minister (Roeslan Abdulgani) on corruption charges, an order that was countermanded by Nasution.

Lubis was involved in failed attempts to send West Java-based troops to Jakarta to overthrow Nasution and was sacked after failing to comply with a summons to army headquarters. He disappeared for a while before turning up in Sumatra at a meeting of all the commanders on that island.

On December 20, 1956 Lieutenant Colonel Achmad Husein, a West Sumatra officer, took power from the local governor, Ruslan Mulyoharjo. Two days later in North Sumatra Colonel Simbolon "temporarily suspended" relations with the Jakarta government. Not long afterward Lieutenant Colonel Barlian took power from the governor of South Sumatra. The three officers then broke off relations with the Ali government in Jakarta.

In early 1957 the rebellions spread to the eastern island of Sulawesi where the governor, Andi Pangeran, and the military commander of Eastern Indonesia, Lieutenant Colonel Sumual, demanded more autonomy from Jakarta, the right to levy taxes at regional levels, central government funds for development in Eastern Indonesia, and an improvement in the living conditions of soldiers in the region. On March 2, 1957, they announced the formation of a regional movement known as *Perjuangan Semesta* (Total Struggle). Some two weeks later, the central government declared a state of martial law throughout the country.

Meanwhile, the West Irian issue remained unresolved and was attracting increased attention in Indonesia. In November 1957, an Indonesian call for the UN to order the Dutch to negotiate on West Irian was rejected, giving rise to anti-Dutch protests throughout Indonesia and further heightening the political temperature. Days later a group of Muslim zealots, who were thought to be associated with Lubis and other regional dissidents, attempted to assassinate Sukarno. The incident appears to have been the last straw for Nasution who finally abandoned attempts to reach a compromise with the regional commanders.

The crisis assumed full-blown proportions in February 1958. A revolutionary government of the Republic of Indonesia (*Pemerintah Revolusioner Republik Indonesia*—PRRI) was established, based in Padang, Central Sumatra. Its proponents were discontented military officers, some leading Masyumi politicians, and the University of Indonesia economist and leading Socialist Party (PSI) figure, Sumitro Djojohadikusumo.

After feeling reassured by the army's swift crackdown on the PKI in 1948, the United States had by this time become concerned about the Communist resurgence in the 1950s and an increasing willingness on Sukarno's part to associate himself with the party. The Central Intelligence Agency, in the guise of a private US firm, began providing rifles and ammunition before the US government went even further, backing the provision of B26 bombers and P51 fighters by Taiwan.[3] Bombing missions were flown against government troops from the Philippines (where the United States maintained large air and naval facilities) and an American citizen was shot down while carrying out a bombing raid over Ambon in May 1958.

However, the United States (and its allies) had seriously misunderstood the situation. Rather than backing an anti-Communist movement that was in a life-and-death struggle with a strong Communist one, such as in Vietnam, many of the rebels were ambivalent about taking up arms against other Indonesians and they appear to have expected the situation to be resolved through negotiation in a typical Indonesian compromise of some sort.

Faced, for once, with a technical military problem Nasution acted quickly. He efficiently assembled and commanded a combined land, sea and air operation that was impressive, given that the air force and navy had only really come into being when in 1950 they inherited World War II–era assets from the former colonial forces. By late 1958 it was clear that the insurgencies had been suppressed.

This was a major accomplishment for Nasution. His decisive and effective action was instrumental in saving his country from an American-backed proxy war that might have engendered enduring bitterness and division if it had been prolonged.

In a major change to the political landscape, the central government subsequently banned Masyumi and the Indonesian Socialist Party. Rebel leaders who included former prime minister and PSI leader Syahrir and the leading Masyumi figure and former leader of the revolutionary emergency government in Sumatra, Sjafruddin Prawiranegara, were arrested. As mentioned earlier, Dr. Sumitro Djojohadikusumo fled to Malaysia where he remained for many years.

Unlike the October 17, 1952 Affair, where Nasution had sometimes been accused of being in alliance with the PSI, he now stood with Sukarno and against the PSI. Whereas in 1955 Masyumi had supported Nasution's reappointment as army chief of staff, Nasution had opposed important elements of this party by suppressing the rebellions. Importantly, he had eliminated his main rivals for the leadership.

His focus upon the revolts had not impeded him from giving attention to concepts associated with "people's resistance." This is evident in his first Order of the Day which emphasized the need for a "people's army" and "people's defence":

> They must safeguard the sovereignty [of the nation] . . . against internal uprisings and subversive actions from the outside. They must plan the military sector in the context of advancing the unfinished 1945 Revolution. They must gradually form "a People's Army with the Soldier of 1945 as its core, to pioneer People's Defence to safeguard the State of the Proclamation [of Independence] against any possible internal or external aggression."[4]

Penders and Sundhaussen point out that the three sentences quoted above were so important to Nasution that they appeared identically in articles in the daily *Pedoman* on November 1 and 3, 1955, in his Order of the Day, and in Sukarno's Armed Forces Day speech of October 5, 1955.[5]

Nasution's reference to "People's Defence" aimed at overcoming "internal uprisings" indicates that he was already interested in using "people's war" strategies and apparatus against internal opponents. Obvious targets were the *Darul Islam* and other insurgents then active in various parts of the country. However, the PKI may well have interpreted it as a warning about its own activities as Nasution's reinstatement was preceded by press speculation of an army crackdown on that party. For example, in November 1955 the Indonesian national news agency, Antara, carried a report from the US Christian Science Monitor to the effect that the reinstatement of Nasution was likely to lead to a crackdown on the PKI. The article stated that the army was "expected to play an even more active political role here following the success of the Communist Party in this young Republic's first general election on September 29."[6]

Nasution had presaged the formation of an inspectorate general of territorial affairs and people's resistance in *Fundamentals of Guerrilla Warfare*.[7] His planning for the introduction of an organisation of this type to implement some of the reforms set out in his Order of the Day was made clear immediately after his reinstatement[8] and an inspectorate general of territorial affairs and people's resistance was subsequently formed as part of his shake-up of the structure of the army.[9]

Preparations for the establishment of the inspectorate general were under way as early as February 1956, as evidenced by a press announcement of officer postings, including that of Major Pamurahardjo to work under the chief of staff for "arrangements under the purview of the Inspector General of Territorial [Affairs]."[10] The first inspector general (officially appointed on May 23, 1956) was Colonel Sadikin, the *Siliwangi* commander in the final year of the revolution.[11] His anti-Communist credentials included commanding the forces involved in suppressing the Madiun Affair and his appointment as commander of the Madiun military area in September 1948.[12]

According to a January 1956 army document, the new inspectorate general was to:

> assist in a return to a people's army concept, organise training schemes for veterans, village guards and school cadets, prepare for the return to civilian life of older men discharged from the army, and maintain close relations between the army and the general populace.[13]

The time was right for Nasution to reemphasize people's defense as his reputation as a guerrilla warfare strategist was on the rise. In 1953, soon after he commenced his period on the inactive list, he had published his influential *Fundamentals of Guerrilla Warfare* and the first volume of *TNI* was completed in 1955 and published shortly after his reinstatement. In his campaign speeches on behalf of IPKI he had referred to the "guerrilla struggle" and castigated the prominence in the 1950s of Indonesians who had earlier been neutral or sided with the Dutch.

Promoting, as they did, an image of harmony between soldiers and civilians in support of the lofty ideal of upholding the state against external attack, his books appeared at an opportune time in fragmented and crisis-ridden Indonesia. It also helped that memories of General Sudirman were being rekindled. For example, when senior officers gathered in Yogyakarta to sign the Charter of Army Unity in 1955 they made a pilgrimage to Sudirman's grave. Sudirman had not lived to become embroiled in the conflicts, disillusion and turmoil that affected the army and political life in general after the transfer of sovereignty. He had opposed the resumption of negotiations with the Dutch in 1949 and the terms of the Round Table Agreement, which were increasingly being regarded as onerous, demeaning, and (in the case of the retention of West Irian by the Dutch) neocolonial.

In his first Order of the Day, Nasution referred to Sudirman's last message to the army in August 1949 in which he described the army as the "only national property of the Republic" which had emerged from the struggle for independence "unimpaired and unchanged" as it had never surrendered to the Dutch. The army therefore had an obligation "to defend persistently the survival of the Proclamation of 17 August 1945." Penders and Sundhaussen consider that the inclusion of this message was "ominous" and conveyed a clear antipathy toward politicians at a time when their prestige had become very low.[14]

In August 1953 Sukarno had joined in expressing disillusionment with Western-style liberal democracy. He called for a form of democracy that would embody Indonesia's "soul," elements of which were *gotong royong* and consultation aimed at achieving consensus, rather than voting.[15] In 1954, he had called for the formation of an "Indonesian National Congress" to mobilize support for the return of the territory of West Irian. In January 1955, an *Angkatan '45* [Generation of '45] Committee formed a Congress Committee to advance the proposal but became bogged down in party politics.[16]

During 1956 the president made a series of speeches in which he criticized the multiparty system and proposed changes to the political system that culminated in his proposal to introduce means of interest representation through functional groups. In early August 1956, he attacked the party system and called for all political forces to unite. A week later he expressed concern that the elections had not produced a more stable set of political forces.[17]

In late October, Sukarno went further, calling for the parties to be "buried," and for "guided democracy" and a single state party to replace them. As regional unrest, political uncertainty and economic malaise worsened, Sukarno announced that he would soon bring forth a "political conception" or *konsepsi* that would provide an overall solution to the country's problems.

Sukarno made his *konsepsi* address to the nation in February 1957. In it he repudiated liberal democracy and called for a return to what he regarded as "traditional" non-confrontational methods of interest representation.

> The principles of Western democracy, the parliamentary democracy of the western countries, incorporate the concept of an active opposition, and it is precisely the adoption of this concept that has given rise to the difficulties we have experienced over the past eleven years. By accepting this concept, we have come to think in a manner which is alien to the Indonesian way of life.[18]

Reflecting his emphasis on "traditional" values, he proposed the formation of a *gotong royong* cabinet with membership from the four major political parties to emerge from the general elections.

Sukarno had originally discovered the functional group idea in the 1930s[19] and began to promote the idea of corporatist forms of representation through functional groups as an alternative to the parties after a tour of Eastern

European countries in 1956. In his *konsepsi* speech he announced that he would call into existence a *Dewan Nasional* or national council comprising representatives of functional groups in society. In a move that was clearly aimed at downgrading the importance of parliament, he stated that because these groups were "functional in society" they would therefore be "a reflection of society, just as the Cabinet is a reflection of parliament."[20] The various "functional groups" which were to be given membership in the *Dewan Nasional* would include representatives of labor, youth, intellectuals, farmers, journalists, religious scholars, business, women, artists and minorities.[21] Cabinet ministers and the armed forces chiefs of staff were also to be members of the *Dewan*.

The more conservative political parties vehemently opposed the inclusion of the PKI[22] and some were also wary of the functional group concept because of its potential to weaken the role of the parties and the parliament. Nevertheless, Sukarno inaugurated the *Dewan Nasional* in July 1957.[23]

Suwirjo of the PNI was charged with forming a *gotong royong* cabinet but failed in his mission. Sukarno himself subsequently formed an extra-parliamentary cabinet led by Prime Minister Djuanda, although it failed to include Masyumi and the PKI.[24]

The principle of including societal groups in legislative bodies had been provided for in the defunct 1945 Constitution. In addition to providing executive powers to the president, Article Two of that document provided for the inclusion of groups representing occupations or interests within the upper house of parliament.[25] The clarification to the 1945 Constitution defines groups (*golongan-golongan*) as associations including worker's groups, farmers, youth organizations, cooperatives and other collective associations. However, the idea of this form of representation was jettisoned when the interim liberal-democratic constitution was adopted in December 1949.

The 1945 Constitution only referred to "groups" or *golongan* and not functional groups and its drafters clearly never intended the armed forces—which did not exist at the time this document was drafted—to be categorized as a group. However, it became apparent to Djokosutono (who was advising the president on constitutional matters)[26] and then Nasution that a reintroduction of the 1945 Constitution and a reinterpretation of the meaning of *golongan* might leave the door open for the armed forces to acquire a legally sanctioned political role by gaining representation in the legislature. Over time, Nasution also became aware that the army could employ the functional group concept to form civil-military cooperation bodies based upon shared function, rather than ideology, from the mass organizations of the parties.

The following passage from Nasution's *Towards a People's Army* is typical of his explanations of and justifications for the army's new political role:

The military men are now not only [part of the] State apparatus technically but also are functional groups. They can become ministers. The Armed Forces must understand clearly the difference between [being part of] the State apparatus and functional group[s]. . . . The Armed Forces' functional group cooperates side by side with political groups, functional groups in the field of religion, material and spiritual development.[27]

He had called for a return to the 1945 Constitution in his IPKI campaign material and Professor Djokosutono clearly played a role in advising him on this feature of the Constitution.

Based upon his personal acquaintance with Djokosutono, Daniel Lev (the author of the seminal work *The Transition to Guided Democracy*)[28] believed that Nasution's corporatist ideas were influenced:

on the one hand by Djokosutono's digging up of Italian fascist ideas, and on the other by his (Nasution's) concern to find a formula that rendered the army equal to or superior to the political parties, which were the main obstruction to Nas's vision of military guidance of the state.[29]

Lev happened to be present at Djokosutono's residence when one of Nasution's officers visited:

He was a lieutenant, I think, who simply ran errands for Nas and came to pick up letters or reports or to give Djoko requests from Nas. Djoko gave the young officer some paper, and when he had left told me that Nas had long ago asked for some formulation of the army's position and also for some ideas about managing the state in a more orderly fashion. That would have been in late 1957 or 1958. When Djoko and I talked about these issues, it must have been in mid or late 1959 or so. Thus, we were actually talking about history. . . . The answer to the first problem was "the army's middle way," *jalan tengah tentara*; the second resulted in the *golongan karya* [functional groups], chief of which was of course the army.[30]

In later years Nasution claimed that it was on President Sukarno's initiative, rather than his, that the army was classified as a functional group. When interviewed by Australian ABC Television in the early 1990s, he contended that he had never intended the military to become so dominant in day-to-day political life. He asserted that he had only intended the army to become involved in "the broad guidelines of state policy" but had been overruled by Sukarno who had told him that the military must do more because it was a functional group, and that was how the army had come to occupy seats in the legislatures.

Nasution appears to have presaged the concept of the army adopting a "middle way" between participation in politics while not taking over the state in *Fundamentals of Guerrilla Warfare*.[31] In old age, he complained that the style of military intervention the army had adopted under Suharto's New Order regime no longer accorded with his "middle way" formulation.[32] Nasution seems to have been selective in his memory of these events but much of what took place in the frenetic political atmosphere of the time is still unclear.

Sukarno said in his *konsepsi* speech that he did not consider the armed forces to be functional groups, although the veterans clearly were.[33] However, by July of that year Sukarno was clearly on the side of giving the armed forces this classification, declaring that the *Dewan Nasional* would comprise:

> persons from the following groups: workers, peasants, intelligentsia, artists, women, Christians, Muslims, national entrepreneurs, the army, navy and air force.[34]

A well-timed series of articles by Colonel Suhud Prawiroatmodjo in the Jakarta daily *Merdeka* in February 1957 indicate that the army leadership was beginning to think of the army as a *golongan* in its own right prior to Sukarno's *konsepsi* address. Suhud was a former PETA officer who later wrote about the rigors of PETA training and the ethos that the Japanese sought to implant in PETA trainees.[35] He was steeped in Javanese traditionalism and after his retirement in the late 1950s established a successful plantation in East Java where he sought a Javanese spiritual basis to growing traditional Indonesian crops.[36]

His articles show that the army leadership was beginning to associate corporatist / functional modes of interest representation with "people's resistance" by linking the idea of the army as a *golongan* with its formative experience as a guerrilla force. The army headquarters appears to have wanted to use them to condition public opinion toward the idea of the army acting as a *golongan* or group within society, alongside other social forces. In a similar vein to arguments Nasution had put forward in *Fundamentals of Guerrilla Warfare*, Suhud based this claim on the army being a stakeholder in the revolution and not just a tool of the state.

He began by asserting that Indonesian military personnel had greater rights to participate in political life than members of armies in other countries because of the Indonesian Army's unusual origins:

> It was not the State that took the initiative in forming and creating its military; moreover, it was not the State that preceded and led [the military]. Rather, it followed [developments] and only then regulated, step-by-step, the growth of the military with various formal regulations.[37]

He sought to root the idea in the military administration of 1949 which he described as a "Totalitarian Military Government that subordinated the civil government which was also totalitarian in nature as an absolute necessity in defending and saving the State of the Republic of Indonesia."[38]

After Sukarno announced his *konsepsi,* Prawiroatmodjo followed up with another article in which he claimed that the army was a *golongan* with similar rights to participation in the political process as other social groups:

> The TNI as the armed freedom fighter *pejuang* group of citizens was born at the same time and is equal to other groups of citizens, such as political groups or parties, economic groups, religious and cultural clubs or associations and other social groups or agglomerations. These groups all stand shoulder to shoulder in shaping the State and its apparatus, in jointly regulating structures of life, in driving out threats from any source, both external and internal."[39]

Prawiroatmodjo went on to display a remarkable degree of prescience in calling for the army to adopt a "middle way" in involving itself in non-military affairs:

> If power in the military and political fields is held by one person in the one pair of hands as was the case with Caesarism and Bonapartism there will clearly be no conflict between military and political elements. In order to prevent this sort of Caesarism and Bonapartism, Clausewitz proposed following a middle way. Make the commanders members of the cabinet so that they can take part in cabinet discussions and decisions regarding important matters.[40]

There is a strong probability that Nasution was behind the colonel's articles. The similar lines of argument that he had run in *Fundamentals of Guerrilla Warfare* point to this, and although Simatupang has written that Nasution was by no means "a keen student of Clausewitz"[41] (as Penders and Sundhaussen assert)[42] he liked to quote the Prussian military theorist's dictum on the need for civilian and military elites to work closely together toward clearly defined goals.[43] His history of antipathy toward civilian control over the military in crisis situations went back to his opposition to the Regional Defense Councils during the revolution.

Nasution writes that he only announced that the army would adopt a "middle way" after he learned that the president would accede to his recommendation to return to the 1945 Constitution:

> Accordingly, in my graduation address at the Military Academy in Magelang I officially affirmed the TNI opinion [of its place] in national life: it could not be just an "instrument [that was responsive to] civilians" like in the Western democracies, and it also could not be a "military regime" which monopolised power, but would follow a middle way as [provided for] in the 1945 Constitution which Professor Djokosutono later termed "the army's middle way."[44]

Lev writes of Nasution and like-minded officers placing a considerable amount of pressure on Sukarno and the parties. In particular, he describes Nasution maneuvering and applying pressure on the parties while Sukarno was on an overseas trip in mid-1959, and upon Sukarno when he returned.[45]

In November 1958, the *Dewan Nasional* completed deliberations on a new electoral law in which half the seats in the DPR would be reserved for functional groups that were to be nominated through a National Front, thus seeking to detach the mass organizations from the parties. The list of functional groups proposed included general categories or functions such as youth, women and artists. Significantly, it also included the armed forces and the veterans as functional groups.[46]

The proposal was put to the embattled House of Representatives but no agreement could be reached. Many party leaders opposed representation through functional groups and fears were expressed that such a corporatist style of representation could lead to fascism. It was also argued that functional groups in themselves would not achieve any greater degree of consensus than the parties had done and there was still a great deal of uncertainty about how groups would be categorized and recognized as little work had apparently been done to refine the concept since it was mooted in 1957.[47]

Finally, Sukarno, with the full endorsement of Nasution, proposed to the body which had been established to frame a permanent constitution (the *Konstituante*) that the 1945 Constitution be restored. A heated debate ensued in that committee over the status of Islam within the state. Three votes were taken on whether to return to the 1945 Constitution and each time a majority was in favor. However, on each occasion the majority fell short of the two-thirds needed to approve a draft constitution.

The army leadership piled on the pressure, placing a ban on all political activities. It then stepped up the tension with a series of statements from military officers suggesting that the president should reinstate the 1945 Constitution by decree, including a statement to that effect by a new Youth-Military Cooperative Body (*Badan Kerja Sama Pemuda-Militer*—BKS)[48] that was comprised of the army and the youth mass organizations of the four major parties to emerge from the general elections. On July 5, 1959, with the full support of the army, Sukarno reintroduced the 1945 Constitution by presidential decree and the Guided Democracy era began.

The army's categorization as a functional group under the 1945 Constitution was a most significant milestone in the history of military intervention in Indonesia. The formation of the Youth-Military Cooperative Body and then other "cooperative groups" for different sectors of society such as labor, peasants, fishermen and religious scholars, was also important because it indicated that Nasution was now attempting another string to his "middle way" bow of intervening in politics. He had turned his attention to weakening the parties and particularly the PKI which had enjoyed a great deal of success in forming large mass organizations and mobilizing them in its support.

Unlike this more limited development, in 1958 outright military coups were launched in Pakistan and Burma. There were constant rumors and press speculation about the possibility of one happening in Indonesia and Sukarno took advantage of the situation to force concessions from the parties.[49] However, it would have been difficult for Nasution to take a more direct route to power by staging an outright coup.

By the mid-to-late 1950s there was an oppressive atmosphere surrounding the regional revolts and the imposition of martial law that was becoming detrimental to the prestige of the army. Sukarno was becoming increasingly assertive and popular and demonstrations in his support (often organized by the PKI) took place frequently. The perennial problems of command and control and a lack of support for Nasution's reemergence as chief of staff within sections of the army officer corps were also deterrents to staging a coup. He lacked direct command and control over troops who could intervene decisively in the capital as the Jakarta district was under the military command of the *Siliwangi* Division, from which Nasution had long since separated, and they could not be relied upon to present a united front. There was also the possibility of one of the other Java-based divisions and particularly the Central Java *Diponegoro* Division staging a counter coup had the *Siliwangi* managed to seize power in Jakarta.

Another factor which worked against the possibility of the army leadership or a faction within it staging a coup was that they could not necessarily trust the other services, particularly the air force. Air Commodore Suryadarma, the air force chief, was an old rival of Nasution who, as previously noted, had surrendered to the Dutch in 1948. He and his wife had sympathies with the political left and the air force was believed to be heavily infiltrated by the PKI. While not having a large amount of striking power it could be expected to cause problems in any coup attempt by the army.

Whereas in the early 1950s the army was divided into administrators and solidarity makers, Lev has identified the existence of radical and moderate groups within the army in the mid-to-late 1950s. Generally, the moderates were from the Javanese divisions. Such officers tended to be loyal to Sukarno and to feel that the army should be a "driving force behind the civilian administration" rather than attempt to rule by themselves. On the other hand, the radicals tended to be from the outer islands and less impressed with the civil administration. Of course, as Lev argues, there were divisions within both the Java-based and outer-islands-based officer corps, personal factors played a role in determining the loyalties of officers, and it is not possible to categorize officers as radicals or moderates simply on the basis of their ethnic origin or unit affiliations.[50]

An interview Lev conducted with General Yani, a future army chief of staff, is revealing of the attitudes of the officers before some regional commanders rebelled against the central government and Nasution in 1957:

> One group of officers wanted a very quick change in the government [in 1956–1957], one that if necessary would go ahead without the President. This group ended up in the rebellion. The second group was more moderate, and it . . . is now the leadership of the army. This second group realised that there could be no very rapid change—i.e., no military coup—and certainly not one that left out the President. These officers realised that the President was essential, that there was no other political leader with the influence of the President over the masses and over other political groups in the country.
>
> Also, this moderate group took the view that if the President were pushed aside, unity in the army would be endangered. Above all, the most important factor is army unity; it is essential to the nation and to the welfare of the army as a participant in the life of the nation.
>
> There was no unity in the army between these two major groups, and the moderates realised that a military coup would prevent unity from being achieved, since the differences between the two groups would then be thrown into stark relief. The moderate group also feared . . . government by coup. Because there was no unity in the army, the first coup would eventually set off another coup by an opposing group and so on ad infinitum. This is what the moderate group wanted to prevent at all costs.[51]

The suppression of the regional rebellions had brought about greater unity and coherence within the officer corps, in that the "moderates" had prevailed over the "radicals," but it had also strengthened the position of the president. In Lev's words:

> Army leaders were never able to forge the true consensus in the officer corps that would make it an effective political organisation with well-defined and articulated goals. . . . And so long as differences continued to exist within the officer corps, it was more convenient to recognise the authority of President Sukarno than to risk exacerbating internal disunity by assuming more political responsibility.[52]

Lev concludes that "Like the civilian elite which it was to some extent succeeding, the officer corps became a political group with visible interests to defend. The antagonism between the army elite and the PKI must be understood partly in these terms."[53]

Operating from a powerful position as the enforcer of martial law but constrained by these factors, Nasution sought to take advantage of Sukarno's evolving ideas for guided democracy by taking the BKS concept a step further in January 1958. While Sukarno, the PKI and other nationalist forces expressed outrage at the refusal of the Dutch to hand over the territory of West Irian, he appears not to have been as emotionally committed.[54] However, he saw the need and opportunity to deal the army into the growing Sukarno- and PKI-led campaign to force the Dutch to concede by consolidating the army's BKS civil-military cooperation organizations into a newly formed West Irian National Liberation Front (*Front Pembebasan Nasional Irian Barat*—FNPIB) of which he was chairman.

NOTES

1. McVey, 1971 *Op. Cit.*, p. 152, 153.
2. Simbolon might at first have been inclined to go along with the planned rotation, but became caught up in the political power plays within Sumatra that culminated in the PRRI regional rebellion. For an interesting (although perhaps hagiographic) account of his life, see P. Bangun, *Kolonel Maludin Simbolon: Liku-liku Perjuangannya dalam Pembangunan Bangsa* (translated title *Colonel Maludin Simbolon: Twists and Turns of his Struggle in the Development of the Nation*), Jakarta, Pustaka Sinar Harapan, 1996.
3. Ernst Utrecht, *The Military and the 1977 Election*, Townsville, Qld., James Cook University of North Queensland, South East Asian Studies Committee, 1980, p. 87, 89. For an authoritative and comprehensive account of these actions by the CIA, see Audrey R. Kahin and George McT. Kahin, *Subversion as Foreign Policy: The Secret Eisenhower and Dulles Debacle in Indonesia*, New York, Free Press, 1995.
4. Penders and Sundhaussen, *Op. Cit.*, p. 106.
5. Ibid.
6. *Antara*, November 18, 1955.
7. A. H. Nasution, *Fundamentals*, p. 84.
8. Penders and Sundhaussen, *Op. Cit.*, p. 110. Consistent with his persistence in creating a more professional officer corps, at the same time Nasution established an inspectorate general of education and training to upgrade the professional skills of officers. Ibid.
9. *Reorganisasi TNI-AD Tahun 1984*, pp. 15, 16. "Sekitar Mutasi-mutasi di AD: Pengisian jabatan Teras SUAD selesai" ("Transfers in the Army: Filling of senior officer appointments in Army General Staff Complete"), *Suluh Indonesia*, June 6, 1956.
10. "Pemindahan pejabat-pejabat Perwira" ("Transfer of officers"), *Pikiran Rakyat*, February 25, 1956. Pamurahardjo was one of three officers listed as being assigned to this duty.
11. "Insp. Jend. Pemeriksaan Umum untuk sehatkan A.D." ("An Inspectorate-General of General Inspection to make Army healthy"), *Merdeka*, July 21, 1956.
12. Bachtiar, *Op. Cit.*, p. 269, 270.
13. Penders and Sundhaussen, *Op. Cit.*, p. 110.
14. Ibid., p. 107.

15. Reeve, *Op. Cit.*, p. 113.
16. Ibid.
17. Ibid., p. 115.
18. Guy Pauker, "The Role of Political Organisations in Indonesia," *Far Eastern Survey*, September 1958, p. 139.
19. Lev, *Op. Cit.*, p. 24.
20. Sukarno, "Safeguarding the Republic of the Proclamation" in Feith and Castles, *Op. Cit.*, p. 87, 88.
21. Ibid.
22. Lev, *Op. Cit.*, p. 18.
23. Ibid., p. 24. As it turned out, the parties with the exception of Masyumi, tended to retain their influence on the functional groups within the *Dewan Nasional* through party-associated functional group appointees. "The PNI and the PKI largely shared the labor, peasantry, youth and journalist categories.... NU monopolized the Islamic religious representation. Six or seven of [the] Council members with political party connections would, when necessary, firmly defend the interests of their parties against the encroachments of Guided Democracy." Ibid., pp. 27–8.
24. Nevertheless, supporters of these parties were included. Ibid.
25. *The 1945 Constitution of the Republic of Indonesia*, p. 7. The main roles of this chamber (the People's Consultative Assembly—*Majelis Permusyawaratan Rakyat*—MPR) were to determine broad guidelines of state policy and select mandate holders, in the form of a president and vice president, to implement them.
26. See D. Reeve, "The Corporatist State: The Case of Golkar," in A. Budiman (ed.), *State and Civil Society* p. 161 for an exploration of the possibility that Djokosutono and his close colleague and fellow constitutional lawyer, Professor Supomo, influenced Nasution to accept the functional group concept.
27. A. H. Nasution, *Towards a People's Army*, Jakarta, Delegasi, 1964, p. 22.
28. D.S. Lev, *The Transition to Guided Democracy*: Indonesian Politics, 1957–1959. Ithaca, NY: Modern Indonesia Project, Southeast Asia Program, Department of Asian Studies, Cornell University, 1966.
29. Excerpt from email from Daniel Lev, August 18, 2004.
30. Ibid.
31. Nasution, *Fundamentals*, *Op. Cit.*, p. 97.
32. *Riding the Tiger*, Australian ABC television documentary series, 1992.
33. See Leo Suryadinata, *Military Ascendancy and Political Culture: A Study of Indonesia's Golkar*, Athens, Ohio, Center for International Studies, 1989, p. 7.
34. Ibid.
35. Anderson, 1972 *Op. Cit.*, pp. 22–24.
36. The plantation is at Kaliklatak, at the eastern end of Java. His widow remarked to a journalist that he was "a real Javanese. He believed in the saying, 'Put before you the ocean, behind you the mountains, in between the land will bring you happiness.'" Ron Gluckman, "The Best Joe in Java," www.gluckman.com, accessed January 2005.
37. "Colonel Suhud Prawiroatmodjo, Kedudukan T.N.I. Dalam Masyarakat (I): Kedudukan Menurut Hukum Formil" ("Colonel Suhud Prawiroatmodjo, The Position

of the TNI in Society (I): The Position According to Formal Law") *Merdeka*, February 18, 1957.

38. Ibid.

39. "Colonel Suhud Prawiroatmodjo, "Anggota T.N.I. Menyongsong Konsepsi Bung Karno: 1. T.N.I. Menuju Keutuhan Bangsa dan Keutuhan Negara"), ("Colonel Suhud Prawiroatmodjo, Members of the TNI Welcome Bung Karno's Concept: 1. The TNI [Striving] Towards the Integrity of the Nation and the Integrity of the State"), *Merdeka*, March 5, 1957.

40. "Kedudukan T.N.I." ("The Position of the T.N.I."), *Merdeka*, February 21, 1957 *Op. Cit.*

41. Simatupang, 1996 *Op. Cit.*, p. 102. Cribb, 2001 *Op. Cit.*, p. 146.

42. Penders and Sundhaussen, *Op. Cit.*, p. 49.

43. For example, see Nasution, *Memenuhi Panggilan Tugas*, Vol One, 1990, p. 220.

44. Nasution, *Memenuhi Panggilan Tugas*, Vol Four, *Op. Cit.*, pp. 303–304. Nasution, *Memenuhi Panggilan Tugas*, Vol Four, *Op. Cit.*, p. 91.

45. Lev, *Op. Cit.*, pp. 269–277

46. Ibid., p. 126

47. Lev, *Op. Cit.*, p. 219.

48. Ibid., 273.

49. See Lev, *Transition, Op. Cit.*, p. 189, 190, 201, 204 for a discussion of the ways in which Sukarno used the possibility of a coup to force concessions from the parties.

50. Ibid., p. 71.

51. Ibid.

52. Ibid.

53. Ibid., p. 74.

54. Penders and Sundhausen, *Op. Cit.*, pp. 149–150.

Chapter 9

Civil-Military Cooperation Bodies

Nasution's involvement in the establishment of the BKS Civil-Military cooperation bodies provides a glimpse of the rapidly changing currents of Indonesian politics that he sought to navigate through and exploit in the final years of the 1950s. Reeve interprets Nasution's behavior in forming them as "vigorous but derivative, grasping eagerly at the developments in Sukarno's political thinking."[1] While this is true, Nasution was far from derivative in placing the BKS groups within his renewed "people's resistance" apparatus. Importantly, neither Sukarno (nor the PKI) could claim to have taken meaningful parts in the "people's resistance" campaigns against the Dutch, and his use of this apparatus was both a convenient way of intervening in politics at the grassroots by seeking to co-opt the party mass organizations and a reminder that many in the army saw themselves as important stakeholders in the revolution and not just tools of the state.

This association between army-led "people's resistance" and corporatist means of interest representation was to influence the political behavior of the Indonesian Army during its uneasy power-sharing relationship with President Sukarno under Guided Democracy, and then during the three decades of the New Order regime. It entailed the linking of an idea that originated outside the army, representation through functional groups, and "people's resistance" which was associated with the army's own core concepts and experiences.

The functional group idea and the use of the army's people's resistance apparatus to form the BKS organizations were strangely compatible. Whereas Sukarno sought to dampen the relevance and power of the parties by providing for interest representation through functional groups, the strategies for "people's resistance" that Nasution developed during the revolutionary period provided a pretext and means of mobilizing civilian communities that was not associated with a particular party or ideology and was linked in the minds of many officers with the military administration in which they, rather than the parties, were in charge.

However, due, undoubtedly, to the Machiavellian and rapidly changing political maneuvering that took place as Indonesia lurched from crisis to crisis, the timing of Nasution's reemphasis on "total people's resistance" and its association with the functional group concept has often not been made clear.

In his *Indonesian Doctrine of Territorial Warfare and Territorial Management,* Guy Pauker does not mention Nasution's establishment of the inspectorate general in 1956.[2]

Lev notes a connection between the BKS initiative and territorial warfare but only describes it in very general terms, and he does not link it with the inspectorate general:

> The theoretical basis of the effort was the concept of territorial warfare, the basic doctrine of defence strategy to which Nasution had committed the Army. Possibly originating in Japanese occupation ideas and undoubtedly influenced by revolutionary experience, territorial warfare, as Nasution explained it, was essentially a guerrilla strategy in which each area of the country would be prepared to defend itself, independent of central direction, against outside attack. This would require not only proper logistics and tactics but also considerable social, economic, and political preparation, in which the Army would necessarily assume the leading organisational role. The political implications of the doctrine are obvious and, after 1957, tended to take precedence over its military significance.[3]

Reeve and other researchers (for example Yong Mun Cheong[4] and Leo Suryadinata[5]) have written extensively about the emergence of functional groups in Indonesia. However, they have not identified an association between territorial warfare/people's resistance and the army's involvement in corporatism at the very outset of the army's formation of the BKS organizations.

Reeve, who quotes Pauker's *Doctrine of Territorial Warfare* extensively in his *Golkar of Indonesia,*[6] provides a comprehensive and valuable account of the association between the army's territorial warfare apparatus and its support for the functional group concept from 1958. He notes the establishment of the inspectorate general "after [Nasution's] reappointment as Chief of Staff" in *Golkar of Indonesia*[7] but implies in a subsequent paper (*The Corporatist State: The Case of Golkar*) that the inspectorate was established after the various BKS were formed.[8]

On the other hand, Supriyatmono explicitly associates the BKS initiative with "total people's resistance":

> From Nasution's point of view, the Civil-Military BKS were a joint working forum for the military and the functional groups or mass organisations, which

would also reflect the close relations between the military and the civilians or between the TNI and the people, which at the same time was based on "territorial warfare" or total people's resistance. [9]

The responsibility of the inspectorate general for the BKS initiative was made explicit in an instruction issued by Nasution to the inspector general regarding the establishment of the first BKS in July 1957. In his capacity as chief of army staff and (martial law) military authority, Nasution directed the Inspector General for Territorial Affairs and People's Resistance to:

in the shortest possible time carry out a meeting, the intention of which is to invite all existing youth organisations to consider a program which has been agreed by the four core organisations.[10]

Clearly, this instruction gave the inspector general, as a member of the Daily Staff of the [martial law] Military Authority, a central role in the BKS enterprise.[11]

To some extent, these organizations owed their existence to the Legion of Veterans of the Republic of Indonesia (LVRI). This body was formed in 1956 outside the direct auspices of the inspectorate general but with the involvement of Major Pamurahardjo. It was this officer who went on to develop the BKS initiative from his position within the inspectorate general of Territorial Affairs and People's Resistance.[12]

Pamurahardjo was most unlike the cautious and conservative Nasution. He was a politically active officer of the 1945 generation with links to the "national communist" *Murba* Party and President Sukarno. He would prove to be yet another subordinate who was difficult for Nasution to control.

Pamurahardjo confirmed the link between the LVRI and the BKS initiative when interviewed in 1996. He was closely involved in the formation of the LVRI and "gained experience and the inspiration" for the BKS initiative from the LVRI exercise. Obviously proud of his role, he described the first of the BKS organizations, the Youth-Military Cooperation Body, as a "pure endeavour" and asserted that a range of organizations "from the extreme left to the extreme right" were willing to belong to it because its focus was on Dutch "subversion" and the campaign to "restore" West Irian to the republic.

He implied that the first of the functional groups that he formed, the Youth-Military Cooperation Body (*Badan Kerja Sama Pemuda-Militer*—BKS-PM), was a more focused organization than the LVRI, whose sole objective was the unification of all the veterans' organizations and the denial of them to political enemies such as the PKI.[13] However, the basic elements of the army's efforts to establish a single veterans' association (the separation of mass organizations for veterans from party control and their affiliation with an army-backed agency) were part of a pattern which was continued (rather than initiated) when he began to establish the BKS functional groups in June 1957.

Reeve has noted that Sukarno's intention in coming up with the functional group idea was to detach the mass organizations "from the parties and to draw them together on the bases of common 'functional' interests and of commitment to his own grand vision."[14] A proportional representation, rather than a district electorate system, prevailed in Indonesia and this tended to concentrate the attention of the party leaderships and parliamentarians on what might now be called "the beltway." The mass organizations were often more vital and in touch with grassroots Indonesia than the often remote and Jakarta-centric parties themselves.

Pauker has vividly described the fissiparous and poorly organized nature of Indonesian political parties and organizations (except for the PKI) and the lack of ability of the party leaders (again with the exception of the PKI) to directly coordinate their mass organizations.[15] Many conservative Indonesians were concerned about the PKI's clearly superior organizational skills at the village level where most Indonesians lived, as Donald Fagg, who carried out research into the social structure of a town in Central-East Java in 1953–1954, points out:

> In their untiring, well-planned, well-organised and well-financed activities the Communists seemed a few years ago unrivalled in the small towns and villages of Java. Other organisations, outclassed in terms of initiative, sense of direction and material means, were either put in the position of going along or had to leave the field to the Communists.[16]

Guy Pauker, who had close relations with army officers, observed in 1958 that the leadership saw a need to develop the BKS initiative to compete with the organizational skills of the PKI:

> Developments in the last two years indicate that the army, unlike the non-Communist political organisations, is increasingly aware of and familiar with the value of organisational techniques through which to reach and integrate the intermediate social strata.
>
> Clearly the army was establishing control over the activities of the auxiliary organisations of the political parties and other voluntary organisations, though not over the parties themselves.[17]

Guillermo O'Donnell notes that authoritarian regimes establish state corporatist structures "to control or to prevent the emergence of autonomous organisational bases, leaders and goals that might carry its political activation beyond the limits acceptable to the new bourgeois and state-based sectors."[18] In attempting to establish army-backed quasi-state corporatist bodies in the form of the BKS functional groups a decade before the army achieved outright power Nasution was acting in a highly precocious manner.

Like the regimes that establish state corporatist structures, Nasution appears to have hoped that the BKS initiative had the potential to suppress forces that threatened the social order by taking over the mass organizations of the parties on the pretext that there was a need to unify all the divergent streams of opinion (*aliran*) of Indonesia behind an overriding and inclusive nationalism, as defined by the army. This is evident in reactions of contemporary researchers. For example, Lev states that Nasution intended to prise the mass organizations away from the parties, organize them on a functional basis and channel all their activities through the cooperation bodies. In doing so, a measure of control would be exerted over them and they would be to some extent depoliticized and stripped of ideology.[19]

However, a highly distinctive feature of the BKS initiative that sets it most apart from those of the regimes O'Donnell describes was its association from the outset with Nasution's concepts of "people's resistance." Had Nasution not formed the Inspectorate General of Territorial Affairs and People's Resistance, Pamurahardjo would have lacked a pretext and a context to form the BKS-PM. Pamurahardjo asserts that it was his duty as the head of People's Resistance within the inspectorate general to foster "people's resistance" to Dutch subversion and rally the people behind the West Irian cause.[20]

An East Javanese former PETA officer, Pamurahardjo had taken part in the Battle of Surabaya and commanded a unit that took part in the late 1948 to early 1949 return of republican units to East Java following the Dutch assault on Yogyakarta in December 1948. In Yogyakarta, he served as President Sukarno's military adjutant.

An example of the type of political activities this officer involved himself in is the confiscation of the Jakarta Club, a successor to the colonial-era *Harmonie* Society that had been a haven for the Dutch elites. Although it was demolished decades ago, the club building was so well-known that the area in which it was located is still known as Harmonie. Its continuing presence in the form of the Jakarta Club was an affront to those who resented the large numbers of Dutch nationals in Indonesia and their control of major sectors of the economy.

Pamurahardjo states that he turned his attention to the *Harmonie* building on Independence Day 1957:

> on 17 August, Proclamation Day, I convened a meeting of all of the *pemudas*, and after that meeting we held a people's demonstration [*aksi rakyat*], with all of the *pemudas*, after we held the meeting. The first place we occupied was Harmonie.[21]

In an apparent attempt to inject a note of morality into the decision to occupy the building and humiliate its members, Pamurahardjo said that one of the reasons he acted was to bring an end to wife-swapping there.[22]

Like Sukarno but unlike Nasution, the *Murba*-leaning Pamurahardjo was inclined toward radical nationalist policies.[23] He had remained close to Sukarno and for a time was also reasonably close to Nasution. In the aftermath of the October 17 Affair he was one of a small group of East Javanese officers who attempted to lobby his old East Java *Brawijaya* command on Nasution's behalf.[24] Soon after Nasution's reinstatement he was one of a few officers who undertook to safeguard Nasution from possible actions against him by dissident officers.[25]

Immediately after being appointed to the inspectorate general in early 1956, this officer drew upon his political interests and involvements, and particularly *Angkatan '45*'s West Irian campaign.[26] This was to lead to the formation of the Youth-Military BKS.

Pamurahardjo remarked that he agreed with President Sukarno on the need to reduce the influence of the parties,[27] although he was fervently anti-PKI while the president was much more prepared to accommodate it. Pamurahardjo also states that he specifically avoided involving the parties themselves in the BKS-PM as he was concerned that they would politicize the organization, as they had tried to do with the veterans.[28] Instead, he concentrated his attention on the youth mass organizations of the parties.

Interestingly, Pamurahardjo denies that the functional group concept was a factor in the formation of the BKS-PM,[29] and it is possible that at its outset the army leadership were not fully aware of all its ramifications for military intervention. In later years Nasution wrote that the BKS initiative was intended as a means of support for the army in Indonesia's struggle to "regain" West Irian[30] and that he initially incorporated the youth organizations of the four big parties in the Youth-Military BKS in line with Sukarno's call in 1956 for a "four-legged" *gotong royong* cabinet drawn from the PNI, Masyumi, NU and PKI.[31]

Reeve's comment "That the head of the BKS, for youth was the *Angkatan 45-Kongres Rakyat* [People's Congress] figure, Major Pamurahardjo, suggests that Sukarno had been able to intervene [in the BKS initiative initially]"[32] is supported by Pamurahardjo's assertion that he was encouraged in his activities by the president:

The idea emerged from the youth. . . . The youth and us, the army group [*golongan*]. For this we needed to form a home front. A home front with which we could clean up subversive elements. To form this home front, we had to, amongst other things, have as its core our fundamental social forces. . . . Then, Bung Karno [Sukarno] and I—in my capacity as a member of the Inspectorate

General of Territorial affairs and People's Resistance—I had responsibility for the People's Resistance section—I was the Head of the Governmental Affairs Section—I discussed this matter with Bung Karno. Yes, Bung Karno agreed but as a Government person he couldn't act in the manner we desired. And then he handed it over to me to settle this matter. Bung Karno himself handed it over to me. "You yourself take action. As the Government, I can't." And that is when I began to assemble the *pemudas*, 120 organisations, from the far Left to the far Right. But its core [organisations] were four [in number]. Its core [organisations] were four [in number], the winners in the general elections.[33]

In assembling the *pemudas*, Pamurahardjo was calling upon a component of society that had sometimes played leading roles in the independence struggle and in 1956 the president was increasingly urging them to carry out regeneration and "finalise" the revolution of 1945. In February 1956, the *Merdeka* daily, whose editor B.M. Diah was close to the president, ran an editorial on the role of youth that reflected these concerns:

> In recent times, several newspapers have devoted attention to the role that might be played by our youth in bringing about order in this country of ours. Now, when it is evident that the results of the general elections will not provide an antidote to the political illness that our people have suffered, the question which arises in our hearts is what contribution can be made by the leaders of our younger generation in bringing greater order to matters of state. This is a question that needs to be raised at an important moment in our history. Since 1945 we have observed a deterioration taking place which is not uncommonly blamed on our older generation who have lost their revolutionary spirit in leading this nation, [and] who are frightened to make mistakes and therefore are happy not to do anything.[34]

By now, disappointment in the outcome of the general elections, the regional revolts, the ongoing *Darul Islam* insurgency, Dutch intransigence over West Irian, the resurgence of the PKI, and a decline in the economy had created a febrile political and security situation that various actors, including an increasingly assertive Sukarno and elements within the martial law-empowered army, were attempting to exploit. Both Sukarno and the army officers were testing the limits of their roles and powers as the situation unfolded.

Pamurahardjo's somewhat conspiratorial work in 1956 and early 1957 that culminated in the BKS initiative provides a glimpse into some of the maneuvering that took place within this unpredictable and constantly changing environment. It illustrates the extent to which Sukarno was prepared to circumvent the army chain of command by communicating directly with Pamurahardjo, and Nasution's attempts to control and exploit the opportunities for military intervention that were being made available by his volatile Head of People's Resistance.

This officer turned his attention to "anti-subversion" youth organizations which were to become the member organizations of the Youth-Military BKS in early 1956. They emerged within the context of the trials of two Dutch nationals, Jungschlaeger, the former head of NEFIS—Netherlands Expeditionary Forces Intelligence Service—and currently a senior employee of the Dutch-owned KPM (*Koninklijke Paketvaart Maatschappij*—Royal Shipping Line), and Schmidt (a former KNIL officer) on charges of subversion.[35] The trials became linked with Dutch insistence on retaining sovereignty over West Irian and allegations that the major Dutch enterprises in Indonesia were actively involved in subversive activities.

On February 23, 1956, a major public meeting was held at Independence Square in relation to the trial. Significantly, the representative of the freedom fighters was Major Pamurahardjo who was "still active in the military."[36] Three weeks earlier on February 1 some 100 Jakarta youth from a variety of organizations had demonstrated in front of the Jakarta District Court, demanding the death penalty for Schmidt[37] and a resolution was taken to the president by a delegation including Major Pamurahardjo.[38]

On March 16, organizations involved in the February 23 public meeting held a further meeting in the *Pemuda* Building. The daily *Suluh Indonesia* reported that the youth organizations that attended this meeting had taken part in "the Gigantic Anti Foreign Subversive Movements Meeting (*Rapat Raksasa Anti Subversip Asing*) some time ago."[39]

The campaign against Jungschlaeger suffered a setback when he died suddenly, apparently of natural causes, in late April.[40] However, the continuation of the Schmidt trial resulted in further demonstrations.[41]

The term *Badan Kerja Sama* was used to refer to a group which gathered outside the Jakarta District Court when Schmidt was sentenced to life imprisonment on October 16, 1956:

> Meanwhile, the huge crowd which had congregated outside the Jakarta State Court building . . . shouted after learning of the sentence passed by the Judge and as Schmidt was removed under very tight escort from the Court building: "Long live the *Badan Kerja Sama menentang aksi subversif.*" [Cooperation Group to oppose foreign subversion][42]

The atmosphere within which this *Badan Kerja Sama menentang aksi subversif* came into being was one of tension, excitement and expectation of imminent change in the lead-up to President Sukarno's *konsepsi* speech, and support for the *konsepsi* from the army leadership. A few days later an announcement was made that another public anti-subversion meeting would be held in Jakarta on February 10 by a joint committee known as "The Anti Subversive Movements Gigantic Meeting Committee." The stated aim of the meeting was to "oppose subversive movements and to analyse the current situation."⁴³

The meeting issued a statement along the now familiar lines of "affirming the existence of a danger which has been created by subversive movements in regions of Indonesia [that] threatens the safety of the Republic of Indonesia."⁴⁴ However, the headline in the daily *Merdeka* focused on the fact that the meeting had supported President Sukarno's *konsepsi*.⁴⁵

In February 21, 1957 when Sukarno's *konsepsi* was announced, the term *Badan Kerja Sama* reemerged in the Jakarta media. *Merdeka* reported that the *Badan Kerja Sama Pemuda dan Pelajar Anti Gerakan Subversif* (The Youth and Student's Cooperation Body to Oppose Subversive Movements) had issued a statement calling upon all groups of "Youth, Secondary School Students, University Students, Workers, Peasants, Veterans and all levels of society to enthusiastically welcome President Sukarno's *konsepsi*."⁴⁶ The BKS called upon the Indonesian people to:

> flock to the State Palace to hear the address by the Head of State in which the *konsepsi* will be announced at 8 pm. tonight. People outside Jakarta should congregate in the houses of neighbours where there are radios and those who have radios should ensure that they can easily be heard by the public.⁴⁷

That this latter *Badan Kerja Sama* was a more substantial entity is evidenced by the fact that it issued a press statement. As was the case in its reporting of the *Badan Kerja Sama menentang aksi subversif*, *Merdeka* did not cite the names of individuals and organizations associated with the *Badan Kerja Sama Pemuda dan Pelajar Anti Gerakan Subversif* or even the name of a spokesperson, raising the possibility that the newspaper was aware of the involvement of highly placed individuals or organizations in this BKS but was not able or willing to name them.

By July 1957 the only *Badan Kerja Sama* to be referred to in the Indonesian media was the officially inaugurated Youth-Military BKS-PM. According to Pamurahardjo, he and two other youth leaders had the idea of forming the BKS-PM. Following initial discussions, they took a proposal to form a civil-military group to a meeting of youth organizations but Pamurahardjo did not involve Nasution at that stage because this would have made the youth groups "suspicious."

> At the time, I had not sought permission from Nasution. After they [the youth organisations] met and agreed I took . . . Nasution didn't know anything about it. I told him that these four core organisations were willing. It had taken place outside army premises and outside the army. Because if it had begun in the army it would never have been completed. Because they [the youth organisations]

would have been suspicious. Had it been Nasution they would have been suspicious. They wouldn't have wanted to. Finally, the four core party youth organisations were willing to meet with us and we conducted our negotiations outside [the army]. But the topic wasn't what you might think. The only topic that I put forward was West Irian. West Irian—the thinking of the army hadn't extended that far. We said that West Irian was a long way away but it must return [to Indonesia]. How can we bring about the return of West Irian? Are you all going to just stay quiet? They agreed [with me]. For West Irian, we will unite! Then I formed a committee—this was still outside the army. I was the only military person with four people from the core organisations. They agreed and we formulated a document, a sort of decree—no, not a decree but a document of association. After they expressed willingness—these four people—we took it to other *pemudas*. It developed into 120 organisations. They all agreed.[48]

Pamurahardjo's statement that Nasution was kept in the dark while he carried out the spadework in forming the BKS-PM contradicts most accounts of the BKS initiative, which assign the army chief a central role. Pamurahardjo is known to have become antagonistic toward Nasution in later life and this might have colored his recollection of events in 1957, but his involvement in *Angkatan '45* and the anti-subversion movements in 1956 and his closeness to President Sukarno support his claim, as does the degree of autonomy he evidently enjoyed in running the BKS-PM in the second half of 1957.

It seems likely that to some extent Nasution was carried along by the flow of events and allowed Pamurahardho to take the initiative, as he had done with his subordinates in the *Bandung Lautan Api* and October 17, 1952 Affair. He owed his reinstatement to Sukarno who had dismissed him in the past, was close to Pamurahardjo and sympathized with that officer's radical nationalist leanings. Nasution's outsider status might have weighed upon him as well, as both Sukarno and Pamurahardjo were not only ethnically Javanese but came from East Java.

However, there is little doubt that the idea of mobilizing the youth under the leadership of the army appealed to him. It was in conformity with his involvement in the youth movements of the Japanese occupation period, and his apparent youthful admiration for Baldur von Schirach and the Hitler Youth movement.[49] It also accorded with his distaste for the politically affiliated *laskar* organizations and the firm steps he took to co-opt them into the army or disband them. The prospect of detaching the youth organizations from what he saw as the fractious and divisive parties must have seemed very inviting.

Nasution later wrote that the initiative was in accordance with the functional group idea outlined in the *konsepsi*, and was associated with "total people's resistance":

I formed the Cooperation Groups that were later united in the West Irian National Liberation Front. And during that period the President began with his *konsepsi* political reform.

My first step was the formation of the *BKS Pemuda-Militer* in June 1957, that was implemented by Lieutenant Colonel Pamurahardjo. [all the BKS organizations] were formed in line with the President's *konsepsi* on the existence of groupings in the community based on their professions or particular field of employment.

The doctrine of territorial management had already been applied at the village level in the guerrilla period and almost throughout the whole of the archipelago during the period of restoration of security.... Now this was being done at the national level because the TNI was being compelled by national developments to participate actively in national [territorial] management.[50]

An army document shows that in launching the BKS-PM, Nasution directed Pamurahardjo's superior officer, the Inspector General of Territorial Affairs and People's Resistance (Colonel Sadikin), to invite "all existing youth organisations" to join a Youth-Military Cooperation Body.[51] Nasution's concern that the BKS address problems of national unity is clear in his address at the launch of the Youth-Military BKS in July 1957:

The condition of our society provides a clear picture that at present our people are fragmented into various groups and streams [*aliran*]. [It is] as if only particular groups are entitled to live on Indonesian soil. However, this was not the aim and intention of the struggle of the people of Indonesia. The fruits of our struggle were for all the Indonesian people.

I therefore thank Almighty God that tonight a desire to [work] together has been reached amongst the youth who represent the four (4) major *aliran* in our society.

A joint desire which indicates an intention to UNITE, AN INTENTION TO STRUGGLE TOGETHER, AN INTENTION TO PAVE THE WAY FOR PEACE IN OUR NATION.

Without considering differences of opinion and *aliran* but only with the fullest capacity to pave the way for PEACE IN OUR NATION.[52]

Nasution's concern for "peace in our nation" can be interpreted as a reference to the deteriorating regional situation. However, it is more likely that he was concerned about threats to "peace" at the grassroots of society by radical elements and particularly the PKI. His reference to the fruits of the independence struggle being denied by fractious and fissiparous *aliran*-oriented parties was redolent of his IPKI speech in which he spoke of people who had been united in the guerrilla struggle being divided by the parties, even to the point of penetrating families.[53]

The BKS-PM attracted considerable media attention through its leading role in organizing the celebrations for Youth Pledge Day on October 28, 1957. The ceremonies, that were organized by the BKS-PM, culminated in a youth festival in Banteng Square, Jakarta, and a torch-lit procession through a number of major streets around the State Palace.[54]

Merdeka reported that young street thug (*crossboy*) organizations had taken part in the parade. Feith notes that *Murba* identities had courted the support of such underworld groups, and that Colonel Mustopo—who became Pamurahardjo's replacement as head of the BKS—had also done so. It will be recalled that Feith identified the role of Colonel Mustopo in mobilizing Jakarta street gangs in support of Nasution in the October 17, 1952 Affair.[55]

The Youth Pledge Day celebrations turned out to be violently anti-Dutch, an outcome that was no doubt intended when Pamurahardjo explicitly appealed for crossboys "to participate in the youth struggle" on October 21.[56] The BKS-PM went on to form a special subcommittee of the Youth Pledge Commemorative Committee known as the Sub-Committee for Channelling Crossboys. Presaging the *Golkar*-associated *Pemuda Pancasila* thuggish group of the New Order period—who claimed that they were attempting to rehabilitate criminals—the justification for the involvement of crossboys was that they were also *pemudas* "and their activities should be channeled toward the appropriate struggle of the *pemudas* which will enable them to contribute their energies to their nation and people."[57]

That a car was seen on fire near the Netherlands High Commission was perhaps an indication of the success with which the crossboys were "channelled." Attempts to intimidate the Dutch legation and community continued. The procession of 28 October was followed by an outbreak of graffiti on Dutch-owned buildings and vehicles, criticizing Dutch attitudes to the West Irian question and urging that West Irian be "seized." As *Merdeka* described it, the procession:

> which was organised by the BKS-PM . . . was preceded by a squad of motor cyclists [and] escorted by fully-armed troops from the Military Forces, the Corps of Music, and squads from all sorts of student and youth mass [organisations]. . . . The atmosphere was that of a sea of fire which symbolised the spirit of the youth of the capital. . . . It can be reported that when the procession arrived in West Merdeka Square in front of the Netherlands High Commission an effigy of a Dutchman was burned and that despite that atmosphere no incident whatsoever occurred because of the tightness of supervision by the instruments of the state. Meanwhile, a car was seen to be on fire in that area.[58]

In the latter part of 1957 the Indonesian government raised the political temperature of the already heated West Irian issue. On October 3, Foreign

Minister Subandrio issued a warning to the Dutch that Indonesia would adopt "another course" in pursuit of its West Irian. [59] On November 18 and 19, in the lead up to a discussion of the West Irian question in the United Nations, a mass rally in Jakarta was attended by "political, military and youth organisations" from throughout the country that directly threatened Dutch interests in Indonesia.

Palmier notes that the rally adopted four resolutions:

> first, nationalisation of Dutch-owned enterprises; second, repatriation of Dutch nationals who do not contribute to Indonesia's reconstruction program; third a ban on the entry of Dutch nationals into Indonesia; fourth, withdrawal of permits issued to Dutch nationals practising the liberal professions.[60]

Perhaps the highlight of the year that Pamurahardjo led the initiative was the role that he played in a rash of takeovers of Dutch enterprises in December 1957—starting with the KPM shipping line—after further negotiations on West Irian failed to yield progress. The takeovers were followed by the mass exodus of Dutch citizens who, as one of them put it, "went back to Holland from which they had never come."[61] According to Louis Fischer, Sukarno later stated explicitly that he ordered the takeovers.[62] Feith writes that the source of the takeovers is unclear . . . although it is clear that a major role was played by Lieutenant Colonel Pamurahardjo."[63] Lev provides the most accurate summation of what took place:

> The take-overs begun with Sukarno's encouragement, and a few leaders of the recently established Youth-Military Cooperation Body . . . were involved in the action. But if the takeovers were not entirely spontaneous, nor were they fully planned. Neither [Prime Minister] Djuanda, who did not agree with the take-overs, nor Nasution was entirely aware of what was happening, and policy during the tense days of early December was largely ad hoc.[64]

Pamurahardjo states that he set the ball rolling with the takeover of the KPM shipping line. As the major inter-island service in Indonesia, KPM was a continuing symbol of Dutch economic control over the major sectors of the economy. Whether the KPM and Jungschlaeger had been involved in subversion or not, it is clear that some Indonesians were suspicious that the former senior intelligence officer's access to Dutch-owned ships and Dutch masters had provided an ideal means of distributing weapons and other material to groups (had he intended to do so). The trials became linked with wider allegations that the major Dutch enterprises were actively involved in subversive activities as Jungschlaeger and Schmidt were alleged to have been complicit in a range of subversive activities, including fostering the *Darul Islam* cause.[65]

By the time of the takeover of the KPM, Pamurahardjo had expanded the scope of the BKS-PM to include peasants and workers, although no official inauguration of new BKS-style organizations had taken place at this stage. Prior to the meeting on the KPM takeover, Pamurahardjo had contacted members of labor unions (*buruh*) and according to press reports the organization which decided to mount the takeover on the night of December 2 styled itself the *Front Buruh-Tani*-BKS-PM—the BKS-PM-Peasants-Workers Front.[66]

The formation of this front, before a BKS organization for peasants and workers was formally established, resembled the fleeting emergence of shadowy *Badan Kerja Sama* organizations prior to the establishment of the BKS-PM. By December a Workers-Military Cooperation Body had been inaugurated and a Peasant-Military Cooperation Body was formed in 1958. The BKS-PM returned to its earlier role and composition. All these bodies were under the control of Pamurahardjo who in early 1958 became the first chairman of the umbrella organization for the BKS organizations, the West Irian National Liberation Front.

Previous research into the confiscations identifies that the Djuanda cabinet was hostile to the takeovers, if only because of the likely adverse impact on the economy. For example, Donald Hindley writes: "Hearsay has it that many members of the cabinet, and probably including Djuanda, were opposed to such drastic action against the Dutch partly because they feared the economic disruption that was expected to ensue."[67] Louis Fischer recalls an interview with Prime Minister Djuanda in which he clearly registered his opposition to the takeovers.[68]

Pamurahardjo's account accords with these observations. According to Pamurahardjo, the Djuanda government knew of the meeting and dispatched the veterans affairs minister, Chaerul Saleh [69] and the Minister for Information and Chairman of the Committee of Action for the Liberation of West Irian, Sudibyo, to prevent the confiscation from taking place.

Hindley assesses that the PKI was initially reluctant to become involved in the confiscations and that it followed that Sukarno who was "one if not *the* prime mover" in the confiscations.[70] Pamurahardjo's account of the takeover of the KPM headquarters supports Hindley's assessment. He states that some representatives of PKI mass organizations at the meeting held immediately prior to the confiscation were concerned not to upset Sukarno's efforts to form a "four-legged cabinet" which would include the PKI.

According to Pamurahardjo, the government representatives at the meeting were unsuccessful in their efforts to prevent the takeover of the KPM, although they were supported by some PKI-associated activists and something of a fracas broke out. True to Nasution's form of sometimes being carried along by events and strong personalities, Pamurahardjo recalls that although Nasution did not instigate the confiscation of the KPM he was again prepared to allow his subordinate to make the running. Pamurahardjo recalls that when the two government representatives reported back to Djuanda the prime minister ordered Nasution to arrest him.

> At three in the morning the cabinet decided to arrest me. Chaerul Saleh and Sudibyo reported to the Prime Minister. "These people from the West Irian National Liberation Front [71]can no longer be controlled. It would be best if the Chairman were arrested." The Chairman was [me]—Lieutenant Colonel Pamurahardjo.[72]

Pamurahardjo reported to the residence of Lieutenant Colonel Dahyar, the commander of the Greater Jakarta City Military Command, where Dahyar, Nasution, Chaerul Saleh, Sudibyo and an adjutant were awaiting him. Pamurahardjo remembers that Chaerul Salah had earlier been mocked by the *pemudas* at the Proclamation Building meeting for apparently forsaking his previous hard line on the seizure of foreign assets in Indonesia. [73] The government representatives demanded that the action be stopped but Nasution prevaricated before finally handing the matter over to Pamurahardjo who returned to the meeting at 5 a.m. Pamurahardjo asserts that he then ordered that the takeover proceed [74] but it might also be the case that his role was to signal to the activists that Nasution and the army would not attempt to stop them from implementing their plans.

He also states that Sukarno did not explicitly order the confiscation but registered his approval by smiling when afterward he reported to the president:

> I went to Bung Karno. After I ordered it to go ahead—the takeover—I went to Bung Karno. I said "Pak Karno I request your forgiveness. I have been in conflict with the Djuanda cabinet." [Sukarno replied:] "Yes I have heard about everything. A report from Chaerul Saleh. What has happened?" [I told him that] "At 6 o'clock in the morning the Dutch enterprises were taken over. We have occupied the enterprises." He didn't reply. He didn't do anything. He just smiled. That was a sign that I could keep on going.[75]

The seizing of the KPM headquarters was followed by confiscations of Dutch assets throughout Indonesia. Ultimately the army took over the confiscated assets, principally to prevent the PKI from doing so. The profits from the enterprises considerably boosted the army's finances and those of many of the officers involved in their management.

Pamurahardjo recalls that the BKS-PM's involvement in the confiscation of the KPM headquarters met with some opposition within the army general staff. He states that at 10 a.m. on December 3 he reported to a full meeting with Nasution and the general staff where the Director of Army Intelligence, Sukendro, was concerned that the takeover could "lead to terror." [76] However,

Nasution's accommodating attitude had not changed since the meeting in Colonel Dahyar's residence and, according to Pamurahardjo, had been strengthened by the president's tacit approval. In Pamurahardjo's words, "In the end, it was all handed over to me."[77]

According to Pamurahardjo, the leading role that the general staff allocated to him extended to placing a transport officer, Colonel Suwondo, as manager of the KPM. He states that after attending the army headquarters he proceeded to the KPM building. There he ordered the director, de Geus—who expressed considerable anger at the takeover—to assemble the Dutch employees of the company. Pamurahardjo states that he advised them that Suwondo would henceforth manage the enterprise.[78]

The takeover of the KPM was popular with the public and the Djuanda cabinet appears to have been left with no other option but to acquiesce and somewhat grudgingly give its support. [79]

Pamurahardjo might have inflated his role and that of the Inspectorate General in the confiscation of the KPM Headquarters, or Sukendro and the army headquarters might have sought to conceal it from the public. The first *Merdeka* report of the takeover, datelined December 4, states in its headline and text that the Minister for Shipping, the Minister for Information and the BKS-PM knew nothing at all about the takeovers, which had been carried out by the KPM workers themselves:

> In response to a question by [the national news agency] *Antara*, Minister for Information Sudibyo in his capacity as Chairman of the Committee of Action for the Liberation of West Irian stated that the takeover of the KPM building was [carried out] without the knowledge of the Committee of Action for the Liberation of West Irian. The Minister also affirmed that the incident was in no way connected with the BKS-PM.[80]

The report emphasized that it was the KPM Union, acting on its own initiative, which was solely responsible for the takeover. The *Merdeka* article reports that a KPM Union delegation cut telephone links to the building, assembled the directors of the KPM (president director de Geus and directors Ter Brake and Brandt), and read a proclamation (signed by representatives of the All-Indonesia KPM Union) to the effect the company was "in the hands of the Indonesian KPM workers." The report also states that de Geus and the other directors were ordered to leave the building, "pale of face, their hands shaking, and walking slowly" after a skirmish over the ownership of a file.[81]

That no mention was made of Pamurahardjo's presence in the removal of KPM director de Geus and his staff from the company's headquarters could be due to confusion on the part of reporters, government censorship, or to exaggerations or distortions in his account. However, that Sudibyo was questioned about the BKS-PM's involvement gives some support to Pamurahardjo's version of this event. Furthermore, other media reports indicate that Pamurahardjo gained the cooperation of the union workers involved. The following day a union official, A.M. Datuk, made a statement on behalf of the expanded BKS-PM.[82] *Merdeka* reported that the "Action Committee of the BKS-PM-Peasants-Workers Front" was in control "of the Dutch enterprises which were taken over by their workers in the capital city on Tuesday [December 3] and will be handed over to the Government in the form of a Supervisory Team [appointed by] the Military Authority."[83] Datuk stated that a number of worker representatives would be included in the supervisory team.

That Pamurahardjo had assumed a leading role in the takeovers in cooperation with some unionists and was in conflict with a Committee of Action for the Liberation of West Irian, which had been formed by the Djuanda cabinet and was chaired by information minister Sudibyo, is indicated by a report of a meeting held on December 4 between the BKS-PM-Peasants-Workers Front and several ministers, including the First Deputy Prime Minister and the ministers for veterans affairs, information, finance, justice, mobilization of the people, and industry, and the Greater Jakarta Military Authority:

> A.M. Datuk explained that at the meeting last night Minister for Information, Sudibyo, in his capacity as Chairman of the Committee of Action for the Liberation of West Irian had provided clarification concerning the Actions to Liberate West Irian and afterwards Lieutenant Colonel Pamurahardjo, in his capacity as Chairman of the BKS-PM-Peasants-Workers Front, also spoke.
>
> It was further explained that at the meeting the BKS-PM-Peasants-Workers Front had proposed to the Chairman of the Committee of Action for the Liberation of West Irian that coordination be arranged in dealing with Actions for the Liberation of West Irian by cooperating with the BKS-PM-Peasants-Workers Front.[84]

Pamurahardjo's unofficial action front continued its involvement in the takeovers. On December 7, the "BKS-PM-Peasants-Workers" were said to be in control of the once beautiful old colonial-era (and now sadly vanished) *Hotel Des Indes (Duta Indonesia)*, following its takeover by "workers under the leadership of the Hotel and Tourism Union"[85]

By this stage the BKS-PM-Peasants-Workers organization appears to have been paying lip service, at least, to the government's Committee of Action for the Liberation of West Irian:

> In regard to this incident the Military Authority was informed and latest reports indicate that control of the Hotel des Indes has been taken over by the BKS-PM-Peasants-Workers and accountability has also been made to the Committee of Action for the Liberation of West Irian.[86]

That the BKS-PM was thought to be a leading player in a number of takeovers that followed that of the KPM headquarters is evident in the remark: "Concerning these actions, *Antara* has not yet obtained clarification from the BKS-PM and the Military Finance Authority, and the bank worker's union is not yet prepared to provide any information."[87]

Like Pamurahardjo, Hindley writes that the PKI was cautious about the takeovers at first,[88] and continued to be so even after the confiscation of the KPM headquarters generated a rash of others.[89] Conversely, the anticommunist Arnold Brackman states that on the first day of the takeovers affiliates of the large PKI-associated SOBSI Union "seized Dutch estates, banks, and trading companies. . . . and the following day occupied the offices of three more Dutch banks and other properties."[90] Fischer goes further, writing of Communists racing "through the country with firebrands. They exploited every opportunity to inflame passions against the Dutch, against the [regional] rebels, and against their political enemies. Anyone who doubted the desirability of expelling Dutch enterprises was condemned."[91]

Throughout his career, Nasution had demonstrated an ingrained repugnance for chaos and disorder and he expressed concern that events not get out of hand or play into the hands of the PKI as early as December 6 when he exhorted Indonesians to "Act in accordance with the flaming spirit of 1945 while avoiding excessive and wild actions." On December 12, the Greater Jakarta Military Authority announced that Dutch estates in that area which had been taken over by workers were for the time being placed under the control of a Committee of Control of Dutch Enterprises/Greater Jakarta Military Authority. Included in the membership of the committee were representatives of workers' organizations at the Greater Jakarta level and the Greater Jakarta BKS-PM.[92] On December 13 Nasution forbade any further takeovers of Dutch enterprises and decreed that the military would take control of all the seized assets.[93]

The PKI continued its cautious line, welcoming Nasution's measure as "good." However, a proposal by the party that workers participate in the management councils within the enterprises was categorically rejected by the army.[94]

Nasution continue to try to control events as much as possible and give the appearance of being fully in charge. He played the nationalist anti-Dutch subversion card by forbidding former members of the Netherlands Expeditionary Forces Intelligence Service (NEFIS) to work in confiscated Dutch assets[95] while drawing upon the West Irian campaign to distance the PKI's organizations from the confiscated assets by announcing that "within the framework of perfecting the return of West Irian" he had instructed regional military authorities throughout Indonesia to take over all Dutch enterprises in their regions.[96] He warned the entire community and "particularly the workers to heed the importance of these determinations of the (martial law) Central Military Authority."[97]

In 1958, Pamurahardjo established a number of other BKS organizations and an umbrella organization for these organizations, the West Irian National Liberation Front. However, by the middle of that year the initiative became embroiled in a financial scandal over a West Irian Struggle Fund that collected contributions for the West Irian cause.[98] He was suddenly removed as its secretary general in August 1958 and "exiled" to remote Kalimantan.[99] His replacement was the eccentric and underworld-linked Brigadier General Mustopo[100] while President Sukarno's brother-in-law, Achmadi, became the Deputy Secretary-General.[101]

The organizations also began to encounter concerted resistance from some of the parties. At first, the PKI appears to have had few qualms about allowing its mass organizations to join the BKS-PM. A former member of the PKI's youth organization (*Pemuda Rakyat*) who was involved in this organization's affiliation with the BKS-PM recalled that the party was confident of being able to withstand any attempts on the part of the army to influence its members. Indeed, it hoped to exploit the opening provided by the BKS-PM to spread its influence within the army.[102]

As the anti-PKI intentions of the army became increasingly apparent, elements within some other parties might have seen some benefit in the BKS initiative. However, a growing awareness that the army was a threat to all the parties was no doubt reinforced in 1957 when Nasution instigated a strong anti-corruption drive and prohibited senior civil servants from becoming party members.

Roccamora writes that these measures adversely affected right-wing senior PNI functionaries because of the reliance of that party on civil servants whose corrupt activities had benefited many of them during the various PNI-led governments:

> On the whole, the army campaign to restrict the activities and undermine the prestige of the political parties also weakened these leaders' positions within the PNI. This being the case, leftist elements in the PNI leadership, especially those in the *ormas* (mass organizations) who benefited from their participation in the various army-organised *Badan Kerja Sama*, tended to see the army at this time as an ally.[103]

In addition to the financial scandal, many of the officers assigned to manage the BKS organizations and the West Irian National Liberation Front were not up to the task of influencing the party mass organizations.[104] After initially cooperating, the PKI was the first party to reject the idea after a year of involvement[105] and many of the other parties became antipathetic toward the organizations. By the time Pamurahardjo was removed, President Sukarno had also become wary of the initiative.

Nasution's attempt to establish quasi-state corporatist institutions before the army had achieved undisputed power over the state can be seen in retrospect to have doomed it to failure. Nasution's BKS initiative could only prosper while martial law remained in force and with the president's acquiescence.

As creatures of the army's martial law powers, the reputation of the Front and its constituent BKS organizations suffered as unrest grew about the duration and harshness of martial law and the army's ability to pressure the parties into cooperating diminished. Sukarno, who had gained a degree of influence in the Front through the appointment of Achmadi as a deputy chairman, began to express frustration with the inroads the army was making into many areas of national life.[106] He became concerned that Nasution was attempting to use the West Irian National Liberation Front to develop a political vehicle of his own that might in time rival his powers.

Sukarno also became opposed to Nasution's intent to use the functional group idea to de-ideologize society and put a brake on changes to the social order. For Sukarno, interest representation through functional groups had not meant a return to a static representation of the past. Lev has portrayed him as a dreamer, an idealist and a revolutionary.[107] He intended to unlock the "dynamic" forces in Indonesian society while developing what he saw as authentic means of interest representation that united in their commitment to his own revolutionary zeal.

A number of interest groups circled the Front as they sought to follow the lead of Sukarno. For example, in November 1958, the PNI leader, Suwiryo, proposed that a new Pancasila Front be created which would comprise "all *golongan* and individuals . . . *buruh*, peasants, women, *pemuda*, students, politicians, intellectuals, artists, the religious, state instrumentalities which truly possess the spirit of the proclamation of 17 August 1945 and are therefore loyal to Pancasila and a free and active [foreign] policy." The statement conspicuously failed to mention the army as one of the *golongan* that might be included in the Pancasila Front and made no reference to the various BKS organizations and the West Irian National Liberation Front. On the other hand, politicians were to be included.[108] Six months after decreeing the introduction of Guided Democracy in July 1959, the president acted to curb the growing influence of the army by announcing the absorption of the West Irian National Liberation Front into a new National Front that would not be controlled by the army. The BKS initiative was wound up when martial law was lifted in 1963 and the BKS organizations were ultimately unsuccessful in their primary aim of levering the mass organizations away from the parties.

Nevertheless, they had some enduring legacies. For example, the Youth-Military BKS presaged the New Order's attempt to control the younger generation through such organizations as *Pemuda Pancasila*,[109] and the Worker-Military BKS set the scene for the regime's establishment of a monolithic organization of workers, the All-Indonesia Organisation of Workers (*Serikat Pekerja Seluruh Indonesia*—SPSI).

The most durably significant aspect of the BKS initiative was the precedent it set in associating corporatist and anti-party thinking with Nasution's principles of "total people's resistance." As the BKS initiative declined, Sadikin and the Inspectorate General began to conduct activities that were aimed at mobilizing populations for self-help projects such as working bees[110] that were redolent of the *gotong royong* and *sinoman*-type activities discussed in earlier chapters. Such community assistance activities were to be taken up by the army under the banner of "civic mission" and became increasingly associated with the army's territorial role from the early 1960s.

In December 1958, as the army was conducting mopping-up operations against PRRI/Permesta troops and continuing its struggle against the *Darul Islam* insurgency, Nasution made a major statement on the army's renewed commitment to territorial affairs, including the role the BKS/West Irian National Liberation Front were to play within the territorial organization:

> In relation to the BKS [organisations], they will be organised within the framework of the Territorial organisation as permanent bodies which will receive colours [unit flags] from the Supreme Commander.
>
> In relation to the [West Irian] National [Liberation] Front, efforts will be intensified for its formation in operational areas as a means of assembling National potentials.[111]

Further indications of the links between the West Irian National Liberation Front/BKS initiative and "total people's resistance" were evident in the following month when the visiting former partisan leader President Tito of Yugoslavia awarded Mustopo and Nasution the Star of the People's Army of Yugoslavia Class II in a ceremony involving the various BKS organizations.[112]

That the Front was increasingly being seen by the army leadership as integrally involved in seeking the participation of the people in preparations for and the conduct of "total people's resistance" is evident in the involvement of the WINLF in an institution known as the *Pancasila* Development Research Centre which had the task of providing education in five basic areas aimed at "facilitating" the WINLF's command [structure]: "the intensification of People's Defence, security, development, education and the welfare of the people."[113]

While the army was undertaking these activities the BKS/West Irian National Liberation Front initiative remained under threat. Sukarno appointed a *Dewan Harian* (Daily Board) that first met on January 20, 1961 to discuss the incorporation of the West Irian National Liberation Front and the various *Badan Kerja Sama* organizations into his own National Front.

Nasution stated that whether the West Irian National Liberation Front and the *Badan Kerja Sama* were dissolved or not, their work would continue. The link between these institutions and concepts of territorial warfare was underlined when it was announced that the BKS would work through the Inspectorate General of Territorial Affairs and People's Resistance.[114]

A further association between the BKS organizations and the concept of mobilizing groups for "total people's resistance" was made when Nasution determined that the army would have the task of mobilizing "functional potentials."[115] This was an attempt to maintain the BKS initiative by another name and the army subsequently formed three new "Bodies for the Fostering of Functional Potentials" (*Badan Pembina Potensi Karya*—BPPK).[116] As had been the case with the BKS organizations, these bodies reported to the Inspector General of Territorial Affairs and People's Resistance (led by Colonel Sokowati) and to the branch of the general staff that replaced it in a reorganization in 1961.

Reeve writes that "From 1961 on the BPPKs operated as a rival to the *Front Nasional*," were "criticised as such by Sukarno and increasingly attacked by the PKI and Partindo (*Partai Indonesia*) in 1962."[117] This final phase of the BKS project ended when the BPPKs were dissolved on the lifting of martial law in 1963.[118]

Despite these setbacks, Nasution continued to press for a more powerful role for functional groups. In addition to the BKS entities and some smaller functional groups, three major army-sponsored functional groups had been formed by 1962.

Principal among them was the SOKSI (*Sentral Organisasi Karyawan Seluruh Indonesia*—The All-Indonesian Central Organisation of Workers), that largely comprised workers in the formerly Dutch-owned enterprises taken over by the army. SOKSI was an amalgam of twenty-five organizations representing workers and management in government-owned industries and plantations and was a direct counterpart to the PKI-dominated SOBSI Union. Like the Worker-Military BKS, SOKSI paved the way for the New Order's corporatization of labor unions.

The second of the major groups was MKGR (*Musyawarah Kekeluargaan Gotong Royong*—The Mutual Assistance Familial Consultative Organisation) that was established in 1960. It was originally active in social and religious fields but evolved into a quasi-political organization.

The third was Kosgoro (*Koperasi Simpan Tabung Gotong Royong*—the Mutual Assistance Savings Cooperative) that was founded in 1957. It was at first only open to former members of TRIP (*Tentara Republik Indonesia Pelajar*—Republic of Indonesia Student Army) but soon expanded its activities into the political field and began to accept non-TRIP members. All three bodies were headed by senior army officers[119] and came to be known collectively as the *Trikarya*.[120]

In 1964 the army formed the predecessor of the *Golkar* Party, the secretariat general of functional groups (*Sekretariat Bersama Golongan Karya*—Sekbergolkar), largely based upon these three bodies. The number of *Golkar* member organizations steadily increased from 64 in late 1965 to 128 in 1966 and 262 in 1967.[121] The sudden increase in 1966 and 1967 was due to the advent of the New Order regime and the attention it was beginning to pay to developing Sekbergolkar into its political vehicle.

While a discussion of these developments is outside the scope of this book, it is noteworthy that the most influential officer in this process was Major General Sokowati, who was elected general chairman of *Golkar* in 1967.[122] Sokowati had replaced Sadikin as Inspector General of Territorial Affairs and People's Resistance in November 1958.[123]

Army headquarters staff organizations in Jakarta were revamped in the early 1960s when the army further emphasized "total people's resistance" and sought to use these concepts to facilitate military intervention.[124] In 1961 Nasution replaced the Inspectorate General of Territorial Affairs and People's Resistance with a new fifth branch of the general staff—Section V (*Staf Umum Angkatan Darat*—SUAD V)[125] of which Sokowati was the head.

Upgrading the Inspectorate to a section of the general staff was a very significant step as most armies only have four branches (Operations, Intelligence, Personnel and Logistics).This showed that the army now regarded its territorial doctrines and apparatus as having similar importance to the four staff sections that most armies embraced, and that it was not afraid to embark on initiatives that were shaped by local, rather than international, experience. Sokowati's seamless transition from Inspector General of Territorial Affairs and People's Resistance to Head of SUAD V and later to Head of *Golkar* indicates the association that existed in the minds of the army leadership between the army's management and sponsorship of functional groups and the doctrines for military intervention that it began to develop around the strategies for "total people's resistance" that Nasution introduced in the 1940s.

Throughout this hectic period, Nasution seems to have had relatively little time for family life. He does not mention Sunarti a great deal in his accounts of the mid-to-late 1950s and she doesn't give much attention to this period in her recollections of life with her husband. Weekends in Bandung and a close relationship with his in-laws seem to have largely ceased as he sought to influence and control fast-changing events and ideas in the political hot house of Jakarta.

Nasution clearly relished many aspects of his increasingly important role within the bubble of power and prestige that he now occupied. Sunarti describes the pleasure they took in overseas visits, including one to Australia in 1961.

Figure 9.1 Visiting the library of The University of Melbourne, Australia, in 1961. The University's Vice Chancellor, Sir George Paton, is standing between Sunarti and Nasution. *Source*: National Archives of Australia.

She was particularly pleased when his treatise on guerrilla warfare received international recognition:

> From Paris, Pak Nas and party visited the Federal Republic of Germany. We stayed in a hotel that faced the busy Rhine river. It turned out that his "Fundamentals of Guerrilla Warfare" had been translated into German with the title *Der Geurillakrieg*, published by Bruckenbauer Verlag in Cologne. (A review appeared in the magazine *Wehrkunde* in May 1961.)[126]

However, he was riding a tiger in the form of Sukarno who could draw upon support from the PKI, rivals within the army, and senior officers in the other services who were receiving new and powerful equipment and resented their more junior status. His relations with the president were never intimate and Sunarti writes that he always regarded the austere and devout Nasution as "rather different," such as:

> when there was a medal presentation to the Crown Prince of Japan and his wife who were visiting Indonesia. The ceremony took place at sunset. After greeting the Crown Prince and his wife Pak Nas acquired some *wudu* water so that he could pray. The President instructed Pak Suhardjo, the Head of the Palace Household, to accompany him to [the President's son] Guntur's room.[127]

Nasution's devotion to his religion and family also set him apart from some of his senior officers. The politically astute Sukarno was to out maneuver him and replace him with a more pliable officer.

NOTES

1. Reeve, 1985 *Op. Cit.*, p. 144.
2. Guy Pauker, *The Indonesian Doctrine of Territorial Warfare and Territorial Management*, Santa Monica, Ca, The Rand Corporation, 1963. Presumably, this is because Pauker's focus in the early 1960s was on the then unfolding doctrine of territorial warfare and territorial management and the influence on this process of a committee on army doctrine established in 1958,
3. Lev, *Op Cit*, pp. 65–6.
4. Yong Mun Cheong, *Op. Cit.*
5. Suryadinata, *Op. Cit.*, p. 8. Suryadinata states that the Department of Defense and Security was responsible for forming the BKS organizations but at the time there was no such department in Indonesia (there was only a Department of Defense). Rather, Nasution specifically gave the inspectorate general of Territorial Affairs and People's Resistance the task of forming these organizations. Suryadinata also asserts that the BKS organisations were intended to be the foundation of the West Irian National Liberation Front. As discussed in this chapter, the process of forming this Front was not as clear-cut as this.
6. See various footnotes, Reeve, 1985 *Op. Cit.*, pp. 204–205.
7. "In 1958 Nasution appointed an Army Doctrine Committee and its ideas were elaborated by task forces, and seminars at the Army Staff and Command School from 1960 and 1962. As part of Nasution's reorganisation after his reappointment as Army Chief of Staff, he had also created an Inspectorate General of Territorial Affairs and People's Resistance, with the tasks of supervising and assisting the chief of staff in the supervision and coordination of powers held under martial law, of planning the

initial stages of the concept of territorial warfare, and of handling relations between the army and civilians." Ibid., p. 186.

8. "In the late 1950s the 'cooperation bodies' were set up on the initiative and under the direct supervision of Nasution as army chief of staff. This activity was institutionalized with the creation of the inspectorate general of Territorial Affairs and People's Resistance, headed by Colonel Sokowati (who later became chairman of Sekber Golkar in 1966)." Reeve, 1990 *Op. Cit.*, p. 167. According to *Who's Who in Indonesia*, Colonel Sokowati was appointed inspector general of Territorial Affairs and People's Resistance in 1959, some three years after it was formed. O.G. Roeder, *Who's Who in Indonesia*, Revised 2nd Edition, Jakarta, Gunung Agung, 1971, p. 510. In *Siapa Dia, Op. Cit.*, H.W. Bachtiar, records that Sokowati's appointment took place in 1958. However, as stated earlier in this chapter, the Inspectorate General was inaugurated on May 23, 1956. The first inspector general of Territorial Affairs and People's Resistance was Colonel Sadikin.

9. H. Supriyatmono, *Nasution, Dwifungsi ABRI dan Kontribusi ke Arah Reformasi Politik* (translated title: *Nasution, the Dual function of the Armed forces and His Contribution to Political Reformation*), Surakarta: Sebelas Maret University Press in cooperation with Yayasan Pusaka Nusatama. 1994, p. 99.

10. *Surat Keputusan No.: Kpts/P.M./015/1957* issued by the Ministry of Defense Army Staff (*Kementerian Pertahanan Staf Angkatan Darat*), July 5, 1957, National Archives No. AN # 250.

11. Ibid.

12. The Legion of Veterans was formed on the basis of organizations of former freedom fighters, many of which were attached to the parties. Yong Mun Cheong's 1975 article, *The Indonesian Army and Functional Groups, 1957–59*, explores the similarities in the processes adopted in forming the first BKS and those used in 1956 in prising the veterans' organisations away from the parties and forming them into the army-backed and controlled *Legiun Veteran Republik Indonesia*. Yong Mun Cheong, *Op Cit.*

13. Interview with Pamurahardjo, *Op. Cit.*

14. Reeve, 1985 *Op. Cit.*, p. 139.

15. G. Pauker, "The Role of Political Organisations in Indonesia," *Far Eastern Survey*, September 1958, pp. 138–140.

16. Excerpted from Ibid., pp. 141–142.

17. Ibid.

18. "Corporatism and the Question of the State" in G. Davis (ed.), *"What is Modern Indonesian Culture?" Papers presented to the Conference on Indonesian Studies, 29 July—1 August 1976*, Indonesian Summer Studies Institute.p. 67.

19. Lev, *Op. Cit.*, p. 65.

20. Interview with Pamurahardjo, *Op. Cit.*

21. Ibid. In something of a prelude to a moralistic and anti-Western approach taken by the BKS movement in 1958, that included a campaign against a hula hoop craze. Yong Mun Cheong, *Op. Cit.*

22. Interview with Pamurahardjo, *Op. Cit.*

23. Feith described Pamurahardjo as *Murba* oriented. Feith, 1962 *Op. Cit.*, p. 584.

24. Nasution, *Memenuhi Panggilan Tugas*, Vol Three, *Op. Cit.*, p. 175.
25. Ibid., p. 309.
26. Associated with this group "were a number of non-party persons of a radical nationalist orientation, mostly former members of the Student Armies of the Revolution, the most prominent being Achmadi, A.M. Hanafi, Major 'Mas' Isman, Lt. Col. S. Parman, Major Pamurahardjo, and Chaerul Saleh. These latter figures came to dominate the *Angkatan 45* by 1956 although there was little progress in turning that loose association into a working organisation." Reeve, 1985 *Op. Cit,*, p. 114.
27. Interview with Pamurahardjo, *Op. Cit.*
28. Ibid.
29. Ibid.
30. A. H. Nasution, *Memenuhi Panggilan Tugas*, Vol. 4, p. 124.
31. Pamurahardjo states that he selected the four core organizations for the BKS-PM from the youth organizations of these parties because of the support they had received in the elections. Interview with Pamurahardjo, *Op. Cit.*
32. Reeve, 1985 *Op. Cit.*, p. 147.
33. Interview with Pamurahardjo, *Op. Cit.*
34. "Peranan golongan muda" ("The Role of the Young"), *Merdeka*, February 2, 1956.
35. Jungschlaeger and Schmidt were charged with complicity in a number of subversive activities, including fostering the *Darul Islam* cause. See, for example, the *Merdeka* article "Lanjutan perkara Schmidt: Schmidt perencana siasat dalam gerakan Darul Islam" ("Further to the Schmidt case: Schmidt was the planner of tactics in the Darul Islam movement"), November 9, 1955. Leslie Palmier provides extensive information on the trials in L. Palmier, *The Dutch in Indonesia,* London, Oxford University Press, 1962.
36. "Rapat raksasa anti Van Empel dikundjungi puluhan ribu manusia" ("Giant anti-Van Empel meeting attended by scores of people"), *Merdeka* February 23, 1956.
37. "Pemuda-pemuda Jakarta Adakan Demonstrasi: Menuntut hukuman mati bagi pembunuh pemuda-pemuda Indonesia" ("Jakarta Youth Hold Demonstration: Demand the death penalty for the murderers of Indonesian young people"), *Merdeka,* February 1, 1956.
38. "Rapat raksasa anti Van Empel dikundjungi puluhan ribu manusia" ("Giant anti-Van Empel meeting attended by scores of people"), *Merdeka* February 23, 1956, *Op. Cit.*
39. The reason for the meeting was to discuss reports that comments on the Jungschlaeger case from "overseas in general (including the International Council of Jurists) and the Netherlands in particular . . . that Jungschlaeger had not been involved in a subversive movement aimed at bringing down the state." "Pemuda perhatikan reaksi-reaksi perkara Jungschlaeger" ("Youth pay attention to reactions to the Jungschlaeger case"), *Suluh Indonesia*, March 17, 1956.
40. "Dokter yang merawat al. Jungschlaeger diperiksa DA" ("Doctor who treated Jungschlaeger questioned by D.A."), *Suluh Indonesia*, April 24, 1956.
41. "Nyonya Bouman minta Schmidt dibebaskan" ("Mrs Boumann requests Schmidt be freed"), *Merdeka*, September 11, 1956.

42. "Schmidt dijatuhi hukuman seumur hidup" ("Schmidt sentenced to life imprisonment"), *Merdeka*, October 17, 1956.

43. "Rapat Umum Anti Subversif di Jakarta" ("Public Anti-Subversion Meeting in Jakarta"), *Merdeka*, February 6, 1957.

44. "Rapat raksasa anti subversif dukung konsepsi Presiden" ("Giant anti-subversion meeting supports President's Concept"), *Merdeka*, February 11, 1957.

45. Ibid.

46. "Menyambut Konsepsi" ("Welcoming the Concept"), *Merdeka*, February 21, 1957.

47. Ibid.

48. Interview with Pamurahardjo, *Op. Cit.*

49. Jenkins, *Op. Cit.*, p. 226.

50. Nasution, *Memenuhi Panggilan Tugas,* Vol Four, *Op. Cit.*, p. 124.

51. In his capacity as army chief of staff and (martial law) military authority, Nasution directed the Inspector General for Territorial Affairs and People's Resistance to "in the shortest possible time carry out a meeting, the intention of which is to invite all existing youth organisations to consider a program which has been agreed by the four core organisations." *Surat Keputusan [Written Directive] No.: Kpts/P.M./015/1957* issued by the Ministry of Defence Army Staff (*Kementerian Pertahanan Staf Angkatan Darat*), July 5, 1957, National Archives No. AN # 250.

52. *Amanat KASD Dalam Pertemuan Program Kerdja Sama Penguasa Militer—Pemuda Massa [Address by the Army Chief of Staff to the Meeting of the Military Authority—Mass Youth [Organisations] Cooperation Program]*, pp. 1–2.

53. Penders and Sundhaussen, *Op. Cit.*, Appendix 2, p. 238.

54. The celebrations got under way on October 23 "with slides in the cinemas, the placement of posters along the main roads, pamphlets dropped from aircraft, and a meeting at the State Palace on 27 October." The BKS-PM called on all citizens to hoist the national flag, for all schools to hold special ceremonies and for youth organizations to hoist the national flag as well as that of the BKS-PM. "Pesta Pemuda Puncak Peringatan Hari Sumpah Pemuda: Didahului dengan pawai pemuda berobor," *Merdeka*, October 28, 1957.

55. Feith, 1962, *Op. Cit.*, p. 262.

56. "BKS-PM ajak 'Crossboys' ikut dalam perjuangan pemuda," *Merdeka*, October 23, 1995.

57. Ibid.

58. "Patung 'Belanda' dibakar . . . Komisaris Agung: 100,000 massa-pemuda memeriahkan pawai obor," *Merdeka*, October 29, 1957; Jakarta Raya: Gedung-gedung Belanda dan Mobil-mobil Dicoreti Tulisan-tulisan: Panitia Pembebasan Irian Barat minta perhatian organisasi-organisasi, *Merdeka*, October 29, 1957.

59. "The only question is whether the United Nations is the place where its solution may be worked out, or whether we must embark on another course, even at the risk of aggravating conditions in South-East Asia and perhaps invite 'cold war' tensions to muddy further the waters of peace in that region of the world." As George and Audrey Kahin point out, this statement clearly reflected Sukarno's views on the matter. A. Kahin and G. McT. Kahin, *Op. Cit.*, p. 109.

60. L. Palmier, *Op. Cit.*, p. 101.

61. Rueful remark frequently made by Mr Cornelis van Herwijnen who loved Indonesia but migrated to Australia after the take-overs and taught at the Royal Australian Air Force School of Languages in the 1960s. Many departing Dutch citizens did not feel at home in The Netherlands and migrated to other countries including the United States and Australia where they formed community organisations that reflected their Indies heritage, such as Tempo Doeloe (in Australia).

62. Louis Fischer, *The Story of Indonesia*, New York, Harper, 1959, p. 300.

63. Feith, 1962 *Op. Cit.*, p. 584.

64. Lev, *Transition, Op. Cit.*, p. 34.

65. See, for example, the *Merdeka* article "Lanjutan perkara Schmidt: Schmidt perencana siasat dalam gerakan Darul Islam" ("Further to the Schmidt case: Schmidt was the planner of tactics in the Darul Islam movement"), November 9, 1955.

66. "KPM dapat berjalan lancar: Tenaga-tenaga Indonesia akan gantikan Belanda jika mereka undurkan diri, kata jurubicara BKS-PM" ("KPM able to continue smoothly: Indonesian staff will replace Dutch if they withdraw, says a spokesman for the BKS-PM"), *Merdeka*, December 5, 1957.)

67. D. Hindley, *The Communist Party of Indonesia, 1951–1963*, p. 267.

68. L. Fischer, *Op. Cit.*, p. 230.

69. The *Murba*-associated and former close colleague of Tan Malaka, Chaerul Saleh, was appointed minister for veterans affairs in Prime Minister Djuanda's essentially PNI-NU "Business Cabinet" [*Kabinet Karya*] in April 1957.

70. D. Hindley, *Op. Cit.*, p. 267.

71. Pamurahardjo is apparently referring to the association he says that he had formed with the *buruh* as the West Irian National Liberation Front was not formed until early 1958.

72. Interview with Pamurahardjo, *Op. Cit.*

73. He had been associated with Tan Malaka, the national communist who inspired the *Murba* Party's philosophies, in the latter part of the Japanese occupation, and had been involved in the efforts by *pemuda* to persuade Sukarno and Hatta to proclaim Indonesia's independence in August 1945. He was imprisoned for his involvement in the kidnapping of Prime Minister Sutan Syahrir in June 1946 and exiled from Indonesia from 1952 until 1956, when he was called back by Sukarno.

74. Interview with Pamurahardjo, *Op.Cit.*

75. Ibid. Later in the interview, Pamurahardjo remarked with evident satisfaction: "Bung Karno was very pleased."

76. Sukendro was the director of army intelligence throughout the 1950s.

77. Interview with Pamurahardjo, *Op. Cit.*

78. Ibid.

79. "The Government understands that actions undertaken by all levels of society ... is a current of emotion which has been flowing for some time and has now become a flood which we are obliged to channel together and as well as possible so that it really becomes a national potential which is tightly organised and disciplined in order to achieve our national aim of the return of West Irian into the authority of the Republic of Indonesia." Title not available, *Merdeka*, December 6, 1957.

80. "KPM disita dan dijadikan milik RI—Inisiatip pengoperan dilakukan oleh kaum buruh KPM sendiri—Menteri-menteri Pelayaran, Penerangan dan BKS-PM tidak tahu-menahu," *Merdeka*, December 4, 1957.

81. Ibid.

82. "Buruh, Tani, Wanita, Pemuda dan Veteran berdiri di belakang Pemerintah," *Merdeka*, May 2, 1958 refers to Datuk as a member of the KBKI 1 May Committee.

83. "KPM dapat berjalan lancar: Tenaga-tenaga Indonesia akan gantikan Belanda jika mereka undurkan diri, kata jurubicara BKS-PM," *Merdeka*, December 5, 1957.

84. Ibid.

85. "Pengoperan milik-milik Belanda berjalan terus," *Merdeka*, December 7, 1957.

86. Ibid.

87. Ibid.

88. "On December 3, workers began taking over Dutch concerns. The initial actions apparently were taken by members of KBKI, PNI's trade-union federation, but SOBSI quickly joined in with enthusiasm." D. Hindley, *Op. Cit.*, p. 267.

89. "The PKI leaders, probably afraid that the workers' action might frighten the national bourgeoisie and the army into an alliance with Masyumi, called on the workers in the seized enterprises to avoid 'adventurist' acts, to maintain firm work discipline, to assist the new management 'with all their energy,' and to help prevent sabotage." See Ibid., p. 267.

90. A. Brackman, *Indonesian Communism: A History*, New York, Frederick A. Praeger, p. 243.

91. L. Fischer, *Op. Cit.*

92. "Perusahaan-perusahaan Belanda di ibukota dioper Buruh: Berada dibawah Panitia Penguasa Perusahaan Belanda/Penguasa Militer Jakarta Raya," *Merdeka*, December 12, 1957.

93. H. Feith, 1962, *Op. Cit.*, p. 584.

94. D. Hindley, *Op. Cit.*, p. 267.

95. As noted earlier, Jungschlaeger, one of the two Dutch nationals tried for subversion in 1956, had been a member of NEFIS.

96. "KSAD larang gunakan tenaga-tenaga bekas Nefis: Beleh kerahkan tenaga-tenaga ahli Belanda untuk lancarkan perusahaan-perusahaan yang sudah dioper," *Merdeka*, December 14, 1957.

97. Ibid.

98. "KSAD sahkan Dana Perjuangan Irian Barat" ("Army Chief of Staff authorizes the West Irian Struggle Fund"), *Merdeka*, December 7, 1958.

99. Interview with Pamurahardjo, *Op. Cit.*

100. Two unidentified officers from within the Front were arrested because they could not "account for irregularities in regard to material and financial matters." "Dua perwira A.D. ditahan: Karena tak bisa pertanggungjawabkan keuangan FNPIB: Tindakan koreksi ke dalam" ("Two Army officers detained: Because they cannot account for West Irian National Liberation Front funds"), *Merdeka*, September 5, 1958. On September 8, Mustopo issued a statement that the arrests were not being made arbitrarily but on the basis of clear evidence. "Anggota Front Nasional tidak perlu merasa

takut: Kalau tak punya salah, kata Brig. Jend. Mustopo" ("Members of the National Front have no need to feel afraid: If they have not done anything wrong, says Brig, Gen. Mustopo"), *Merdeka*, September 8, 1958. Concern about missing funds within the Front came into the open on August 27, when the newly installed Secretary General, Mustopo, told the press that the Front was not (supposed to be) a center for people seeking "money, licences, rank, influence or [to carry out] party activities." Indicating that there was public concern over the financial management of the Front, he stated that "should any members of the public feel that they have been disadvantaged by the West Irian National Liberation Front they can make a personal submission to the Secretary-General" "Front Nasional satu-satunya markas perjuangan rakyat: Untuk bantu penguasa Perang dan Pemerintah—Bukan markas buat cari uang dan lisensi, pangkat, pengaruh dan kegiatan partai-partai" ("National Front the one and only headquarters for the struggle of the people: To assist the Military Authority and the Government—Not a headquarters to seek money and licences, ranks, influences and party activity"), *Merdeka*, August 27, 1958. The scandal involving the West Irian Struggle Fund continued to dog the WINLF in November 1958, when Nasution called for greater financial probity. "Letkol. Tituler Achmadi Pejabat Sekjen FNPIB," *Merdeka*, November 24, 1958.

101. "Brigadier Jenderal Dr. Mustopo Sekjen FNPIB" ("Brigadier General Dr. Mustopo Secretary General of the West Irian National Liberation Front"), *Merdeka*, August 15, 1958. On September 12 an announcement was made that Brigadier General Gatot Subroto (deputy army chief of staff) had been appointed by Nasution as deputy chairman of the West Irian National Liberation Front. "Gatot Subroto Wakil Ketua Front Nasional," *Merdeka*, September 12, 1958.

102. Interview with Hardoyo, January 1995. Hardoyo was detained for many years because of his PKI links after the September 30, 1965 Affair which ended with the downfall of Sukarno and the banning of the PKI.

103. J.E. Rocamora, *Nationalism in Search of Ideology: The Indonesian Nationalist Party, 1945–1965*, Qezon City, University of the Philippines, Center for Advanced Studies, 1975, pp. 333–4. Roccamora also makes the point that after leftist elements within the PNI began to gain control over that party, "continued army moves against the political parties brought these leaders to a position where they now had to fight back." Ibid., p. 334.

104. Yong Mun Cheong writes that "Army officers sent to head the BKS were either inexperienced or incompetent. Organising and leading functional groups already affiliated to and heavily influenced by political parties was a difficult job at best." Yong Mun Cheong, *Op. Cit.*, p. 99.

105. Lev, *Op. Cit.*, p. 66.

106. For example, in December 1958, in his capacity as commander-in-chief of the Armed Forces, Sukarno instructed Nasution to leave the work of civilians to the civil authorities. "Amanat Presiden di Hadapan Peperpu—Peperda: Presiden Sukarno Peringatkan APRI Serahkan Pekerjaan-pekerjaan Sipil pada Instansi-instansi Sipil" ("Address by the President to the Central War Authority—Regional War Authorities: President Sukarno Warns Armed Forces to Hand Over Civilian Functions to Civil Agencies"), *Merdeka*, December 16, 1958.

107. Lev, *Op. Cit.*, pp. 46–48.

108. "P.N.I. Usahakan Bentuk Front Pancasila: Untuk Membantu Pelaksanaan Demokrasi Terpimpin Bung Karno" (PNI Strives to Form Pancasila Front: To Assist Implementation of Bung Karno's Guided Democracy"), *Merdeka*, November 26, 1958.

109. Like the youth organizations organized by the New Order regime, the BKS-PM mobilized *jago* or thuggish elements of society in support of the army's political objectives. During the New Order such elements became known as *preman* while in the 1950s they were know somewhat quaintly as crossboy. Pamurahardjo involved crossboy elements when the BKS-PM took a leading role in organizing the celebrations for Youth Pledge Day on October 28, 1957 ("Pesta Pemuda Puncak Peringatan Hari Sumpah Pemuda: Didahului dengan pawai pemuda berobor" ("Youth Festival Peak of Youth Pledge Day Commemorations"), *Merdeka*, October 28, 1957.A week before the celebrations this officer made an explicit appeal to crossboy "to participate in the youth struggle" ("BKS-PM ajak 'Crossboys' ikut dalam perjuangan pemuda," *Merdeka*, October 23, 1995) and the BKS-PM went so far as to form a special subcommittee of the Youth Pledge Commemorative Committee known as the Sub-Committee for Channelling Crossboys. Pamurahardjo's rationale for involving crossboys ("their activities should be channeled toward the appropriate struggle of the *pemuda* which will enable them to contribute their energies to their nation and people.") (Ibid.) was similar to that of the *Golkar*-associated *Pemuda Pancasila* of the New Order period—who claimed they were not *preman* but were attempting to rehabilitate criminals. Interview with Pamurahardjo, *Op. Cit.* For a thorough account of the role of *Pemuda Pancasila*, including its relations with the New Order regime and Suharto himself, see Loren Ryter, "Pemuda Pancasila: The Last Loyalist Free Men of Suharto's New Order," *Indonesia* 66 (October 1998) pp. 45–73.

110. There are several newspaper accounts of these activities. In July 1958, Merdeka reported that the BKS—*Buruh Militer* would hold a "Week of Action to Increase Productivity." The BKS-BUMIL stated that in the wake of the takeovers of Dutch assets it would no longer just consider the interests of workers but would strive to increase productivity in the interests of national development. "BKS-BUMIL Akan Mengadakan Pekan Aksi Pertinggi Produksi" ("Worker-Military BKS to Hold a Week of Activities to Increase Production"), *Merdeka*, July 25, 1958. In August the minister for Civil-Military Cooperation announced that a revised National Front would move to implement "concrete" objectives. The second of three major objectives of the WINLF was to "carry out development which was inspired by a feeling of sacred *kerja bakti* [work of devotion—often in the form of a working bee] in the interests of the nation and people." In the same month Mustopo associated the West Irian National Liberation Front with more basic aspects of "total people's resistance" by referring to the WINLF's role in forming "a strong basis [for a] home front in confronting the challenge of the danger of subversion from within and outside the country." and the "importance of a 'people's army' and 'people's defence' in Indonesia." "Yang masih kantongi uang Dana Irian Barat: Supaya segera menyerahkan pada FNPIB" ("Those who are still pocketing the West Irian Fund: Hand it over to the West Irian National Liberation Front"), *Suluh Indonesia*, August 28, 1958.

111. "Keputusan-keputusan Rapat Peperpu dan Peperda: Operasi Keamanan Lebih Diperhebat—Brigade-brigade Pembangunan Diaktivir di Daerah-daerah" ("Decisions of Central Authority and Regional War Authorities: Security Operations to be Further Stepped Up—Development Brigades to be Activated in Regions"), *Merdeka*, December 15, 1958. The wording of this passage was somewhat ambiguous in that it was not entirely clear whether it was the BKS or the territorial organization which was to be permanent—*Mengenai BKS-BKS segera akan diatur dalam rangka organisasi Territorial yang permanent dan akan mendapat panji-panji dari Panglima Tertinggi*. The balance of probabilities indicated that it was the BKS which were intended to be permanent. The reference to the supreme commander indicates that Nasution presumed that President Sukarno himself would present colors (unit flags) to the various BKS.

112. "Brigjen Mustopo di Hadapan BKS-BKS" ("Brig. Gen. Mustopo in Front of the BKS Organisations"), *Merdeka*, January 8, 1959. Mustopo's medal was pinned to his uniform by the youngest member present from the Womens'—Military BKS. As Ruth McVey points out, in the years prior to the advent of the New Order regime the Indonesian Army had excellent relations with Yugoslavia, "which was seen as nonaligned, acceptable to respected Western opinion, and opposed by the Indonesian Communists." R. McVey, "The Post-Revolutionary Transformation of the Indonesian Army," *Op. Cit.*, p. 169, f.n. 169. That the Yugoslav Army, like the Indonesian Army, had emerged as a territorial warfare force could be added to McVey's list. As stated in previous chapters, a former senior officer in Tito's World War II Yugoslav Army, Dushan Kveder, wrote a tract on territorial warfare (Kveder, *Op. Cit.*). It became influential in Indonesian Army circles.

113. "Brigjen Mustopo di Hadapan BKS-BKS" ("Brig. Gen. Mustopo in Front of the BKS Organisations"), *Merdeka*, January 8, 1959, *Op. Cit.*

114. Reeve, 1985 *Op. Cit.*, p. 181.

115. Ibid.

116. These bodies, respectively, covered material, religious and spiritual functional groups and were chaired by Lieutenant Colonel Amir Murtono (material), Lieutenant Colonel Harsono (religious) and Mohd. Isa Idrus (spiritual). Ibid., p. 182.

117. Ibid., pp. 181–2.

118. Ibid., p. 185.

119. SOKSI was led by Lieutenant Colonel Suhardiman, Kosgoro by Lieutenant Colonel Mas Isman and MKGR by Lieutenant Colonel R.M. Soegandhi. Panggabean, *Op. Cit.*, p. 391.

120. For information on these bodies, see Suryadinata, *Op. Cit.*, pp. 13–14.

121. Ibid., p. 23.

122. See Reeve, 1985 *Op. Cit.*, for a comprehensive account of this process.

123. "20 Orang Perwira Masuk Kursus 'C' SSKAD: Dalam Rangka Mempertinggi Mutu dan Pembangunan Angkatan Darat" ("20 Officers Enter 'C' Course: Within the Framework of Improving the Quality and Development of the Army"), *Merdeka*, September 24, 1958.

124. *Reorganisasi TNI-AD Tahun 1984* (*Reorganisation of the Army 1984*).

125. Ibid. In 1963, two additional branches were added to the Army General Staff. According to Pauker, Section V now managed the army's territorial warfare function

and Section VI its involvement in forming and managing functional groups. As Pauker put it, both sections were aimed at enabling the Indonesian officer corps "to play a major role in the government of the country and to mobilise extensive popular support, of a political nature, behind army policies." Pauker, 1963 *Op. Cit.,* p. 22. On the other hand, the army's own document states that Section VI was to manage the placement of officers in organizations outside the army. *Reorganisasi Angkatan Darat, Op. Cit.,* p. 18. Whatever the case, the fact remains that the Indonesian Army retained a specialist section or sections on the Headquarters Staff that looked after the army's more conventional territorial functions and its involvement in functional groups and this organization had its origins in the old Inspectorate General of Territorial Affairs and People's Resistance that founded the BKS initiative.

126. Sunarti, *Op. Cit.,* p. 121.
127. Ibid., p. 148.

Chapter 10

Territorial Warfare and Territorial Management

In 1962 Sukarno succeeded in sidelining Nasution to a resurrected but relatively powerless armed forces chief of staff appointment. Nasution had attempted to assert control over the rapidly developing navy and air force by pressing for the creation of a position of armed forces commander which would entail command of the army, navy, air force and police. He eventually accepted the dual appointments of minister for defense and the newly created position of armed forces commander (*Panglima* ABRI), relinquishing the army chief of staff appointment. However, he was about to be out-maneuvered and seems not to have seen it coming. At the (manipulated) urging of the pliant and left-leaning Omar Dhani, who had replaced Suryadarma as air force chief of staff, the president subsequently converted the positions of "chiefs of staff" of the four services to "commander" (*panglima*) while changing Nasution's military appointment from *panglima* to armed forces chief of staff.

Operational command and control gravitated to the four commanders who, under the restored 1945 Constitution, were formally accountable to Sukarno as president and supreme commander. The position of armed forces chief of staff held relative little power as it was largely administrative in nature and did not entail direct command and control of troops, while Nasution's other position of minister for defense was also lacking in real influence. The more personally and culturally congenial Achmad Yani (who was Javanese, like Sukarno, and regarded as more flexible than Nasution) was appointed army chief of staff. While Yani was very concerned about the influence of the PKI he was nevertheless more prepared to work more closely with the president than Nasution had been.[1]

Sunarti writes that by the early 1960s relations between Nasution and Sukarno had become increasingly tense, with the president expressing resentment at Nasution's (and Sunarti's) opposition to his polygamy and sexual promiscuity. She recalls that the Army Wives Association had been shocked when the president took Hartini as his second wife in July 1953: "It was hard for women's freedom fighter organisations, including the Persit organisation, to accept and approve of Bung Karno's marriage to Ibu Hartini."[2] She also records that in late 1962 and 1963 the president had become annoyed because of Nasution's opposition to him taking a second wife.[3]

Like her husband, Sunarti was a fierce opponent of officers engaging in extramarital sex:

> There was a senior officer—he is dead now—who was playing around. I asked him why he was doing this. His reason was that his wife had affairs before he did. I said to him—that officer—that it was not gentlemanly to say that his wife was having extramarital sex. If he really didn't like his wife, he should just tell her so. Eventually he said that he wanted to divorce his wife. I didn't believe his excuse. And finally, I was right and the officer remarried. At first, we didn't recognise the second wife and only did so after a few years.[4]

She recalls that some other officers, including Yani, were not as keen on enforcing moral standards:

> Before Yani was appointed Army Chief of Staff we had a shock when he, his wife, and all the [Army Headquarters] Assistants [to the Chief of Staff] dined at the Bogor Palace with the President and Ibu Hartini. This was a 180-degree reversal from past [policy] that an army officer was not allowed to take a second wife without the approval of his commander.
>
> Pak Nas had repeatedly given a choice to officers in that situation. Give up the second wife and receive a promotion or resign. This was in accordance with the aspirations of women's groups at that time.[5]

By this time, the Nasution had a second daughter, Ade, who was born in 1960. Nasution's rather puritanical approach, the unusually small size of their family, and the many years that separated the births of their daughters had given rise to "deplorable" rumors that Nasution was not the father of their two daughters "because, they said, Pak Nas was unable to father children."[6] Of course, there were deeper elements to the tensions between the two men. Sukarno had become wary of being dominated by the army and Nasution was dismayed at the president's increasing closeness to the PKI, and for indulging in frivolity at the palace while the economy collapsed around him.[7]

A group of pro-Sukarno officers within the army became prominent from this time, especially the commander of the West Java *Siliwangi* Division, Major General Ibrahim Adjie.[8] His command of that strategically located division made the prospect of a coup against Sukarno less likely.

The West Irian issue, which became increasingly inflamed in the early 1960s, appeared to accord increased prominence to the army when a decision was made to insert troops to infiltrate the territory. However, a successful outcome would also benefit the PKI that had campaigned strongly on the issue since the mid-1950s.

To bolster its chances of seizing the territory or at least forcing the Dutch to succeed, Indonesia sought access to modern weapons systems for its armed forces. US military assistance had fallen to a relatively low level during the period of CIA support for the PRRI/Permesta rebels and was largely directed at the army.

Nasution was instructed to look to the Soviet Bloc for assistance and in the final decade of the president's rule Russia and its satellites provided the air force and navy with a substantial arsenal of Mig-21, -19, -17 and -15 fighters, TU-16 and IL-28 bombers, SA-2 Guideline surface-to-air missiles, and a Soviet-provided early warning radar network. MI-4 and larger MI-6 helicopters were also Russian supplied and the transport fleet was largely comprised of Soviet-manufactured four-engine AN-12s and smaller IL-14s. The navy took possession of a trophy ship in the form of a Sverdlov-class cruiser named the Irian, Riga Class frigates, fast missile-equipped patrol boats, and a small fleet of Whisky Class diesel-electric submarines. The army's tanks and other armored vehicles were also manufactured in the Soviet Bloc.

Sukarno's campaign of international negotiations and military action finally paid off in 1962 when the Dutch, under pressure from the Kennedy administration, agreed to hand the territory over to Indonesia pending an "act of free choice" supervised by the United Nations. In 1969 Opsus (*Operasi Khusus*—Special Operations), a foreign liaison and political manipulation unit located within General (later president) Suharto's Kostrad (Army Strategic Reserve Command), ensured support for the plebiscite through controversial tactics and the territory was officially ceded to Indonesia.

However, Indonesia quickly became embroiled in another international conflict. Sukarno and his foreign minister Subandrio began to voice concerns about the decolonization process in which neighboring Malaya was to join in a federation with British protectorates in North Borneo to form the new nation of Malaysia. As the economy descended further into chaos and the PKI launched "unilateral" actions in support of land reform that led to open fighting in rural Java, particularly with Muslim groups, an undeclared war began in Borneo in which Indonesian troops came into conflict with British, Australian and local forces.

Many army officers supported the confrontation of Malaysia, including Nasution who seems to have been concerned that he and the army had suffered when they had not initially warmed to the West Irian campaign. Some genuinely feared the establishment of Malaysia on professional-military grounds because, as Mrazek points out, the fall of Singapore had precipitated the invasion of the Netherlands Indies in World War II.[9]

Within this increasingly febrile atmosphere, Sukarno placed the air force commander Omar Dhani in charge of the anti-Malaysia *Komando Siaga* (Alert Command). Within the army, a group of senior officers, including General Yani, became worried that confrontation would benefit the PKI by diverting the army's attention into a probably unwinnable campaign against a technically superior British and Commonwealth force in Malaysia. Eventually, General Suharto became Dhani's deputy in January 1965 and began to slow the operation down.

In August and September 1964, the Opsus liaison and political manipulation unit, led by Lieutenant Colonel Ali Murtopo, was used by Suharto, under the direction of Yani, to open secret contacts with British and Malaysian officials. In November, Murtopo and another Kostrad officer travelled to Bangkok to conduct secret negotiations to limit confrontation.[10] That the army was prepared to conduct its own foreign policy initiative was indicative of the suspicions and tensions which were becoming unbearable in the last days of Guided Democracy.

Within the army, the territorial doctrine remained dominant but under increasing pressure from proponents of mobile, offensive forces. Officers in the rapidly developing navy and air force were demanding "a greater share in all fields of military policy and doctrine."[11] Complaints were made that the military doctrine was still a "land forces infantry doctrine (that) is determined by the territorial spirit and thus accords the principal role to the land forces only."[12]

An indication of the growing strength of the advocates of a mobile, offensive doctrine was the declaration of the *Tri Ubaya Cakti* (Three Sacred Endeavors) doctrine in April 1965 after an army seminar was held in Bandung. Following Sukarnoist policy lines, *Tri Ubaya Cakti* declared that Indonesia had a defense role throughout Southeast Asia in the wake of the impending departure of "neocolonialists." The territorial doctrine was to remain integral to Indonesia's defense posture but its focus would be directed toward the army's involvement in politics and the economy while its operational significance was to be downplayed.[13]

This apparent setback to territorialism was a cause of satisfaction to the PKI who, as Mrazek states, had long regarded the doctrine as "the main danger to its own position and to social progress and change in general."[14] The attitude of the PKI was that territorial warfare was "a doctrine of capitulation to the Western powers,"[15] had resulted in a conflict between the principle of "popular defence" and the need to develop modern and capable armed forces, and had relegated the navy and air force to secondary positions.[16]

The PKI considered that the territorial sections of the army should be replaced by a "fifth force" of volunteers while the professional armed forces should be mobile and offensive,[17] a concept which would have had the effect of creating functional rivals to the army and placing at risk its significant economic assets and role in politics and civil administration. The navy tentatively supported the army but China promised to provide arms for the establishment of a Fifth Force and in July 1965 the air force began training civilians from the PKI's mass organizations.

However, many within the army were prepared to stand fast in defense of its territorial defense strategies and structures and they did so from a position of relative strength. The new fifth branch of the general staff placed the territorial function on an equal footing with the other four branches at army headquarters and in 1958 Nasution had moved to strengthen the system of territorial commands and the territorial administrative apparatus. He took steps to reduce the authority of individual commanders so that they would be more responsive to central direction by dividing the seven existing *Tentara dan Territorium* into sixteen (later seventeen) smaller territorial commands. These were termed military area commands (*Komando Daerah Militer*—Kodam).[18]

The "shadow administration" the Dutch had complained about in 1949 was now much more deeply entrenched. Many of the Kodam headquarters were in provincial capitals and each covered a single densely populated province or several smaller ones. This gave commanders the ability to shadow their civilian administrative counterparts more closely. Over time the system was expanded into Korem (*Komando Resort Militer*) or military provincial commands, equating them roughly to a province in more populated areas or a number of provinces in outlying regions. Further down the hierarchy were Kodim (*Komando Distrik Militer*) military district commands, which were generally equivalent to *Kabupaten* or regency administrative districts, and Koramil (Komando *Rayon* Militer) military sector commands which usually corresponded with the *Kecamatan* or subdistrict level of administration.

The reorganization had greatly expanded Nasution's opportunities to dispense patronage as the number of command appointments and promotion opportunities available to the officer corps increased substantially.[19] He was also aiming to use these structures to exert greater control over the activities of the PKI throughout the country.[20]

Beyond these organizational changes, strategic thinkers within the army were developing a new Doctrine of Territorial Warfare and Territorial Management. Soebijono, who was involved in this initiative, writes that it was intended to enable the army to extend its reach deep into the rural villages to counter the PKI at the grassroots:

Another step that the Armed Forces took to counter the strength of the PKI, particularly in the regions, was the enhancement of the territorial organization in accordance with a new Doctrine of Territorial Warfare. At the end of 1962 at the [Ministry of Home Affairs] sub-district level Military Sector Commands were established and from 1963 Village Development Non-Commissioned Officers were placed in the villages.[21]

The army had first focused on the villages in the independence war and then used its martial law powers to restore its presence at this level of society in an effort to influence rural populations that were showing a tendency to vote for the PKI. Lev writes that in Java the army's use of these powers at the grassroots was to cause friction with the *pamong praja*. He notes that the army had initially worked with the *pamong praja* on the island of Java and used them as intermediaries with the masses and that both benefited from this arrangement as they were unsympathetic to the parties and had little commitment to the parliamentary system. However, within two years the army's local territorial commands began to penetrate down to the villages that had been the traditional domain of the *pamong praja*, who turned for assistance to the parties.[22]

Lev also notes, however, that Nasution came to the *pamong praja*'s rescue when parliament passed a new decentralization law in 1957 (Law No. 1/1957) that would have seen the already declining *pamong praja* eliminated altogether in favor of elected local councils. In regional and municipal elections in that year the PKI improved on its surprisingly good performance in the general elections two years earlier, causing even more consternation within the *pamong praja*. He writes that an alliance of mutual interest developed between the corps and the army that saw Nasution demand that the law be reconsidered. New regional administration laws enacted in 1959 greatly strengthened the *pamong praja* and weakened the control of local government bodies by the parties.[23]

Again, Nasution had asserted a partnership between the army and the *pamong praja* but it was an increasingly lopsided one. The imposition of martial law saw the introduction of committees in the regions comprising the regional commander, the head of the *pamong praja* in the area, members of the regional assembly (*Dewan Perwakilan Daerah*—DPD) and the regional chief of police. Legge points out that this "naturally constituted a limitation of authority upon the freedom of local authorities."[24]

Throughout the period of martial law a pattern of government was developed at the provincial level in which territorial management decisions were made by a committee of four or *Catur Tunggal* [Four in One] comprising the "territorial military commander, the civil governor, the chief of police, and the district attorney."[25] Under martial law the military commander, rather than the civil governor, chaired these meetings. These arrangements were a direct throwback to the system Nasution devised in 1948 where territorial commanders became military governors in times of war.

The army increasingly inserted its presence into the *pamong praja*'s traditional domain of the rural village. Civic mission programs were developed which were intended to win "hearts and minds" by improving conditions for village populations through the construction of roads and public buildings.

As noted earlier, the army had first used such strategies in the early 1950s in West Java, where the *Darul Islam* insurrection continued after the transfer of sovereignty. In the mid-1950s the commander of the Tasikmalaya-based 11th Infantry Regiment, Major Suwarto, formulated an integrated military, economic and sociopolitical strategy to separate *Darul Islam* insurgents from local communities.[26] This officer gradually assumed Nasution's mantle as the army's main territorial warfare strategist. Like Nasution, Suwarto was a former Royal Military Academy cadet.[27] He had been an officer in Nasution's *Siliwangi* Division during the revolution where he acquired first-hand experience of waging "total people's resistance." Like other *Siliwangi* officers (including Nasution) he became interested in concepts of "total people's resistance" after reading Edgar Snow's *Red Star Over China* in 1946.[28]

He was apparently a charismatic and highly intelligent officer[29] who held views associated with the now outlawed PSI.[30] His ideas on counterinsurgency gained wide attention in April 1956 when he announced a "Five-Year Plan" to finalize the *Darul Islam* rebellion. He expressed the hope that the government formed after the elections would "take it over" to "assist the people and release them from the depths of despair that they have suffered thus far."[31]

In a similar vein to the concepts of "total people's resistance" developed by Nasution in the revolutionary period, Suwarto's strategy accorded a leading role to the army in the mobilization of all governmental apparatus and the people, as reported by *Merdeka*:

> He [Suwarto] affirmed that in his "five-year plan to restore security," the restoration of security had to be carried out in a planned and integrated manner. All the machinery and apparatus of the state and the people were to be mobilised in order to participate in accordance with their respective capacities, with the military [acting as] exponents.[32]

By 1958, when the army was finding it difficult to deal with rebel troops after they retreated from urban centers and resorted to guerrilla warfare,[33] Nasution formed the Army Doctrine Committee (of which Suwarto was an influential member) which recommended that territorial warfare be the basis of Indonesia's defense doctrines.[34]

Suwarto was to become deeply involved in attempts by the United States to influence the Indonesian Army. From the early 1960s the Indonesian Army Staff and Command School became increasingly involved in developing doctrines of internal security and national development. Suwarto undertook training at Fort Leavenworth in the United States in 1959 and on his return, became the deputy commandant of Seskoad.

By this time he had become associated with Guy Pauker, who was then working for the US Rand Corporation "think tank" which had redirected its activities from a conventional defense focus to other areas, including "economic, social and political affairs overseas" because of "Cold War competition," meaning competition "with the Soviet Union."[35] Pauker had made extensive contacts within the army leadership during visits to Indonesia from the mid-1950s with a team from the Massachusetts Institute of Technology.

In late 1959, following the failure of PRRI/Permesta rebellions and in the hope that Nasution and the anti-communist officers would provide a bulwark against the rising influence of the PKI,[36] the United States agreed to the sale of fifty military aircraft including ten transports, and allowed Indonesia to make other private purchases. It was within this context of heightened US concern about Indonesia's relationship with communist countries and renewed cooperation between the US government and elements of the Indonesian Armed Forces that Suwarto, at Pauker's invitation, visited the Rand Corporation in the United States in 1962.

Pauker subsequently stated that Suwarto learned "all sorts of things about international affairs" at Rand and saw how Rand "organises the academic resources of the country as consultants." Suwarto returned to Indonesia with the "new idea" of inviting some top Indonesian US-trained economists at the University of Indonesia to lecture at Seskoad. Ransom observes that

> In effect, this group became the army's high level civilian advisers. They were joined at Seskoad by other PSI and Masyumi alumni of the university programs—Miriam Budiardjo from Pauker's MIT study group, and Selosoemardjan from Kahin's program at Cornell, as well as senior faculty from the nearby Bandung Institute of Technology, where the University of Kentucky had been "institution building" for AID [US Agency for International Development] since 1957.[37]

The "mini Rand" created under Suwarto influenced a generation of officers who passed through the school.

At this point, Djokosutono went further than striving to prevent the University of Indonesia's economics faculty from being taken over by "leftists on the teaching staff."[38] He and a cohort of US-educated economists within the faculty became involved in the efforts by the United States to promote anti-communism within the army and nurture sympathetic army officers. The faculty developed cooperative arrangements with the Ford Foundation and the University of California, Berkeley, during Djokosutono's tenure[39] and he joined other faculty staff in giving lectures at Seskoad.

According to Utrecht, the lectures of the staff from the University of Indonesia reflected "a growing impatience [within the military] with the prevalence of civil authority over its affairs and an increasing propensity to, itself, interfere deeper in civil administration." "On balance it may be concluded that during the final eight years of Sukarno's rule, the military dictatorship of 1966 was being prepared in Seskoad."[40] According to David Ransom "contingency plans" were developed at Seskoad that aimed to prevent a PKI takeover of the country in the event of Sukarno's sudden death.[41]

It was at Seskoad and under Suwarto's direction that territorial warfare doctrines were refined and developed into what became known as the Doctrine of Territorial Warfare and Territorial Management. At an operational level, a three-phase plan was formulated. At first, attempts would be made, primarily by the navy and air force, to repel an external threat. However, these branches of the armed forces were bound to fail given their lack of capability. In the second phase the army would play a predominant role, constantly inflicting damage on the enemy while avoiding engagements which would entail its own destruction and preparing for a counter-offensive to drive the enemy out. The counter-offensive was to be the third phase.[42]

In countering insurgencies within the country, the revised doctrine of territorial warfare concentrated on obtaining the support and assistance of local communities. This required villagers to carry out such duties as surrounding guerrilla redoubts in a *pagar betis* (wall of feet) during military operations to alert the army to any attempt by guerrillas to break the encirclement. Army officers attributed such tactics to their eventual success against the *Darul Islam* insurgents in mid-1962.[43]

The operational aspects of the new territorial warfare doctrines developed by Suwarto and others were to be supported by an associated doctrine of territorial management. This envisaged the army having a wide interventionist role in virtually all areas of national life so that it would be better able to mobilize the civilian populace for territorial warfare.

The doctrine was to describe territorial warfare as "a form of warfare which is total in nature. It utilises all national forces in a total fashion. . . ."[44] The definition of "national forces" included "the national potential in the military, political-economic-social, spiritual, and civic (or people's) fields."[45] To achieve a resilient defense capability there needed to be "territorial management" (*pembinaan wilayah*) to supervise all these areas.[46]

Whereas preparing for territorial warfare was the army's pretext for leading and mobilizing the population, territorial management aimed to nurture the attributes of an ideal Indonesian citizen and provided guidelines for intervening in non-military affairs in the cause of managing the human and other resources needed for territorial warfare.

The doctrine of territorial management was intended to provide the army with an ongoing "leading role in civil affairs" after martial law was lifted in 1963.[47] Suwarto hoped to maintain this leading role through courses and seminars aimed at acquainting "a substantial number of senior officials to understand the relationship between Territorial Warfare and Territorial Management, hoping that this would create enough consensus between civilian and military authorities to help them close ranks."[48]

As Robert Elson points out, the Indonesian Army's new doctrines, based as they were on the experience of the armed struggle, led to the emergence of an interventionist doctrine that emphasized "total people's resistance":

> Taking as their starting-point the idea of a territorial army ensconced with the people, set out by Nasution in the late 1940s and after, Suwarto's [Seskoad] group drew out its implications for the Army's relationship with Indonesia's broader society. The notion was not just that the army should be amongst the people, but that it should also seek to *manage* [Elson's italics] affairs within its territorial areas, including the idea that there should be developed a parallel army administration side by side with the civilian territorial administration controlled by the Ministry of Home Affairs, with a mandate to check and supervise these authorities.[49]

Elson's comment that the army intended to "manage affairs within its territorial areas" harked back to Nasution's strategies for the military administration which envisaged the army leading and mobilizing civilian populations with the *pamong praja* as its junior partner. With this clearly in mind, the doctrine recommended that "Close cooperation between the commanders of Military Regions and the governors/chiefs of First-Level Regions must be initiated in peacetime."[50] The military territorial command structures were also to shadow civil administrations at the regency and sub-district levels.[51]

Moreover, rather than tie its doctrine of territorial management exclusively to the internal threat, the Indonesian Army drew upon its origins as a "people's resistance" force. It put forward a hypothetical (and most unlikely) threat of invasion as a rationale for mobilizing the population and making other preparations to wage a war of "total people's resistance."

This transformation of doctrines that had originally been directed toward defending the country against the Dutch into a rationale for military intervention across the archipelago and down to the grassroots of society was a particularly unusual and even ingenious approach to military intervention.

In the early 1960s Pauker went further, describing the "political conception underlying the doctrine of Territorial Warfare and Territorial Management" as "shrewd and even brilliant."[52]

Territorial management had a conservative agenda that accorded closely with the thinking outlined in Supomo's 1945 address to the BPUPKI or the aims of the aristocratically led PIR party. Territorial management stressed political stability, national unity, a harmonious blending of the elements in the war potential of a nation. It warned that "the infiltration of foreign ideologies into the body of the people can endanger the well-being of the state and the unity of the people"[53] and aimed to suppress "antagonistic elements" including "individualism and liberalism," "international communism," "negative religious fanaticism," and "atheism."[54]

The doctrine also advocated that territorial managers use a range of methods to change the attitudes of different social groups: "the educated upper group (the elite, the wealthy) many of whom are found within the currents of liberalism, individualism and feudalism," "the common people" "many of whom are found within the Communist ranks"; the "orthodox group of people, many of whom are found in fanatical religious movements"; and "those groups of citizens who are inspired by feelings of regional separatism and narrow ethnocentrism."[55]

A paper on territorial warfare by the Inspectorate General for Territorial Affairs and People's Resistance emphasizes this concern for stability and the belief that *Pancasila* would act as an antidote to "foreign" ideologies that would be detrimental to the achievement of social stability:

> The objective of control in these [the political and psychological] fields is to strengthen the people's powers of moral defence. This is encouraged by indoctrinating them in the ideology of the *Pancasila* and by achieving political stability. Conscious indoctrination in the *Pancasila* will provide a powerful defence against the penetration of foreign ideologies which are raging throughout the world at this time and whose influence is increasing. The infiltration of these foreign ideologies into the body of the people can endanger the well-being of the state and the unity of the people.[56]

The doctrine represented the final stage in the transformation of Nasution's strategies for "people's war" into overt means of military intervention that accorded with Nasution's own social conservatism and his concern to put a brake on threats to the social order through an emphasis on organicist thinking. That the doctrine was influential long after Nasution's direct influence over the army had evaporated entirely is evident in the following excerpts from Seskoad's core publication for students, *Vademikum*, issued at the height of the Suharto New Order regime in 1987.[57]

According to this publication, the first two areas of vulnerability at the national level were:

1. Communism, which in its essence does not tolerate the participation of all citizens within the political system.
2. Liberalism, which in its essence emphasizes individualism in an extreme manner, which disturbs social harmony and balance and a sense of community.[58]

Elsewhere, the manual counselled territorial staff to impart a sound understanding of *Pancasila* to foster "loyal and moderate" religious teaching and to develop a culture of consultation and consensus as means of making decisions and resolving issues. It referred to "the spirit of the preamble to the 1945 Constitution" as "containing characteristics of openness and the provision of opportunities for new social energies and dynamics to participate within the system. Thus, in a strategic manner social changes and dymanism can be absorbed and integrated into the system."[59]

Vademikum contained similar advice on how to communicate with different social groups, such as intellectuals and the Muslim community, and another section advised officers on how to handle the "Chinese problem" "through implanting a spirit of Indonesian nationality and eradicating characteristics of exclusivism within citizens of Chinese descent."[60]

Sociopolitical operations had objectives that accorded particularly closely with the traditional values espoused by Supomo and taken up by Nasution. They included consultation and "*gotong royong / kekeluargaan.*"[61] Javanese was often used to describe or name particular concepts, with Indonesian translations offered. An example is *tut wuri handayani* (to influence and provide impetus from behind).[62]

The *Catur Tunggal* committees of the 1960s had by this time been replaced by Regional Leadership Consultation Committees (*Musyawarah Pimpinan Daerah—Muspida*). These were to be chaired by province governors and *bupati*s (depending upon the level of government) and membership included the local military and police commanders and the head of the attorney general's office. The committees were to "facilitate the implementation of development throughout all parts of the nation and develop political stability and national unity."[63]

Under the new doctrines that emerged from the 1960s, top marks at Seskoad were given to officers who did well in territorial, rather than operational, subjects, and future assignments for such officers tended to be more prestigious and lucrative. For example, David Jenkins wrote in 1983:

Assignments given to officers who have completed the course at Seskoad reflect the pre-eminent position of the territorial apparatus. While the top ten or twelve graduates may be selected by the intelligence service to serve as military attaches, those immediately below them are generally given Korem [territorial] commands."[64]

Jenkins also described how officers were specifically trained to intervene in such activities as influencing the outcome of general elections:

As part of their course work, mid-career officers at Seskoad study the mounting of a territorial intelligence exercise during the run-up to a general election. They decide the groups to target and what sort of psychological operations should be launched against them. . . . inevitably in these exercises the political parties are listed as targets, with special attention being paid to which members of these groups are of particular interest. The "targets" also include informal leaders in the community—a man who stands up and commands attention at the local mosque, a student leader, and so on.[65]

Clearly, Suwarto's use of Nasution's strategies as the basis for the Doctrine of Territorial Warfare and Territorial Management resulted in a highly unusual, durable and pervasive form of military intervention.

In the political reform (*reformasi*) era following the collapse of the Suharto regime the army severed its ties with *Golkar*, distanced itself from the functional group concept and set about restructuring its doctrines so that they emphasized external, rather than internal, defense. The experience of East Timor's transition to independence was a particular indication of a need for change. The army had organized militia bands in that territory under the banner of "people's resistance" whose behavior was so barbaric that it attracted world attention. Cribb has argued persuasively that the violent behavior of many Indonesian troops in East Timor stemmed from deference and timidity on the part of the Indonesian population that had its origins in the separate and leading role of the army in pursuing "people's warfare" during the armed struggle against the Dutch. He postulates that soldiers often became enraged when East Timorese civilians failed to show such deference.[66]

However, regional conflicts in parts of Indonesia provided a rationale for dampening this process, and for a reversion to old habits in the form of the army establishing new territorial commands, rather than closing them down. In this climate, from 2002 the army leadership began to strongly and frequently defend the territorial structures and territorial management role as being indispensable in maintaining national unity. For example, in 2002, the army chief of staff, Lieutenant General Ryamizard Ryacudu (who is minister for defense in the current Widodo administration) made the following statements in a media interview:

> We don't need to copy the defense models of other countries, because they are not yet appropriate for application in our nation. Here in Indonesia the nature of the state has not been finalised as it has in advanced countries. We are still facing a number of problems, particularly social conflict and separatism in some regions. Because of that, what is needed [is thinking about] how to enhance the resources that we possess—human and materiel.
>
> It has been put to the test, how this country is still standing and how rebellions have been able to be eradicated. So, don't experiment with concepts of defence. Trial and error can have good results, but if it fails it will be fatal. Imagine if this country was threatened and we didn't have an established concept, because we were still dismantling and replacing it.[67]

Ryacudu's views about the territorial commands were met with concern on the part of human rights advocates, such as Munir Said Thalid:

> Now that the basic tasks of the army are becoming so extensive, the army is becoming like a nation in its own right because they can fight at any level, based upon their own assessments about safeguarding the sovereignty and symbols of the state. There was a statement from Ryamizard who said, for example, that he would maintain the territorial commands which have long been criticised. He said that dismantling the territorial commands was the same as dismantling the Unitary State of the Republic of Indonesia.[68]

The interview concluded with the somewhat wry and pointed observation that perhaps the term *Negara Kesatuan Republik Indonesia* (Unitary State of the Republic of Indonesia) had been superseded by *Negara Kodam Republik Indonesia* (Military Area Command State of the Republic of Indonesia). Munir died in late 2004 while on a Garuda Airlines flight to the Netherlands. Tests showed that he had been poisoned. A.M. Hendropriyono, a former four-star special forces general who ran the National Intelligence Agency at the time of Munir's murder, was widely suspected of involvement but has never been brought to trial.[69]

NOTES

1. For an account of Sukarno's sidelining of Nasution, see Crouch, 1978 *Op. Cit.*, pp. 344–345.
2. Sunarti, *Op. Cit.*, p. 70.
3. Ibid., p. 139.
4. Ibid., pp. 222–223.
5. Ibid., pp. 146–147.
6. Ibid., p. 139.
7. Ibid., p. 148.

8. Jenkins, *Op. Cit.*, p. 3.
9. R. Mrazek, *Op. Cit.*, p. 95.
10. Hamish McDonald, *Suharto's Indonesia*, Fontana, Melbourne, 1980, pp. 35–38.
11. R. Mrazek, *Op. Cit.*, p. 135.
12. Ibid., p. 137.
13. Ibid., p. 150.
14. Ibid., p. 155.
15. Ibid.
16. Ibid.
17. Ibid.
18. The seven *Tentara dan Territorium* were split into the following sixteen (seventeen after the incorporation of West Irian) *Komando Daerah Militer* (KODAMs):Kodam I/Iskandarmuda—AcehKodam II/Bukit Barisan—North SumatraKodam III/17 Agustus—West SumatraKodam IV/Sriwijaya—South Sumatra and JambiKodam V/Jaya—Greater JakartaKodam VI/Siliwangi—West JavaKodamVII/Diponegoro—Central JavaKodam VIII/Brawijaya—East JavaKodam IX/Mulawarman—East KalimantanKodam X/Lambung Mangkurat—South KalimantanKodam XI/ Tambun Bungai—Central KalimantanKodam XII/Tanjung Pura—West KalimantanKodam XIII/Merdeka—North and Central SulawesiKodam XIV/Hasanuddin—South and Southeastern SulawesiKodam XV/Pattimura—Maluku and Irian JayaKodam XVI/Udayana—West Lesser SundasKodam XVII/Cenderawasih—Irian Jaya (formed in August 1962)
19. Sundhaussen, *Op. Cit.*, p. 125.
20. Panggabean observes that the ratification of this doctrine and the rapid proliferation of territorial commands that took place from the early 1960s was "a thorn in the side of the PKI," Panggabean, *Op. Cit.*, p. 280.
21. Soebijono *Op. Cit.*, p. 30.
22. Lev, *Op. Cit.*, p. 62.
23. Ibid., f.n. 29. For a discussion of moves toward regional autonomy at the time, including extracts of Law No 1/1957 see J.D. Legge, *Central authority and Regional Autonomy in Indonesia: A Study in Local Administration 1959–1960, Op. Cit.*
24. Ibid., p. 205. Legge goes on to point out that the extent to which regional military commanders exerted their influence through these committees "varied from area to area and upon the regional commander himself." "There was a more restricted limit in fact than there was in theory to the emergency powers of the army and there was no detailed military intervention in civil administration." Ibid., pp. 205–206.
25. Pauker, 1963 *Op. Cit.*, p. 30.
26. Sundhausen, *Op. Cit.*, p. 138.
27. Bachtiar, *Op. Cit.*, p. 423.
28. Pauker, *Op. Cit.*, pp. 8–9.
29. See, for example, Molly Bondan's brief but respectful account of her association with Suwarto during the revolution in Yogyakarta in J. Hardjono and C. Warners (eds.) *In Love with a Nation: Molly Bondan and Indonesia*, Picton, Charles Warner, 1995, p. 89. Panggabean wrote respectfully and affectionately about Suwarto's role

in developing army doctrine after that officer's death from cancer in September 1967. Panggabean, *Op. Cit.*, p. 279, 280, 363.

30. Jenkins, *Op. Cit.*, p. 203, f.n. 35.

31. "T.T.-III jalankan 'Rencana 5 Tahun' pemberantasan Gerombolan D.I." ("T.T.-III Carries out 'Five-Year Plan' to Eradicate D.I. Bandits"), *Merdeka*, April 16, 1956.

32. Ibid.

33. Pauker, 1963 *Op. Cit.*, p. 16.

34. This was endorsed by the Provisional People's Consultative Congress (*Majelis Permusyawaratan Rakyat Sementara*—MPRS) in December 1960. Panggabean, *Op. Cit.*, p. 280.

35. *Rand's History: Fifty Years of Service to the Nation*, www.rand.org.org/history, p. 5, accessed September 2001.

36. "AS Taroh Harapan Pd. Nasution" ("US Pins its Hopes on Nasution"), *Merdeka*, April 17, 1958.

37. Ransom. *Op. Cit.*, p. 102.

38. "No Ivory Tower," www.fordfoundation.org, accessed June 2005.

39. http://www.fe.ui.ac.id/tentangfeui/sejarah/, accessed June 2005.

40. E. Utrecht, *The Military and the 1977 Election*, Townsville, Qld.: James Cook University of North Queensland, South East Asian Studies Committee, p. 78.

41. Ransom, *Op. Cit.*, p. 76.

42. John Keegan, "Indonesia" in *World Armies*, London, MacMillan, 1979, p. 272.

43. Pauker, 1963 *Op. Cit.*, p. 33.

44. Ibid., p. 55.

45. Ibid. pp. 140–170.

46. Ibid.

47. Ibid., p. 30.

48. Ibid.

49. R.E. Elson, *Suharto: A Political Biography*, Oakleigh, Vic., Cambridge University Press, 2001, pp. 76–77.

50. Translation of Document No. NS 1124–01, Pauker, 1963 *Op. Cit.*, p. 109.

51. "The same principles [of establishing territorial command boundaries] should be applied in deciding on the regional boundaries of military districts and second-level regions." Ibid., p. 109.

52. Ibid., p. 46.

53. "Basic Thoughts on Territorial Management by the Department of the Army Inspectorate General for Territorial Affairs and People's Resistance," pp. 301–302.

54. Book 1, "Concept of the Doctrine of Territorial Warfare," Ibid., p. 144.

55. Ibid., pp. 145–146.

56. "Basic Thoughts on Territorial Management, Ibid., pp. 301–302.

57. Seskoad, *Vademikum* (Third Edition), Authorized Vide Directive from the Commandant of Seskoad No. SKEP/5/II/1987 dated February 28, 1987.

58. Ibid., p. 194.

59. Ibid., pp. 195–196.

60. Ibid., pp. 197–198.

61. Ibid., p. 207.

62. Ibid.
63. Ibid., p. 205.
64. Jenkins, *Op. Cit.*, p. 44.
65. Ibid.
66. See Cribb, 2002 *Op. Cit.*
67. "KSAD Ryamizard Ryacudu: Komando Teritorial Masih Relevan" ("Army Chief of Staff Ryamizard Ryacudu: Territorial Commands Still Relevant"), *Kompas*, July 13, 2002.
68. "Rapat PangKodam di Aceh: Hati-hati Angkatan Darat Bangkit Lagi!" ("Kodam Commanders Meeting in Aceh: Watch Out or the Army Will Rise Again"), Daily Reports of Current Affairs in Indonesia, Radio Netherlands, April 1, 2003. (iiasnt.leidenuniv.nl:8080/DR/2003/04/DR_2003_04_01/OneFile)
69. *The Conversation* media service (September 29, 2014) provides a brief account in English of this officer's possible involvement in Munir's murder (http://theconversation.com/solving-munirs-murder-case-a-test-for-indonesias-president-elect-31293).

Chapter 11

Old Age and Legacy

By the time the bloody and chaotic political upheavals of September/October 1965 took place the economy was in ruins:

> There was rampant inflation; industrial production dropped to 20 percent of its capacity; gold and foreign exchange reserves were completely exhausted; foreign debt had risen to $2.4 billion; money circulation had increased by 100 percent in 1963, by about 150 percent in 1964 and in the first nine months of 1965 made a jump of 240 percent; and it proved impossible to draw up a budget for 1965. The government came to a virtual standstill and the underpaid government workers showed up only for a couple of hours at their jobs and then went to earn extra money in one or more other jobs. The economic down-turn was felt strongest in the towns, where there was famine in the pauperised *kampungs* [urban villages] and where hordes of children searched the garbage dumps for something edible.[1]

There were severe shortages of all sorts of imported goods and the newspapers were cobbled together with motley collections of typefaces. The postal system had largely ceased to function and in most parts of Jakarta rubbish was disposed of by piling it into concrete containers by the roadside and burning it, or just dumping it by the roadside or in the stagnant and massively polluted rivers and canals. The telephone system had deteriorated to the point where callers had to dial repeatedly before (sometimes) finally getting through. The water pipes in the capital were in such poor state that most relied upon wells that tapped artesian supplies. Electricity was intermittent and the State Electricity Company (*Perusahaan Listrik Negara*) was often referred to sarcastically as the *Perusahaan Lilin Negara* (the National Candle Company). Those who could afford it installed diesel generators.

Sharp declines in education standards had resulted in poorly trained doctors being turned out, particularly by many of the newer universities that sprung up after the Dutch departed. Many older educated Indonesians were appalled at the decline in hospital management, hygiene and facilities.[2]

Sunarti recalls her father's bitter disappointment with Sukarno that preoccupied him on a visit to Europe with Maria in 1963:

> This was the first time that Mother had been to Europe in forty years of married life. A fortnight before they were due to return I had a premonition that Father would die and I asked him to come home. When he came down the steps from the aircraft I felt as if he was no longer there. Two weeks later Father died. I should note here that Father had wanted to come home to Indonesia to meet with Bung Karno to ask why he was always chasing after women and forgetting about the real struggle.[3]

Although many officers were personally loyal to Sukarno, tensions increased between members of the army leadership and the president that were to culminate in his downfall. In May 1965, a telegram sent to London by the British ambassador (the so-called Gilchrist letter) was leaked. It mentioned "local army friends" and the PKI quickly spread rumors that a Council of Generals had been formed to overthrow the president, whose health was declining.

The transformative rupture between anti-communist officers and the president occurred on the night of September 30, 1965. Troops went to the houses of Yani and five other senior generals, requesting them to accompany them immediately to a meeting with the president. Those who resisted were killed while the others were abducted to Halim air base on the outskirts of Jakarta where they were killed by volunteers who were being trained by the air force within the China-backed Fifth Force program.

Their attempt to abduct Nasution failed when Sunarti urged him to escape and told the soldiers that he had been out of town for a few days. He managed to flee over a back fence of his house, breaking his ankle as he fell into a neighbor's yard, but little Ade Nasution was shot in the spine when a maid tried to carry her to safety.[4]

The following day General Suharto (who remained in command of Kostrad but had not been included in the list of generals to be abducted) moved to establish control over the army. After hiding for a time, Nasution joined him as he set about countering what became known as the "30 September Movement." A chaotic and drawn-out process ensued that culminated in the end of Sukarno's long tenure as president and the establishment of the New Order, the regime that Suharto led for thirty-two years.

During this period, massive student and other street protests demanded that Sukarno be put on trial for suspected involvement in the "coup," and elements of the army and Muslim groups carried out massive and widespread killings of people suspected of Communist Party membership or involvement. By the end of the 1960s the PKI, which had been one of the largest Communist parties in the world, was all but eliminated.

That Nasution did not emerge as the leader of the anti-September 30 forces puzzled many observers. Throughout his life and career, he had proved that he was a man of great strength of character and resilience. His unrelenting efforts during the struggle against the Dutch to place the army on a more professional footing while emphasizing that asymmetric warfare was the only realistic option open to it was of great service to the republic, as was his concerted action in the face of the Madiun insurgency. His effective command of the forces involved in suppressing the CIA-backed regional rebellions in the 1950s was also of great service to his country. His loyalty to the *Pancasila* state and determination to suppress the *Darul Islam* insurgency, despite his personal piety, played an important part in upholding aspirations for a unitary, secular republic. However, in a reference to Shakespeare's Hamlet, by the 1970s and 1980s he was sometimes referred to as The Wavering Prince for his behavior in the days after the attack and Jenkins has written that "Military men, particularly those around Suharto, sought to focus attention on his seeming immobility at several critical points in the nation's history, most particularly in the wake of the 1965 coup attempt."[5]

In the early 1980s Jenkins interviewed Suharto's then vice president, Adam Malik, who said that he joined Nasution at Ade's hospital bedside on the evening of October 1. Malik claimed that he had urged Nasution (to whom he was related) to go to Suharto's Strategic Command Headquarters and take over because he was the senior general. Nasution refused because he would not leave his daughter, even though Malik and his wife, Nelly, assured him they would look after the little girl.[6]

Of course, by then Malik was firmly ensconced within the Suharto regime and his remarks should be treated with some caution.

Nasution later denied the veracity of this account, writing that Malik only visited the hospital once, on October 5, and that no such conversation took place at that time. Rather, he claims that the conversation recalled by Malik ocurred after 11 March 1966 (when Suharto effectively took the reins of power from Sukarno but was having difficulty forming a cabinet). However, by then Sukarno had dismissed him from his Cabinet post and the armed forces. Believing that Suharto had acquired sufficient powers to form a cabinet, Nasution sent a letter to him to that effect but Suharto had already reached a comprise with the President. Nasution also recalled that although many thought of him as the second most senior officer in the military (after Sukarno) his removal from command of the army in 1962–1963 meant that he was outside the chain of command and no longer had operational command and control of any military force or unit at the time of the coup.[7]

Jenkins also cites assertions from within the regime that Suharto offered Nasution command of the army on more than one occasion. However, Nasution denied this when asked by Jenkins.[8]

Shocked by the attack on his family home, his narrow escape from assassination, and the wounds sustained by his daughter, he might have been concerned that he would be unlikely to attract genuine support from the wily Suharto and other senior military officers who had command and control of substantial military units. He might also have expected the relatively unknown Suharto to be a short-term leader and that he would take over the army and perhaps the presidency in the long term based upon his credentials, experience and seniority. Crouch writes that senior army officers might have considered it better to keep Nasution "in the background" pending the wresting of power from Sukarno, who remained a potentially powerful force for some time after the events of September 30, because the president would never agree to him taking command.[9]

There is a subplot to the relationship between Nasution and Suharto that might have impinged upon these events. While Suharto was deferential at the time, there are grounds for surmising that he deeply resented Nasution. The Sumatran had been a junior KNIL officer and clearly played a leading role in the revolutionary armed struggle against the Dutch while Suharto had only been a sergeant in the KNIL and not as prominent during and after the revolution. Perhaps most significantly, in 1959 Nasution had removed him from command of the Central Java *Diponegoro* Division, apparently because of involvement in the corrupt use of charitable foundations (*yayasan*s).[10] Vatikiotis believes that this humiliation "still rankled" with the Kostrad commander.[11]

However, Nasution's seeming reluctance to assert himself on this occasion might have been another manifestation of a tendency to stand back in some crisis situations and allow subordinates to make the running. In the *Bandung Lautan Api* episode of 1946 he had allowed his subordinate officers to take the initiative and in the October 17, 1952 Affair he had merely introduced them to Sukarno and not aired his own views. Pamurahardjo's account of the takeover of the KPM shipping line indicates that Nasution adopted a rather passive stance in the formation of the BKS organizations and when this firebrand officer became centrally involved in the rupture in economic and political relations with the former colonial power. Out-maneuvered by Sukarno in the early 1960s, he seems to have submitted rather meekly to being "kicked upstairs" to become armed forces chief of staff and defense minister. The founding president figured centrally in all but the first of these examples and it is possible that Nasution was in such awe of Sukarno that he felt unable to oppose him in highly critical situations.

Opportunities for a relatively poor boy from an obscure village in Sumatra to obtain an education, let alone train as a military officer, were extremely limited in the Dutch colonial system and against the odds he made the best of those available to him through sheer brilliance and hard work. However, a childhood spent far from his family in boarding school dormitories might have given rise to insecurities and vulnerabilities. His relatively humble origins and outsider status as a Sumatran in a predominantly Javanese milieu might also have caused him to be hesitant and wrong-footed on occasions when dealing with men like Sukarno who had emerged from more privileged and perhaps unfathomable Javanese *priyayi* backgrounds.

Eventually, he accepted appointment as the chairman of the Provisional People's Consultative Assembly (*Majelis Permusyawaratan Rakyat Sementara*—MPRS) that called upon Sukarno to account for his actions and then appointed Suharto as acting president and then president. He became increasingly disaffected with the Suharto regime in the early 1970s and retired from the army in 1972.

In 1980, he signed a petition, together with forty-nine other leading Indonesians (the Petition of 50—*Petisi 50*) protesting about Suharto's interpretation and use of *Pancasila* to criticize opponents. He was banned from leaving the country for some years but, as always, found consolation in his home in Menteng where he:

> retained, in his family life, a quiet harbour from the storms of politics. He lived unpretentiously with his Eurasian wife and two daughters in a suburban villa in Jakarta. They did not take part in the social round. After the death of his daughter—from bullets intended for him—and the murder of his colleagues, Nasution retired into grief and bitterness.[12]

An exception was made to the travel ban when Sunarti won the 1981 Ramon Magsaysay Award for her untiring work for charitable causes and he accompanied her to Manila to receive it. The information on Sunarti on the Magsaysay web sums up her achievements:

> Indonesians sometimes say: "If you want something planned, talk with the men. If you want something done, talk with the women." In this spirit, Mrs. Nasution pursued her work independent of her husband's military career, although on occasion their relationship has opened doors. Reaching far beyond her initial work with soldiers' families, her efforts have been directed with continuity and fidelity to the larger needs of the country.
>
> The Indonesian National Council on Social Welfare which was organized by Mrs. Nasution and her associates today includes twenty-three national nongovernmental groups, eighteen provincial coordinating councils of social welfare, seventeen schools with social work faculties and nine national government

agencies. Working together are the Muhammadiyah and Aisyiyah—major Muslim organizations for men and women, respectively, the Red Cross, Bishops' Conference, National Council of Churches, Hindu Dharma Council, several federations for the handicapped and similar nonprofit associations.

The organizational approach Mrs. Nasution initiated in Jakarta eighteen years ago became the model. The National Council guides and assists member organizations in recruiting volunteer workers and experts, organizing workshops, collecting funds and distributing donated food, clothing and medicines. The council also assists in placing children in families, schools and jobs, and in marketing handicrafts, vegetables and fruits for cooperatives. Management guidance is provided to homes for the disabled, sick, destitute and orphans. The council helps draw up the welfare portion of the government's National Development Plan, working closely with the departments concerned to achieve equitable distribution of welfare. All is accomplished by a headquarters of fifteen paid staff and fifty-five volunteers.

Through her energy, initiative and vision, Mrs. Nasution has infused her colleagues in their own organizations with purpose and professionalism. Much remains to be done, but the cadre of social workers she has inspired now has tools to aid Indonesia's least fortunate.[13]

The lift in the travel ban came after a concerted attack upon Sunarti by the First Lady, Mrs. Tien Suharto, who was often referred to as *Ibu Tien Persen* (Madame Ten Per Cent) for the rake-offs she was alleged to take from those seeking to do business with the regime. Jenkins has written that Mrs. Suharto tried to engineer a takeover of Sunarti's Coordinating and Supervising Body by the Department of Social Welfare and replace her with Nelly Malik.

Sunarti soon demonstrated a steely resolve by meeting with the vice president and emerging with a promise that his wife would not take part in such a move. She then gained support from General Surono, the Coordinating Minister for People's Welfare, who had once been an aide to her husband. Finally, she spoke to a high official in a government bank about plans by the regime to "cut her money" and was assured that it was not in her name and would not be touched.[14] The outcome was that the formidable Mrs. Suharto suffered a rare defeat and Sunarti retained her leadership of her charitable organizations.

Increasingly embraced by many opponents of the Suharto regime, Nasution gradually adopted a political stance that was at odds with some of his attitudes in the 1950s and 1960s. He began to assert that he had wished the army to avoid "petty politics" and had only wanted it to become involved in "the broad guidelines of state policy." Rather disingenuously, in view of his formulation of the "middle way" approach and concerted efforts to include military personnel in the legislatures and many areas of governmental administration, it was at this point in his life that he began to assert that it was President Sukarno who had insisted that the army involve itself in the legislatures in the mid-to-late 1950s.[15]

In his final years the regime softened its stance toward him. It appears that President Suharto wished to be promoted to the rank of five-star general but realized that it would be awkward to do so without granting the same status to Nasution and (posthumously) to General Sudirman. In 1997 he was promoted to Great General or *Jenderal Besar*, a rank equivalent to Field Marshal in armies with a British tradition or General of the Army in the United States, together with Suharto and the late *Panglima Besar*. He was again allowed to travel abroad, this time to seek medical treatment. He died in 2000, soon after the fall of Suharto, and did not live to see the democratization that has since taken place.

Until the last few years of his life he received a steady flow of visitors, always sitting under a large portrait of Ade in his house in Jakarta where the furniture and décor had hardly changed since the early 1950s. He continued to write his many accounts of the formation of the army, the revolutionary years, and his involvements in Indonesian politics.

Sunarti, who died in March 2010, recalled that he wrote largely from memory, only calling on research staff to find details on: " names, dates, places or troop numbers. But he didn't need to ask for information on all the strategies and the way operations had taken place because they were still lodged in his memory."[16] He could remember all the details of his "monumental" Strategic Order No 1/1948 that laid down the basis for the struggle against the Dutch in 1949: "Anyone who took part in the Second Independence War certainly witnessed how the Dutch military were gasping for breath because they had run out of energy."[17]

Nasution's Strategic Order No. 1/1948 was "monumental" in more than a strictly military sense as it embodied an emerging political orientation that owed a great deal to his personal and family life. Unlike the prewar elites of Vietnam, China and other societies where Communist movements had used "people's war" to achieve national liberation, Nasution's unique principles of guerrilla warfare and his transformation of them into a means of military intervention in politics in the 1950s helped protect the traditional elites with whom he allied himself after marrying into the Gondokusumo family. Like them, he lived in financial comfort in his home country into his old age.

Nasution's beloved home in Menteng has been transformed into a museum in his memory, but comments about it on the Tripadvisor website focus more on the bloody events of September 30, 1965 than Nasution's military career and his principles of "people's resistance" that helped to wear down the Dutch and became a powerful means of military intervention in politics over the three decades that the New Order ruled Indonesia.

Indonesians have enthusiastically embraced democracy in recent years, their archipelagic and multiethnic country has not succumbed to balkanization (except for movements in Aceh and Papua), and it has made substantial economic progress. However, the army's "shadow administration" territorial commands remain in place and it cannot be ruled out that the style of military intervention that Nasution pioneered might reemerge should there be a security crisis at some time in the future. As previously noted, Ryamizard Ryacudu, the army commander who declared his support for the territorial system in 2002, is minister for defense in the current Widodo government and in June 2016 President Widodo declared his categorical support for the army's territorial commands.[18]

In the second decade of the new millennium as countries like France and Great Britain deployed armed troops to patrol the streets in the face of terrorist attacks and Islamists seized and held the town of Marawi in The Philippines, the sensitivities that remain in Indonesia about adopting such measures and their potential to be used by the military to assert control over civilian populations were canvassed in media reports in June 2017, such as the following article in Singapore's *Straits Times*:

> President Joko Widodo's recent call for the military to have a bigger role in Indonesia's war on terror has been greeted with support from many lawmakers, but also trepidation by rights groups.
>
> Certain members of the national police commission (Kompolnas) have even warned that giving the armed forces, or *Tentara Nasional Indonesia* (TNI), more powers in domestic counter-terrorism may be unconstitutional and lead to abuses. "If this law is ignored, it will affect the criminal justice system in Indonesia, disrupt the order of civil society, and perpetuate human rights violations," said Kompolnas commissioner chief Poengky Indarti.
>
> But coming after the twin suicide bombings in East Jakarta that killed three policemen on May 23, and amid fears of a spillover from the fighting in Marawi city in southern Philippines, the call makes sense.[19]

There have been increasing tendencies within some Islamic organizations to challenge the secularity of the *Pancasila* state in recent years, giving impetus to what Nasution (and his old patrons within the traditional elites) would have seen as dangerous and divisive divisions within society. As this book was prepared for publication in mid-2017 it was not difficult to imagine an Islamist force overwhelming the police and seizing a town or district in Eastern Indonesia, the army being called to respond, and its territorial commands and strategies of "people's resistance" again being employed to mobilize support for its operations.[20] If the army was to prevail against the insurgents it is likely that many Indonesians and Western governments would applaud it for doing so.

It seems likely that Nasution's ambivalent legacy will continue to reverberate long into the future in the country that he loved and worked hard to establish, defend and shape to fit his vision of the proper relationship between the state (including the military) and society.

NOTES

1. L.J. Giebels, *Op. Cit.*, Location 8018/10815 (e-book).
2. Personal discussion in 1970 with a prominent Dutch-trained ear nose and throat specialist who blamed his wife's death in Jakarta's main hospital on incompetent and inadequate treatment.
3. Sunarti, *Op. Cit.*, p. 224.
4. There are many accounts and versions of what has become known in Indonesia as the September 30, 1965 Movement. Benedict Anderson and Ruth McVey's *A Preliminary Analysis of the October 1, 1965, Coup in Indonesia*, Interim Reports Series, Ithaca, NY: Cornell Modern Indonesia Project is comprehensive and describes the sequence of events and personalities involved. John Roosa's *Pretext for Mass Murder: The September 30th Movement and Suharto's Coup d'Etat in Indonesia*, Madison, WI: University of Wisconsin Press, 2006, includes new material on the involvement of sections of the PKI, the commander of the *Cakrabirawa* palace guard, Lieutenant Colonel Untung, and some air force officers in the planning that led to the events of September 30.
5. Jenkins, *Op. Cit.*, pp. 243–244.
6. Ibid.
7. A. H. Nasution, *Memenuhi Panggilan Tugas Vol. 6, Masa Kebangkitan Order Baru*, CV Haji Mas Agung, Jakarta, 1988, p. 270.
8. Jenkins, *Op. Cit.*, pp. 243–244.
9. H. Crouch, *The Army and Politics in Indonesia*, Ithaca, NY: Cornell University Press, 1978, p. 231.
10. M. Vatikiotis, *Indonesian Politics Under Suharto*, London: Routledge, p. 15.
11. Ibid., p. 21.
12. Bruce Grant, *Indonesia*, Melbourne University Press (Third Edition), 1996, p. 103.
13. *Biography, Johanna Sunarti Nasution, The 1981 Ramon Magsaysay Award for Public Service*, "http://www.rmaf.org.ph/Awardees/Citation/CitationNasutionJoh.htm." www.rmaf.org.ph/Awardees/Citation/CitationNasutionJoh.htm, accessed June 2005.
14. Jenkins, Op. Cit., pp. 220–222.
15. Interview with Nasution, Riding the Tiger, ABC Television, 1,993.
16. Sunarti, Op. Cit., p. 221.
17. Ibid., p. 222.

18. Jokowi Klarifikasi Isu Pembubaran Komando Teritorial (Jokowi Clarifies the Territorial Command Issue), http://www.jpnn.com/news/jokowi-klarifikasi-isu-pembubaran-komando-teritorial, 29 June 2,017.

19. "Indonesian Military Role in Terror Fight Prompts Debate," Straits Times, Singapore, June 9, 2,018.

20. Such a development was canvassed in the Melbourne, Australia, daily The Age on July 21, 2017: "The terrorist 'caliphate' on Australia's doorstep."

Glossary

PRIVATE

Abangan	syncretic/nominal Muslims, influenced by pre-Islamic beliefs
adat	customary practices, law
AHM	Military Law Academy
Akademi Hukum Militer	See AHM
aliran	stream or current—of belief / religion / ideology
anak	child, subordinate, protégé
angkatan	generation, cohort, branch of the armed forces
Angkatan '45	Generation of '45
Angkatan Perang Ratu Adil	See APRA
APRA	Army of the Just King
asrama	dormitory style living quarters / pre-Islamic Hindu-Buddhist school
bapak	father, appellation for older / more senior man, title before name of older / more senior man
bapak-anak	Father-child [relationship]
Badan Keamanan Rakyat	See BKR
Badan Kerja Sama	Cooperation Bodies
Badan Kerja Sama Sipil Militer	Civil-Military Cooperation Bodies
Bekas Pejuang Islam Bersenjata	Muslim Former Armed [Freedom] Fighters
Badan Pembina Potensi Karya	See BPPK
Badan Penyelidik Usaha Persiapan Kemerdekaan Indonesia	See BPUPKI
Bandung lautan api	Bandung sea of fire
Barisan Pemuda	Youth Brigade
Barisan Tani Indonesia	See BTI
BB	European branch of the territorial civil service
Bersiap!	Get ready!

255

Binnenlands Bestuur	See BB
Binter	Territorial Management
BKR	People's Security Agency
BPUPKI	Preparatory Body for Indonesian Independence
BPPK	Body for the Fostering of Functional Potentials
BTI	Indonesian Peasants' League
Budi Utomo	Noble Endeavor (priyayi-based organisation for the advancement of Javanese society)
Bupati	Regent / Head of Regency (Kabupaten) Administrative Area
buruh	laborer / manual worker
Camat	Head of Kecamatan Administrative Area
Corps Reserve Officieren	See CORO
CORO	Reserve Officers Training Corps
Darul Islam	Abode of Islam (muslim movement)
Departemen Pertahanan dan Keamanan	See Dep Hankam
Dep Hankam	Department of Defence and Security
desa	rural village
Dewan Nasional	National Council
Dewan Pertahanan Daerah	See DPD
diplomasi	diplomacy (negotiations and diplomatic measures)
DPD	Regional Defence Council
dwi fungsi	dual function (of the armed forces during the Suharto period)
FDR	People's Democratic Front
FNPIB	West Irian National Liberation Front
Front Nasional Pembebasan Nasional Irian Barat	See FNPIB
Front Demokrasi Rakyat	See FDR
fungsional	functional
golongan	group
golongan fungsional	functional group
golongan karya	functional group
Hizbullah	Army of God (militia)
Hokokai	People's Loyalty Organisation
IJTP	Inspectorate-General of Territorial Affairs and People's Resistance
Inspektorat Jenderal Teritorium dan Perlawanan Rakyat	See IJTP
gerpolek	guerrilla (warfare), politics and (the) economy
gotong royong	mutual assistance / cooperation
hankamrata	total people's defense and security
hanrata	total people's defense
hansip	civil defense
Ikatan Pendukung Kemerdekaan Indonesia	See IPKI
IPKI	League of Upholders of Indonesian Independence

Glossary

jalan tengah	middle way (policy of the army)
Kabupaten	Regency Administrative Area – see also Bupati
karya	work, function
karyawan	worker, functionary
kawula gusti	servant-master / patron-client / unity of outer–inner world / macrocosmos-microcosmos
Kebatinan	Javanese Mysticism / Mystical Beliefs
Kecamatan	Administrative Area (sub-district of a Kabupaten or Kotamadya)
Keibodan	Vigilance Corps
kekeluargaan	family or family-like relationship
kelurahan	village administrative district (headed by a lurah)
kemerdekaan	independence, freedom
Kenpeitai	Military Police
Keresidenan	See Residen
Kewedanaan	See Wedana
KL	Royal (Netherlands) Army
KNIL	Royal Netherlands Indies Army
KNIP	Central Indonesian National Committee
Kodam	Military Area Command
Kodim	Military District Command
KODM	Military District Command
Komando Cadangan Strategis Angkatan Darat	See Kostrad [1]
Komando Daerah Militer	See Kodam
Komando Distrik Militer	See Kodim
Komando Onder Distrik Militer	See KODM
Komando Rayon Militer	See Koramil
Konstituante	Constitutional Assembly
Korem	Military Provincial Command
Komando Resort Militer	See Korem
Komando Strategis Angkatan Darat	See Kostrad [2]
Komite Nasional Indonesia Pusat	See KNIP
Koninklijk Nederlands Indisch Leger	See KNIL
Koninklijk Leger	See KL
Koninklijke Paketvaart Maatschappij	See KPM
Konsepsi Politik	Political Conception
Koramil	Military Sector Command
Kostrad [1]	Army Strategic Reserve Command
Kostrad [2]	Army Strategic Command
Kotamadya	Municipality (mid-sized city)
KPM	Royal Shipping Company
laskar	irregular soldier/unit
Legiun Veteran Republik Indonesia	See LVRI
Lembaga Ketahanan Nasional [1]	See Lemhannas [1]

Lembaga Pertahanan Nasional ²	See Lemhannas ²
Lemhannas ¹	National Resilience Institute
Lemhannas ²	National Defence Institute
Lurah	Village Head
LVRI	League of Veterans of the Republic of Indonesia
Madjelis Sjuro Muslimin Indonesia	See Masjumi
Markas Besar Komando Jawa	See MBKD
Masjumi	Council of Indonesian Muslim Associations
MBKD	Java Command Headquarters
merdeka	Independent, free
mufakat	Consensus
murba	common, ordinary, the proletariat
Muslihat	trick, ruse, tactics, strategy
musyawarah	Consultation
Nahdatul Ulama	see NU
negara	State
NICA	Netherlands Indies Civil Administration
NU	Council of Muslim Scholars
organisasi masa	see ormas
ormas	mass organisation(s)
Pager Desa	Village Guerrilla Troops
Pak	contraction of Bapak—appellation for older / more senior man, title before name of older / more senior man
pamong desa	village administration personnel (lit. guardians of the village)
pamong praja	civil service (after independence—lit. guardians of the state)
Pancasila	Five Principles (of the Indonesian state)
Panglima	Commander
Panglima Besar	Commander-in-Chief
pangreh praja	civil service (before independence—lit. rulers of the state)
Panitia Persiapan Kemerdekaan Indonesia	See PPKI
Parindra	Greater Indonesia Party
Partai Indonesia Raya	See Parindra
Partai Komunis Indonesia	See PKI
Partai Nasional Indonesia	See PNI
Partai Sosialis Indonesia	See PSI
Partai Persatuan Indonesia Raya	See PIR
Pasukan Gerilya Desa	See Pager Desa
Pasundan	Sundanese (West Java ethnic group) area
PDRI	Emergency Government of the Republic of Indonesia
pejuang	(freedom) fighter

Glossary

Pembela Sukarelawan Tanah Air	See Peta [1]
Pembela Tanah Air	See Peta [2]
Pembinaan Teritorial	See Binter
Pemerintah Darurat Republik Indonesia	See PDRI
Pemerintah Revolusioner Republik Indonesia	See PRRI
pemuda	Youth
Pemuda Rakyat	People's Youth (PKI-associated mass organization)
Pemuda Sosialis Indonesia	See Pesindo
Penguasa Militer	(Martial Law) Military Authority
pepolit	political education
Perbepsi	All-Indonesia Association of Former Armed Fighters
Persatuan Bangsa Indonesia	Indonesian Unity Party (later merged with Budi Utomo to form Parindra)
Persatuan Bekas Pejuang Bersenjata Seluruh Indonesia	All-Indonesia Association of Former Armed Fighters
Persatuan Perjuangan	See PP
perjuangan	armed struggle
pertahanan sipil	See Hansip
pesantren	Muslim boarding school—see also santri
Pesindo	Indonesian Socialist Youth (organisation)
Peta [1]	Volunteer Defenders of the Homeland
Peta [2]	Defenders of the Homeland
PIR	Greater Indonesia Union Party
PKI	Indonesian Communist Party
PNI	Indonesian Nationalist Party
PP	Struggle Union
PPKI	Preparatory Committee for Indonesian Independence
priyayi	Javanese aristocratic / administrative class
PRRI	Revolutionary Government of the Republic of Indonesia
PSI	Indonesian Socialist Party
re-dan-ra	reorganisation and rationalisation (of the army)
Rechtshoogeschool	Law School—predecessor to the Faculty of Law, University of Indonesia
Republik Indonesia	See RI
Republik Indonesia Serikat	See RIS
Residen	Head of a Residency administrative district (Keresidenan)
RI	Republic of Indonesia
RIS	United States of Indonesia
Rukun Tani	Farmers' Organisation (Parindra-affiliated)
rust en orde	peace and order
santri	orthodox practicing Muslim / student in a traditional Muslim boarding school (pesantren)
Seinendan	Youth Corps
Sekbergolkar	Joint Secretariat of Functional Groups

Sekretariat Bersama Golongan Karya	See Sekbergolkar
semangat	spirit / fighting spirit
Sekolah Staf dan Komando Angkatan Darat	See Seskoad
Sentral Organisasi Buruh Seluruh Indonesia	See SOBSI
Sentral Organisasi Karyawan Indonesia	See SOKSI
Seskoad	Army Staff and Command School
Siliwangi	West Java Division / Military District
sinoman	mutual assistance / cooperation
sishankamrata	total people's defence and security system
SOBSI	Central All-Indonesia Workers Organisation (PKI-associated union)
SOKSI	Central All-Indonesia Organisation of Functionaries (military-backed union)
Staf Umum Angkatan Darat	See SUAD
STM	Military Sub Territory
SUAD	Army General Staff
Sub Territorium Militer	See STM
Surya Wirawan	Parindra youth wing
T & T	Territorial Command (lit. Troops and Territorial Command)
Tentara Keamanan Rakyat [1]	See TKR [1]
Tentara Keselamatan Rakyat [2]	See TKR [2]
Tentara Nasional Indonesia	See TNI
Tentara Pelajar	Student Army
Tentara Republik Indonesia	See TRI
Tentara dan Territorium	See T & T
TKR [1]	People's Security Army
TKR [2]	People's Salvation Army
TNI	Indonesian National Army
TRI	Army of the Republic of Indonesia
UNCI	United Nations Commission for Indonesia
Volksraad	People's Council (powerless parliament formed by the Dutch)
Wedana	Head of an administrative area known as a Kewedanaan
wehrkreis	military district

Bibliography

BOOKS AND CHAPTERS OF BOOKS

Abeyasekere, S. (1976) *One Hand Clapping: Indonesian Nationalists and the Dutch 1939–1942*. Clayton, VIC: Centre of Southeast Studies.

Anderson, B. R. O'G. (1972) *Java in a Time of Revolution. Occupation and Resistance, 1944–1946*. Ithaca, NY: Cornell University Press.

———. (1990) "Old State, New Society," in Anderson, B. R. O'G. (ed.). *Language and Power: Exploring Political Cultures in Indonesia*. Ithaca, NY: Cornell University Press.

———. (1990) "The Idea of Power in Javanese Culture" in Anderson, B. R. O'G. (ed.). *Language and Power: Exploring Political Cultures in Indonesia*. Ithaca, NY: Cornell University Press.

Anderson, B. R. O'G & Audrey Kahin (1982) *Interpreting Indonesian Politics: Thirteen Contributions* Kahin A *to the Debate*. Ithaca, NY: Modern Indonesian Project, Cornell University Press.

Bachtiar, H. (1988) *Siapa Dia?: Perwira Tinggi Tentara Nasional Indonesia Angkatan Darat (TNI-AD)* (translated title: *Who is He? Senior Officers of the Indonesian Army*). Jakarta: Penerbit Djambatan.

Bangun, P. (1996) *Kolonel Maludin Simbolon: Liku-Liku Perjuangannya dalam Pembangunan Bangsa* (translated title: *Colonel Maludin Simbolon: Twists and Turns of his Struggle in the Development of the Nation*). Jakarta: Pustaka Sinar Harapan.

Basrie, C. (1998) *Bela Negara: Implementasi dan Pembangunannya. Penjabaran Pasal 30 UUD 1945* (translated title: *Defending the State: Its Implementation and Development. Elaboration of Section 3 of the 1945 Constitution*). Jakarta: U.I. Press.

Benda, H. J. (1958) *The Crescent and the Rising Sun: Indonesian Islam under the Rising Sun*. The Hague: W. van Hoeve.

Boileau, J. M. (1983) *Golkar – Functional Group Politics in Indonesia*. Jakarta: Yayasan Proklamasi (CSIS).

Booth, A. (1998) *The Indonesian Economy in the Nineteenth and Twentieth Centuries. A History of Missed Opportunities*. London: Macmillan.
Bourchier, D. and Hadiz, V. (2003) *Indonesian Politics and Society: A Reader*. London: Routledge Curzon.
Brackman, A.C. (1963) *Indonesian Communism: A History*. New York: Frederic A. Praeger.
Breman, J. (1982) "The Village on Java and the Early Colonial State," *Journal on Peasant Studies*, 9, 4.
Britton, P. (1996) *Professionalisme dan Ideologi Militer Indonesia*: Perspektif Tradisi-tradisi Jawa dan Barat (translated title: *Military Professionalism in Indonesia: Javanese and Western Military Traditions in Army Ideology to the 1970s*). Jakarta: LP3ES.
Budiman, A. (ed.) (1990) *State and Civil Society in Indonesia*. Clayton, VIC: Centre of Southeast Asian Studies, Monash University.
Caldwell, M. & Utrecht, E. (1979) *Indonesia, An Alternative History*. Sydney: Alternative Publishing Cooperative Limited.
Clancy, G.B. (1992) *A Dictionary of Indonesian History Since 1900: Over 500 People, Events and Ideas that have Contributed to the History of Indonesia this Century*. Sydney: Sunda Publications.
Clune, F. (1940) *To the Isles of Spice with Frank Clune: A Vagabond Voyage by Air from Botany Bay to Darwin, Bathurst Island, Timor, Java, Celebes and French Indo-China*. Sydney: Angus and Robertson.
Cote, J. and (2005) *Recalling the Indies: Colonial Culture and Postcolonial*, in Westerbeek, L. (ed.). Amsterdam Identities, Aksan.
Cribb, R. (2002) "From Total People's Resistance to Massacre: Explaining Military Violence in East Timor," in F. Colombijn and J.T. Lindblad (eds.), *Roots of Violence in Indonesia*. Leiden: KITVL Press.
———. (1991) *Gangsters and Revolutionaries: The Jakarta People's Milita and the Indonesian Revolution 1945–1949*, North Sydney, NSW: Asian Studies Association of Australia in association with Allen and Unwin.
Crouch, H. (1978) *The Army and Politics in Indonesia*. Ithaca, NY: Cornell University Press.
———. (1991) "The Military in Malaysia," in V. Selochan (ed.), *The Military, the State and Development in Asia and the Pacific*. Boulder: Westview Press.
Dahl, R.A. (1970) *Modern Political Analysis*. Englewood Cliffs, N.J.: Prentice-Hall
———. (1971) *Polyarchy, Participation and Opposition*. New Haven: Yale University Press.
———. (1986) *Democracy, Liberty and Equality*. Oslo: Norwegian University Press.
Dahm, B. (c1969) *Sukarno and the Struggle for Indonesian Independence*. Ithaca, NY: Cornell University Press. Translated from the German by Mary F. Somers Heidhues.
Davis, C. (1979) "What is Modern Indonesian Culture?" in G. Davis (ed.), *Papers Presented to the Conference on Indonesian Studies, 29 July–1 August 1976, Indonesian Summer Studies Institute, Madison, Wisconsin*, Ohio University, Centre for International Studies.

Debray, R. (1977) "Guerrilla Doctrine Today," in W. Laqueur (ed.), *The Guerrilla Reader: A Historical Anthology*. New York: New American Library.

Djamily, B. (1978) *Hidup dan Perjuangan Adam Malik: Wartawan, Politisi, Diplomat, Negarawan* (translated title: *The Life and Struggle of Adam Malik: Journalist, Politician, Diplomat, Statesman*). Kuala Lumpur: Pustaka Melayu Baru.

Djojohadikusumo, M. (1970) *Kenang-Kenangan dari Tiga Djaman: Satu Kisah Kekeluargaan Tertulis* (translated title: *Memories of Three Eras: A Family Story*). Jakarta: Indira.

Elson, R.E. (2001) *Suharto: A Political Biography*. Oakleigh, VIC: Cambridge University Press.

Emmerson, D.K. (1976) *Indonesia's Elite: Political Culture and Cultural Politics*. Ithaca, NY: Cornell University Press.

Ebury, S. (1994) *Weary: The Life of Sir Edward Dunlop*. Penguin Books, Australia.

Feith, H. (1958) *The Wilopo Cabinet, 1952–1953: A Turning Point in Post-Revolutionary Indonesia*. Ithaca, N.Y., Modern Indonesia Project, Southeast Asia Program, Department of Far Eastern Studies, Cornell University.

———. (1962) *The Decline of Constitutional Democracy in Indonesia*. Ithaca, NY: Cornell University Press.

Feith, H. and Castles, L (eds.) (1970) *Indonesian Political Thinking 1945–1965*. Ithaca, NY: Cornell University.

Fischer, L. (1959) *The Story of Indonesia*. New York: Harper.

Fitzgerald, C.P. (1964) *The Birth of Communist China*. Harmondsworth, Middlesex: Penguin.

Forty, G. (2002) *German Infantryman at War*. Hersham, UK: Ian Allen Publishing.

Gaffar, A. (1992) *Javanese Voters: A Case Study of Elections Under a Hegemonic Party System*. Yogyakarta: Gadjah Mada University Press.

Gede, Ide Anak Agung. (1991) *Renville*. Jakarta: Sinar Harapan.

Geertz, C. (1959) "The Javanese Villagers," in G.W. Skinner (ed.). *Local, Ethnic and National Loyalties in Village Indonesia*. Ithaca, NY: Cornell University Project, Interim Report Series.

———. (1960) *The Religion of Java*. New York : The Free Press of Glencoe.

Giebels, L.J. (2015) *Sukarno: A Political Biography*, Amazon Kindle e-books.

Gondokusumo, D. (1947) *Sosiologi* (translated title *Sociology*). Jakarta: Menara Pengetahuan Yogyakarta, G.C.T. Van Doorp and Co. C.V. (Third Edition).

Gondokusumo, D. (1951) *Parlemen Indonesia* (Translated title: The Parliament of and Amelz Indonesia). Jakarta : Bulan Bintang.

Grant, B. (1996) *Indonesia*. Melbourne University Press, Carlton. (Third Edition).

Hardjono, J. and (1995) *In Love With a Nation: Molly Bondan and Indonesia*. In Warner, C. (eds.). Picton: Charles Warner.

Hefner, R.W. (1985) *Hindu Javanese: Tengger Tradition and Islam*. Princeton, NJ: Princeton University Press.

Heijboer, P. (1998) *Agresi Militer Belanda: Merebutkan Pending Zamrud Sepanjang Khatulistiwa 1945/49* (translated title: *The Dutch Military Aggression: Seizing the Girdle of Emeralds around the Equator*). Jakarta: Gramedia Widiasarana Indonesia in cooperation with Koninklijk Instuut voor Taal, Land-en Volkenkunde (KITLV). Translated by W.S. Karnera.

Hindley, D. (1964) *The Communist Party of Indonesia 1951–63*. Berkeley, CA: University of California Press.

Hoadley, S. J. (1975) *The Military in the Politics of Southeast Asia: A Comparative Perspective*. Cambridge, MA: Schenkman Publishing Co.

Howard, M. (1993) *Clausewitz: Mahaguru Strategi Perang Modern* (translated title: *Clausewitz: Great Teacher of Modern Warfare* – originally published in English under the title *Clausewitz*). Jakarta: Pustaka Utama Grafiti,

Huntington, S.P. (1957) *The Soldier and the State*. Cambridge, MA: The Belknap Press of Harvard University Press.

———. (1966) "Civilian Control of the Military: A Theoretical Statement" in Eulau, H., Eldersveld, S., and Janowitz, M., *Political Behavior: A Reader in Theory and Research*, New York: Free Press.

———. (1968) *Political Order in Changing Societies*. New Haven, CT: Yale University Press.

Hutagalung. W. *Tiga Episode Perang Kemerdekaan* (translated title: *Three Episodes in the War of Independence*). Forthcoming publication, www.hamline.edu/apakabar/basisdata/2000/01/0400.html, accessed January 2005.

Idris, K. (1996) *Bertarung dalam Revolusi* (translated title: Fighting in the Revolution). Jakarta: Pustaka Sinar Harapan.

Jackson, K.D. (1978) "Bureaucratic Polity: A Theoretical Framework for the Analysis of Power and Communications in Indonesia" in Karl S. Jackson and Lucien W. Pye (eds.). *Political Power and Communications in Indonesia*. Berkeley: University of California Press.

Janowitz, M. (1962) *The Military in the Political Development of New Nations*. Princeton, NJ: Princeton University Press.

Jenkins, D. (1984) *Suharto and His Generals: Indonesian Military Politics 1975–1983*. Ithaca, NY: Cornell Modern Indonesia Project, Southeast Asia Program, Cornell University.

Higgins, B. and Jean Higgins (1963) *Indonesia: The Crisis of the Millstones*. Princeton, NJ: Van Nostrand.

Kahin, G.M., (ed.) (1963) *Major Governments of Asia*. Ithaca, NY: Cornell University Press.

Kahin, G.M. (1952) *Nationalism and Revolution in Indonesia*. Ithaca, NY: Cornell University Press.

Kahin, A.R. and Kahin, G.M. (1995) *Subversion as Foreign Policy: The Secret Eisenhower and Dulles Debacle in Indonesia*. New York: New Press.

Keegan, J. (1979) "Indonesia," in Keegan, J. (ed.) *World Armies*. London: Macmillan.

Kennedy, C.H. (1991) "Civil-Military Interaction: Data in Search of a Theory," in C.H. Louscher, D. Kennedy and *Civil Military Interaction in Asia and Africa*. Leiden, New York: D. Louscher (eds.) E.J. Brill. Kolopaking, R. T.W. (1997) *Sejarah Dinasti Kanjeng Raden Adipati Tumenggung Kolopaking 1677–1832: Pendopo Panjer Roma Kebumen*. Leiden, New York: EJ Brill, 1991.

Kumar, A. (1980) "The Peasantry and State on Java: Changes of Relationship, Seventeenth to Nineteenth Centuries," *Indonesia: Australia Perspectives*. Canberra: Australian National University.

Kurasawa, A. (1993) *Mobilisasi dan Kontrol*. Jakarta: Gramedia. (Translated title: *Mobilisation and Control*. Translation by Hermawan Sulistyo.)

Legge, J.D. (1961) *Central Authority and Regional Authority in Indonesia: A Study in Local Administration*, Ithaca, NY: Cornell University Press.

———. (1964) *Indonesia*. Englewood Cliffs, NJ: Prentice Hall.

———. (1972) *Sukarno*. Sydney: Allen & Unwin.

Lev, D.S. (1966), *The Transition to Guided Democracy*: Indonesian Politics, 1957–1959. Ithaca, NY: Modern Indonesia Project, Southeast Asia Program, Department of Asian Studies, Cornell University.

Linz, J. (1975) "An Authoritarian Regime: Spain," in *Cleavages, Ideologies and Party Systems*, Greenstein, F., and Polsby, N. (eds.). *Handbook of Political Science*, Volume 3. Reading, MA: Addison-Wesley.

Lowenberg, P. (Spring 2000) *Writing and Literacy in Indonesia*, Studies in the Linguistic Sciences Volume 30, Number 1.

Lowry, R. (1993) *Indonesian Defence Policy and the Indonesian Armed Forces*. Canberra: Strategic & Defence Studies Centre, Australian National University.

Lucas, A. (1991) *One Soul, One Struggle*. Sydney: Allen and Unwin.

MacFarling, I. (1996) *The Dual Function of the Indonesian Armed Forces*. Canberra: Australian Defence Studies Centre.

MacIntyre, A. (1991) *Business and Politics in Indonesia*. North Sydney: Asian Studies Association of Australia in association with Allen and Unwin.

Mao Tse Tung (1963) *Selected Military Writings of Mao Tse Tung*. Peking: Foreign Languages Press.

McDonald, H. (1980) *Suharto's Indonesia*. Blackburn, Vic: Fontana Books.

McVey, R. (1969) "Nationalism, Islam and Marxism: The Management of Ideological Conflict in Indonesia," Introduction in Sukarno, *Nationalism, Islam and Marxism*. Ithaca: Cornell Modern Indonesia Project.

McVey, R. (1992) "The Case of the Disappearing Decade," in D. Bourchier and J.D. Legge (eds.) *Democracy in Indonesia 1950s and 1990s*. Clayton: Monash University.

Moertopo, A. (1973) *Some Basic Thoughts on the Acceleration and Modernization of 25 Years' Development*. Jakarta: Centre for Strategic and International Studies.

Mrazek, R. (1978) *The United States and the Indonesian Military 1945–65: A Study of Intervention*. Prague: Oriental Institute in Academic.

Mukmin, H. *TNI Dalam Politik Luar Negeri: Studi Kasus Penyelesaian Konfrontasi Indonesia-Malaysia* (translated title: *The TNI in Foreign Policy: A Study of the Settlement of Confrontation Between Indonesia and Malaysia*). Jakarta: Sinar Harapan, 1991.

Mulder, N. (1992) *Individual and Society in Java; A Cultural Analysis*. Yogyakarta: Gadjah Mada University Press.

Nasution, A.H. (1982) "Bertugas Dengan Sri Sultan," in Atmakusumah (ed.), *Tahta Untuk Rakyat: Celah-celah Kehidupan Sultan Hamengku Buwono IX* (translated title: *A Throne for the People: Details of the Life of Sultan Hamengku Buwono IX*). Jakarta: Gramedia.

———. (1994) "Di Saat-Saat Kritis" (translate title: "At Critical Moments") in A. Katoppo (ed.), *80 Tahun Bung Karno* (translated title: *80 Years After the Birth of Bung Karno*). Jakarta: Pustaka Sinar Harapan.

———. (undated) *Fundamentals of Guerilla Warfare and the Indonesian Defence System Past and Future*. Jakarta: Information Service of the Armed Forces.

———. (1971) *Kekarjaan ABRI* (translated title: *The Functional Role of the Armed Forces of the Republic of Indonesia*). Jakarta: Seruling Masa.

———. (1995) "Kita Belum Cukup Dewasa" (translated title: "We are Not Yet Sufficiently Mature") in *Para Tokoh Angkat Bicara* (translated title: *Leading Figures Rise to Speak*) Book One. Jakarta: Pustaka Utama Grafiti.

———. *Memenuhi Panggilan Tugas* (translated title: *Answering the Call of Duty*). Jakarta: CV Haji Masagung/Gunung Agung, Jakarta. Published by the same publisher and in the same location in the following nine volumes.

———. (1983a) Volume 2: *Kenangan Masa Gerilya* (translated title: *Memories of the Guerrilla Period*).

———. (1983b) Volume 3: *Masa Pancaroba Pertama* (translated title: *The First Period of Change*).

———. (1984) Volume 4: *Masa Pancaroba Kedua* (translated title: *The Second Period of Change*).

———. (1985) Volume 5: *Kenangan Masa Orde Lama* (translated title: *Memories of the Old Order Period*).

———. (1986) Volume 6: *Masa Kebangkitan Orde Baru* (translated title: *The Period of the New Order's Resurgence*).

———. (1988a) Volume 7: *Masa Konsolidasi Orde Baru* (translated title: *The Period of Consolidation of the New Order*).

———. (1988b) Volume 8: *Masa Pemancangan Orde Pembangunan* (translated title: *The Period of Setting Out the Development Order*).

———. (1989) Volume 2a: *Kenangan Masa Gerilya* (translated title: *Memories of the Guerrilla Period*) (2nd ed.).

———. (1990) Volume 1: *Kenangan Masa Muda* (translated title: *Memories of Youth*) (2nd edn.).

———. (1993) Volume 9: *Bagi Pejuang Tiada Tugus Akhir dan Tiada Akhir Tugas* (translated title: *For a Patriot There is No Final Duty and No End to Duty*).

———. (1994) Volume 2b: *TNI Berposisi Antigerilya* (translated title: *The TNI Adopts an Anti-Guerrilla Position*).

———. (1970) *TNI* (Volume One). Jakarta, Seruling Masa.

———. (1968) *TNI* (Volume Two). Jakarta, Seruling Masa.

———. (1971) *TNI* (Volume Three). Jakarta, Seruling Masa.

———. (1955) *Tjatatan-Tjatatan Sekitar Politik Militer Indonesia.* (translated title: *Notes on Indonesian Military Policy*). Jakarta: publisher unknown.

———. (1964) *Towards a People's Army*. Jakarta: Delegasi.

Nasution, J.S. *Pak Nas dalam Kenangan* (translated title: *Pak Nas Remembered*) as told to and written by Ramadhan K.H. and Sukiarta Sriwibawa. Jakarta: Pusat Sejarah dan Tradisi TNI.

Nishihara, M. (1972) *Golkar and the Indonesian Elections of 1971*. Ithaca, NY: Modern Indonesia Project, Cornell University.

Nitisastro, W.and Ismael, J.E. (1959) *The Government, Economy and Taxes of a Central Javanese Village*. Ithaca, NY: Southeast Asia Program, Department of Far Eastern Studies, Cornell University.

Nordlinger, E.A. (1977) *Soldiers in Politics: Military Coups and Governments*. New Jersey: Prentice Hall.

O'Donnell, G. (1976) "Corporatism and the Question of the State" in G. Davis (ed.), *"What is Modern Indonesian Culture?" Papers presented to the Conference on Indonesian Studies, 29 July–1 August 1976*, Indonesian Summer Studies Institute.

Padmodiwiryo, S. (1995) *Memoar Hario Kecik: Autobiografi Seorang Mahasiswa Prajurit* (translated title: *Memoirs of Little Hario: The Autobiography of a Student-Soldier*). Jakarta: Yayasan Obor.

Palmier, L. (1962) *Indonesia and the Dutch*. London: Oxford University Press.

Panggabean, M. (1993) *Berjuang dan Mengabdi* (translated title: *Struggling and Serving*). Jakarta, Pustaka Harapan.

Pauker, G. (1963) *The Indonesian Doctrine of Territorial Warfare and Territorial Management*. Santa Monica, CA: The Rand Corporation.

Paxton, R. (2004) *The Anatomy of Fascism*. New York: Alfred Knopf.

Pfennig, W. (c1990) "The Military in Southeast Asian Politics: Some Introductory Remarks and Questions," in W.S. Heinz, W. Pfennig and V.C. King (eds.), *The Military in Politics: Southeast Asian Experiences*. Clayton, VIC: Centre for Southeast Asian Studies, Monash University.

Polomka, P. (1971) *Indonesia Since Sukarno*. Harmondsworth, Middlesex: Penguin Books.

Pour, J. (1993) *Benny Moerdani-Profil Prajurit Negarawan* (translated title *Benny Moerdani: A Profile of a Soldier Statesman*). Jakarta: Yayasan Kejuangan Panglima Besar Sudirman.

Penders, C.L.M. (ed.) (1977) *Indonesia: Selected Documents on Colonialism and Nationalism, 1830–1942*. St Lucia, QLD: University of Queensland Press.

Penders, C.L.M. and 1985) *Nasution: A Political Biography*. St Lucia: Sundhaussen, U. (University of Queensland Press.

Prasetyo, A. and Hadad, T (1998) *Jenderal Tanpa Pasukan, Politisi Tanpa Partai: Perjalanan (eds.) Hidup A. H. Nasution* (*A General Without Troops, A Politician Without a Party: The Life Journey of A. H. Nasution*). Jakarta: Pusat Data dan Analisa Tempo : Institut Studi Arus Informasi.

Pringgodigdo, A.K. (1949) *Sejarah Pergerakan Rakyat Indonesia* (translated title: *History of the Movement of the People of Indonesia*). Jakarta: Dian Rakyat, 8th edition, 1978.

Pye, L. (1962) "Armies in the Process of Political Modernisation," in John J. Johnson (ed.) *The Role of the Military in Underdeveloped Countries*. Princeton: Princeton University Press.

Ransom D. (1975) "Ford Country: Building an Elite for Indonesia," in Weissman S. (ed.) *The Trojan Horse: A Radical Look at Foreign Aid.* Palo Alto, California: Ramparts Press.

Rapaport, A. (ed.) (1968) Carl Von Clausewitz, *On War.* London: Penguin.

Rapoport, D.C. (1962) "A Comparative Theory of Military and Political Types," in *Changing Patterns of Military Politics.* New York: Free Press.

———. (1982) "The Praetorian Army: Insecurity, Venality and Impotence," in Kolkowicz, Roman. & Korbonski, Andrzej (eds.). *Soldiers, Peasants and Bureaucrats: Civil-Military Relations in Communist and Modernizing Societies/* London: George Allen & Unwin.

Reeve, D. (1985) *Golkar of Indonesia: An Alternative to the Party System.* Singapore and New York: Oxford University Press.

———. (1990) "The Corporatist State: The Case of Golkar," in A. Budiman (ed.), *State and Civil Society in Indonesia.* Centre of Southeast Asian Studies, Monash University, Melbourne.

Reid, A.J.S. (1974) *Indonesian National Revolution 1945–50.* Hawthorn, VIC: Longman.

Ricklefs, M.C. (1981) *A History of Modern Indonesia.* London: Macmillan Education.

Riggs, F. (1966) *Thailand: The Modernisation of a Bureaucratic Polity.* Hawaii: East-West Center Press.

Robison, R. (1986) *Indonesia: The Rise of Capital.* Sydney: Allen and Unwin.

Rocamora, J.E. (1975) *Nationalism in Search of Ideology: The Indonesian Nationalist Party, 1945–1965.* Quezon City: University of the Philippines, Center for Advanced Studies.

Roeder, O. G. (1969) *The Smiling General: President Soeharto of Indonesia.* (Revised 2nd edition). Jakarta: Gunung Agung.

———. (1971) *Who's Who in Indonesia.* Jakarta: Gunung Agung.

Roosa, J. (2006) *Pretext for Mass Murder: The September 30th Movement and Suharto's Coup d'Etat in Indonesia.* Madison, WI: University of Wisconsin Press.

Said, S. (1992) *genesis of power: General Sudirman and the Indonesian Military in Politics 1945–49.* North Sydney: Allen and Unwin.

Seskoad (1990) *Serangan Umum: 1 Maret 1949 di Yogyakarta Latar Belakang dan Pengaruhnya* (translated title: *The General Offensive of 1 March 1949 on Yogyakarta: Its Background and Influence*). Jakarta: Citra Lamtoro Gung Persada.

Shils, E. (1962) "The Military in the Political Development of New States" in John J. Johnson (ed.). *The Role of the Military in Underdeveloped Countries.* Princeton: Princeton University Press.

Simandjuntak, M. (1994) *Pandangan Negara Integralistik* (translated title: *Views on the Integralistic State*). Jakarta: Grafiti.

Simatupang, T.B. (1961) *Laporan Dari Banaran* (translated title: *Report from Banaran*), second edition. Jakarta: Pembangunan.

———. (c1972) *Report from Banaran: Experiences During the People's War.* Ithaca, NY: Modern Indonesia Project, Cornell University. Translated by B. Anderson and Elizabeth Graves; with an introduction by John R.W. Smail.

Simatupang, T.B. (1996) *The Fallacy of a Myth*. Jakarta: Pustaka Sinar Harapan. Translated and introduced by Peter Suwarno.

Soebijono (1992) "Dwifungsi ABRI Sebagai Konsep Politik," in Soebijono et al. (eds.), *Dwi Fungsi ABRI*. Yogyakarta: Gadjah Mada University Press.

Soeharto (1989) *Soeharto: Pikiran, Ucapan dan Tindakan Saya. Separti Dipaparkan kepada G. Dwipayana and Ramadhan K.H.* (translated title: *Soeharto: My Thoughts, Words and Deeds. As told to G. Dwipayana and Ramadhan K.H*). Jakarta: Citra Lamtoro Gung Persada.

Soetanto, H. (1994) *Perintah Presiden Soekarno: Rebut Kembali Madiun. Siliwangi Menumpas Pemberontakan PKI/Moeso 1948* (translated title: *President Soekarno's Order: Seize Back Madiun. The Siliwangi Suppress the PKI/Moeso Revolt of 1948*. Jakarta: Pustaka Sinar Harapan.

Stepan, A. (ed.) (1973) *Authoritarian Brazil: Origins, Policies, and Future*. New Haven: Yale University Press.

Strachan, H. (1997) *The Politics of the British Army*, Oxford, Clarendon Press, New York, Oxford University Press.

Sudarno, et al. (1993) *Sejarah Pemerintahan Militer dan Peran Pamong Praja di Jawa Timur Selama Perjuangan Fisik 1945–1950* (translated title: *The History of the Military Administration and the Role of the Pamong Praja in East Java during the Period of Physical Struggle 1945–1950*). Jakarta: Balai Pustaka.Sunarti See Nasution, J.S.

Sundhaussen, U. (1982) *The Road to Power: Indonesian Military Politics, 1945–1967*. Kuala Lumpur and New York: Oxford University Press.

Supriyatmono, H. (1994) *Nasution, Dwifungsi ABRI dan Kontribusi ke Arah Reformasi Politik* (translated title: *Nasution, the Dual function of the Armed forces and His Contribution to Political Reformation*). Surakarta: Sebelas Maret University Press in cooperation with Yayasan Pusaka Nusatama.

Suryadinata, L. (1989) *Military Ascendancy and Political Culture: A Study of Indonesia's Golkar*. Athens, OH: Center for International Studies.

Suryohadiprojo, S. (1996) *Kepimpinan ABRI: Dalam Sejarah dan Perjuangannya* (translated title: *The Leadership of the Armed Forces of the Republic of Indonesia: Throughout its History and Struggle*). Jakarta: Intermasa.

Sutherland, H. (1979) *The Making of a Bureaucratic Elite: The Colonial Transformation of the Javanese Priyayi*. Singapore: Heineman (ASAA Southeast Asia Publications Series.).

Swift, A. (1989) *The Road to Madiun: The Indonesian Communist Coup of 1948*. Ithaca, NY: Cornell University Press.

Tanter, R & Young, K. eds. (1989) *The Politics of Middle Class Indonesia*. Clayton, VIC: Centre for South East Asian Studies, Monash University.

Tantri, K. (1960) *Revolt in Paradise*. London: William Heinemann.

Tjokropranolo (1992) *Jenderal Sudirman* (translated title: *General Sudirman*). Jakarta: PT Surya Persindo.

———. (1995) *General Sudirman. The Leader Who Finally Destroyed Indonesia Colonialism*. Canberra: Australian Defence Studies Centre, University of New South Wales. Translated by Ian MacFarling, et. al.

Utrecht, E. (1980) *The Military and the 1977 Election*. Townsville, Qld: James Cook University of North Queensland, South East Asian Studies Committee.

van de Kroef, J. (1965) *The Communist Party of Indonesia: Its History, Program and Tactics*. Vancouver, Canada: University of British Columbia.

Van Dijk, C. (1981) *Rebellion Under the Banner of Islam: The Darul Islam in Indonesia*. The Hague: M. Nijhoff.

van Doorn, A.A. (1992) 'Kelampauan Adalah Kekinian Yang Kental: Konflik Belanda-Indonesia dan Bertahannya Pola Kolonial' (translated title: "The Past is the Very Much in the Present: The Dutch-Indonesian Conflict and the Maintenance of the Colonial Pattern," in A.B. Lapian and P.J. Drooglevel (eds.), *Menelusuri Jalur Linggarjati: Diplomasi dalam Perspektif Sejarah* (translated title: *Tracing the Linggarjati Path: Diplomacy in Historical Perspective*). Jakarta: Grafiti.

Vatikiotis, M. R. J. (1993) *Indonesian Politics under Suharto*. London: Routledge.

Ward, K. (1974) *The 1971 Election in Indonesia - An East Java Case Study*. Clayton, Vic: Centre for Southeast Studies, Monash University.

Weber, M. (1930) *The Protestant Ethic and the Sprit of Capitalism*. London: Unwin University Books. Translated by Talcott Parsons.

ARTICLES AND PAPERS

Anderson, B.R. and McVey, R.T. *A Preliminary Analysis of the October 1, 1965, Coup in Indonesia*. (1971) Interim Reports Series. Ithaca, NY: Cornell Modern Indonesia Project. ISBN 0–87763–008–9. OCLC 21079

Carmody, S.P. *The Importance of General Sudirman's 'Route Gerilya' for the Indonesian People*, unpublished essay, Yogyakarta, 1982. (Translated into Indonesian under the title *Pentingnya 'Route Gerilya' yang Dipimpin oleh Panglima Besar Sudirman bagi Bangsa Indonesia*.)

Castles, L. Pengalaman Demokrasi Liberal di Indonesia (1950–1959*) Seminar Pendidikan Demokrasi dan Dialog Sipil-Militer 11 June 1998*. (translated title: "The Experience of Liberal Democracy in Indonesia (1950–1959)." *Education on Democracy and the Civil-Military Dialogue Seminar 11 June 1998*) www.csps-ugm.or.id/artikel/Ndilance.htm. Accessed 2004.

Cribb, R. "Military Strategy in the Indonesian Revolution: Nasution's Concept of 'Total People's War' in Theory and Practice," *War and Society*, Volume 19, Number 2, 2001: 143–54.

Cribb, R. "Opium and the Indonesian Revolution," *Modern Asian Studies*, Volume 22, Number 2, 1988: 701–22.

Crouch, H. "Patrimonialism and Military Rule in Indonesia," *World Politics*, Volume 31, Number 4, 1979: 571–87.

Howe, R.H. "Max Weber's Elective Affinities: Sociology within the Bounds of Pure Reason," *The American Journal of Sociology*, Volume 84, Number 2, September 1978: 366–85.

King, D.Y. (1982) "Indonesia's New Order as a Bureaucratic Polity, a Neopatrimonial Regime or a Bureaucratic-Authoritarian Regime: What Difference Does

It Make?" in B. Anderson and A. Kahin (eds.), *Interpreting Indonesian Politics: Thirteen Contributions to The Debate*, Interim Reports Series (Publication No. 62). Ithaca, NY: Cornell.

Kveder, D. "'Territorial War': The New Concept of Resistance," *Foreign Affairs*, Volume 32, Number 1, October 1953: 91–108.

Lev, D.S. "The Political Role of the Army in Indonesia," *Pacific Affairs*, Volume 36, Number 4, Winter 1963–1964: 349–64.

McVey, R. 'The Post-Revolutionary Transformation of the Indonesian Army (Part 1)," *Indonesia*, Number 11, April 1971.

———. 'The Post-Revolutionary Transformation of the Indonesian Army (Part 2)," *Indonesia*, Volume 13, April 1972: 147–182.

Moedjanto, G. Pemikiran Bung Karno Menuju Pancasila: Catatan Bung Karno Seratus Tahun (translated title: *The Thinking of Bung Karno Prior to the Formulation of Pancasila: 100 Years After the Birth of Bung Karno*). Indomedia Bernas Website, accessed February 2005.

Moore-Colyer, R. "Towards Mother Earth: Jorian Jenks, Organicism, the Right and the British Union of Fascists," *Journal of Contemporary History*, Volume 39, Number 3, July 2004: 353–71.

Morefield, J. "Hegelian Organicism, British New Liberalism and the Return of the Family State," *History of Political Thought*, Volume 23, Number 1, 2002: 141–70.

Pauker, G. 'The Role of Political Organisations in Indonesia', *Far Eastern Survey*, September 1958.

Pauker, G. "Southeast Asia as a Problem Area in the Next Decade," in *World Politics* Volume Two, April 1959.

Ryter, L. "Pemuda Pancasila: The Last Loyalist Free Men of Suharto's New Order," *Indonesia* 66, October 1998.

Touwen-Bouwsma, E. *Japanese minority policy; The Eurasians on Java and the dilemma of ethnic loyalty*, in Bijdragen tot de Taal-, Land- en Volkenkunde, Japan, Indonesia and the WarMyths and realities 152 (1996), no: 4, Leiden.

van der Kroef, J. "'Guided Democracy' in Indonesia," *Far Eastern Survey*, Volume XXVI, Number 8, August 1957: 113–24.

Yong Mun Cheong. "The Indonesian Army and Functional Groups," *Journal of Southeast Asian Studies*, Volume VII, Number 1, March 1976, 92–101.

Yordan, C.L. "Instituting Problem-Solving Processes as a Means of Constructive Social Change" *Online Journal of Peace and Conflict Resolution*, accessed January 2005.

Young, K.R. "Political Geography," *Indonesia – The Structure and the Drivers*, paper presented to the Centre for Defence and Strategic Studies, June 2004.

UNPUBLISHED ACADEMIC WORKS

Bourchier, D. (1996) *Lingeages of Organicist Thought in Indonesia*, unpublished PhD thesis, Monash.

McKemmish, S. (1976) *A Political Biography of General Nasution*, unpublished MA thesis, Monash.

Ramage, D.E. Ideological Discourse in the Indonesian New Order: State Ideology and the Beliefs of an Elite, 1985–1993, PhD Dissertation, University of South Carolina, 1993.

WORKS OF LITERATURE

Anwar, C. "Krawang Bekasi" in Jassin, H.B. *Chairul Anwar, Pelopor Angkatan '45* (translated title: *Chairul Anwar: Pioneer of the Generation of '45*), Jakarta: Gunung Agung, 1978.
Kayam, U. *Sri Sumarah dan Bawuk Cet 1*. Jakarta: Pustaka Jaya, 1975.
———. *Para Priyayi; Sebuah Novel*. Jakarta, Pustaka Utama Grafiti, 1992.
Mihardja, A.K. *Atheis*. St. Lucia, Qld, University of Queensland Press, 1972. (Translated from the Indonesian by R.J. Maguire.)
———. *Keretakan dan Ketegangan* (Translated title: *Fissures and Tensions*). Jakarta: Perpustakaan Perguruan Kem. P.P. dan K., 1956.

NEWSPAPERS AND OTHER MEDIA

Antara, Jakarta news agency, 18 November 1955.
Riding the Tiger, Australian Broadcasting Corporation (television production), 1992.
Indonews, Internet news site, 20 March 2000.
Kompas, *Jakarta daily, 1 June 2001, 13 July 2002*.
Madjalah Tengah Bulanan BKS - Tani Militer, No. 1, Year 1, December 1960.
Merdeka, Jakarta daily, various issues, 1950, 1951, 1955, 1956, 1957, 1958, 1959.
Pikiran Rakyat, Bandung daily, various issues, 1951, 1956.
Prisma, Jakarta magazine, 10 October 1994.
Radio Netherlands, Daily Reports of Current Affairs in Indonesia, Internet news site, 1 April 2003
Straits Times, Singapore, 8 June 2017.
Suluh Indonesia, Jakarta daily, various issues, 1956, 1957, 1958
Tempo, weekly magazine, Jakarta, 9–15 October 2000.
Tempo, Jakarta daily Internet site, check date internet from ch 6.
The Age, Melbourne daily, 13 November 2004.
The Age, Melbourne Daily, 20 June 2017.
The Australian, Sydney daily, 22 October 2003
The Economist, International weekly magazine published in London, 9 December 2004.

INDONESIAN ARMY TRAINING PUBLICATIONS

Seskoad, Harsojo, Aspek Pembangunan Masyarakat [Aspects of Community Development], 1983.

Seskoad, *Dwi Fungsi ABRI: Sistem Khas Indonesia* [The Dual Function of the Armed Forcees: Indonesia's Own System].

Seskoad, *Naskah Departemen tentang Perkiraan Keadaan untuk Kursus Reguler Staf Umum dan Komando TNI-AD 1993* [Departmental Notes on the Appraisal of Situations for Army Command and Staff Regular courses 1993].

Seskoad, *Pedoman Dasar Kerukunan Hidup Beragama* [Basic Guidance on Harmony in Religious Life], Preparatory Course for Armed Forces and Police Staff Colleges, 1991/1992 Academic Year.

Seskoad, Pembangunan Daerah dan Perlunya Pola-Pola Interdependency re Regionalisme-Baru [Regional Development and the Need for Patterns of Interdependency in regard to New Regionalism], by Dr. Edi Swasono, 1983

Seskoad, *Perintah Siasat No: 1 Panglima Besar TNI 9 November 1948* [Strategic Order No. 1 by the Commander-in-Chief of the TNI 9 November 1948] , written by Major General Bambang Triantoro, Commanding General, Army Training and Education Development Command, 1 October 1981.

Seskoad, Sekitar Pertempuran Surabaya 10 November 1945 [On the Battle of Surabaya 10 November 1945].

Seskoad, *Vademikum* (Third Edition), 28 February 1987.

DOCUMENTS

Amanat KASD Dalam Pertemuan Program Kerdja Sama Penguasa Militer - Pemuda Massa, National Archives Jakarta Document No. 250, undated [1957].

Michael Wilson, Recorded Interview with T K Critchley, 25 November 1993, Oral History Section, Australian diplomacy 1950–1990 oral history project, National Library of Australia.

Military Assistance Training. Hearings before the Subcommittee on National Security Policy and Scientific Developments of the Committee on Foreign Affairs. House of Representatives, Ninety-First Session, October 6,7,8, December 8, and 15, 1970.

"The Situation in Vietnam," 1 October 1964, U.S. Department of State, Office of the Historian, Foreign Relations of the United States, 1964–1968, Volume 1, Vietnam (Washington DC), Document Number 368.

Reorganisasi TNI-AD Tahun 1984, Dispenad, Jakarta, 1986/

Pritchett to Critchley and Department of External Affairs, Cablegrams, The Hague 6 K340, Batavia, 12 September 1949, www.info.dfat.gov.au

Surat Keputusan No.: Kpts/P.M./015/1957 issued by the Ministry of Defence Army Staff (*Kementerian Pertahanan Staf Angkatan Darat*), 5 July 1957, National Archives, Jakarta, document Number 250.

WEBSITES

ABRI website, accessed June 1998.

Apa Kabar? website, 1998 (www.hamline.edu/apakabar?), accessed June 2005.

Arus Bawah, arus.kerjabudaya.org, accessed 22 January 2005.
Biography, Johanna Sunarti Nasution, The 1981 Ramon Magsaysay Award for Public Service, www.rmaf.org.ph/Awardees/Citation/CitationNasutionJoh.htm, accessed June 2005.
Faculty of Economics, University of Indonesia website (www.fe.ui.ac.id), accessed January 2005.
Gadjah Mada University website (web2.ugm.ac.id), accessed December 2004.
Gluckman, R. *The Best Joe in Java*, www.gluckman.com, accessed January 2005
Indonesia's History and Background, Asianinfo.org, accessed December 2004. www.javapalace.org, accessed 27 December 2004.Library of Congress Country Studies studies.us/Indonesia/8.htm accessed 27 December 2004.www.lowensteyn.com/indonesia/nationalist.html, accessed January 2004.1945 Constitution of the Republic of Indonesia, Department of Information, 1989http://asnic.utexas.edu/asnic/countries/Indonesia/ConstIndonesia:html, accessed June 2005.http. jpnn.com/news, 28 June 2016
No Ivory Tower, www.fordfoundation.org, accessed June 2005.
Panduan Memilih Perguruan Tinggi (www.pdat.co.id), accessed December 2004.
Josko Petkovic, "Dede Oetomo Talks on *Reyog Ponorogo*," in http://wwwsshe.murdoch.edu.au/intersections/issue2/Oetomo.html, accessed February 2005.
Rand's 50 Years, www.rand.org.org/history, accessed September 2004.
Sejarah Terjadinya Kebumen, www.kebumen.go.ed, accessed December 2004.
"Seminar Cagar Budaya di Sastra Unair," http://www.warta.unair.ac.id/fokus/index.php?id=183, accessed January 2005.
www. sshe.murdoch.edu.au/intersections/issue2/Oetomo.html, accessed February 2005.
Tapol Bulletin, http://tapol.gn.apc.org/166–7head.htm, accessed 3 September 2003.
http://theconversation.com, 9 September 2014, accessed 25 June 2017.
Wahana Selamat Jalan Prof Dr. Wertheim, www.hamline.edu/apakabar/basisdata/1998/11/06/008.html, accessedFebruary 2005.
https://profil.merdeka.com/indonesia/r/r-p-soeroso/, accessed July 2017.www.warta.unair.ac.id/fokus/index.php?id=183, accessed January 2005.

DICTIONARIES AND TRANSLATION REFERENCES

Baker, M. (1992) *In Other Words: A Coursebook on Translation*. London: Routledge.
Larson, M.L. (1984) *Meaning-Based Translation: A Guide to Cross-Language Equivalence*. Lanham, MD: University Press of America
Newmark, P. (1987) *A textbook of translation*. London, Prentice-Hall.
Poerwadarminta, W.J.S. (1944?) *Baoesastra Indonesia Djawi*. Jakarta, Gunseikanbu Kokumin Tosyokyoku (Bale Pustaka).
Stevens, A.M. and A. Ed. (2004) *A Comprehensive Indonesian-english Dictionary*. Athens, Ohio: Schmidgall-Tellings, Ohio University Press.
Tim Penyusun. (2008) *Kamus Besar Bahasa Indonesia*. Jakarta: Balai Pustaka (Compiling Team) Fourth Edition.

Index

abangan (syncretic masses) 15, 16, 73, 167, 168, 173n82
Abeyasekere, Susan, 12n3, 33n69, 36, 45n7
Achmadi, 211, 212, 219n26, 223n100
Anderson, Benedict R. O'G, 13n11, 18, 31n17, 46nn36, 42, 45, 54, 58, 62, 74, 80nn23, 29, 83n123, 118n118, 253n4

Badan Kerja Sama. *See* BKS
Bandung Lautan Api. *See* Nasution, A. H.
Batak (ethnic group), 1, 2, 12n2, 28, 35, 86, 177
Binnenlands Bestuur, 15
BKS (organisations), 186, 188, 189, 193–204, 206, 208–15, 217n5, 218nn12, 21, 219n31, 220n54, 221n66, 222nn80, 83, 223n104, 224nn109, 110, 225nn111, 125, 248
bersiap!, 48, 49, 56, 59, 76
BKR, 56
Bourchier, David, vii, 11, 13n11, 41, 45n9, 50, 52, 157, 159, 171n34, 172n53
Brackman, Arnold, 54, 55, 86, 113n5, 210
Budi Utomo, 19, 20, 35
Bumi Putera, 22, 39, 154

Candradimuka (academy), 132
civil-military cooperation groups. *See* BKS
Clune, Frank, 25, 91, 129
cooperating and non-cooperating nationalism, 6–8, 18–21, 27–29, 31n19, 35, 37, 38, 52, 72, 86, 95, 102, 109, 123
Cribb, Robert, 7, 10, 13n7, 62, 70, 104, 143, 148n66, 239
Critchley, T. K., 17, 30n10, 96, 112, 130
Crouch, Harold, 135, 248

Darul Islam, 24, 78, 110, 128, 136, 140, 141, 147n33, 158, 179, 199, 205, 213, 219n35, 221n65, 233, 235, 247
Djojhohadikusumo, Margono, 109, 118n128
Djojohadikusumo, Sumitro, 118n128, 157, 160, 178, 179
Djokosutono, Professor, 11, 12, 153–160, 162, 170n20, 182, 183, 185, 190n26, 234, 235
Dutch in Indonesia, 2, 4, 5, 17, 121, 176, 197, 205

Ebury, Sue, 37, 38, 45n16
Elson, Robert, 236

Fagg, Donald, 196
Feith, Herbert, vii, viii, 92, 122, 123, 134, 146nn1, 9, 18, 147n33, 148nn66, 67, 150n96, 155, 162, 163, 169, 172n63, 204, 205, 218n23
Fischer, Louis, 205, 206, 210
functional groups/interest representation, 7, 10, 11, 162, 163, 175, 181–84, 186, 190nn23, 26, 193–98, 202, 212, 214, 215, 218n12, 223n103, 225, 226n125, 239
Fundamentals of Guerrilla Warfare (book), 10, 72, 90, 101, 108, 116n62, 118n134, 142–45, 165, 179, 180, 183–85, 216

general elections (1955), 5, 7, 74, 124, 155, 160, 163, 166–69, 172n63, 173n77, 181, 186, 199, 219n31, 232, 233
Giebels, L. J., 32n56, 253n1
Golkar, 11, 163, 172nn50, 53, 190n25, 194, 204, 214–16, 218n8, 224n109, 239
Gondokusumo, Maria (Rademaker): Dutch origins, 16, 75, 246;
Indonesian nationalist views, 17, 21, 22;
and Nasution, A. H., 39, 41;
and Sunarti (Gondokusumo/ Nasution), 22, 39
Gondokusumo, R. P. Sunario:
Bumi Putera Insurance Company, 22, 39;
and Djody Gondokusumo, 11, 13n11, 157, 171n34;
early life and aristocratic rank, 16, 115n37;
education in The Netherlands, 15, 16;
nationalist views, 16, 19, 20;
family networks, 11, 91, 92, 115n37;
and Nasution, A. H., 6, 10, 27–30, 35, 37, 39, 43, 75, 76, 93, 127, 154, 155;
and Nasution, J. S., 22, 75, 127, 246;

Japan/Japanese occupation, 35, 37–39;
priyayi social status, 2, 11, 16, 30n5;
and Sutomo, Dr, 20–22
Grant, Bruce, 253n12
guerrilla warfare. See people's resistance/territorial warfare

Hamengku Buwono, Sri Sultan, 57, 91, 92, 102, 111, 112, 123, 125, 133, 134, 149n92, 164, 172n65
Hardoyo, Mas, viii, 223n101
Hatta, Mohammad, 4, 6, 28, 42, 44, 48, 52, 55, 60, 61, 80n23, 86, 87, 93–96, 123–24, 135, 138, 154, 175, 177, 221n73
Headquarters Java Command/MBKD, 98, 100, 103, 105, 125, 133, 168
Heijboer, Pierre, 66, 67, 70, 71, 78, 96
Hindley, Donald, 206, 210, 222n88

IPKI. See Nasution, A. H.
Indonesian Communist Party. See PKI
Inspectorate General of Territorial Affairs and People's Resistance, 143, 179, 180, 194, 195, 197, 198, 208, 213–15, 217nn5, 7, 218n8, 226n125, 237

jalan tengah. See middle way
Japanese invasion and occupation, 1, 2, 4, 17, 27, 37, 38, 43, 44, 48, 49, 50, 52, 87
Javanese (language/culture), 2, 15, 16, 19, 50, 52, 56–58, 62, 105, 114n14, 156, 167, 184, 190n36, 227, 238, 249
Johana Nasution. See Nasution, Johana Sunarti
Jungschlaeger, Leon, 200, 205, 219nn35, 39

Kahin, George McT, 30n1, 74, 81n62, 99, 100, 102, 106, 107, 146n10;
Audrey, 189n3, 220n59

Kartasasmita, Didi, 57
Kartamihardja, Achdiat, 26
Kartawinata, Arudji, 56
Kawilarang, 134, 169, 177
Kayam, Umar, 30n3
KNIL, 24, 27, 35, 39, 41, 42, 44, 56–58, 62–64, 75, 88, 91, 101, 112, 121–23, 125, 127, 128, 132, 133, 147nn37, 38, 157
KODAM, 171n48, 231, 240, 241n18
KODM, 70, 90
KODIM, 231
KORAMIL, 231
KOREM, 231, 239
Kolopaking, Sumitro, 103, 106–8, 118nn118, 121, 156, 157, 161–63, 170, 170n24
Kolopaking, Sunario, 156, 157, 160, 162
Kurasawa, A., 46n41
Kveder, Dushan, 66, 69, 225n112

Laqueur, Walter, 72
laskar organisations, 48, 53, 54, 57–60, 63, 69, 72, 73, 76, 82n108, 85, 88, 93, 94, 109, 114n16, 137, 163, 202
Legge, John, 89, 114n14, 232, 241nn23, 24
Legion of Veterans. *See* LVRI
Lev, Daniel, vii, 8, 159, 174n96, 183, 186–88, 194, 197, 205, 212, 232
Lubis, Zulkifli, 166, 169, 176–78
LVRI, 195

MacFarling, Ian, 112, 171n33
McKemmish, Susan, 12, 24, 58, 113, 115n46, 123, 147n37
McVey, Ruth, 87, 110, 118n130, 132, 134, 135, 148n67, 167, 169, 225n112
Madiun Affair, 60, 73, 88, 93, 94, 96, 98, 99, 109, 113, 156, 166, 180, 247
Malaka, Tan, 54, 55, 61, 62, 65, 72–74, 92, 109, 122, 136, 165, 221nn69, 73

Malaysia (includes Malaya), 3, 6, 5, 15, 17, 118n128, 129, 160, 179, 229, 230
Mangkupradja, Gatot, 139
Markas Besar Komando Jawa/MBKD. *See* Headquarters Java Command
middle way (of the army), 143, 159, 183–86, 250
Musso, 86, 93
Mustopo, Colonel, 133, 204, 213, 222n99, 223nn99, 100, 224n109, 225nn110, 111

Nasution, Abdul Haris:
Bandung Lautan Api, 60, 61, 69, 134, 176, 202, 248;
birth and early childhood, 2, 23;
caution/hesitancy, 61, 121, 125, 126, 134, 202, 247, 248;
cooperating nationalism, 6–8, 27–29, 35, 38, 108, 109, 123;
and Djokosutono, Professor (*See* Djokosutono, Professor);
Dutch officer training, 27, 29, 35, 127;
desertion from KNIL, 38, 39;
early military ambitions, 24, 25;
education in Sumatra and Bandung, 23–25;
father, 23, 24, 155;
German Nazi regime, 35, 36, 40, 202;
and Gondokusumo, Sunario (*See* Gondokusumo, Sunario);
and IPKI, 74, 108, 153–55, 161–65, 168–70, 172nn53, 62, 174n96, 180, 183, 203;
Japan/Japanese occupation, 1, 29, 30, 35, 38–43;
and KNIL, (see KNIL);
and Kolopaking, Sunario (*See* Kolopaking, Sunario);
laskar organisations (*See* laskar organisations);

legal/administrative matters, 11, 98, 101, 105, 106, 153, 155–60, 162, 182, 183, 185;
lurah (village heads), 43, 68, 72–74, 76, 90, 104, 105, 116n62, 144, 164;
Madiun Affair (*See* Madiun Affair);
Mandailing Batak ancestry, 23;
Military Administration, x, 90, 92 94, 98, 101–6, 109–111, 116nn62, 64, 124, 125, 132, 144, 153, 157, 158, 162, 165, 184, 194, 236;
and Nasution, J. S., 1, 5, 6, 9, 10, 23, 28, 29, 39, 57, 60, 74–77, 92, 93, 97, 111, 125–29, 134–35, 145, 146, 154, 155, 162, 175, 215–17, 227, 228, 246, 249–51;
pamong praja (*See* Pamong Praja);
PETA (*See* PETA);
PKI (*See* PKI);
and political parties, 7, 9, 28, 47, 57, 59, 72, 73, 78, 85, 90, 110, 111, 124, 133–35, 144, 145, 153, 161–65, 175, 176, 182, 183, 185, 186, 190nn23, 24, 191n49, 193, 194, 196–98, 202–4, 211–13, 223n102, 232;
people's resistance/warfare (*See* people's resistance/territorial warfare);
reorganisation and rationalisation (*See* reorganisation and rationalisation);
regional defence councils, 71, 90, 97;
and Soeroso, R. P. (*See* Soeroso, R. P.);
and Sukarno (*See* Sukarno);
Siliwangi Division (*See* Siliwangi Division);
Strategic Order 1/48, 88, 89;
and territorial commands (*See* territorial commands);
territorial warfare (*See* separate entry)
Nasution, Johana Sunarti (Gondokusumo):

birth and early childhood, 2, 15, 21, 22;
charity work, 17, 18, 22, 145–46, 249, 250;
Dutch ancestry, 17, 129;
education, 28, 39, 75;
Eurasian status, 75, 76;
guerrilla struggle, 9, 76–78;
memoir, 9;
and Nasution, A. H. (*See* Nasution, A. H.);
Pesindo, 60;
priyayi ancestry, 15;
and Sukarno, 9, 145–46, 175, 217, 227, 228, 246
Netherlands Indies, 1, 2, 4, 17, 19, 25, 26
Netherlands Military Mission, 121, 128, 130–32, 137, 147n48
non-cooperating nationalism. *See* cooperating and non-cooperating nationalism

October 17, 1952 Affair, 12, 121, 127, 133–35, 137, 142, 146n18, 148n67, 153–55, 158, 159, 166, 169, 176, 177, 179, 198, 202, 204, 248
O'Donnell, Guillermo, 196, 197
Organicism, 7, 9–12, 21, 49, 52, 53, 72, 91, 109, 164, 165

Padmodiwiryo, Suhario, vii, 22, 32n39, 41, 105, 106, 131, 137, 149n87, 158,
Palmier, Leslie H., 219n35
Pamurahardjo, vii, 180, 189n10, 195, 197–212, 219nn23, 26, 221n70, 224n108, 248
Pamong Praja, 11, 47, 53, 59, 67, 72–74, 80, 85, 88, 91–94, 101–4, 108, 109, 115n42, 116n65, 117n96, 122, 136–38, 141, 144, 153, 161–65, 168, 169, 172n63, 232, 233, 236

Pangreh Praja, 15, 16, 19, 30nn2, 3, 39, 42, 43, 46n41, 47, 52, 72, 91, 109, 137, 155
Parindra, 19, 21, 22, 31n19, 39
Parindra (1950s), 155
Partai Indonesia Raya. *See* Parindra
Partai Komunis Indonesia. *See* PKI
Partai Nasional Indonesia. *See* PNI
Pauker, Guy, 82n98, 136, 159, 194, 196, 217n2, 225n125, 234, 236, 237
people's resistance/territorial warfare:
  early 1950s, 131, 132, 135–44, 158;
  hardships of guerrilla warfare, 9, 95, 96;
  impact on civilians, 105;
  international influences, 68;
  socially conservative, 12, 53, 67, 69, 72–74, 79, 90, 93, 99–101, 103, 104, 109–112;
  (and) Tan Malaka, 55, 61, 68, 73;
  territorial warfare 66, 67, 70, 71;
  use against Dutch, 54, 64, 66–68, 70–72, 76, 79, 87–90, 94, 103, 104, 112
people's war. *See* people's resistance
Penders, C. L. M. and Sundhaussen, Ulf, 10, 11, 13n11, 28, 58, 99, 144, 169, 171n34, 172n65, 179, 181, 185
Pesindo, 54, 59, 60
PETA, 41, 44, 55, 57, 62, 63, 69
PKI, 5, 20, 53, 54, 73, 86, 87, 93, 94, 96, 97, 101, 109, 113, 156, 166–68, 175, 176, 178, 179, 182, 187–90, 190n23, 193, 195, 196, 198, 199, 203, 206, 207, 210–12, 214, 217, 222n88, 223n102, 227–32, 235, 241n20, 246, 247, 253n4
PNI, 20, 52
Prawiroadmodjo, Suhud, 184, 185, 190n37
priyayi administrative class 2, 7, 11, 12, 15, 16, 19, 22, 30nn2, 3, 42, 50, 52, 73, 109, 122, 156, 168, 173n82, 249

Ramage, D., 173n77
Ransom, David, 234, 235
re-dan-ra. *See* reorganization and rationalisation (of the army)
Reeve, David, 160–63, 169, 172nn50, 53, 193, 194, 196, 214, 218n8, 219n26
regional and municipal elections (1957), 168, 232
Reid, Anthony, 31n19, 88, 98, 105, 109
reorganization and rationalisation (of the army), 85, 87, 88, 92, 94, 100, 128, 131, 132, 136, 144, 149n85, 214
Ricklefs, M. C., 80
Rijadi, Slamet, 110
Rocamora, J. E., 211, 223n102
Ryamizard, Ryacudu, 239, 251

Sadikin, 137, 140, 141, 180, 203, 213, 215, 218n8
Said, Salim, 55, 58, 61, 101, 106, 113n7, 115n43
Saleh, Chaerul, 55, 206, 207, 219n26, 221n68
santri (Muslims), 15, 20, 73, 110, 167, 168
sapta marga, 132
Sarekat Islam, 19, 20
Schmidt, Captain, 200, 206, 219n35
Seskoad, 160, 234–36, 238
Siliwangi Division, 58–70, 77, 85, 88, 89, 93, 94, 98, 104, 110, 128, 134, 137, 139, 140, 145, 163, 180, 187, 228, 233
Simandjuntak, Marsillam, 79n1
Simatupang, Tahi Bonar, 35, 36, 63–65 69, 85, 95, 97, 98, 110, 112, 123, 126, 127, 130, 133–35, 161, 185
Simbolon, Maludin, 134, 169, 177, 189n2
Sjahrir, Sutan, 6, 52, 60–63, 65

Sjarifuddin, Amir, 54–56, 60, 62, 63, 65, 85–88, 93
Soebijono, 94, 115n43, 173n75, 231
Soeroso, R. P., 30n4, 39, 91, 92, 95, 114n31, 155, 187
SUAD V, 215, 216
Subroto, Gatot, 135, 138, 154, 170, 223n100
Sudarno, 98, 103, 111
Sudirman, Panglima Besar, 57, 58, 60–62, 85, 86, 92, 94–97, 111, 112, 127, 154, 180, 250
Sudirohusodo, Wahidin, 19
Sukarno, President, 4–7, 9, 11, 12, 18, 20, 24, 26–28, 31n17, 42, 44, 48, 50–52, 55, 60–62, 86, 91, 93, 95, 96, 106, 111–13, 118, 122–24, 126, 129, 132–35, 139, 142, 145, 153, 154, 159, 162, 163, 165, 168, 169, 175, 176, 178, 179, 181–89, 193, 195, 198, 199, 202, 205–7, 212, 214, 216, 221n72, 223nn101, 105, 225n110, 227–30, 246, 248–50
Sumohardjo, Urip, 56, 57, 60, 64, 85, 86
Sunarti. *See* Nasution, Johana Sunarti
Sundhaussen, Ulf, see Penders, C.L.M. and Sundhaussen, Ulf
Supomo, Prof., 49, 50, 53, 153, 155, 156, 160, 190
Supriyatmono, 194, 195
Suryadarma, 85, 95, 187, 227
Suryadinata, Leo, 190n33, 217n7, 225n119
Suryohadiprojo, Sayidiman, 160, 171n48, 172n50

Sutherland, Heather, 19, 20, 30n2, 117n113, 161, 165
Sutoko, 59, 61, 62, 64, 134, 137, 154
Sutomo, Dr, 19–21
Suwarto, 140, 233–36, 241n29

territorial commands, 69, 70, 72, 89–91, 137, 231, 240, 242n51
territorial warfare. *See* people's resistance/territorial warfare
territorial warfare and territorial management (Doctrine), 10, 94, 194, 217n2, 231, 232, 237, 239
Thalid, Munir Said, 240
Thamrin, M. H., 20, 21, 37
TKR, 56
TRI, 62
TNI, 63, 67, 68, 70, 88, 99, 100, 101, 112, 121, 127, 132, 136, 141, 147n38, 149n85, 157, 160, 161, 165, 185, 195, 203, 252
TNI (book), 59, 72, 165, 180
total people's resistance. *See* people's resistance

Utrecht, Ernst, 189n3, 235

van Mook, Hubertus, 48, 77

West Irian. *See* West Papua
West Papua (formerly Irian Jaya, Dutch New Guinea), 4, 5, 20, 113, 123, 129, 177, 178, 180, 181, 189, 195, 197–200, 202–14, 217, 221n78, 224, 229, 241, 251
Widodo, Joko, 239, 251

About the Author

Barry Turner is a former intelligence officer in the Royal Australian Air Force. He became fascinated with Indonesia after undergoing an intensive Indonesian language training course in 1967. He was posted to the Australian Embassy in Jakarta from 1969 to 1972 where he met military personnel who had served in the struggle for independence and where much of the infrastructure from the Dutch colonial period remained in place. He became interested in the country's transition from colonial status under the Dutch to independence and after leaving the RAAF became an academic, gaining a PhD for a dissertation entitled *Nasution: Total People's Resistance and Organicist Thinking in Indonesia*, on which this book is based. He has continued to visit Indonesia regularly and has run workshops and courses for the Indonesian Ministry of Defense and the University of Indonesia. He has largely retired from academic life but retains the honorary appointment of adjunct professor at RMIT University in Melbourne.

www.ingramcontent.com/pod-product-compliance
Lightning Source LLC
Chambersburg PA
CBHW070019010526
44117CB00011B/1644